Bali

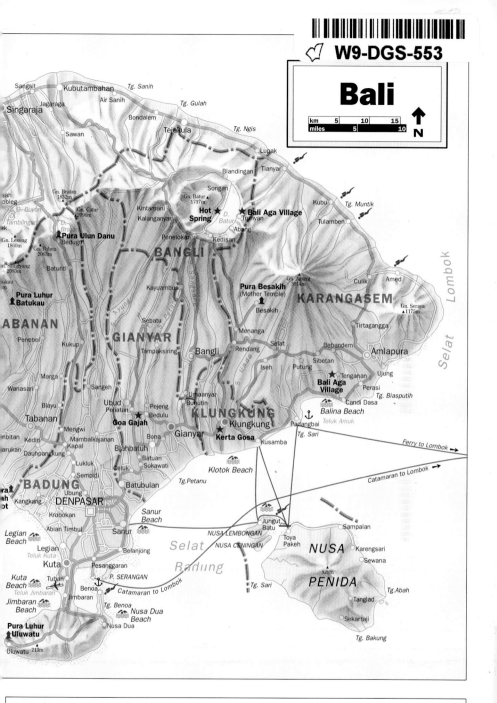

Some Indonesian map terms

Air (Yeh) – Spring
Atas – Far (as in Ruebas Atas)
Bawah – Near (as in Ruebas Bawah)
Besar (Bsr.) – Greater or "Big"
Danau (D.) – Lake
Gunung (Gn.) – Mountain
Jalan (Jl.) – Street

Kecil (Kel.) – Lesser or "Little"
Kepulauan – Archipelago
Laut – Sea
Pulau (P.) – Island (also, locally,
   Nusa, Gili, Mios and others)
Pulau-Pulau – Islands
Pura – Temple

Puri – Palace
Samudra – Ocean
Selat – Strait
Sungai (S.) – River
  (sometimes Kali or Yeh)
Taka – Atoll or bank reef
Tanjung (Tg.) – Cape
Teluk (T.) – Bay, also Gulf

BALI

Edited by
ERIC OEY

PERIPLUS
EDITIONS

DS
647
.B2
B29
1996

BALI is divided into eight regencies for administrative purposes, corresponding to the old Balinese kingdoms. A ninth kingdom, Mengwi, existed until the end of the 19th century. The nine traditional realms are treated separately in this book to give a better historical and cultural frame of reference to the major sights.

Badung	**Klungkung**	**Mengwi**
Gianyar	**Karangasem**	**Tabanan**
Bangli	**Buleleng**	**Jembrana**

© 1996 by Periplus Editions (HK) Ltd.
3rd edition, first reprint
ALL RIGHTS RESERVED
Printed in the Republic of Singapore
ISBN 962-593-028-0
Publisher: Eric Oey
Editorial revisions: Joan Suyenaga, Martijn de Rooi
Production: Mary Chia, Thomas G. Oey
Cartography: Violet Wong

INTERNATIONAL DISTRIBUTORS:

Belgium Uitgeverij Lannoo NV, Kasteelstraat 97,
B-8700 Tielt

Germany Brettschneider Fernreisebedarf GMBH,
Hauptstrasse 5, D-85586 Poing

Hong Kong and Taiwan Asia Publishers Services Ltd.,
16/F Wing Fat Commercial Building, 218 Aberdeen Main
Road, Aberdeen, Hong Kong

Indonesia C.V. Java Books, P.O. Box 55 JKCP, Jakarta 10510

Japan Charles E. Tuttle Inc., 21-13, Seki 1-Chome, Tama-
ku, Kawasaki, Kanagawa 214

Netherlands Nilsson & Lamm bv, Postbus 195, 1380 AD
Weesp, The Netherlands

Singapore and Malaysia Berkeley Books Pte. Ltd., 5 Little
Rd, #08-01, Singapore 536983

Thailand Asia Books Co. Ltd., 5 Sukhumvit Road Soi 61,
Bangkok 10110

U. K. GeoCenter U.K. Ltd., The Viables Center, Harrow
Way, Basingstoke, Hampshire RG22 4BJ

U.S.A. NTC Publishing Group (Passport Guides), 4255 W.
Touhy Avenue, Lincolnwood, Illinois 60646-1975

The Periplus Adventure Guides Series

BALI

JAVA

SUMATRA

KALIMANTAN *Indonesian Borneo*

SULAWESI *The Celebes*

EAST OF BALI *From Lombok to Timor*

MALUKU *Indonesia's Spice Islands*

IRIAN JAYA *Indonesian New Guinea*

UNDERWATER INDONESIA
A Guide to the World's Greatest Diving

SURFING INDONESIA *(1996)*

BIRDING INDONESIA *(1997)*

TREKKING INDONESIA *(1997)*
A Guide to Nature and National Parks

WEST MALAYSIA *and Singapore*

SABAH & SARAWAK *with Brunei Darussalam*

While we try to ensure that all information in our guides is accurate and up-to-date, the authors and publisher accept no liability for any inconvenience, injury or loss sustained by any person using this book. We welcome comments and corrections from readers. Please address all correspondence to: Periplus (Singapore) Pte. Ltd., 5 Little Rd, #08-01, Singapore 536983.

CAPTIONS:
Cover: The renowned dancer Cok Ratih during a tooth-filing ritual. By Amir Sidharta.
Pages 4–5: Worshipping at Pura Luhur, Batukau. By Kal Muller.
Pages 6–7: The spectacular Kecak dance. By R. Ian Lloyd.

Contents

12 CONTENTS

PART III Central Bali: Gianyar

PART IV Kintamani and Bangli

PART V Klungkung Regency

PART VI East Bali: Karangasem

PART I

Island of the Gods

Even today, there is a certain magic about Bali. The longer one stays on the island, the more one is impressed by the many exquisite sights and the scores of talented and charming people one encounters. All the tourist hype aside, Bali truly is exceptional.

The island of Bali indeed presents a modern paradox — an ancient, traditional society that is still incredibly alive and vital. While the basic conservatism of the Balinese has enabled them to preserve many of their past achievements, it has never hindered the acceptance of new and innovative elements, whether home-grown or foreign.

How are we to account for the island's fabled cultural wealth? A fortuitous congruence of circumstances — accidents, really, of geography and history, seem responsible.

First and foremost, Bali is extraordinarily blessed by Nature. Lying within a narrow band of the tropics where wet and dry seasons fall roughly into balance — providing both adequate rainfall and long periods of sunshine — the island's soils, topography and water resources are all remarkably well-suited to human habitation. As a result, Bali has been civilized since very early times.

This is also the only island in "inner Indonesia" that has enjoyed centuries of more or less uninterrupted cultural continuity. While other traditional states in the region suffered major disruptions due to Islamization and Dutch colonization, Bali was isolated, left to go her own way.

As a result, this is the only area of Indonesia that remains "Hindu" today — retaining elements of the great fusion of indigenous and Indian cultures which took place over a thousand years ago. When Bali was finally colonized by the Dutch, at the turn of this century, the European invaders were so fascinated by what they found here that a concerted effort was made to preserve and foster the island's traditional culture.

Balinese society remains strong and vital, moreover, because it promotes family and communal values. This is indeed the key — a self-strengthening system in which religion, custom and art combine with age-old child-rearing techniques and deeply-entrenched village institutions to produce an exceptionally well-integrated society. Feelings of alienation from parents and peers, so common now in the West, are rare in Bali.

Children are carried everywhere until they are at least three months old, held at all times in the warm, protective embrace of family, friends and neighbors. Elaborate rituals are performed at frequent intervals to ensure their well-being. Every aspect of village life is organized to the nth degree — the individual's rights and responsibilities within the community being carefully defined by tradition.

Despite all this, it should be noted that traditional Bali was far from perfect. For the majority of Balinese peasants, it was in fact a world wracked by warfare, disease, pestilence and famine. In this century, moreover, Bali was continuously plagued by political violence, over-population and poverty.

Bali's unique culture should in fact be viewed as a response to difficult, uncertain conditions. Its strong village institutions served as bulwarks against the ever-present threat of disaster; their inherent flexibility was a guarantee of survival in the face of often overwhelming odds.

The rapid changes now occurring on the island must be seen from this historical perspective. Certainly there are problems, some perhaps as serious as those faced in earlier times. But the Balinese are eternal optimists, fervently believing that their "Island of the Gods" enjoys a very special place indeed in the grander scheme of things.

Overleaf: *Traditional and modern Bali seem to peacefully and even playfully co-exist, in a painting by I Made Budi of Batuan.* **Opposite:** *A pemangku or temple priest, with child. Photo by Kal Muller.*

GEOGRAPHY

An Island Built by Volcanoes

Every aspect of Bali's geography and ecology is influenced by the towering range of volcanic peaks that dominate the island. They have created its landforms, periodically regenerated its soils, and helped to produce the dramatic downpours which provide the island with life-giving water. The Balinese recognize these geophysical facts of life, and the island's many volcanoes, lakes and springs are considered by them to be sacred.

Bali is continually being formed by volcanic action. The island lies over a major subduction zone where the Indo-Australian plate collides with the rigid Sunda plate — with explosive results. A violent eruption of Mt. Agung (3,142 m before the eruption; 3,014 m now) in 1963 showered the mountain's upper slopes with ash and debris that slid off as mudflows, killing thousands of people and laying waste to irrigation networks and rice-

fields that had been built up over many years. Mt Batur (1,717 m) to the west is also active, with greater frequency but less violence.

A mild, equatorial climate

Lying between 8 and 9 degrees south of the equator, Bali has a short, hot wet season and a longer, cooler dry season. The mountains are wet year round, averaging 2,500 to 3,000 mm (100 to 120 inches) of rain annually, with warm days and cool nights. The lowlands are hotter and drier, but fresh and persistent winds make the climate less oppressive here than elsewhere in the equatorial zone.

The wet season lasts from November to March, and though there are only five or six hours of sunshine a day, this is also the hottest time of year (30-31° C by day, 24-25° C at night). The dry season is from April to October, when southeasterly winds blow up from the cool Australian interior (28-29° C by day, and a pleasant 23° C at night), with seven or eight hours of sunshine daily.

By itself, the rainfall in the lowlands is not enough for wet rice cultivation. In other parts of Indonesia, particularly Java, flood waters following heavy rains can be collected behind dams, but the steep, narrow valleys of Bali offer no good dam sites. Over the centuries, the Balinese have instead devised many sophisticated irrigation systems which optimize the water available from rain and rivers.

Bali's volcanic soils are in fact not natural-

RIO HELMI

ly well-suited to wet rice cultivation. They are deep, finely textured and well-drained, so water soaks through them rapidly. While this reduces the risk of floods, it wastes precious water. Paradoxically, the solution is vigorous and repeated ploughing, which actually renders the soils less permeable. Irrigated areas, moreover, receive a supply of nutrients from river water enriched by domestic effluents.

Man has extensively modified the natural vegetation of Bali. The moist primary forest which is its natural vegetation now covers

only 1,010 sq km or 19 percent of Bali's total area, mainly in the western mountains and along the arc of volcanic peaks from Agung to Batukau. About a quarter of the forest is protected in four nature reserves, the largest of which is Bali Barat National Park (196 sq km. Further reserves are planned to protect another quarter of the island's forests.

An island of great contrasts

Bali may be small, but its physical geography is complex, creating an island of great contrasts. In simple outline, three major areas emerge — the mountains, the coastal lowlands and the limestone fringes. The mountains are lofty and spectacular, dominated by Mt Agung and its neighbors, Abang and Batur. Dramatic lava flows on the northeastern flanks of Agung are Bali's newest landforms, showing what the entire island probably looked like a million years ago.

The western mountains provide the last major wildlife sanctuary. Cultivation is here limited to coastal areas that are very dry in the north, but more prosperous and fertile in the south. Coconut groves, cattle pastures and rainfed fields line the foothills while ricefields are found along the coast. Unique canals vanish into foothill tunnels excavated as protection from landslides. In the extreme southwest, the new Palasari Dam forms the island's only manmade lake. On Bali's western tip, the coral reefs and clear waters

around Menjangan Island provide fantastic scuba diving.

The southern lowlands formed the cradle of Balinese civilization. Here it is possible to grow two or more irrigated rice crops per year. Based on this agricultural surplus, eight small but powerful kingdoms arose, symmetrically lining the parallel north-south river valleys that shaped their early growth.

In contrast to the south, the north coast hosted only a single kingdom, centered on the less extensive but equally productive ricelands around Singaraja. Terracing here continues well into the hills, on slopes which elsewhere would be regarded as a severe erosion hazard. In Bali, these terraces stand as firm as masonry because of peculiar clay minerals within the soil. Further east, the dry coast is relieved by several major springs which emerge from fissures in the lava flows. The spring water is used for irrigating table grapes, a crop that thrives here.

The southern limestone fringes stand in complete contrast to the rest of Bali. These are dry and difficult to cultivate. The Bukit Peninsula south of the airport has impressive southern cliffs and many large caves. Across the sea to the east, Nusa Ceningan, Nusa Lembongan and Nusa Penida are dry limestone islands with scrubby vegetation and shallow soils. Villagers on Penida have built ingenious catchments to collect rainwater. Springs also emerge from the base of its high southern cliffs, and villagers scramble down precarious scaffolds to collect water. Just as water is the measure of richness in the interior, so is it the measure of survival around the periphery. In Bali, water is truly sacred.

— *Stephen Walker*

Opposite: *The dramatic cone of Mt Agung, at 3,014 m, Bali's highest peak.* **Above, left:** *Bali's volcanoes dominate the landscape and are considered by the Balinese to be sacred.* **Above, right:** *Stands of primary forest near Bedugul.*

AGRICULTURE

Rice Culture: Nourishing Body and Soul

Nature has endowed Bali with ideal conditions for the development of agriculture. The divine volcanoes, still frequently active, provide the soils with great fertility. Copious rainfall and numerous mountain springs supply many areas of the island with ample water year-round. And a long dry season, brought on by the southeasterly monsoon, brings plentiful sunshine for many months of the year. Bali is, as a result, one of the most productive traditional agricultural areas on earth, which has in turn made possible the development of a highly intricate civilization on the island since very early times.

Rice as the staff of life

Wet-rice cultivation is the key to this agricultural bounty. The greatest concentration of irrigated ricefields is found in southern-central Bali, where water is readily available from spring-fed streams. Here, and in other well-watered areas where wet-rice culture predominates, rice is planted in rotation with so-called *palawija* cash crops such as soybeans, peanuts, onions, chili peppers and other vegetables. In the drier regions corn, taro, tapioca and beets are cultivated.

Rice is, and has always been, the staff of life for the Balinese. As in other Southeast Asian languages, rice is synonymous here with food and eating. Personified as the "divine nutrition" in the form of the goddess Bhatari Sri, rice is seen by the Balinese to be part of an all-compassing life force of which humans partake.

Rice is also an important social force. The phases of rice cultivation determine the seasonal rhythm of work as well as the division of labor between men and women within the community. Balinese respect for their native rice varieties is expressed in countless myths and in colorful rituals in which the life cycle of the female rice divinity are portrayed — from the planting of the seed to the harvesting of the grain. Rice thus represents "cul-

ture" to the Balinese in the dual sense of *cultura* and *cultus* — cultivation and worship.

Irrigation cooperatives (subak)

Historical evidence indicates that since the 11th century, all peasants whose fields were fed by the same water course have belonged to a single *subak* or irrigation cooperative. This is a traditional institution which regulates the construction and maintenance of waterworks, and the distribution of life-giving water that they supply. Such regulation is essential to efficient wet-rice cultivation on Bali, where water travels through very deep ravines and across countless terraces in its journey from the mountains to the sea.

The *subak* is responsible for coordinating the planting of seeds and the transplanting of seedlings so as to achieve optimal growing conditions, as well as for organizing ritual offerings and festivals at the *subak* temple. All members are called upon to participate in these activities, especially at feasts honoring the rice goddess Sri.

Subak cooperatives exist entirely apart from normal Balinese village institutions, and a single village's ricefields may fall under the jurisdiction of more than one *subak*, depending on local drainage patterns. The most important technical duties undertaken by the *subak* are the construction and maintenance of canals, tunnels, aquaducts, dams and water-locks.

AMIR SIDHARTA

Other crops

One often gets the impression that nothing but wet-rice is grown on Bali, because of the unobstructed vistas offered by extensive irrigated ricefields between villages. This is not so. Out of a total of 563,286 hectares of arable land on Bali, just 108,200 hectares or about 19 percent is irrigated ricefields (*sawah*). Another 157,209 hectares are non-irrigated dry fields (*tegalan*) producing one rain-fed crop per year. A further 134,419 hectares are

forested lands mostly belonging to the state, and 99,151 hectares are devoted to cash crop gardens (*kebun*) with tree and bush culture. Compared with the figures for 1980, a gradual decrease in the total area under cultivation may be noted, resulting mainly from population pressures and tourism development. This includes a real estate and building boom in the coastal resort areas and tourist handicraft villages such as Celuk and Ubud.

Other crops include Balinese coffee, famous the world over for its delicate aroma and still an important export commodity. Lately, the production of cloves, vanilla and tobacco has also stepped up, and in mountainous regions such as Bedugul, new vegetable varieties are under intensive cultivation to supply the tourist trade. Other export commodities include copra and related products of the coconut palm.

For subsistence cultivators, the coconut palm in fact remains, as before, a "tree of life" that can be utilized from the root right up to the tip. It provides building materials (the wood, leaves and leaf ribs), fuel (the leaves and dried husks), kitchen and household items (shells and fibers for utensils), as well as food and ritual objects (vessels, offerings, plaited objects, food and drink).

The 'green revolution'

Recent changes in Balinese agricultural practices have brought about fundamental

changes in the relationship of the Balinese to their staple crop. Rice production can no longer be expanded by bringing new lands under cultivation. Nor is mechanization a desirable alternative, given the current surplus of labor on the island. For these reasons, the official agricultural policy since the mid-1970s has been to improve crop yields on existing fields through biological and chemical means.

The cultivation of new, fast-growing, high-yielding rice varieties, in concert with the application of chemical fertilizer, herbicides and pesticides, lies at the core of the government's agricultural development program (BIMAS). Further aims are to improve methods of soil utilization and irrigation, and to set up new forms of cooperatives to provide credit and market surplus harvests. Over 80 percent of Bali's wet-rice fields are now subject to these intensification steps.

Since 1984, Indonesia has been able to meet most of its own rice needs, thus relieving some of the pressures responsible for the original "green revolution." As a result, an ecologically more meaningful "green evolution" is now possible, and rice varieties better suited to local conditions and better able to find an anchor in the traditional system of faith are being introduced to the island.

Since 1988, many fields now display new altars for Sri, and the hope is that her rice cult — one of the basic elements of Balinese civilization and culture — will remain strong well into the future.

— *Urs Ramseyer*

Opposite: *The goddess of rice, Bhatari Sri is honored with offerings in a simple ceremony.*
Above, left: *The transplanting of young rice shoots into a flooded field is regulated throughout Bali by traditional irrigation cooperatives (*subak*).*
Above, right: *The agricultural bounty provided by wet-rice cultivation is the basis for the island's intricate and ancient civilization.*

BIRDING

An Insider Looks at Bali's Colorful Birds

Well, did you see the birds in Bali
When you were staying there last year,
Or was your time assigned entirely
To seeing sights and swilling beer,
Sifting sand or shifting gear?

The hobby of birdwatching is above all a delightful recreation, and no longer merely the province of collectors and academics. And what better place than Bali to indulge the urge? What pleasanter island, what wilder domain, and what fresher air in which to nurture it?

We are lucky in Indonesia. The zoogeographic range embraces not only both hemispheres but also the Oriental and Australian regions, which are divided by the Wallace Line running between the islands of Bali and Lombok. Extending from the mountain forests of Sumatra to those of New Guinea, there rests a largely unpeopled clime and an unrivalled diversity of avian life.

Bali alone boasts something like 300 different bird species, including of course migrants, from massive Hornbills and Storks to diminutive Sunbirds and Spiderhunters — to say nothing of one of the world's rarest and most beautiful birds, the Rothschild's Myna (also known as the Bali Starling), which occurs only in Bali.

Our view of such marvels, moreover, need not be confined to the aviary. There lies the wild, readily accessible to all, even to those who inhabit, for example, the crowded tourist beach resorts or the city of Denpasar — whence an hour's drive at most to Ubud or Bedugul — and indeed there is more than enough to feast the eyes here without the need to venture beyond the garden gate.

Within my very own garden situated in the central foothills of Bali, I have seen something like eighty different types of bird. On one side, there extends a dense curtain of greenery, mainly of flowering shrubs, coconut palms and fruit trees, with here and

there a shady acacia and clump of bamboo, the whole surmounted by a towering cotton-tree. This is the resort of a host of arboreal birds, the most remarkable being the Black-naped Orioles and Ashy Drongos; the former a glorious golden-yellow with a broad black band through the eye to the nape, and the latter an unrelieved dark grey with deeply forked tails, always prominently perched and admirable for their acrobatic hawking of insects.

Beneath the canopy, the Magpie Robins endlessly disport and vent a rich vocabulary of imprecations and sweet fluting calls, whilst the restless Pied Fantail dashes to and fro, pirouettes and trips the light fantastic, characteristically flirting its tail the while. Always in evidence are the ubiquitous Yellow-vented Bulbuls, chattering and chortling, as they race each other from palm to palm.

Of the smaller birds, the most commonly occurring are the Bar-winged Prinias and Ashy Tailorbirds, alternately creeping and darting through the bushes in search of grubs; the vivid Scarlet-headed Flower-peckers and metallic blue-throated Olive-backed Sunbirds, busily rifling the hibiscus blossoms to sate their appetite for minute insects and nectar; and the cheerful greeny-yellow Common Iora, which hops about in the thick crown of a *rambutan* tree, now and again betraying its presence with a long drawn-out mellow whistle, slowly increasing

FRANK JARVIS

FRANK JARVIS

in pitch and ending abruptly on a lower note: *tweeeeeeeeeeeeeeeeeeee-tyou*.

To the east is an open expanse of terraced ricefields, gently ascending to a ridge. And here, according to the season, is the haunt of Watercock and Cinnamon Bittern, of Ruddy-breasted Crake and flocks of stately snowy-white Plumed and Little Egrets. Consorting with the latter and usually distinguishable by the buffy-rufous patches of their nuptial plumage, are the Cattle Egrets; while scattered about in frozen attitudes, some Javan Pond Herons stare warily at passers-by, the breeding birds richly adorned in buff and cinnamon and black, which is curiously transformed to white when they erupt into flight.

Overflying the fields are Swiftlets and Swallows, and tiny tumbling Fantail-Warblers, whilst swarms of marauding Munias wheel this way and that to escape the clappers, before descending in a mass to ravage another patch of unguarded grain. There patiently sits the little Pied Bushchat, rather resembling a miniature Magpie Robin in appearance, and likewise perched and keenly espying its prey, is the spectacularly caparisoned Javan Kingfisher, whose radiant presence makes such an indelible impression on all who behold it. Like others of its tribe, it may be found along the river-beds of verdant ravines, but it also frequents the paddy-fields where it may more readily be observed, perched atop a slender pole or the thatched roof of a small shrine, sacred to Dewi Sri, goddess of agriculture and fertility.

To live thus, surrounded by birds, not to say invaded by them, is a joy and an everlast-

ing revelation. Other regular visitors include the Magpie Robins, those conspicuously pied and vocal denizens of all the gardens of the East. In pops the Ashy Tailorbird, insignificant mousy grey thing, rufous face peering inquisitively about, tail cocked vertically. The coast is clear. Bounding sprightly gaited over the boards, it hops on a cushion, inserts its narrow pointed bill, and extracts a scrap of *kapok* stuffing. A cautious backward look, more poking and prodding till the bill stuffed with white fluff, for all the world like the thief that it is and sporting instant whiskers and a beard in order to avoid detection. A final cursory glance, and away to add some comfort to a miraculously stitched leafy nest in the hedgerow.

Then what are those elegant little olive-grey-brown birds, clambering about in the variegated copper-leaf and croton bushes yonder, every so often emitting a plaintive: *twee-wee-wee*, succeeded by utterances of quite explosive force? Notice the long white-tipped tail feathers, white throats and upper breasts, twin white wing bars, amber eyes and lemon-yellow bellies. They are the Bar-winged Prinias or Wren-Warblers, which seem to thrive in any habitat from montane forest to coastal mangrove, and especially in ornamental gardens. Yet their geographic range is confined to Sumatra, Java and Bali. Nowhere else may they be found.

— *Victor Mason*

FRANK JARVIS

Opposite: *The celebrated Bali Starling* (Leucopsar rothschildi)*, the island's rare endemic. Only about 200 individuals are still found in the wild, mainly around Menjangan Island.* **Above:** *The colorful Javan Kingfisher* (Halcyon cyanoventris).
Right: *Various species of munias, all of which are known here by the Balinese name* prit.

Artifacts and Early Foreign Influences

The early history of Bali can be divided into a prehistoric and an early historic period. The former is marked by the arrival of Austronesian (Malayo-Polynesian) migrants beginning perhaps three to four thousand years ago. The Austronesians were hardy seafarers who spread from Taiwan through the islands of Southeast Asia to the Pacific in a series of extensive migrations that spanned several millennia. The Balinese are thus closely related, culturally and linguistically, to the peoples of the Philippines and Oceania as well as the neighboring islands of Indonesia.

Stone sarcophagi, seats and altars

Though precious little is known about the long, formative stages of Balinese prehistory, artifacts discovered around the island provide intriguing clues about Bali's early inhabitants. Prehistoric grave sites have been found

AMIR SIDHARTA

in western Bali, the oldest probably dating from the first several centuries B.C. The people buried here were herders and farmers who used bronze, and in some cases iron, to make implements and jewelry. Prehistoric stone sarcophagi have also been discovered, mainly in the mountains. They often have the shape of huge turtles carved at either end with human and animal heads with bulging eyes, big teeth and protruding tongues.

Stone seats, altars and big stones dating from early times are still to be found today in several Balinese temples. Here, as elsewhere in Indonesia, they seem to be connected with the veneration of ancestral spirits who formed (and in many ways still form) the core of Balinese religious practices.

Also apparently connected with ancestor worship is one of Southeast Asia's greatest prehistoric artifacts — the huge bronze kettledrum known as the "Moon of Pejeng." Still considered to have significant power, it is now enshrined in a temple in the central Balinese village of Pejeng, in Gianyar Regency. More than 1.5 meters in diameter and 1.86 meters high, it is decorated with frogs and geometric motifs in a style that probably originated around Dongson, in what is now northern Vietnam. This is the largest of many such drums discovered in Southeast Asia.

Hindu-Javanese influences

It is assumed (but without proof so far) that the Balinese were in contact with Hindu and Buddhist populations of Java from the early part of the 8th century A.D. onwards, and that Bali was even conquered by a Javanese king in A.D. 732. This contact is responsible for the advent of writing and other important Indian cultural elements that had come to Java along the major trading routes several centuries earlier. Indian writing, dance, religion and architecture were to have a decisive impact, blending with existing Balinese traditions to form a new and highly distinctive culture.

Stone and copper plate inscriptions in Old Balinese are known from A.D. 882 onwards, coinciding with finds of Hindu- and Buddhist-inspired statues, bronzes, ornamented caves, rock-cut temples and bathing places. These are found especially in areas close to rivers, ravines, springs and volcanic peaks.

At the end of the 10th and the beginning of the 11th centuries there were close, peaceful bonds with Indianized kingdoms in east Java, in particular with the realm of Kadiri (10th century A.D. to 1222). Old Javanese was thereafter the prestige language, used in all

ERIC OEY

Balinese inscriptions, evidence of a strong Javanese cultural influence. In 1284, Bali is said to have been conquered by King Krtanagara of the east Javanese Singhasari dynasty (1222-1292). It is not certain whether the island was actually colonized at this time, but many new Javanese elements manifest themselves in the Balinese art of this period.

According to a Javanese court chronicle known as the Nagarakrtagama (dated 1365), Bali was conquered and colonized in 1334 by Javanese forces under Gajah Mada, the legendary general or *patih* of the powerful Majapahit kingdom who established hegemony over east Java and all seaports bordering the Java Sea during the mid-14th century. It is said that Gajah Mada, accompanied by contingents of Javanese nobles, called *aryas*, came to Bali to subdue a rapacious Balinese king. A Javanese vassal ruler was installed at a new capital at Samprangan, near present-day Klungkung in east Bali, and the nobles were granted apanages in the surrounding areas. A Javanese court and courtly culture were thus introduced to the island.

The separation of Balinese society into four caste groups is ascribed to this period, with the *satriya* warrior caste ruling from Samprangan. Those who did not wish to participate in the new system fled to remote mountain areas, where they lived apart from the mainstream. These are the so-called "original Balinese," the Bali Aga or Bali Mula.

Around 1460, the capital moved to nearby Gelgel, and the powerful "Grand Lord" or Dewa Agung presided over a flowering of the Balinese arts and culture. Over time, however, the descendants of the *aryas* became increasingly independent, and from around 1700 began to form realms in other areas.

Reconstructing the past

Because ancestor veneration plays such an important role in Balinese religion, many groups possess family genealogies, known as *babad*. In such texts, the *brahmana*, *satriya* and *wesya* clans trace their ancestry to Majapahit kings, while the Bali Aga claim descent from even earlier Javanese rulers. There are also groups which claim as their ancestors Javanese Hindus and Buddhists who are said to have taken refuge in Bali from invading Muslim forces. This probably gave rise to the story that entire Hindu-Buddhist populations of Java, with their valuables, books and other cultural baggage, fled to Bali after the fall of Majapahit. We do not know if this is true, as even up to the present day it is a common for families to re-write and improve their *babad*, depending on their circumstances.

— *Hedi Hinzler*

Opposite: *A huge prehistoric sarcophagus in the shape of a turtle, in the Archaeological Museum in Pejeng.* **Above:** *The "Moon of Pejeng" — the largest prehistoric kettledrum in Asia.*

TRADITIONAL KINGDOMS

History in a Balinese Looking-Glass

Most of what we know about Bali's traditional kingdoms comes from the Balinese themselves. Scores of masked dance dramas, family chronicles and temple rituals focus on great figures and events of the Balinese past. In such accounts, the broad outline of Bali's history from the 12th up to the 18th centuries is an epic tale of the coming of great men to power. These were the royal and priestly founders of glorious dynasties — some mad, some fearsome, some lazy and some proud — who together with their retainers and family members determined the fate of Bali's kingdoms, as well as shaping the situation and status of the island's present-day inhabitants.

It is possible to see the Balinese as both indifferent to history and yet utterly obsessed by it. Indifferent because they are not very interested in the "what happened and why" that make up what we know as history, while at the same time they are obsessed by stories concerning their own illustrious ancestors.

Balinese "history" is in fact a set of stories that explain how their extended families came to be where they are. Such stories may explain, for example, how certain ancestors moved from an ancient court center to a remote village, or how they were originally of aristocratic stock although their descendants no longer possess princely titles. In short, they provide evidence of a continuing connection between the world of the ancestors and present-day Bali.

Major events are thus invariably seen in terms of the actions of great men (and occasionally women), yet to view them as mere individuals is deceptive. They are divine ancestors, and as such their actions embody the fate of entire corporate groups. Above all, they are responsible for having created the society one finds in Bali today.

Each family possesses its own genealogy that somehow fits into the overall picture. Some focus on kings, their followers or priests as key ancestors. Others see the family history in terms of village leaders, blacksmiths (powerful as makers of weapons and tools) or villagers who resisted and escaped the advance of new rulers.

The fact that such stories sometimes agree with one another should not necessarily be taken as proof that this is what really happened. There are many gaps, loose ends and inconsistencies — often pointing to the fact that generations of priests, princes and scribes have recast these tales about the past to serve their own ends. The stories must be retold, nevertheless, in order to know what is open to dispute.

Ancestors and origins

The story begins in ancient Java, in the legendary kingdoms of Kadiri and Majapahit where Javanese culture is regarded (by Javanese, Balinese and Western scholars alike) as having reached its apex. From these rich sources flowed the great literature, art and court rituals of Hindu Java, that were later transplanted to Bali.

One of the prime reasons for holding such rituals was to elevate Hindu-Javanese leaders to the status of god-like kings who were in contact with the divine forces of the cosmos. As these Javanese kingdoms expanded to take over Bali, they brought with them their art, literature and cosmology. At the same time, the Javanese also absorbed vital elements of Balinese culture, eventually spreading some of these throughout the archipelago and elsewhere in Southeast Asia.

The great Airlangga, descendant of Bali's illustrious King Udayana, is said to have ascended the east Javanese throne and to have founded the powerful kingdom of Kadiri in the 11th century. Thus it was proper that his descendants would later install priests and warriors from Java to rule over Bali. Foremost among these was the son of a priest, Kresna Kapakisan, who became the first king of Gelgel (now in Klungkung Regency) in the mid-15th century.

The transition to Gelgel from a previous court center at Samprangan (now in Gianyar Regency) was made by a cockfighting member of the Kapakisan dynasty, who became embroiled in a struggle for the throne and attempts to save the kingdom from the mismanagement of his elder brother, or so the account goes. There is little reason to doubt this version of events, yet there are huge gaps in the story of how power moved from Java to Gelgel in previous centuries, and the

relation of the Kapakisan line to earlier kings appointed by the Javanese conquerors.

Bali's "Golden Age"

Most Balinese trace their ancestry back to a group of courtiers clustering about the great King Baturenggong, a descendant of Kapakisan, who is seen to have presided over a Balinese "Golden Age" in the 16th century. Balinese accounts describe him as: "A king of great authority, a true lion of a man, who was wise in protecting his subjects and attending to their needs, and an outstanding warrior of great mystical power, always victorious in war." European records do not mention him by name, but attest to the wealth and influence of a Balinese kingdom which at this time had a more centralized and unified system of government than was the case in subsequent centuries.

Of equal if not greater importance in the collective Balinese memory of this era is the super-priest Nirartha. He is remembered for his great spiritual powers — a man who could stop floods, control the energies of sexuality through meditation, and write beautiful poetry to move mens' souls. In the genealogies it was he who founded the main line of Balinese high priests — those whose worship is directed to Siwa, Lord of the Gods. His name is associated with many of Bali's greatest temples, and a corpus of literature produced by himself and his followers.

In Balinese eyes, the descendants of King Baturenggong and Nirartha presided over a period of decline, even though Baturenggong's son, Seganing, upheld some of his father's greatness and, after the texts, fathered the ancestors of Bali's key royal lines. Balinese sources tell of the destruction of Gelgel by a rebellious chief minister, Gusti Agung Maruti, who was distinguished by possessing a tail and an overweening thirst for power. After his defeat by princes who established themselves in the north and south of the island, new independent kingdoms arose from the ashes of Gelgel. The Gelgel dynasty itself survived, albeit in a much reduced state, as the kingdom of Klungkung — maintaining some of its moral and symbolic authority over the rest of the island, but having direct control of only its immediate area.

Slave trading and king-making

To the outside world, as to later Balinese writers, the period following Gelgel's Golden Age was one of chaos — in which fractious kings ruled from courts scattered about the island. This was not necessarily so in contemporary Balinese terms, where the new states must have represented a more dynamic way of conducting the affairs of state and external trade. Bali became famous on the international scene at this time as a source of slaves, savage fighters, beautiful women and skilled craftsmen.

According to traditional accounts, the fate and status of present-day Balinese families was also largely determined at this time. Kingdoms rose and fell with alarming rapidity, clans split and were demoted or even enslaved, aspiring princes waged war and organized lavish ceremonies. Such human dramas were punctuated by a series of natural disasters, such as earthquakes, epidemics and volcanic eruptions.

Bali's principal export throughout the 17th and 18th centuries was slaves. Warfare and a revision of Bali's Hindu law codes helped provide a steady supply of slaves to meet an ever-increasing overseas demand. War captives, criminals and debtors were sold abroad indiscriminately by Balinese rulers, who maintained a monopoly on the export trade. In north Bali, Europeans were even invited in to oversee the trade, and the Dutch in particular purchased large numbers of Balinese to serve as laborers, artisans and concubines in their extensive network of trading ports — especially their capital at Batavia (now Jakarta), where Balinese slaves made up a sizeable portion of the population. Balinese were even sent to South Africa, where in the early 18th century they constituted up to a quarter of the total number of slaves in that country.

Likewise, Balinese wives and concubines were very much favored by wealthy Chinese traders, for their industriousness and beauty, and the fact that they had no aversion to pork, unlike the Muslim Javanese. An early 19th-century trader noted that Balinese women were among the most expensive slaves, costing "30, 50 and even 70 Spanish dollars, according to her physical qualities." The same observer later comments that the Balinese "regard deportation from their island as the worst possible punishment. This attitude results from their strongly-held conviction that their Gods have no influence outside Bali and that no salvation is to be expected for those who die elsewhere."

The principal kingdoms which emerged during this period were Buleleng in the north, Karangasem in the east and Mengwi in the southwest. At various times, these realms expanded to conquer parts of Bali's neighboring islands. Mengwi and Buleleng moved westward into Java, where they became embroiled in conflicts with and between rival Muslim kingdoms. The Dutch came to play an ever larger role in these conflicts, until eventually the Javanese rulers discovered that they had mortgaged their empires to the gin-drinking Europeans. The Balinese were finally pushed out of eastern Java by combined Dutch and Javanese forces.

In the east, Karangasem conquered the neighboring island of Lombok, and at one point even moved into the western part of the next island, Sumbawa. It also annexed Buleleng, and knocked at the gates of Bali's august, but largely impotent central kingdom, Klungkung.

By the beginning of the 19th century, the island's changeable political landscape had stabilized to an extent, as nine separate kingdoms consolidated their positions. A massive eruption of Mt. Tambora on Sumbawa in 1815 — the largest eruption ever recorded — proved to be a catalyst. A tide of famine and disease swept Bali in the wake of the eruption, shredding the traditional fabric of Balinese society, and with it many of the fragile political structures of the two previous centuries.

Paradoxically, Tambora's devastating eruption brought in its aftermath a period of unprecedented renewal and prosperity. Deep layers of nutrient-rich ash from the volcano made Bali's soils fertile beyond the wildest imaginings of earlier Balinese rulers. Rice and other agricultural products began to be exported in large quantities, at a time when vociferous anti-slavery campaigns throughout Europe were bringing an end to Bali's lucrative slave trade.

Two other factors served to transform the island's political and economic landscape. The first was a dramatic decrease in warfare, as ruling families focused more and more on internecine struggles and competing claims for dynastic control, and the monopolies on duties, tolls and corvee labor that came with it. The second was the changing nature of foreign trade, particularly with the founding of Singapore as a British free trade port in 1819. To Singapore went Bali's pigs, vegetable oils and rice. Back came opium, Indian textiles and guns. Bali was now integrated with world markets to an degree unknown in the past, a fact that did not escape the ever watchful eyes of colonial Dutch administrators in Batavia.

— *Adrian Vickers*

Overleaf: *Gusti Bagus Jlantik, king of Karangasem, with his wife and daughter, photographed in 1923.* **Below:** *A vintage 1930s portrait of all eight Balinese kings gathered in the Gianyar palace grounds.*

COLONIAL ERA

Conquests and Dutch Colonial Rule

In the 19th century, Europe took up the fashion of empire building with a vengeance. Tiny Holland, once Europe's most prosperous trading nation, was not to be left behind, and spent much of the century subduing native rulers throughout the archipelago — a vast region that was to become the Netherlands East Indies, later Indonesia.

A steady stream of European traders, scholars and mercenaries visited Bali in this period. The most successful of the traders was a Dane by the name of Mads Lange, one of the last of the great "country traders" whose local knowledge and contacts permitted them to operate on the interstices of the European colonial powers and the traditional kingdoms of the region.

A literary character

Lange was perhaps the prototype for Joseph Conrad's *Lord Jim* — a man who failed to pick the winning side in an internecine dynastic struggle which wracked Lombok in the first half of the 19th century, but who then settled in southern Bali and found a powerful patron in Kesiman, one of the lords of the expanding kingdom of Badung. He soon combined this patronage with a knowledge of overseas markets and familiarity with the largely female-run internal trading networks of Bali, to become extremely rich for a brief period in the 1840s.

The Dutch, determined to establish economic and political control over Bali, became embroiled during this period in a series of wars in the north of the island. They came, as they saw it, to "teach the Balinese a lesson," whereas the words of the chief minister of Buleleng best expressed the prevailing Balinese view: "Let the *keris* decide." The first two Dutch attacks, in 1846 and 1848, were repulsed by north Balinese forces aided by allies from Karangasem and Klungkung, as well as by rampant dysentery among the invading forces. A third Dutch attempt in 1849 succeeded mainly because the Balinese rulers of Lombok, cousins of the Karangasem rulers, used this as an opportunity to take over east Bali.

Not wishing to push their luck, the Dutch contented themselves with control of Bali's northern coast for the next 40 years. As this was the island's main export region, they did succeed in isolating the powerful southern kingdoms and in controlling much of the export trade. Lange's fortunes soon declined as a result, and he died several years later, probably poisoned out of economic jealousy.

The end of traditional rule

Not long after the cataclysmic eruption of Krakatau in 1883, on the other side of Java, a series of momentous struggles began amongst the kingdoms of south Bali — struggles that were to result in a loss of independence for all of them over the next 25 years.

These conflicts began with the collapse of Gianyar following a rebellion by a vassal lord in Negara. The rebellion ultimately failed, as Gianyar was revived by a hitherto obscure but upwardly-mobile prince in Ubud, but it in turn touched off a series of conflicts that produced a domino effect across the island.

The first kingdom to go was once mighty Mengwi, former ruler of east Java, which was destroyed by its neighbors in 1891. The Sasak or Islamic inhabitants of Lombok then rebelled against their Balinese overlords, which gave the Dutch an excuse to intervene and conquer Lombok in 1896.

Greatly weakened by these events, Karangasem and Gianyar both ceded some of their rights to the Dutch, leaving only the independent kingdoms of Badung, Tabanan, Bangli and prestigious Klungkung by the turn of this century.

Shipwrecks, opium and death

The Dutch found excuses to take on these kingdoms in a series of diplomatic incidents involving shipwrecks and the opium trade. These culminated in the infamous *puputans* or massacres of 1906 and 1908 that resulted in not only many deaths, but complete Dutch mastery over the island.

In the 1906 *puputan*, the Dutch landed at Sanur and marched on Denpasar, where they were greeted by over a thousand members of the royal family and their followers, dressed in white and carrying the state regalia in a march to certain death before the superior Dutch weaponry. As later expressed by the neighboring king of Tabanan, the attitude of

AUX INDES NÉERLANDAISES
Le Rajah de Boeleleng, dans l'île de Bali, se suicide avec quatre cents de ses sujets

the unrelenting Balinese ruler of Badung, when asked to sign a treaty with the Dutch, was that "it is better that we die with the earth as our pillow than to live like a corpse in shame and disgrace."

A macabre massacre

In 1908 the bloody *puputan* (meaning "ending" in Balinese) was repeated on a smaller scale in Klungkung. The ghastly scene was one in which, according to one Dutch observer, the corpse of the king, his head smashed open and brains oozing out, was surrounded by those of his wives and family in a bloody tangle of half-severed limbs, corpses of mothers with babies still at their breasts, and wounded children given merciful release by the daggers of their own compatriots.

Ostensibly because they felt guilty about the bloody nature of their conquest, which was widely reported and condemned in Europe, the Dutch authorities quickly established a policy designed to uphold "traditional" Bali. In fact this policy supported only what was was seen to be traditional in their eyes, and only if those bits of tradition did not contradict the central aim of running a quiet and lucrative colony.

Marketing ploys

Preserving Bali largely meant three things to the Dutch: creating a colonial society which included a select group of the aristocracy, labelling and categorizing every aspect of Balinese culture with a view to keeping it pure, and idealizing this culture so as to market it for the purposes of tourism. Although these may sound contradictory, they meshed well together. There were slight hiccups — Balinese who refused to cooperate and did their best to avoid the demands of the Dutch-run state. Some were killed, others were forced to work on road construction projects or to pay harsh new taxes on everything from pigs to the rice harvest.

Indirect rule through royalty

Another aspect of "preserving" Bali was that the traditional rulers were maintained. As on Java, the Dutch adopted a policy of ruling the villages indirectly through them, while running their own parallel civil service to administer the towns. At least this was the general idea, although here too there were some hitches. It took decades before a cooperative branch of the old Buleleng royal family was in place, and many members of the other royal families had to be exiled. In the case of the Klungkung royalty, the exile lasted for some 19 years after the *puputan*.

The royal families of Gianyar and Karangasem adapted best to the new conditions. Gusti Bagus Jelantik, the ruler of Karangasem, embarked on an active campaign to strengthen and redefine traditional Balinese religion. In large part, he did this to

head off the sort of split that had earlier occurred in the north, between modernist commoners or *sudras* who argued for a social status based on achievement, and members of the three higher castes or *triwangsa* who were given hereditary privileges. Ironically this split came about because of a new emphasis on rigidly-defined caste groups under Dutch rule.

The Dutch had to intervene and exile some *sudra* leaders, but modernizing moderates such as the Karangasem ruler realized the need to shape and control the changes taking place in Balinese religion and society. In this, they found ready allies among intellectuals in the Dutch civil service with a passion for Balinese culture, and an international influx of artists, travelers and dilettantes who poured into Bali during the 1920s and 1930s.

Hints of sex and magic

Some, like Barbara Hutton and Charlie Chaplin, were rich and famous and stayed only for a short time. Others, like painter Walter Spies, cartoonist Miguel Covarrubias and composer Colin McPhee, are now famous principally because of their long association with Bali.

The attraction for these well-heeled, well-connected or simply talented Westerners was the developing image of Bali as a tropical paradise, where art exists in overabundance and people live in perfect harmony with nature —

an image tinged with hints of sex and magic that was officially sponsored by Dutch tourism officials. And it was certainly promoted by genuinely enthusiastic reports from those who visited and witnessed the island's intricate life, art and rituals.

The positive contributions of these foreign scholars and artists, working in conjunction with enlightened Balinese and Dutch civil servants, included such institutions as the Bali Museum and the Kirtya Liefrinck-van der Tuuk (now continuing as the Bali Documentation Center).

But there was a negative side as well. Although the Bali lovers claimed to be the complete opposite of colonial authorities, they in fact represented the other side of the coin of Western rule. With the fan dance performances for tourists came forced labor, and in their writings Bali-struck foreigners always conveniently ignored the poverty, disease and injustice that made the colonial era a time of continuous hardship and fear for many Balinese.

— *Adrian Vickers*

Overleaf: *A contemporary illustration from the French newspaper* Le Petit Journal *depicting the puputan of the Raja of Buleleng.* **Opposite:** *The king of Gianyar greets Lt. Schutsal of the 1906 Dutch Expedition.* **Below:** *The king and queen of Karangasem surrounded by family members and various colonial officials.*

KITLV

POST INDEPENDENCE

From Chaos to Tourism Development

The Dutch, complacent in their cocoon of colonial supremacy, were shocked when the Japanese invaded the Indies in 1941, so shocked that they gave up with hardly a fight. More shocking still to the colonialists was the fact that after the war the majority of Indonesians failed to welcome their former rulers back with open arms. *Revolution!* and *Freedom!* had instead become rallying cries around the archipelago, and these were taken up with fierce determination by the Balinese.

Those who had come to believe in colonial "peace and order" and in "Bali The Paradise" were appalled by the intensity of violence and social divisions which wracked Bali in subsequent decades, from the beginning of WWII until the middle of the 1960s. In many ways the violence was worse here than in any other part of Indonesia, a situa-

tion which had its roots in the way that the Dutch had ruled Bali, and the fierce pride and independence of the Balinese people themselves.

Japanese rule, brief as it was, was a period of increasing hardship punctuated by torture and killings. Although the Japanese had initially been welcomed as liberators, members of the Balinese upper class soon found themselves bearing the brunt of a campaign of terror designed to beat them into submission. Military requirements for rice and other products also dictated that the niceties of wooing the Balinese masses into devotion to the Japanese cause eventually gave way to harsher measures.

As the war dragged on and Japan's position became precarious, most Balinese suffered from serious shortages of all basic necessities. At the same time, Balinese youths were radicalized by being made to join paramilitary organizations with strong nationalistic overtones. When the Japanese surrendered, a few Balinese did welcome the Dutch back, but many others acted swiftly to seize the Japanese weapons and take up the struggle for independence. As the Dutch prepared to return with the triumphant Allied forces, preparations were made on Bali for a violent "welcome for the uninvited guests."

Bali's foremost revolutionary was Gusti Ngurah Rai, who led a brave but badly outnumbered and outgunned guerilla group. Some 1400 Balinese fighters died in the struggle, but with few resources Ngurah Rai was defeated and killed. Bali then became the headquarters of the new State of Eastern Indonesia, which the Dutch hoped to later merge into a pro-Dutch federation. Even this state, under the leadership of the Gianyar ruler, Anak Agung Gede Agung (later Foreign Minister of the Republic), turned against the Dutch when they broke their treaty with the fledgling Republic, and so contributed to the achievement of full independence in 1949.

Mayhem and mass murder

Thoughout the 1950s and early 1960s, social divisions which had crystalized during the Revolution continued to widen. Political conflicts and assassinations were rife — the key split being between those who favored the old caste system and traditional values, and those who rejected the caste system as a form of aristocratic "feudalism" designed to oppress the majority. By the mid-1960s the conflict had taken political form as a contest between the Indonesian Nationalist Party (PNI) and the Indonesian Communist Party (PKI). Attempts by the latter to organize a program of land reform exacerbated the already high level of rhetoric and bad feelings, and both sides organized rallies and pressed Balinese to chose one side or the other.

On September 30th, 1965, an unsuccessful leftist military coup in Jakarta resulted in a takeover of the government by pro-Western military leaders under General Suharto. In the wake of the coup, a tidal wave of killings swept Java and Bali, as the military sought first to dismantle the extensive structure of the PKI, and rightist supporters then turned this campaign into one of wholesale slaughter. As many as 500,000 Indonesians died, and up to a fifth of them — 5 per cent of the island's population at the time — may have been Balinese.

Bitter memories

Most Balinese have family or friends who were involved in the conflict in one way or another, but few will talk about it today, so extensive and brutal were the killings. One journalist wrote, "For the next three months [November 1965 to January 1966] Bali became a nightmare... There is no one living in Bali now who does not have a neighbor who was killed and left unburied by the black devils with red berets [followers of the PNI] who roamed about at the time."

A quiet military leader, Suharto emerged as President of Indonesia. His "New Order" government has provided a long period of stability and development, in sharp contrast to the chaotic Sukarno years that preceded it, providing basic health care, food, housing and education to a rapidly growing population of over 190 million people.

Bali has played a key role in Indonesia's recent development. The tourist "paradise" begun by the Dutch has been revised and given modern form, providing a lucrative income for many thousands of Balinese and significant amounts of foreign exchange for the nation.

Under the leadership of Ida Bagus Mantra, a Brahman religious scholar and educationalist who became Bali's governor in 1978, the island's tourist development was relatively steady and controlled throughout the 1980s.

The great challenge of the 1990s is to maintain control over the physical and cultural changes taking place on Bali as the total number of tourists arriving here is expected to triple from two million to over six million.

— *Adrian Vickers*

Overleaf: *Sukarno reading the declaration of independence* (Proklamasi Kemerdekaan) *on 17 August 1945.* **Below:** *Ngurah Rai International Airport in Tuban, a symbol of Bali's modern age of tourism development.*

RIO HELMI

THE VILLAGE

A Place of Communal Order

The Balinese village is a closely knit network of social, religious and economic institutions to which every Balinese belongs. Most Balinese live in villages, yet even those who now reside and work in cities like Denpasar still identify with and actively participate in organizations in the village of their birth.

Spatial organization

Spatial orientation plays an eminent role in all things Balinese. The most important points of reference are *kaja* ("upstream" or "toward the mountain") and *kelod* ("downstream" or "seawards"), although *kangin* (east), *kauh* (west) and the intermediary compass points are of almost equal importance. Note that *kaja* in south Bali lies to the north, whereas in north Bali, on the other side of the mountains, it refers to a southerly direction.

At the heart of every traditional Balinese village (*desa adat*) is the so-called *kahyangan tiga* — the three core village temples that are physically located in close accordance with this system of orientation. Thus the *pura puseh* ("temple of origin") lies nearest the mountains, the *pura bale agung* ("temple of the great meeting hall") lies in the center of the village, and the *pura dalem* (temple of the not-yet-purified deceased and of magically charged and potentially dangerous forces) lies to the seaward side of the village.

Clustered around the *pura desa*, generally between the *pura puseh* and the *pura dalem*, lie the residential quarters of the village, known as *banjar* (sometimes translated as "hamlets" but actually comprising distinctive neighborhoods within the village). These are usually referred to as "eastern," "western" and "central," but are often named according to the dominant profession or caste of their residents. Thus, we find *banjar pande* where smiths live, and *banjar brahmana* where members of the *brahmana* caste predominate.

Each *banjar* has its own meeting hall (*bale banjar*), which is the secular counterpart of the *bale agung* temple. These *bale banjar* are the social centers of the community, often now equipped with ping-pong tables and TV sets and surrounded by small portable foodstalls in the late afternoon.

Each *banjar* is surrounded by ricefields and gardens. The outer boundaries of the village are usually clearly marked by hedges, valleys, streams, forests and the like. There are many local and regional variations in village layout determined by local topography, population density, and so on, but there is a common pattern.

The family compound

In stark contrast to the open social and religious spaces of the village, the family living quarters are enclosed and private. House compounds are surrounded by a wall and from the outside nothing much can be seen.

A family compound consists of several buildings whose location and function are strictly defined and spacially determined. In the mountainward-eastern corner of the compound lies the family temple. Also toward the mountainward side is the *bale gunung rata* or *meten bandung* in which the parents and grandparents usually live.

The *bale dangin* or *bale gede* (the "east" or "great" pavilion) is where family ceremonies such as tooth-filings and weddings are held, but the children may also sleep here. Guests are normally received in the eastern pavilion.

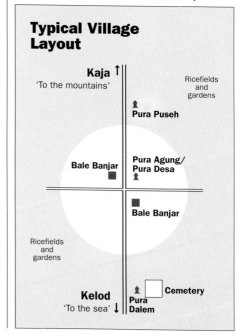

Typical Village Layout

Kaja ↑ — 'To the mountains'
Kelod ↓ — 'To the sea'

Ricefields and gardens

Pura Puseh

Bale Banjar   Pura Agung/ Pura Desa

Bale Banjar

Ricefields and gardens

Cemetery

Pura Dalem

The western pavilion (*bale dauh*) is where children normally sleep. In the seaward or downhill section of the compound we find the more mundane and functional structures — the kitchen (*paon*), rice granary (*lumbung*), pigsty and the bathroom (if there is one).

It is within the house compound that a child is reared and integrated into the ways of village life with the help and care of parents, siblings and, most especially, the grandparents. Male children continue to live here; a girl moves to the compound of her in-laws.

Social and religious organization

The Balinese village may be said to be "semi-autonomous" in the sense that it is largely responsible for its own socio-religious affairs and yet still forms part of wider governmental and religious networks. The *desa adat* is the lowest administrative level of the state. A number of *desa adat* form a "sub-district" (*desa* or *perbekelan*), several of which form a district (*kecamatan*), which in turn make up the regency (*kabupaten*). The boundaries of the latter are for the most part identical with those of the former Balinese kingdoms.

The semi-autonomous status of the village creates the need for a dual village administration — a *kliang adat* or chief responsible for internal village affairs, and a *kliang dinas* who is responsible to the regional government. Below these are several *banjar* chiefs.

The village is further characterized by the existence of numerous groupings, membership in which is only partially voluntary. Before marriage, a person is a member of the boys' or girls' club. These have specific duties in the context of village rituals, and may be regarded as a "training ground" for the person's later participation in village affairs as a married adult. Upon marriage, a Balinese becomes a member of the neighborhood association (*banjar*), the village association, the irrigation society (*subak*), and several other groups such as the local music club, the rice harvest association, and so on.

Every Balinese thus lives within a complex matrix of interconnecting and overlapping associations. He or she has multiple duties to fulfill as members of these various institutions, as well as in the complex rounds of regional, village and family-based ceremonies. It is due to the great complexity of these groups and their attendant support of the individual's personal identity that the village has retained its vital role as the focal point of Balinese life, even in the face of rapid modernization and change.

— Danker Schaareman

Overleaf: *Carrying offerings to a village temple for an* odalan *or anniversary ceremony. Photo by Kal Muller.* **Opposite:** *Diagram showing the schematic pattern of village spacial orientation.* **Below:** *A modern painting in the naive style of the "Young Artists" depicting a Balinese village scene.*

THE TEMPLE

A Sacred Space for God and Man

Above all, the Balinese temple is a sacred space in which the deities are honored with rituals and offerings. Whether a simple enclosure with only one or two tiny shrines, or an elaborate complex with scores of sacred structures, the basic function of each temple is the same — to serve as a site where the Balinese pay reverence to the spiritual powers that play such a large role in their lives.

Temple types

There are literally tens of thousands of temples in Bali, and new ones are being constructed all the time. Throughout much of the year they lie eerily deserted, but on the date of their anniversary festival they come to life in a brief but glorious burst of activity, as the congregation adorns the temple with beautiful ornaments and arrives bearing elaborate gifts, dressed in their finest apparel.

We just have one word for temple, but the Balinese distinguish two important types. A *sanggah* (*merajan* in the refined language) refers to private or family temples, generally translated as "house temples." Each family compound has one, containing shrines to the family's deified ancestors (*sanggah kamulan*). Thus there are several hundred thousand house temples in Bali.

The other word for temple in Balinese is *pura*, originally a Sanskrit term referring to a town or palace. In Bali, the word *pura* has come to refer to a temple in the public domain, generally located on public land. These cannot always be neatly classified, but there are generally three types associated with the three most important foci of social organization on Bali — locale, irrigation cooperative (*subak*) and descent group.

Within the group based on locality are temples of the local village, as well as temples of greater regional and island-wide significance. Irrigation cooperative temples can belong to a single *subak* or to a whole group of *subaks*. And within the group of temples based on descent are temples supported by "clans" of greater or lesser degrees of ancestral depth, variously known as *pura dadia*, *pura kawitan* and *pura padharman*. Altogether there are at least 10,000 temples on Bali belonging to these various types.

Three village temples of special significance are the *kahyangan tiga* ("three sanctu-

ERIC OEY

aries") — the *pura puseh* ("temple of origin"), at the upper end of the village, the *pura desa* ("village temple") or *pura bale agung* ("great meeting hall temple") in the village center, and the *pura dalem* (death temple or "temple of the mighty one") lying near the cemetery and cremation grounds at the lower or seaward end of the village. These temples are linked with the gods of the Hindu Trinity: the *pura puseh* with Brahma the Creator, the *pura desa* with Vishnu the Preserver, and the *pura dalem* with Siwa the Destroyer.

The famous temple sites that tourists visit are regional or island-wide temples. These include the "Mother Temple" of Besakih, high up on the slopes of Mt. Agung, as well as the major temples of Ulun Danu (Batur), Lempuyang, Gua Lawah, Ulu Watu, Batukau, Pusering Jagat (Pejeng), Andakasa and Pucak Mangu. These are nearly all mountain or sea temples, marking the primary poles of the sacred landscape in Bali.

Lesser regional temples, numbering in the hundreds, are sometimes called *pura dang kahyangan* or "temples of the Sacred Ones" because they are associated with legendary priests who brought Hinduism to Bali from Java. Their supporting congregations are drawn from a wide area, and in the past such temples were often supported by local princely houses. Nowadays regional governments have taken on the same role. Important regional temples include Pura Sakenan,

Pura Tanah Lot, Pura Kehen, Pura Taman Ayun and many others.

Shrines and pavilions

A temple may contain just one or two shrines within a small courtyard, or it may contain dozens of shrines and other structures within two, or often three courtyards.

The innermost courtyard is the most sacred. Shrines are usually located here in two rows — one lining the mountain (*kaja*) side and the other lining the eastern (*kangin*) side. Toward the center of the courtyard is a large structure where the gods gather during rituals. Open pavilions for various purposes complete the arrangement.

Among the shrines lining the mountainward side one often finds a pair of small closed shrines (*gedong*) — one with an earthenware dish on its roof, the other with a pointed roof. These honor protective deities of the greatest importance: Dewi Sri, goddess of rice and prosperity, and her consort Rambut Sedana, god of wealth. A small shrine with a deer's head is called *menjangan saluwang* and honors the legendary priest Mpu Kuturan, or a deity called Bhatara Maospahit.

A particularly striking structure is the *meru* or Balinese pagoda, which has an odd number of roofs, up to a maximum of eleven. A *meru* honors a god or a deified ancestor, depending on what kind of temple it is. It was probably introduced from Java during the 14th century.

In the mountainward-eastward corner, between the rows of shrines, there is often an open seat-type shrine. In its fully developed form, adorned with cosmic turtle and serpents, this is called a *padmasana* ("lotus throne") and honors the high god Sanghyang Widhi in his manifestation as Siwa Raditya, the sun god. Modern Balinese Hinduism stresses its monotheistic aspect, and the *padmasana* has recently become more prominent.

Temple festivals are held according to one of two calendrical systems. When it appears on the 210-day *wuku* calendar, a festival is called an *odalan*; when it follows the lunar calendar, it is often referred to as an *usaba*. Various factors, such as local tradition and the size of the ritual, determine whether a festival is officiated by the temple's own priest (*pemangku*) or by a brahmana high priest (*pedanda*).

— *David Stuart-Fox*

Above: *Villagers are blessed with sprinkled holy water during a temple anniversary festival.*

BALINESE HINDUISM

A Life of Ritual and Devotion

The majority of Balinese practice a form of the Hindu religion which they call *Agama Hindu Dharma* ("Religion of the Hindu doctrine"). Also called *Agama Tirtha* ("Religion of the Holy Waters"), it represents a unique amalgamation of foreign Hindu and Buddhist elements that were grafted onto a base of pre-existing, indigenous religious customs. Since independence in 1945, the Balinese have become more self-conscious of their religion and have strengthened their religious organization. This has resulted in the establishment of the Satya Hindu Dharma in 1956, and the Parisada Hindu Dharma Bali in 1959. The state philosophy, Pancasila, is also having an impact on Balinese Hinduism as well.

Hinduism and Buddhism arrived in Bali partly via Java and partly direct from India, between the 8th and 16th centuries. Elements of the two religions have developed further and merged here. The Indian division into four castes has also been adopted, and religious practices are closely connected with social hierarchy. Balinese society is separated into four main groups: *brahmana, satriya, wesya* and *anak jaba* or *sudra,* which are in turn subdivided into many more.

Basic principles

Balinese Hinduism encompasses a vast range of practices and doctrines, dominated by Siwaitic characteristics. Siwa is the main god, manifesting himself as Surya, the Sun. Buddhistic elements in the Balinese *Hindu Dharma* derive from a Tantric form of Mahayana Buddhism (the Buddhism of the "Great Vehicle" — practiced in China, Tibet, Korea and Japan). Only small groups of Balinese Buddhists exist today, mainly brahmans living in the village of Budakling, in Karangasem. However in Banjar, in northwest Bali, a Buddhist monastery has been founded which is strongly influenced by Theravada Buddhism (practiced today in Sri Lanka, Burma and Thailand).

The three basic principles of the Hindu religion are a knowledge of the epics (the *Mahabharata, Ramayana* and commentaries), a knowledge of philosophy and theology, and ritual worship (*puja*) connected with devotion (*bakti*) and offerings (*banten*). The central questions in Balinese Hindu philosophy are: where from and where to? Where does man come from, how can he attain release? In which offspring will he reincarnate? What is the origin of the cosmos and how should one behave to guarantee the continuation of cosmic processes? These questions and their answers can be expressed in visual symbols like a mountain with a tree of life, a lotus pond, or a heavenly nymph.

The stability of the cosmos is expressed by emphasizing the quadrants of the compass and their colors, and the gods with their mounts and attributes. Oppositions like creation-annihilation, good-bad, heaven-earth, and fire-water are visualized in the nadir and the zenith. The swastika, wheel of the sun, is the symbol for the Hindu religion in general.

The five ritual categories

The purpose of every ritual is to cleanse objects and people. Holy water, fire and ash can all be used. This can also be done by rubbing or touching with objects symbolizing purity — for instance eggs, geese, ducks, leaves of the *dabdab* tree. It is believed that one's soul may have accumulated impurities

KAL MULLER

through evil deeds during one's life or previous lives, resulting in punishment in hell followed by rebirth as a miserable creature. In order to avoid this, the deceased and his soul have to be purified by means of fire (the cremation) and holy water. A soul which has been released becomes a god (*dewa, bhatara*).

Many Balinese rituals — tooth-filings, cockfights, cremations and others — can be organized at any time, by anyone who needs them. Many others are held only on specific occasions according to the Balinese calendar. In all, there are literally hundreds of rites and festivals that each person participates in during his lifetime, and a great deal of time and expense is devoted to them.

Yadnya is a term of Sanskrit derivation meaning "worship" or "sacrificial rite" that is collectively applied to all Balinese ceremonies. Each rite may have any number of meanings ascribed to it, but all serve to create a sense of well-being and of community, both of which are important concepts to the Balinese. They are also a means of maintaining a delicate balance among the various forces in the Balinese cosmos. The Balinese themselves distinguish five ritual categories, the so-called *panca yadnya*.

Ritual exorcisms

The first of these, the *bhuta yadnya,* are rites carried out to appease evil forces, personified in the form of ogres, witches and demons, and to cleanse man and his surroundings from their influences. Ritual offerings known as *pacaruan* are set out by housewives every two weeks to appease and banish these baleful influences from the house compound.

An annual *pacaruan* offering ritual on a much larger scale, the Taur Agung, is carried out on the day before Nyepi, the Balinese "New Year." Its aim is the purification of an area from the bad influences that have accumulated during the previous year. The rite is usually carried out at a crossroads, supervised by a *pedanda* high priest. Five sorts of fluids are used — water, *arak* (palm liquor), palm wine, rice wine and blood. Blood is thought to be one of the most purifying ingredients and in most cases has been taken from a cock which has been killed during a ritual cockfight. Afterwards, men carry torches through the village and make a huge commotion beating gongs, bamboo tubes, and so on, to expel the demonic forces. The same is done in every house compound.

More elaborate exorcisms are undertaken once in 5, 10, 25 and 100 years. In 1979 and 1989 elaborate Pancawalikrama rites took place in the temple of Besakih, and the greatest ritual exorcism of them all — the Eka

Opposite: *A* pedanda *or high priest intones sacred mantras during a temple festival.*
Below: *The devotion of worshippers is shown by clasping the hands in a ritual* sembah.

KAL MULLER

KAL MULLER

Dasa Rudra purification of the universe which is held only once every century — was also celebrated in Bali's "Mother Temple" in 1979 to mark the transition to the Saka year 1900.

Rites of passage

The *manusa yadnya* or life-cycle rites are designed to ensure a person's spiritual and material well-being. From conception until after death a person is believed to be in the company of the "four companions" (*kanda empat*). After one's birth these are expressed as personifications of the amniotic fluid, the blood, the vernix caseosa and the afterbirth. The latter is buried by the entrance of the sleeping house and covered with a river stone. The umbilical cord is often kept in a little silver box hung around the neck. The companions will protect if treated well; if not, they may create problems.

Twelve days after birth the ceremonial cutting of the navel string occurs. At this time the child is given a temporary "baby-sitter" — a deity called Dewa Kumara. This deity is instructed by his father, Siwa, to protect the baby until its first tooth appears. A small shrine next to the child's bed is hung with flowers and bananas as an offering for the protecting spirit.

Forty-two days after birth, a ceremony is held to cleanse the mother, who is thought to be impure after birth. On this day also the natural force of a "brother/sister" which has accompanied the baby since birth departs, and the child is now considered to be fully human. Another ceremony is held three months after birth to consolidate the baby's body and soul. At this time, the child's official name is announced and he or she may touch the earth for the first time.

After 210 days, the baby's first "birthday" or *otonan* is celebrated. The hair is cut for the first time and the mother makes an offering in the village temple to announce that her child has arrived in the village.

The next major ceremony occurs as the child reaches the age of puberty. This is the famous "tooth-filing" ceremony whose aim is to symbolically eradicate the animal or "wild" nature in a person — held for girls on the occasion of her first menstruation; for boys when his voice changes. During the ceremony, both upper canine teeth are filed down slightly. A person should now behave as an adult, able to control his or her emotions.

Full adulthood begins after marriage, and the person is then treated as a full-fledged member of the community. If the child is the eldest or youngest son, he will replace his father in carrying out certain village duties.

Completing the cycle and returning the soul safely to the other world are the *pitra yadnya* or ceremonies for the dead (see "Cremations"). After death, the soul of the deceased joins the ancestors, and is worshipped with the gods in special shrines within the mestic animals on Tumpek Andang.

Ritual worship is supervised by specialists — the priests. Their main task is to prepare holy water for the believers. People of higher castes cannot receive holy water from priests belonging to a lower caste. The highest and most distinguished priests are the brahman *pedanda*, who can offer holy water to any person, because they occupy the highest rung in the social hierarchy. Members of the *satriya dalem* and *wesya* castes may use priests from their own class, the *resi*, but they prefer a *pedanda*. The Pasek, Sengguhu, Pande and Bali Aga groups all have their own priests as well, but being so low in the hierarchy, they can only offer holy water to members of their own group.

The so-called *resi yadnya* are rituals to ordain priests. To be ordained as a *pedanda*, a brahman must study with a high priest for many years. A ritual ordination or *padiksan* is then organized for him by the family with the help of other villagers. During the ritual, the candidate undergoes a symbolic death and cremation. Thereafter, he is "reborn" as a pure man. After his ordination, his guru continues to act as his advisor and it is only after another year of study that he is able to perform rituals on his own. Male priests are consecrated along with their wives. This means that the wife may take over the priesthood after the death of their husband.

— *Hedi Hinzler* and *Ida Ayu Agung Mas*

house compound. One hopes to regularly communicate with one's ancestors, and every Balinese has a sense of well-being knowing he or she is protected by them.

Rites for gods and priests

Dewa yadnya ceremonies are performed to honor the divinities. Such ceremonies are a communal responsibility, taking place during temple anniversaries either once every 210 days of the *wuku* year, or once in a lunar-solar year of 360 days. The gods or divine ancestors are then invited to come down to earth and reside in their temples. For at least three days they are feasted and regaled with offerings, music, dance and hymns. Priests perform the rituals to summon the gods; those who support the temple pay their homage.

Apart from these anniversaries, major temple festivals are held on Galungan and Kuningan — two holy days according to the Balinese calendar. Another important festival is Tumpek Uduh — held every 210 days — when useful trees and garden plants are honored with offerings. On this day no tree may be cut nor fruits taken. In a similar way, rituals are performed for household and agricultural tools on Tumpek Landep and for do-

Opposite: *The Eka Dasa Rudra exorcism of the universe held once a century, was last performed in 1979.* **Above:** *A "tooth-filing" ritual.* **Right:** *A bride carried from her house to that of the groom.*

CREMATIONS

Pitra Yadnya: Rites for the Ancestors

Life, death, rebirth. This cyclical conception of existence lies at the very heart of Balinese Hinduism. During each life on earth the eternal soul occupies a temporary vessel — the physical body — which at death must be returned to the *pancamahabhuta*, the five elemental substances: solid, liquid, radiance, energy and ether. Only then can the soul be released and reincarnated. Of all Balinese rituals, the cremation (*pangabenen, palebon*) is the most complex, lasting for many days and culminating with the spectacular burning of not only the corpse, but of vast quantities of valuable ritual objects especially created for the occasion.

Calling the soul

Due to the huge amount of time and expense involved, a cremation is usually postponed for months or even years. In the meantime the body of the deceased is temporarily buried. Family members first wash and groom the corpse, then wrap it in cloths and mats. A raw egg is rolled across it and smashes to the ground, removing all impurities. The body is then transported to the cemetery on a simple bier and buried without a casket.

Once a favorable day has been set, an army of ritual specialists, artists, priests, family members, friends and neighbors of all ages and sexes is mobilized — calling upon an encyclopedia of communal knowledge in the creation of offerings of every imaginable shape, color and ingredient and the performance of a series of elaborate rites.

Before cremation a "soul calling" ritual must be held at the grave. Offerings are made, and as the corpse cannot be returned to the house once it has been buried, the soul is taken home in a *sangah urip* effigy containing soil from the grave. Outside the house a paper and coconut shell lamp — a *damar kurung* — is hung to guide the soul home.

The washing of the corpse is symbolically repeated on an *adegan*, a small board with a human figure drawn on it. The day before the cremation, a priest prays for favorable treatment of the soul in the afterlife. Various types of holy water are made and offerings are purified. The *angenan*, an eggshell lamp mounted on a decorated coconut, serves as a memorial.

The procession

On the day of the cremation, once the sun has passed the zenith, loud *gong* music plays and a lively procession heads off to the cemetery. Dozens of offerings and ritual objects lead the way and the body is carried in a colorful tower (*wadah, bade*) fashioned of wood, bamboo and paper, shouldered by scores of shouting men. Platforms at the base represent the earth, sometimes resting on the cosmic turtle and serpents of the underworld. On the back of the tower may be a winged and fanged face of the son of the earth, and higher up a goose symbolizing purity.

Above these platforms is an open space for the body, and crowning the tower is an odd number of roofs representing the heavens. The caste and clan of the deceased determine the number — 11 for royalty, less for persons of more humble birth. Attached to the front of the tower is a long, white cloth

Right: *An elaborate, 11-tiered tower created for the 1979 cremation of the Cokorda Agung of Ubud.* **Opposite:** *Fire brings release from this world and passage to the next.*

(*lantaran*) held by family members to represent their ties to the deceased. The tower is rotated at each crossroads, to disorient and prevent the soul from returning to disturb the living.

Release through fire and water

Arriving at the cemetery, the body is taken down and a pair of birds set free — symbolic of the soul's release. On a bamboo platform under a high roof stands a wooden sarcophagus (*patulangan, palinggihan*) decorated with cloth and paper, sometimes carried in procession ahead of the tower. The sarcophagus is generally in the shape of a mythical animal such as a bull or winged lion.

The sarcophagus is opened and the body or newly exhumed remains (sometimes simply an effigy) are carried around it and placed inside. The shroud is opened, jars of holy water are poured over the body and shattered. Cloths, letters of introduction to the gods and effigies are piled inside, and the sarcophagus is closed. Offerings are placed below to start the fire and the sarcophagus and corpse are consumed by flames. The tower is burned separately.

Death brings with it the opportunity to fulfill all duties toward the deceased, and there is no public display of mourning if the deceased has lived a long and full life. Weeping near a corpse disturbs the soul, making it unwilling to leave. Grief is expressed in private, however, especially if a young person has died prematurely as the result of serious illness or a tragic accident.

Purification and deification

When the corpse has finally been reduced to ashes, the flames are doused and the family hunts for bone fragments, forming them into a small human shape. The bones are pulverized and placed in an effigy made from a coconut, which is taken on a bier to the sea or river and cast into the waters. Three days later another ceremony removes the ritual pollution brought by death upon the living.

Twelve days after the cremation, the soul of the deceased is purified in a *ngrorasin* rite, often accompanied by rites (*mukur, nyekah, ngasti, maligia*) designed to deify the ancestor. A *sekah* effigy is made for the soul and placed in a high pavilion. In the evening, family members pray and offer their respects. Early the next morning, the image is broken and burned, and the ashes placed in a decorated coconut. A tower (*bukur, madhya*) then transports them to the sea for disposal.

Finally, in the *nyagara-gunung* ceremony the family expresses thanks to the gods of the oceans and the mountains. Offerings are brought to important sea and mountain temples, often including Besakih, after which the deified soul is enshrined in a clan or family temple as a protective ancestral spirit.

— *Garrett Kam*

THE BALINESE CALENDAR

A Cycle of Holy Days and Anniversaries

Except in a number of once-isolated mountain villages and ancient court centers, most of Bali follows both a 12-month lunar calendar and a 210-day ritual cycle. Together these two parallel calendrical systems determine the incredibly complex and busy schedule of holy days and anniversaries observed throughout the island — with many important festivals being determined by the conjunction of particular dates in the two systems. Every day also has associated with it numerous auspicious and malevolent forces which must be considered when selecting dates for everything from construction to cremation.

Two parallel systems

The lunar calendar, similar to that used in parts of India, is based upon phases of the moon. Each 29- to 30-day lunar month (*sasih*) begins on the day after a new moon (*tilem*), with the full moon (*purnama*) occurring in the middle.

Twelve lunar *sasih* months comprise a normal year, with an intercalary 13th month added every two or three years to keep it synchronized with the longer solar year. The years are numbered from the founding of the Indian Saka Dynasty in A.D. 78, so that the year 1900 in Bali began in 1979.

The 210-day *pawukon* cycle, on the other hand, is indigenously Balinese, and its repetitions are not numbered or recorded as years. It may have had its roots in the growing period for rice, but the following Oedipal myth is associated with it as well:

A woman discovers that her husband is in fact her own son, who ran away as a child. Vain with power, he challenges the gods but is defeated — 27 children by his mother and aunt are sacrificed. The 30 weeks (*wuku*) of the calendar are named after these characters.

The 210 days of the *pawukon* "year" are divided into many shorter cycles which run concurrently. The most important of these are the 3- (Pasah, Beteng/Tegeh, Kajeng), 5- (Umanis, Paing, Pon, Wage, Kliwon) and 7-day "weeks," whose conjunctions determine most holy days. Each day has its own deity, constellation and omen that indicate good or bad times for a variety of activities.

The *pawukon* year is also sub-divided into 35-day "months" (*bulan*) determined by a complete cycle of 5- and 7-day weeks. Each

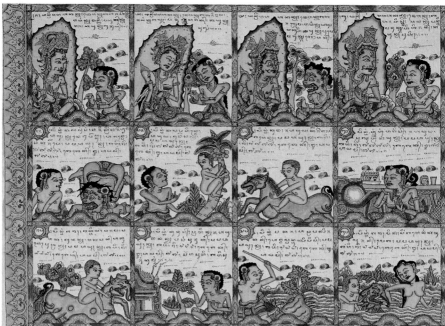

date in the *pawukon* calendar is referred to according to the combination of days in the various weeks, for example: Kajeng Kliwon Menail, Anggarkasih Dukut, Buda Cemeng Ukir. The passage of six *bulan*, a full *pawukon* year, marks a birthday (*otonan*) or anniversary (*rahinan, odalan*).

Sasih holy days

Purnama and *tilem* in the *sasih* calendar are for praying and making offerings, a time when rituals and sacred dances are held in many temples. Temple anniversaries (*odalan*) often take place on the full moon. Siwalatri, the "Night of Siwa," falls on the eve of the new moon of the seventh *sasih*, in January. On this night many Balinese meditate, sing classical poetry and keep all-night vigils in temples of the dead.

The days immediately before the start of the lunar new year are especially full of activity. Processions of offerings and loud *gong* music accompany the icons of every temple to the seacoast for a ritual cleansing (*malasti, makiis, malis*). On the eve of the new year, demon-appeasing sacrifices are held everywhere. That night, a great commotion is made to chase demons away, sometimes accompanied by torch processions of huge bamboo and paper monsters (*ogoh-ogoh*).

The next day is Nyepi, literally "the day of silence," when Bali appears completely deserted. No fires are lit, visiting and entertainment are not permitted, people stay at home to meditate. This continues until the following morning, when normal activity resumes.

Pawukon holy days

Kajeng Kliwon is the only significant conjunction of the 3- and 5-day weeks. Offerings are placed at house entrances to bar demonic forces. Ceremonies and sacred dances are held at temples, many of which celebrate an *odalan* anniversary. On Anggarkasih, when Tuesday coincides with Kliwon, household offerings are made to safeguard its members, and many temple *odalans* take place.

The influence of Buddhism can be seen in the holy days falling on Buda or Wednesday. Buda Umanis is a very auspicious day for ceremonies. Buda Cemeng is a day for praying and meditating. Buda Kliwon is often a particularly holy day (such as Pagerwesi and Galungan), when prayers and offerings are made to ensure the blessings of the gods.

Pagerwesi falls on Wednesday of the week Sinta and means "Iron Fence," a time when humanity must stand firm to protect the

world and its creatures. Rituals begin two days before and prayers are said for the continued well-being of the universe.

Galungan and Kuningan

The days between Galungan (Wednesday of the week Dunggulan) and Kuningan (Saturday of the week Kuningan) are full of celebrations. This 10-day holy period is based on an ancient harvest festival, and it is still forbidden to begin planting at this time.

Each day before Galungan is marked by a special activity— ripening fruits, making offerings, and slaughtering animals. Temples are cleaned and decorated for the upcoming visit of the ancestral spirits. On Galungan eve, *penjor* bamboo poles are set up in front of every house and temple, arcing over roads with flowers, fruits and palm leaf ornaments hanging from them, symbols of fertility.

Nearby altars for offerings are decorated with *lamak* scrolls of delicate palm-leaf cutouts as welcome mats for the ancestors. On Galungan day, prayers are intoned, people visit, and feasts are held. Barongs dance from house to house and receive donations in return for their blessings. On Kuningan day, new offerings and decorations are put out and tools are honored.

— *Garrett Kam*

Opposite: *A pelelintingan, or traditional calendar.*
Above: *Festive* penjor *poles on Galungan eve.*

OFFERINGS

Gifts to Gods, Ancestors and Demons

The many unseen inhabitants of Bali — gods, ancestors and demons — are treated by the Balinese as honored guests through the daily presentation of offerings (*banten*) of every imaginable shape, color and substance. These are first and foremost gifts — expressing gratitude to benevolent spirits, and placating mischievous demons to prevent them from disturbing the harmony of life.

Simple offerings are presented daily as a matter of course, while more elaborate ones are specially produced for specific rituals. After the daily food is prepared, for example, tiny packets are presented to the resident gods of the household before the family eats. Every day, too, the spirits are presented with tiny *canang* — palm leaf trays containing flowers and betel as a token of hospitality.

Being gifts to higher beings, these offerings must be attractive, and a great deal of time and effort is expended to make them so. Leaves are laboriously cut, plaited and pinned together into decorative shapes (*jejaitan*). Multi-colored rice flour cookies (*jajan*) are modeled into tiny sculptures and even into entire scenes which have a deep symbolic significance quite apart from their decorative function. In many ways, therefore, the production of offerings may be regarded as an important traditional art form that still flourishes on Bali.

Materials and preparation

Aside from a few durable elements employed, like coins, cloth and an occasional wooden mask, offerings are generally fashioned of perishable, organic materials. Not only the materials, but also the function of these objects is transitory. Once presented to the gods, an offering may not be used again and similar ones have to be produced again and again each day.

The preparation of offerings is one of the many tasks undertaken by every Balinese woman. Within the household, women of sev-eral generations work together, and in this way knowledge and skills are handed down to the young. To a limited extent, men also cooperate, for it is their task to slaughter animals and prepare most meat offerings.

Many women in Bali even make a living by acting as offering specialists (*tukang banten*). Their main task is to direct the armies of people who collectively produce offerings for large rituals at home or in the communal temple. They are able to coordinate this work because they know the types and ingredients of offerings required for each occasion.

As more and more Balinese women work outside the home in offices or tourist hotels, they have less time to undertake elaborate ritual preparations themselves. This results in an increasing demand for ready-made offerings that many *tukang banten* produce in their own home with the help of women they employ. In spite of this limited commercialization, the meaning and ritual use of offerings is not diminishing in Bali.

Ritual uses

For almost any ritual, the enormous number and variety of offerings required is quite astounding. There are literally hundreds of different kinds — the names, forms, sizes and ingredients of which differ greatly. Furthermore, there is considerable variation from region to region, and even from village to village. The basic form of most offerings is

KAL MULLER

quite similar, however. Rice, fruits, cookies, meat and vegetables are arranged on a palm leaf base and crowned with a palm leaf decoration, called a *sampian*, which serves also as a container for betelnut and flowers.

Certain offerings are used in many rituals, whereas others are specific to a particular ceremony. Basic offerings form groups (*soroh*) around a core offering, and since most rituals can be performed with varying degrees of elaboration depending upon the occasion and the means and social status of

the participants, the size and content of these offering groups vary also according to the elaborateness of the ritual.

The size of an offering may be scaled up or down to match the occasion. For example, an ordinary *pula gembal* contains, among other things, dozens of different rice dough figurines in a palm leaf basket. In more elaborate rituals, this becomes a spectacular construction of brightly-colored cookies, measuring several meters from top to bottom.

Besides the major communal offerings associated with a particular ritual, each family brings its own large and colorful offering to a temple festival. It is a spectacular sight when women of a neighborhood together carry offerings in procession to a temple.

At the temple offerings are placed according to their destination and function. Offerings to gods and ancestors are placed on high altars, whereas demons receive theirs on the ground. An important difference is that offerings to demons may contain raw meat, while those for the gods and ancestors may not. Specific offerings required for a ritual are placed in a pavilion or temporary platform.

During the ceremony, a priest purifies the offerings by sprinkling them with holy water and intoning prayers or mantras. The smoke of incense then wafts the essence of the offerings to their intended destination. The daily presentation of offerings at home takes place in a similar way, through the use of holy

water and fire. After the ritual is over and their "essence" has been consumed, the offerings may be taken home and eaten by the worshippers.

Symbolism

The elements that make life on earth possible are transformed into offerings and thus returned as gifts to their original Creator. But an offering not only consists of the fruits of the earth, but also mirrors its essential structure — decorative motifs often symbolize the various constituents of the Balinese universe.

The colors and numbers of flowers and other ingredients, for example, refer to deities who guard the cardinal directions. The requisite betel on top of every offering symbolizes the Hindu Trinity, as do the three basic colors used — red for Brahma, black or green for Wishnu, and white for Siwa.

Conical shapes, whether of offerings as a whole or of the rice used in it, are models of the cosmic mountain whose central axis links the underworld, the middle world and the upper world — symbolic of cosmic totality and the source of life on earth. Cookies of rice dough represent the contents of the world — plants, animals, people, buildings or even little market scenes and gardens. Pairs of such cookies, like the sun and moon, the mountain and sea, the earth and sky, symbolize the dual ordering of the cosmos in which complementary elements cannot exist without one another. The unity of male and female, necessary for the production of new life, is in many ways represented in the composition of offerings. By recreating the universe through the art and medium of offerings, it is hoped that the continuity of life on earth will be assured.

— *Francine Brinkgreve*

Opposite: *Women bring festival offerings to the temple.* **Above, left:** *Making pula gembal from colored rice dough.* **Above, right:** *Offerings are purified with sprinkled holy water by a river.*

MUSIC

Glistening Tones of the Gamelan

For anyone interested in music — from the casual listener to the professional composer — Bali presents a musical landscape that stretches far beyond the island's diminutive physical dimensions. Few places in the world can boast such a rich and varied musical environment. And while the sheer number and variety of ensembles, performances and compositions is in itself quite extraordinary, it is the superb quality of the music that elevates this tradition into a class all its own.

Over the centuries, Balinese musicians have developed a musical language in which layers of melody and complex figurations are interwoven to produce a unique tapestry of sound. The music is rehearsed to perfect synchrony by musicians in village gamelan percussion orchestras. On almost any evening, one can hear the bell-like tones of the gamelan — from the high, shimmering melodies of the metallophones to the deep, resonant tones of the gongs and drums — drifting across the ricefields as villagers prepare for yet another temple ceremony.

Music in Balinese culture

In Bali there is a fundamental integration of the performing arts into daily social and religious activities. No celebration or gathering is complete without music and dance. In Balinese religious life, where an elaborate calendar requires an extensive range of ceremonies to be performed, there is a consensus that each event must be accompanied by musical performances. Such performances serve to entertain the gods as well as the human participants, enabling both to return home after the ritual with a feeling of well-being and contentment.

Because of the constant and widespread demand for musical performances, a very large number of music and dance troupes is active on the island (one recent estimate put the total at well over 1500). Music is practiced and developed incessantly by these groups in order to maintain a high standard of technique and to develop an integration between musicians and dancers.

This astonishing degree of musical activity not only maintains the tradition, but also extends it. New works are constantly being created and premiered before village audiences eager for new combinations of sound

TOM BALLINGER

and movement. If these pieces are deemed worthy by the players and the audience, they are added to the existing repertoire and may even gain island-wide popularity. The Balinese view this as "a grafting of new flowers onto the old tree" rather than a break with tradition — an attitude that insures the vitality of the arts here.

These ideals find clear expression today in the Indonesian Academy of Music and Dance (STSI) in Denpasar, where many of the island's best performers, composers and choreographers work to develop and transmit their arts to a new generation. STSI also serves as the focal point for an international community of artists and scholars interested in the Balinese performing arts.

Musical organizations

The term gamelan refers not only to the instruments but also to the groups of musicians who play them. People participate in these groups from a very young age, and one is often surprised to hear intricate pieces being performed by children's groups in which the average age is only 12 years. In the villages, such groups may be formed for special festivals only to be disbanded as soon as the festival is over. Most groups play together for a long time, however — some for as long as 40 or 50 years with unchanged membership. Some groups even outlive their original membership and continue to exist as autonomous village institutions for hundreds of years.

Organizationally, music and dance troupes in Bali are deeply rooted in the *banjar* — the fundamental unit of community within the Balinese village or town. Its guiding principle and philosophy is that any group must strive to exist as a coherent unit rather than as a collection of individuals. In Balinese music, this attitude of cooperation is essential, and individual virtuosity is always far overshadowed by the ideal of unity and perfect synchronization of the various parts. Much more so than in Western music, a single part or musician cannot stand alone, but is integral to the whole. For this reason, solo performance is nonexistent in Bali.

Anyone with sufficient interest may join a gamelan, and groups are composed of farmers, merchants, civil servants, etc. Although the academy in Denpasar is giving birth to a new generation of professionals, music remains by and large a non-professional, village endeavor.

While the immediate motivation to form a new group may vary — an upcoming celebra-

tion, a festival competition with another *banjar*, or a specially commissioned hotel performance, for example — in general the Balinese simply love to play, and a first rehearsal often finds more players ready to join in than there are postions in the orchestra. In typical cooperative *banjar* fashion, even the extras take part in the *sekaha* (club), however. They will become helpers (for moving or maintaining the instruments) or alternate players.

With the exception of large hotel or other tourist performances, little money is made from the performances. All proceeds are put into a common fund for tuning and maintenance or acquisition of new instruments, as well as for dance costumes or an occasional dinner for the *sekaha* members. Excess funds are divided among the members just before Galungan, the Balinese New Year.

Instruments and tuning

There is an amazing diversity of musical ensembles and genres found on Bali. Some 15 to 20 different forms have been documented, and the list grows longer as a younger generation of composers experiments with

Overleaf: *The spectacular* kecak, *choreographed by Walter Spies and performed here at Goa Gajah. Photo by Walter Spies; courtesy of The Walter Spies Foundation.* **Opposite:** *A four-piece ensemble consisting of* ugal, kempli *and two* kendang. **Above:** *Village children "practicing."*

TOM BALLINGER

new combinations and types of instruments. The ensembles range in size from the small *gender wayang*, a quartet of musicians who play the demanding accompaniment to the *wayang kulit* shadow play, all the way up to the massive *gamelan gong*, whose 35 or 40 members perform the ancient and stately ceremonial pieces required for village rituals.

A variety of materials are used in the production of instruments. Most gamelan consist of bronze keys in carved wooden frames suspended over bamboo resonators, together

with a number of bronze gongs, drums, cymbals, flutes and an assortment of smaller percussion instruments. But there are bamboo gamelan ensembles as well — entire orchestras composed of bamboo marimbas or flutes.

Perhaps the most impressive of these is the *gamelan jegog*, found exclusively in the western district of Jembrana. In a *jegog* ensemble, the largest bass intruments are made from bamboo tubes measuring up to 12 inches in diameter and 10 feet in length. When struck with a large, padded mallet, they produce low tones of incredible purity and depth that can often be heard for miles around.

The *gamelan selunding* is a rare and sacred ensemble, with keys made of iron and simple trough resonators. Special ceremonies and offerings surround its use, as the keys are thought to possess spiritual powers. Some *selunding* melodies are considered extremely sacred, and may not be played or even hummed except on certain ritual occasions.

In fact, however, all gamelan instruments, no matter how or where they are played, are believed to contain a spiritual power which must be respected with proper offerings and rituals, depending on the occasion and the date within the Balinese calendar. No Balinese would ever think of stepping over an instrument, for example, for fear that the spirit that inhabits it might be insulted.

By far the most common type of gamelan is the *gong kebyar* — a bronze orchestra con-

sisting of a number of metallophones, tuned gongs, cymbals, flutes and drums. As in a Western orchestra, these instrument families are further subdivided depending on the range, musical function and playing technique of the instruments.

For example, the highest-pitched metallophones (*gangsa*) are used to play rapid interlocking figurations and melodies. The mid-range metallophones (*calung* or *jublag*) play the *pokok* or core melody, while the bass instruments (*jegogan*) reinforce the stressed *pokok* tones and mark the longer phrases.

A row of tuned gongs played by four musicians called the *reong* executes another form of figuration and rhythmic accentuation. The *kempli*, a small gong, keeps the beat — a difficult task in this syncopated and rhythmically complex music. The larger gong and the medium-sized *kempur* and *kemong* provide punctuation of the phrases at important junctures. Leading them all is a pair of drummers (accompanied by the cymbal or *cengceng* player), who direct the entire group with changes in tempo, accents and dynamics.

Bronze gamelan instruments are all hand-forged in Bali by highly respected gong smiths using age-old techniques. Each orchestra is laboriously tuned by filing and hammering the keys and gongs to match a pentatonic or 5-tone scale (and more rarely a septatonic or 7-tone scale) that is unique to that particular set of instruments. While all ensembles of a similar type will be tuned to approximately the same scale, there is no uniform standard of reference. This is a clear expression of the Balinese belief in each gamelan's individual spirit. Every ensemble, in other words, has a unique character which must be allowed to emerge from the metal.

Above, left: *A semar pegulingan* ensemble.
Above, right: *Rare* gambang *instruments with keys made of bamboo.* **Opposite:** *Workshop of a famous gong smith, Made Gableran in Blahbatu.*

Each tone in this Balinese tuning system, which may follow either the so-called *pelog* or *selendro* scales found also in Java, has a corresponding tone tuned slightly higher or lower, so that when struck together the two notes produce a pulsating, tremolo effect. This "paired tuning" is responsible for the shimmering quality so characteristic of the Balinese gamelan.

Musical structure

Balinese gamelan music is an intricate blend of sonorities, created in a densely patterned, contrapuntal web of sound. Enhanced by the tremolo effect of the paired tuning system, the music shifts and vibrates rapidly — some have compared it to the nightly choruses of crickets and frogs in the Balinese ricefields.

Working in an oral tradition (no notation is used), musicians have evolved a complex language based on the concept of *kotekan* or interlocking parts. In this system, the intricate melodic figuration of the music is never played by a single musician, but is divided instead into two complementary parts (called *sangsih* and *polos*). When played together the two dovetail to form the composite figuration.

Aside from the sheer sonic complexity that *kotekan* patterning gives the music, it also allows the orchestra to play at dazzling tempos — enough to defy even the most nimble-fingered classical pianist. Adding to the contrapuntual richness of the music is the fact that several kinds of interlocking parts may be played simultaneously in the various families of the orchestra. All of these parts relate directly to a central or core melody (*pokok*) around which they are woven.

In Balinese dance performances, the drums or *kendang* form a critical link between dancers and musicians. Through an intimate knowledge of both dance and music (drummers often perform and teach dance as well as music), the lead drummer is able to provide signals to the other musicians that translate the detailed cues of the dancer's movements into musical gestures.

To achieve the requisite degree of synchronization, both within the music and in its relationship to the dance, requires long hours of rehearsal. As mentioned above, the language of Balinese music has evolved almost entirely without a notational system. Instead, the various parts of each gamelan composition are learned by imitation.

In rehearsals the teacher repeats each musical fragment until, through repetition by the student, it is mastered. The parts are then combined and unified to form a synchronous whole, and the interlocking figurations become a single composite pattern. Practice and years of experience give the piece subtle shadings of dynamics and tempo, and match its movement with every gesture and accent in the dance.

— *Wayne Vitale*

RIO HELMI

DANCE AND DRAMA

Vibrant World of Movement and Sound

Dances and dramatic performances form an important part of nearly every ritual on Bali. They are seen as an integral part of Balinese religion and culture and are employed as an expression of one's devotion to the gods (*ngayah*) as well as a means of instilling centuries-old values in each new generation of Balinese, through the medium of movement, music and words.

Training and taksu

Balinese children are exposed to dance at a very early age. They are taken to performances long before they can walk, and begin to take dance lessons soon after. Most take great pleasure in this, whether or not they perform, as they are just as interested in the learning experience as in the final product.

There are no warm-ups before a lesson begins, and the teacher plunges right into the dance. The movements are not taught individually; the child stands behind the teacher and follows her movements. When the teacher feels that the pupil understands the basic sequence, she will move behind the student, take her wrists or fingers and move them through the desired positions. The student's body must be both full of energy and relaxed — "listening" to the teacher's fingers as much as to her words, which are sol-fa syllables imitating the music.

After many hours of such manipulations, the movements are said to have "entered" the student. He or she then dances alone, with the teacher correcting from behind as needed. Only after completely memorizing a dance will the student practice with a full *gamelan* orchestra.

Balance is essential in Balinese dance, as in everything the Balinese do; rarely do they

Right: *A famous dance teacher, Ni Reneng, corrects the posture of one of her charges.*
Opposite: *Little girls perform the sacred Rejang dance in the village of Bungaya in east Bali.*

trip or fall. Control is also important — the dances demand control of every limb, muscle and emotion. The dancer must learn how to express the character of his or her role as opposed to expressing one's "true self" (a very non-Balinese concept). One could say that dance involves a displacement of the ego.

The most important aspect of dance is that of *taksu* or "divine inspiration" — the electrifying presence that mesmerizes audiences and transports performer and viewer to another time and place. *Taksu* can transform a plain-looking dancer into a great beauty and a technically deficient one into a great artist. A dancer studying Topeng will often sleep with a mask above his bed so he can study and absorb its character. Masks have their own special *taksu*. One who lacks *taksu* is likened to a "weak flame" — and dancers pray to the god of *taksu* before each performance. It doesn't always come though; even the Balinese have "off" nights.

Sacred vs. secular dances

There are literally hundreds of dance forms in Bali, from the starkly simple Rejang to the highly intricate Legong. Concerns about the impact of tourism caused a team of scholars to convene in 1971 to determine which dances were to be deemed sacred and which secular, so as to keep the sacred ones from becoming secularized. The result was that all dances were placed into three categories depending

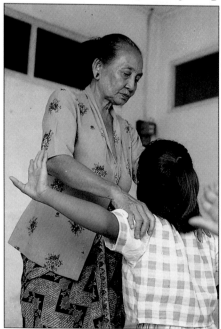

on the area of the temple in which they are performed, and this has now become the standard classification system used for Balinese dance forms.

Wali dances are those performed or originating in the *jeroan* or innermost courtyard of the temple. It is here that the sacred icons are kept and worshipped, and these forms are often group dances with no dramatic elements. They are considered indigenously Balinese, and as with all Balinese dances, are performed to propitiate the ancestral spirits. Rejang, Baris and Sanghyang trance dances all fall into this category.

Bebali dances are ceremonial — performed in the *jaba tengah* or middle courtyard of the temple. This is the meeting point of the divine and the worldly, and these are mostly dance dramas whose stories derive from the Hindu-Javanese epics. These include Gambuh and Wayang Wong.

Balih-balihan dances are secular and performed in the *jaba* or outer courtyard, usually beyond the prescribed sacred space itself (although often this space will be consecrated by a priest before the performance). Into this category fall a number of classical and modern forms like Legong, Baris, Arja, Kebyar, Sendratari and others.

As with most things Balinese, these categories are not rigidly adhered to. Dance dramas may be performed in the *jeroan* and magically-charged sacred dances may be held in the *jaba*. As the Balinese are fond of saying, everything has a place, a time and a circumstance (*desa, kala, patra*) and things vary greatly from district to district, from village to village and even from time to time. The performing arts are no exception, which is why you'll see *barongs* in different villages that are extremely different. This variety is one of the delights of Bali.

Sacred processionals

The most truly indigenous dances of Bali are the sacred *rejang, baris gede* and *mendet*, which are considered temple "offerings" in and of themselves. These are usually performed in stately lines by groups of men or women, with an occasional priest or priestess leading, in the *jeroan* of the temple. The dancers often bear holy water and offerings which they present to the gods.

On the first days of an *odalan* temple festival, the Rejang and Baris Gede are usually performed in the early morning, sometimes in tandem. The **Rejang** dance consists of a procession of females ranging in age from two up to eighty. They move in a slow and stately fashion toward the altar, twirling fans or lifting their hip sashes. Costumes range from simple temple attire (Batuan) to elaborate gold headdresses and richly-woven cloths (Asak and Tenganan).

Baris dances are rooted in courtly rituals of war; the term *baris* refers to a formation of

RIO HELMI

warriors. In the Baris Gede or Upacara, a weapon of some sort is used, while in the Baris Pendet an offering is carried. Various Baris dances are named after the particular weapon involved, and a mock battle between two warriors is often re-enacted. Trance sometimes occurs, and the main function of this dance is devotional — it matters not if the dancers are in unison with one another or with the music, or if they dance with precision. Baris Upacara may be seen in mountain villages near Batur, in the Sanur area, in Tabanan, and now in the Ubud area.

Late at night at the end of a temple festival, a **Mendet** dance is performed by the married women of the village, though in some cases young women and girls join in as well. The women carry woven offering baskets, holy water, or libations of distilled liquor to offer up to the gods on their divine journey home. A procession is formed and they weave around the temple grounds, stopping before each shrine to offer up their gifts. Mendet, like Rejang and Baris Upacara, is not taught but learned in performance.

The divine descent

The word *sanghyang* means "deity" and performers of the sacred **Sanghyang** dances are said to be possessed by specific deities who enable them to perform supernatural feats. Their role is an overtly exorcistic one — they assist in warding off pestilence and ridding

the village of black magic.

Trance is induced through incense smoke and chanting by two groups of villagers — women who sing the praises of the gods and ask them to descend, and a chorus of men who imitate the gamelan using the word "*cak*" and other sounds.

There are many kinds of Sanghyang. In **Sanghyang Dedari**, two pre-pubescent girls (chosen through a "trance test") are gradually put into trance, dressed in costumes very similiar to the Legong (many scholars feel that the Legong developed from this form). They are then carried on palanquins or shoulders around the village, stopping at magically-charged spots such as crossroads, bridges and in front of the homes of people who can transform themselves into *leyak* or witches. After this, the *sanghyangs* lead the villagers back to a dancing arena at the temple or *bale banjar*, where, with eyes closed, they dance for up to four hours. Stories from the Legong repertoire or dramatic forms based on the Calonarang and Cupak are reenacted. In some villages, the *sanghyang dedari* execute the entire dance mounted on the shoulders of men, performing astounding acrobatic feats. This part of the ritual is accompanied by a complete gamelan group, who have been thoroughly trained and rehearsed.

In **Sanghyang Jaran**, a small number of men are put into trance, but their transition is much more violent — they fall, convulsed, to

the ground and rush to grab hobby horses. During the pre-trance chanting, coconut shells have been lit, leaving red hot coals. The trancers are said to be attracted by all forms of fire and onlookers are required not to smoke. The entranced dancers leap into the coals, prancing on top of them, picking up the hot pieces and bathing themselves in fire. The *sanghyangs* are accompanied only by a *kecak* chorus of chanting men.

Both types of Sanghyang may be seen four times a week in Bona, where it is claimed that the performers are indeed possessed, albeit by lesser deities.

Dramatic courtly forms

In the 14th century, Bali was conquered by the great Majapahit kingdom of East Java. As a result, a number of Javanese nobles and courtiers settled in Bali, bringing with them their dances, their caste system and a variety of ceremonies which quickly became interwoven with the rich tapestry of indigenous beliefs and rituals.

The stories of the **Gambuh** dance drama are principally based on the Malat tales concerning the adventures of a Javanese prince, Panji Inu Kertapati, and his quest for the beautiful princess Candra Kirana. However, the dramatic action centers about the courts and the pomp which infuses royal battles. The ideals and manners of 14th century Java and Bali are thus preserved in this form.

The language of Gambuh is Kawi or Old Javanese, which very few Balinese understand. There is little clowning, as more attention is paid to the choreography than to the story. Perhaps because of this, there are only three active village troupes left on the island, all in Batuan. Gambuh is definitely worth seeing, as all Balinese dance and musical forms may be said to stem from it. Gambuh is accompanied by a small ensemble in which four to eight men play meter-long flutes. These, along with a two-stringed *rebab*, provide hauntingly beautiful melodies.

Mask dramas

Topeng literally means "pressed against the face" or mask. All actors in **Topeng** dramas are masked. Refined characters wear full masks; clowns and servants sport a half-mask which facilitates speaking. Topeng is a tremendously popular form in Bali, as it relates local lore and historical tales concerning the royal lineages in scenes of everyday life. Topeng is also immensely entertaining, as the use of humor and clowns is extensive.

KAL MULLER

The first dancers to emerge are the *peng-elembar* or introductory characters — three or four ministers at the court. Next to appear is the *penasar*, by far the most important character in the play. His role is a combination of storyteller, royal servant, stage director, and at times music conductor. He extols the virtues of the king in a sung soliloquoy alternating between Kawi and Balinese. As in many dance dramas, form takes precedence over plot.

His younger brother and sidekick Kartala then comes out and the two engage in slapstick antics. Both the *penasar* and Kartala wear half-masks and speak in colloquial Balinese. The king then appears, moving with delicate steps and thus showing his refined nature. He gestures — as his full mask prevents him from speaking — and the *penasar* translates for him.

Inevitably there is a kingdom to conquer or a person to rescue. The servants of an opposing king appear and more clowning takes place. Often a series of masked dancers with grotesque features appear one at a time under the guise of joining the king's army or going to pay homage at the palace. Here, the audience goes wild. Masks with three sets of

Opposite: *A dramatic Sanghyang Jaran or hobby-horse "fire dance" at Bona.* **Above:** *Sanghyang Dedari. Both are sacred trance dances in which the performers are possessed by specific deities.*

RIO HELMI

teeth, burlesque women — even tourists in cock-eyed berets appear on the scene. If the audience is receptive, these antics could go on for hours. Imbedded in the joking, however, are values of religious piety and honesty that the Balinese treasure. Topeng, along with the *wayang kulit* shadow play, is the primary medium through which Balinese history, values, and even a knowledge of current events are transmitted. In the end, the two factions contend, and the "bad guys" admit defeat.

Prembon

The Balinese love to create new genres by melding together different forms. In the 1940s the king of Gianyar, I Dewa Manggis VIII, summoned his royal dancers and asked them to create a new dance called **Prembon**, taking elements from the Gambuh, Arja (a kind of operatta), Topeng, Parwa (a non-masked form based on the *Mahabharata*) and Baris.

A night of Prembon often begins with a solo Baris and some other *tari lepas* (non-dramatic dance). A story of Balinese kings with characters from all of the above forms is then presented, although it most resembles a Topeng performance. Watching Prembon gives the uninitiated an excellent glimpse of all of these genres in a way that is easier to follow than say, Gambuh or Arja. And often it is the best dancers of each tradition that perform these pieces.

Battling the dark side

Every fifteen days, on Kajeng Kliwon, the dark forces of Bali gather to frolic and inflict illness on unsuspecting souls. These witches or *leyak* are humans who, through the study of black magic, are able to transform themselves into grotesque animals, demons, even flying cars. They haunt crossroads, graveyards or bridges, and this particular day, due to its inauspiciousness for *dharma*, or the correct path, is auspicious for Rangda, queen of the *leyaks*. A performance of the **Calonarang** dance is then often held.

As with many Balinese dance dramas, the story is based on historical sources. In the early 11th century, a powerful Balinese king, Udayana, married an east Javanese princess, Mahendratta. When he found out she had been practicing black magic, he banished her to the forest. No one dared to marry her daughter, even though she was stunningly beautiful — so afraid were they of her mother's magic. To this day the queen, her teeth grown into fangs, her tongue a long flame and her hair full of fire, takes revenge by spreading pestilence throughout the land.

There are many variations on the Calonarang dance, but all involve the Barong — a mythological beast with an immense coat of fur and gilded leather vestments. The most common and sacred is the Barong Ket, a cross between a lion and a bear, although the

Barong Macan (tiger), Barong Bangkal (wild boar), Barong Celeng (pig) and Barong Gajah (elephant) also exist.

The Barong is considered a protector of the village. Of demonic origin, the people have made a beast in his image and transformed him into a playful, benevolent creature. Upon entering, he prances about the stage, shaking his great girth and clacking his jaws. He is often followed by the *telek* and *jauk,* two masked groups of men depicting deities and demons, respectively. They fight, but no one wins (a common theme in Balinese performances).Their role is simply to help restore and maintain balance.

The story then begins with the *condong* (lady-in-waiting) bemoaning the fact that no one will marry her mistress, Ratnamanggali, who then enters and dances. The lights are dimmed and the followers of Rangda enter, holding white cloths whose touch can cause illness. Matah Gede, the witch in human form, then instructs them in deeds of destruction and walks up to her temporary shack on the stage. Two male papaya trees have also been stuck into the ground here, said to represent the *kepoh* tree of the graveyard, a favorite haunt of *leyaks.*

The scene then switches to the village, where many people have died. A group of villagers brings a baby to the cemetery to be buried and the slumber of men in the graveyard is comically disturbed by a *celuluk* — a balding demoness with bulging eyes. This scene is always played to the hilt, with suggestive gestures from her and lewd remarks from the men.

The king and his minister, Mpu Bharadah, then appear and the king asks for advice on how to stop the horrible pestilence plaguing his kingdom. The advisor suggests that his son, Bahula, marry Ratnamanggali to discover how her mother gains her power. This he does, and it turns out that Rangda has stolen a book of holy mantras and recites them backwards. Bahula steals the book and takes it to his father. Mpu Bharadah then confronts Rangda, and a battle of magical wits takes place. Rangda burns the papaya tree and challenges the priest to do the same. He revives the tree and burns Rangda, but brings her back to life, determined that whe will see the evil in her ways. On stage, Rangda can never be killed, only pushed back to the cemetery where she belongs.

The most famous part of this dance drama is the confrontation between Rangda and Barong, involving followers of Barong who attack Rangda with krisses or daggers that are then turned back on themselves. This can also be performed as a separate drama, called simply a **Barong** dance.

Opposite: *A topeng or mask dance performance.*
Above: *The benevolent Barong is carried through the village to rid it of pestilence and evil.*

RIO HELMI

Barong enters, followed by the *telek* and *jauk,* and then Rangda appears, challenging him to a fight. He cannot withstand Rangda's evil power, so the "kris dancers" (*ngunying* or *ngurek*) rush to his assistance and attack Rangda. In a traditional performance, these *ngunying* are in a trance of sorts. The players have reported feeling a heat inside of them and a burning desire to kill Rangda. At times, her power is too much and they fall, apparently lifeless, to the ground. At other times, her power makes them convulse and stab themselves. Some men state that there is a spot, usually on their chest, that itches and they feel compelled to stab it. These men are never allowed to get too far out of control — if they do, their krisses are taken away from them and they are sprinkled with holy water to bring them out of trance.

Barong moves among them, shaking his beard (next to the mask itself, his most holy attribute). After they have all come out of trance, the performance is over and everyone goes home. To the Balinese, the struggle is real enough to be frightening, and the best actors can actually "invite" *leyak* to come to the stage to challenge their own magic.

The exquisite Legong

Perhaps the most famous of Bali's dances, the **Legong** is also by far the most exquisite. Performed by three highly trained young girls, it is said to have been the created by the king of Sukawati, I Dewa Agung Made Karna (1775-1825), who meditated for 40 days and 40 nights in the Yogan Agung temple in Ketewel and saw two celestial angels, resplendent in glittering gold costumes. When he finished his meditations, he summoned the court musicians and dancers and taught them what he had seen, calling it the Sanghyang Legong. This was first performed in the temple with nine masks, and is still performed there every seven months.

Most scholars agree that the Legong grew out of the Sanghyang Dedari. All Legong pieces are for two young girls. Some are totally abstract with no narrative; others tell a story and the *legongs* act out different roles.

In 1932, Ida Bagus Boda, a famous Legong teacher, created the *condong* or female attendant role, which serves as an introduction to the piece. In shimmering costume, her body wrapped like a gilded cocoon, the *condong* makes her entrance. After a solo of about ten minutes, she spies two fans on the ground, scoops them up and turns around to face the two *legongs.* Dancing in complete unison, they take the fans from the *condong,* perform a short piece called *bapang,* and the *condong* exits. It is here that the narrative begins.

Above: *A Legong performance.* **Opposite:** *The famous Mario (I Ketut Maria) from Tabanan, performing the electrifying Kebyar Duduk which he invented and popularized. Photo by Walter Spies.*

The most commonly performed tale is that of a princess lost in the woods of the wicked king of Lasem. He kidnaps her and tries to seduce her, but she spurns his advances. Upon hearing of her fate, her brother, the king of Daha, declares war on the king of Lasem. As they go forth into battle, the *condong* reappears wearing gilded wings — a *guak* (crow) or bird of ill omen. The two kings fight, with evil Lasem invariably meeting death at the hands of King Daha.

Other stories portrayed are *Jobog*, where the two monkey kings Subali and Sugriwa fight over the love of a woman; *Kuntir*, where Subali and Sugriwa are seen in their youth; *Kuntul*, a dance of white herons; and *Semaradhana*, where the god of love Semara takes leave of his wife Ratih and goes to awaken the god Siwa (represented by a Rangda mask) out of meditation. The traditional centers for Legong are Saba, Peliatan and Kelandis. Today one can also see performances in Teges, Ubud and many other villages.

New forms: the Kecak

In the 1930s, when tourism to Bali was just beginning, two western residents, painter Walter Spies and author Katharane Mershon felt that the *"cak"* chorus of the Sanghyang dances, taken out of its ritual context with an added storyline, would be a hit among their friends and other visitors. Working with Limbak and his troupe in Bedulu village, they incorporated Baris movements into the role of the *cak* leader. Eventually the story of the *Ramayana* was added, though it wasn't until the 1960s that elaborate costumes were used.

The **Kecak** dance, as it is now called, involves a chorus of at least 50 men. They sit in concentric circles around an oil lamp and begin to slowly chant: *cak-cak-cak-cak* is the sound they make. Up to seven different rhythms are interwoven, creating a tapestry of sound similar to the gamelan. One man is the *kempli* or time beater and his *"pong"* cuts through the chorus. A *juru tandak* sings the tale of the *Ramayana* as the drama progresses. Tourists call this the "Monkey Dance," because at the end of the play the men become the monkey army sent to rescue Sita. The *cak* sound also resembles the chattering of monkeys.

Kecak is performed solely for tourists. One would never see it in a temple ceremony. Even though it has its roots in the Sanghyang trance dances, the Kecak dancers themselves do not go into trance.

Kebyar: lighting strikes

At the turn of this century, north Bali was the scene of great artistic ferment, as gamelan competitions were common and each club vied to outdo the other. In 1914, Kebyar Legong was born — a new dance for two young women who portray an adolescent youth (the prototype for the dynamic Taruna Jaya, chore-

KAL MULLER

ographed by I Gede Manik in the early l950s). There was no story — the emphasis being instead on interpretation of the music, a new phenomenon. This form swept the island like lightning, which is what *kebyar* literally means. The music is equally electrifying, full of sudden stops, starts and complex rhythms.

Four years later, the king of Tabanan commissioned a *gamelan kebyar* to perform at an important cremation. One member of the audience was so taken with the music that he began to compose and choreograph his own pieces in this style. This was I Ketut Maria (also known as "Mario"), the most famous Balinese dancer of this century.

In l925 Mario debuted his **Kebyar Duduk** — a dance performed entirely while seated on the ground. With no narrative to tell, the Kebyar dancer presents a range of moods — from coquettishness to bashfulness, and from sweet imploring to anger. Mario himself performed this while playing the *trompong* (a long instrument with 14 inverted kettle gongs), using theatrics and flashy moves to coax sound from the instrument.

In l951, Mario was approached by British entrepreneur John Coast and Anak Agung Gede Mantera of Peliatan to create a new piece. They wanted a boy-meets-girl theme for their world tour in 1952. Tambulilingan Ngisap Madu ("a bumblebee sips honey"), now known as **Oleg Tambililingan**, was the result — created for I Gusti Raka, one of the tiny Peliatan *legongs*, and Gusti Ngurah Raka, Mario's prize Kebyar student. It is a story, mimed in abstract terms, of a female bumblee sipping honey and frolicking in a garden. A male bumblebee sees her, encircles her in a dance of courtship and they finally mate.

Into the spotlight: Sendratari

During the political upheavals of the '60s, many new ideas in dance and music were ushered in. A team of Balinese artists at KOKAR (now SMKI, the High School for Performing Arts) in l962 created a new form called **Sendratari**, from *seni* ("art")-*drama-tari* ("dance"). Instead of having dancers speak their lines, as in Gambuh, Topeng and Arja, a *juru tandak* sits in the gamelan and speaks them in Kawi and Balinese. The dancers pantomime the action on stage. Since then, KOKAR and STSI artistes have created new Sendratari very year for the Bali Arts Festival, filling to capacity the open-air theater at the Art Center which seats 5,000. These are lavish spectacles, with casts of hundreds. The stories are usually taken from the *Ramayana* and the *Mahabharata*.

The Arts Festival showcases some of the best dance and music on the island. The festi-

Above: A "frog dance" by I Made Jimat of Batuan — one of many new creations found in Bali.
Opposite: A televised Sendratari performance in the Denpasar Art Center.

val begins in mid-June and runs through mid-July. Schedules are available from the Regional Tourism Office in Denpasar.

Birds and other beasts

This decade has ushered in new forms which are adding to the classical repertoire of Balinese dance. These Kebyar style forms may be popular for a year, a decade or a century — one can never be sure with the Balinese. Most of the new forms are being created by teachers and students at SMKI and STSI.

In 1982 these teachers inserted a bird scene into one of the Mahabharata Sendratari episodes. This team effort was then refined into Tari Manuk Rawa ("long-legged bird dance") in 1982 by I Wayan Dibia, a lecturer at STSI and one of Bali's most prolific modern choreographers. The movements of the bird are stylized; the costumes have cloth wings attached.

Such was the popularity of Manuk Rawa that other bird forms sprung up, notably Tari Kedis Perit ("sparrow dance") by Ni Ketut Arini Alit, and Tari Belibis (a story of a mother swan and her young) and Tari Cendrawasih ("bird of paradise dance") both by Ni Luh Suasthi Bandem, also a lecturer at STSI. Two dances that one can see everywhere are Kijang Kencana (by I Gusti Ngurah Supartha), a "golden deer dance" performed by tiny girls with abundant energy, and Jaran Teji by I Wayan Dibia, a humorous dance of horseback riders that has become a real hit.

New creations

The so-called *kreasi baru* or "new creations" used to refer to the collossal Sendratari productions of the dance schools. Today, however, this term encompasses what in the West would be called "performance art" — which means in Bali, anything quite out of the ordinary. Most of these *kreasi* come out of the academies, SMKI and STSI. There are national festivals every year of new music and modern dance which encourage these forms. Some of the young composers and choreographers are fusing elements of East and West into spectacular and original forms; others are wallowing in mediocre attempts at self-expression and self-indulgence.

One recent form to hit the stage is *dansa* — a rehearsed "disco" dancing of sorts set to pop hits of the day. Often village youth clubs will hold fund-raisers where traditional dances will be interspersed with *dansa* by local girls and boys. This is probably partially due to the influence of the music videos televised nationally very Sunday afternoon.

The tradition of dance in Bali is a strong and a rich one. Even with the influx of modern, Western culture the classical Balinese forms are still the most popular and will undoubtedly remain so for a very long time to come.

— *Rucina Ballinger*

RIO HELMI

TEXTILES

Cloths of Great Power and Artistry

Indonesia enjoys an enviable reputation as a veritable paradise for textile connoisseurs. On Bali, as elsewhere in the archipelago, traditional textiles are much more than simply decorative pieces of cloth. To the Balinese they represent a mark of cultural identity and religious exclusivity, while the use of certain cloths also convey subtle differences of birth, age, sex, title and caste. Traditional fabrics also serve many sacred and ritual functions, distinguishing the holy from the profane and the good from the evil.

Humans are not the only ones who wear clothes — the Balinese clothe almost everything which possesses a head, a body and feet. Buildings, shrines, altars, ancestor stones and statues are all wrapped in costly or magically permeated apparel during rituals. The cotton yarns are said to bring strength to both men and objects, protecting them and warding off harmful influences.

The ritual wardrobe

The ritual or *adat* wardrobe of the Balinese consists of several lengths of cloth of various sizes. These are not tailored, but are used in the form in which they are woven, and then draped artfully around the body. Boys and men wrap a large skirt (*kamben* or *wastra*) around themselves and tie it in such a way that a long fold hangs down in front between the legs, nearly touching the ground. Girls and women wrap their bodies below the waist clockwise as tightly as possible.

In some rituals, an inner cloth is wound around the body as an undergarment (*tapih* or *sinjang*). A *kamben* or *wastra*, which can extend down to the ankles, is then wrapped over the undergarment. The end is tucked in at the waist near the left hip, and the *kamben* is generally secured by a narrow sash wound around the body several times.

Tube skirts (*sarung*) do not belong to the traditional wardrobe, though imported Javanese cloths with batik patterns are commonly used as *kamben*. During the past few years, Balinese weft ikat cloths (*endek*) from Gianyar, Sidemen, Bubunan or Cakranegara (Lombok) have increasingly come into use.

A smaller sash, known as *saput* or *kampuh,* is wound round the hips or the chest by boys and men, falling approximately to the knees. The belt (*umpal*) attached to the end

of this cloth is wrapped around the body and knotted below the upper edge of the *saput*. Another type of sash, known as *sabuk* or *pekekek,* is generally so long that it is wrapped once round the body and then knotted. Men also wear a graceful headcloth, sometimes in the form of a little boat-shaped hat (*destar udang*).

Womens' outer garments consist of a long band similiar to a belt (*sabuk, setagen*) holding the skirt together, and a breast-cloth (*anteng*) wrapped tightly around the upper part of the body. Sometimes a part of the *anteng* will be draped over one shoulder. In former times, women also wore loose shoulder sashes (*selendang*).

Until the 1930s, Balinese women were usually naked above the waist in everyday situations, but always covered the upper parts of their bodies when bringing offerings to the temple or taking part in festive court events. Even though one can still see the traditional bare-shouldered dress at temple feasts and family rituals, this has now been replaced in many parts of Bali by the long-sleeved, lacey *kebayas* that come from Java and are now considered part of the national dress.

Traditional textile forms

The art of Balinese textile decoration is best expressed in men's skirt, chest and head cloths, and women's chest and skirt cloths. Three categories may be distinguished. The first comprises cloths decorated with gold-leaf, called *prada*. These were traditionally produced for royalty and are still used by girls and boys during tooth-filing and marriage ceremonies. The outlines of the design are first drawn on the cloth and coated with glue; the gold-leaf is then applied. Stylized blossoms, plants and birds are the most common motifs; the edges of the cloth are frequently decorated with intertwined swastikas — the symbol of Balinese Hinduism. Other pieces show a distinct Chinese influence.

A second group, just as brilliant and expensive as the *prada* cloths, are the Balinese *songket* brocades. Decorative gold and silver colored weft threads are added when these cloths are on the loom. The range of patterns extends from simple crosses and stars to elaborate compositions with trees, creepers, flowers and snakes.

From a historical point of view the production of brocaded fabrics with ornamental wefts of gold and silver was for centuries the exclusive preserve of the higher castes. Today, brahmana women, along with wives and daughters in the princely *satriya dalem* and *satriya jaba* families, continue to show considerable skill in this art. Centers of *songket* production are still to be found in the

Opposite: *A songket* brocade with supplementary gold wefts. **Below:** *An exquisite example of the traditional Balinese weft ikat, known as* endek.

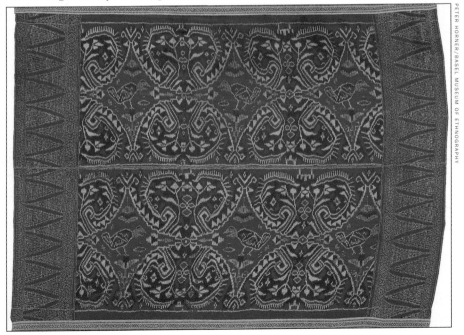

aristocratic and brahmanical neighborhoods of Karangasem (Amlapura, Sidemen), Buleleng (Bubunan, Bratan), Klungkung and Gelgel, Mengwi (Blayu) and Negara (Jembrana).

In 1980, the then governor of Bali, Prof Ida Bagus Mantra, appealed to his fellow citizens to employ Balinese textiles in their ceremonial dress. Apart from promoting village crafts and encouraging the development of the Balinese economy, this has had the effect of reducing the role of these textiles as aristocratic symbols. Anyone of a certain position or wealth is now in a position to flaunt their *songket* publicly at religious and social events. As a result, the demand for *songket* cloth has increased dramatically in the past few years.

The third major type of Balinese textile is weft ikat or *endek*, the weft threads of which are dyed prior to weaving. Areas to be remain uncolored are bound tightly together. Different color combinations may be achieved by repeating the binding and dyeing process several times. Dye is also sometimes applied by hand to the unwoven weft.

Endek is by far the most popular Balinese textile form, and its designs are consquently more reliant on fashion and current trends. The demon heads and *wayang* figures of the older cloths have nearly all been replaced now by finer geometric motifs. The popularity of *endek* is spreading beyond Bali to the rest of Indonesia and abroad as enticing new designs are created.

Magical textiles from Tenganan

The famous double ikat cloths from Tenganan Pegeringsingan rank among the masterworks of Southeast Asian textile art. In double ikat, the weft and the warp threads are both patterned using the ikat method. This is an immensely difficult process, requiring great precision not only in dyeing but also in maintaining the proper tension in the threads on the loom, so that the patterns will align properly.

The showpieces of Tenganan are the so-called *geringsing* cloths, instantly recognizable by their muted colors — red and reddish brown, eggshell and blue-black — achieved by dyeing or over-dyeing with red *sunti* root bark (*Morinda citrifolia*) and *taum* or indigo. It is often claimed that the traditional production of the fabric required blood from human sacrifices. These wild rumors have been refuted many times over, but persist in the tourist literature despite the protests of scholars and the people of Tenganan.

All *geringsing* are made of cotton yarn, decorated with geometrical or floral motifs, lozenges, stars or small crosses. The so-called *geringsing wayang* is best known — large four-pointed stars surrounded by four scorpions divide the main field into semi-circular segments, while inside are buildings, animals and *wayang* figures in the style of ancient east Javanese bas-reliefs, ranging

across the cloth in groups of twos and threes.

Geringsing cloths are said to possess the power to protect against malevolent earthly and supernatural enemies. The fame of the cloths' power has spread throughout Bali, and one wonders whether the independence and wealth of the Tenganan community is not in large part due to a monopoly in the manufacture of these magically potent fabrics.

Geringsing are of importance to all Balinese, irrespective of whether they are used as protective or destructive agents. It is still the custom in quite a few villages to wind the *geringsing* cloths around the seats and sedan chairs in which the gods are carried to the sea or the river to be bathed. Outside of Tenganan, *geringsing* are also used in tooth-filing ceremonies, to wrap around the head, and for cremation purposes.

Narrow cloths called *geringsing sanan empeg* ("broken yoke") are worn by men when a brother has died. During their ritually impure period of bereavement and its associated rites, the cloths are thought to be instrumental in protecting the wearer. It is noteworthy that the people of Tenganan do not use *geringsing* to heal disease in men and animals as is done on other parts of the island. Instead, they use fragments of Indian double ikat which are reputedly just as magical as *geringsing*. These cloths, called *pitola* (also *patola*) *sutra* are woven of silk and were traded to Indonesia for many centuries.

Holy stripes and squares

When the costly and precious *geringsing* and *pitola* weaves are unavailable, luminous red cotton *cepuk* cloths may be substituted. *Cepuk* is used in sacrifices, at cremations, and above all as the protective cloth worn by Rangda dancers. The centers of weaving were formerly Kerambitan and Nusa Penida Island. Today, Tanglad on Nusa Penida is the main production center for *cepuk* cloths, which can be found in the bigger markets all over Bali, sold together with other sacral textiles.

Sacred hip and breast cloths with simple checkered patterns (*polengan*) or small, circular fabrics (*wangsul, gedogan*) are usually worn during rites of passage (especially the three-month birthday, the 210 day birthday and for tooth-filing ceremonies). They define the boundary between the holy and the profane, often acting to shield human beings from the impure, especially when appearing before a priest or priestess to be blessed or to be cleansed. The checkered *poleng* in particular is a symbol of the underworld and is associated with demons and death.

— *Urs Ramseyer*

Opposite: *A magically-charged* geringsing wayang kebo *double ikat from the village of Tenganan.*
Left: *Tenganan women wearing* geringsing *during a festival.* **Above:** *A statue sporting a checkered* kain poleng, *symbol of the underworld.*

BALINESE ART

A Fusion of Traditional and Modern

Modern Balinese "export" art has been charming visitors and collectors around the world for many decades now, and is generally far more popular than the traditional, sacred and ritual pieces that the Balinese originally produced for themselves. One should realize, however, that while displaying many Western and other influences, modern Balinese art has important traditional roots.

Art of the tradition

In the past, Balinese artists were patronized by kings, princes and temple councils. The majority of their works served ritual and magical functions, emphasizing the symbolism of a temple ceremony or domestic sanctuary, or supporting claims of divine authority by the ruler. Traditional calendars, with their attendant astrological symbols, also formed an important category of works.

A major center of traditional painting was and still is located at Kamasan, near Gelgel in Klungkung regency. Village craftsmen here once served rulers who reigned over the whole of Bali. Other centers were located in Gianyar, Bangli, Karangasem, Tabanan, Sanur and Singaraja, where local rulers resided or were influential. After the Dutch took over Bali in the 19th and early 20th centuries, the authority of the rulers waned and new patrons had to be found. As a result, modern influences soon manifested themselves.

Traditional drawings for magical purposes (*rerajahan*) were inscribed with a stylus on palm leaves, potsherds and metal, then blackened with soot. Others on cloth or paper are executed in black ink. The ink was formerly made of soot, and paints were handmade from natural dyes. At present, Chinese ink and imported paints are used. Cloth paintings were only displayed during religious ceremonies; the subject matter being chosen to harmonize with the intent of the ritual.

Artistic conventions were passed down from father to son. There are fixed elements of style, ornamentation and overall composition. Human figures were represented in the so-called *wayang* style, a reference to the leather figures in the *wayang kulit* puppet play. The figures have characteristic clothes, jewelry, coiffures and headdresses, and their facial features and figures indicate their class, age and character. Sky, rocks and ground are

indicated by specific shorthand ornaments. There is no perspective.

Stories are often depicted, the scenes being divided by rock ornaments which act as frames. A back-to-back arrangement of the figures is another way of indicating different scenes. Important scenes are placed in the center and those containing gods are at the top, with demons or animals at the bottom.

The subject matter of traditional paintings derives from religious texts, in particular Old Javanese and Balinese versions of the *Mahabharata* and *Ramayana* epics, the *Pancatantra* fables, Javanese tales about the wandering Prince Panji, and Balinese folktales such as the one about Pan and Men Brayut who were blessed with many children.

The oldest extant Balinese paintings are on two wooden planks in the Pura Panataran and Pura Batu Madeg temples in Besakih. They date from A.D. 1444 and 1458 and depict a small lotus flower and the elephant-headed deity, Ganesa. The next oldest work is the wooden cover of a *Ramayana* manuscript dated A.D. 1826, containing painted scenes

from the epic at the top and sides. Cloth paintings dating from the 1840s can be found in museums in Denmark and Germany, depicting among other things, scenes from the *Ramayana*.

Traditional Balinese art should not be thought of as static. Important innovations occurred at the end of the 19th century. In drawings from Sanur and Singaraja of this period some perspective is used, and figures and scenery are given naturalistic features. More important innovations date from the end of the 1920s, when a naive, naturalistic style incorporating *wayang* elements developed in the Gianyar area. Apart from traditional subjects, scenes from daily life were also depicted on paper in crayon or gouache.

The influence of Western artists

German artist Walter Spies (b. 1895, d. 1942) settled in Campuan, near Ubud, in 1927 and was the first and most influential of a number of Europeans who settled in Bali around this time. Dutchman Rudolf Bonnet (b. 1895, d. 1978) visited Bali in 1929 and settled in Ubud in 1931. The paintings of these two exerted a great influence on local artists. Spies' dense landscapes are characterized by trees with bright leaves, stylized animal and human figures and double or triple horizons. Bonnet painted naturalistic, romantic portraits. The Mexican painter Miguel Covarrubias, who spent the early 1930s in the Sanur area, was

Left: *A* wayang *style painting from Kamasan depicting an episode from the* Mahabharata, *"The Temptation of Arjuna" (artist unknown).*
Above: *A 1928 painting by German artist Walter Spies, entitled "Village Scene." Oil on canvas, 75 x 45 cm.* **Right:** *A work by Dutch artist Rudolph Bonnet entitled "Two Balinese Girls" (1955).*

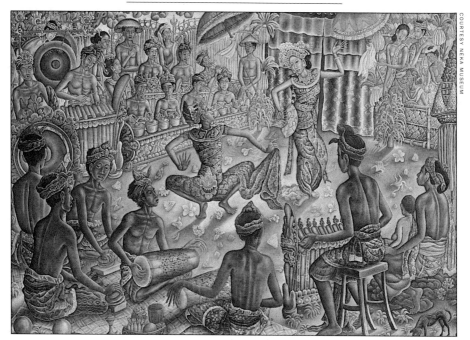

another important figure.

Three modern art centers developed in the 1930s, each with its own characteristic style and subject matter. The first of these was at Ubud, whose style is characterized by refined, polychrome *wayang*-type figures surrounded by Spies-like scenery or Bonnet-like men and women, naked to the waist amidst plants and trees. The figures are harvesting, planting, making offerings and dancing. Witches and scenes from the Old Javanese and Balinese epics were also popular. Famous artists from the Ubud area are: Ida Bagus Kembeng (b. 1897, d. 1952), Ida Bagus Made Poleng (b. 1915), Anak Agung Gede Sobrat (b. 1917), his cousin Anak Agung Gede Meregeg (b. 1902) and Wayan Tohjiwa (b. 1916).

A second center developed around Sanur, whose style is characterized by softly-colored or black-and-white ink drawings with half-*wayang,* half-naturalistic animals in human dance poses, huge insects and birds (for instance I Sukaria, Gusi Made Rundu, I Regig) or naive village scenes and landscapes with trees bearing huge leaves (Ida Bagus Made Pugug, Ida Bagus Rai).

The third center was Batuan, characterized by its stylized half-*wayang*, half-naturalistic figures with pronounced, heavily shadowed vertebra, leafy Spies-like trees, and a very distinctive use of perspective. Originally only black ink and crayon were used on paper. The idea of coloring with crayon came

from the Neuhaus brothers, who began selling Balinese drawings from their art shop in Sanur in 1935. Toda, watercolors, gouache and canvas are used as well. Typical early representatives are Ida Bagus Made Djata(sura) (b. 1910, d. 1946) and Ida Bagus Made Togog (b. 1916, d. 1989).

Some Balinese painters refused to imitate Spies or Bonnet. I Gusti Nyoman Lempad (b. 1875 or 1862, d. 1978) made naturalistic but highly stylized flat human figures with almost no scenery. I Gusti Made Deblog (b. 1906, d. 1987) placed figures clad in *wayang* gear in romantic landscapes.

In the 1930s, many paintings were already being sold to tourists in art shops in Ubud, Denpasar and Sanur. At this time, Spies, Bonnet and the Dutch archeaologist W. F. Stutterheim feared that tourism was having a negative impact on the quality of paintings and drawings being produced, and so with the help of the Cokordas Raka and Gede Sukawati they formed the Pita Maha artists' association in Ubud on January 19, 1936. About 150 painters, sculptors and silversmiths became members, with Lempad playing an important role. The main aim was to organize sales exhibitions in Java and abroad, and to make the artists aware of the importance of quality standards. In this way modern Balinese art began to be purchased by collectors and museums abroad.

The Pita Maha ceased operation in 1942

following the Japanese occupation. Spies died as a prisoner aboard an Allied troop ship; but Bonnet returned to Bali from a Japanese prison camp in 1947 and tried to reorganize the artists. With the help of Cokorda Gede Sukawati, he formed the Ubud Painters' Club (Ratna Warta) and painters from Batuan and Sanur began to work as well as before.

A new style of painting was introduced by Dutch painter Arie Smit (b. 1916), who came to Bali in 1956 and became an Indonesian citizen. In Penestanan near Ubud he taught groups of young boys. Their naive style, characterized by strong colors and primitive, naturalistic human figures soon became well known — their subjects of daily life, festivals, animals and birds are now widely imitated. The group was dubbed the "Young Artists" and recently a third generation has emerged.

Balinese painting today

As Bali opened up to tourists after 1965, young Balinese painters and sculptors as well as many Javanese, Sumatran and Western artists settled in the area between Mas and Ubud. Almost every year a new art style (Pop Art, Macro Art, Magic Realism) emerges and new materials and techniques (batik, silkscreen) have become highly fashionable.

Only a small number of Balinese painters receive formal art training either abroad or at the Indonesian art academies in Yogyakarta (operating since 1950) and Denpasar (founded in 1965). Formally trained artists work in styles and with subjects that differ completely from those of other Balinese painters.

The work of the non-academic painters is still heavily influenced by stories from the epics and folktales, to the extent that many cannot be understood without a knowledge of Balinese literature. All painters, however, are fond of depicting daily Balinese life with its rituals and dramatic performances. Most non-academic painters produce primarily for the tourist market. Many less talented ones, often children, engage in mass production of imitations of works by their more talented colleagues for sale in "art markets" and shops.

Balinese art is now displayed in many galleries and several museums in Bali. Through Bonnet's efforts, a museum for modern Balinese art, the Puri Lukisan, was built between 1954 and 1956 in Ubud. Sales annexes were added in 1972 and 1973. In 1979, an Arts Center, also designed for tourists, was opened in Denpasar. Expositions of paintings and sculptures are now held there, especially in conjunction with the yearly Arts Festival from June to July.

— Hedi Hinzler

Opposite: *"The Bumblebee Dance" by Anak Agung Gede Sobrat of Ubud, one of the original Pita Maha artists.* **Above:** *A painting in the intricate Batuan style by I Made Budi, famous for non-traditional subjects such as tourists and surfers.*

LANGUAGE AND LITERATURE

A Rich Literary Heritage

Three languages are spoken on Bali: Balinese and its dialects, Indonesian, and a kind of Old Javanese called Kawi. Contacts with Hindu-Buddhist Java between the 9th and 16th centuries exerted a strong influence on the language and literature. Later contacts with Muslim Java, with Blambangan, and with Lombok between the 17th and 19th centuries also left their traces. At present the Indonesian language, which derives from Malay and is used in the schools, in the mass media and as the lingua franca of commerce and government, is having a great impact.

Standard Balinese uses different levels, each with its own set of parallel vocabulary, to indicate the caste or status of the speaker vis-à-vis the person spoken to. There are three main levels: *alus* (high), *kasar* (low) and *mider* (middle). This means that a low caste person uses formal high Balinese words in speaking to a person of higher status, while the latter will reply using the low vocabulary. Only several hundred words are covered by these parallel vocabularies, but they tend to be the most commonly used ones.

Indonesian is now spoken and taught at school, and children from six years onwards are thus brought up bilingually with a stress on Indonesian. Moreover, intellectuals and many Balinese parents in towns like Denpasar and Tabanan consider it more fashionable to speak only Indonesian. As a result, knowledge of formal or high Balinese among the younger generation is declining.

Kawi is now mainly a literary language, surviving in spoken form only in the theater. Heroes representing high caste characters from the classical literature express themselves in Kawi, but it is only understood by a few specialists, by *dalangs* and by some of the older people in the audience.

Right: *A priest inscribes a traditional* lontar *palm leaf text with a metal stylus.* **Opposite:** *A 19th century illuminated Balinese manuscript.*

Courtly literary genres

Much of the diversity displayed by Balinese literature today has historical roots. Written sources can be found in the following languages on Bali: Sanskrit, Old Balinese, Old Javanese, Middle Javanese, Balinese, Sasak (from Lombok), Malay and Indonesian.

Sanskrit was used in royal edicts dating from the 9th to the 11th centuries, and still today in hymns (*stuti*, *stawa*) recited by priests. There are many Sanskrit loanwords in Old Javanese, Balinese and Indonesian. Old Balinese was used in edicts issued between A.D. 882 and the early 10th century.

By the end of the 10th century, when close links were established with east Java, Old Javanese was employed in the inscriptions, and it is likely that Javanese literature came to Bali at this time also. Ironically, while Old Javanese is still known and used in Bali, it has all but disappeared on Java. Poems and prose works on religion, grammar, metrics, magic, medicine, history and genealogy are still being produced here in Old Javanese.

During the culturally rich Gelgel period (1550-1600), the kings of Bali kept Balinese or Javanese scribes in their service. These scribes wrote in Middle Javanese, and introduced a whole new genre of laudatory poems on the beauty of women (the queen in particular), or the death of a beloved. They also produced works on politics and ancient history

KAL MULLER

to legitimize the position of the king.

Later east Javanese literature, including stories of Muslim knights such as the *Menak* and *Kidung Juarsa* tales, became known in Bali in the 17th century. When Karangasem took control of western Lombok at the end of the 18th century, Sasak literature was brought to eastern Bali as well. In Karangasem many Sasak words occur in poems.

As Balinese nobles formed their own independent courts and became more powerful around 1700, they began to sponsor works of court literature. Brahman authors were very popular, probably because they knew Old Javanese and were well-versed in religion, politics and the classical literature. The language of these new *kidung* poems was Old Javanese with many Balinese elements added.

A new genre of poetry (Geguritan or Parikan) — epic histories and love stories about Balinese kings, princes and heroes written in Balinese — developed at the end of the 18th century. Folktales, riddles and rhymes were also noted down in Balinese from the end of the 19th century onwards.

When the Dutch began their conquest of Bali early in the 20th century, at a time when the Balinese themselves were constantly at war, a new genre came into being — a poem on the devastation (*rusak* or *uug*) of a realm.

Most works of Old Javanese and Balinese literature are anonymous. The manuscripts consist of *lontar* palm leaves, prepared and cut to size (usually 3.5 to 4.5 cm high and 35 to 50 cm long), and then bound together by means of a string run through perforations in the center or the left hand side of the leaves. An iron stylus is used to inscribe them and the lines are then blackened with soot. Illustrated manuscripts are also known from the late 19th and beginning of the 20th century.

For the most part, Balinese literature is not meant to be read silently but to be sung and recited. It is read during rituals and in theater performances; certain passages are sung or adapted for the *wayang* or the stage. There are also special clubs (*seka bebasan*) devoted to the singing and recitation of poems.

New ideas, new language

With the increase of Western influence during the 1920s and 1930s, many Balinese, especially the Brahmans, came to feel that the Balinese were becoming alienated from their religion and culture. To counter this, they composed religious treatises in Balinese. Treatises on Balinese script, grammar and language were also produced under the influence of Dutch scholarship.

After the revolution, Balinese authors began to write novels in Indonesian, and later also poetry. A Balinese literary movement came into being as well. The Balai Penelitian Bahasa in Singaraja, now in Denpasar, began a Balinese folktale series in 1978.

— *Hedi Hinzler*

WAYANG KULIT

A Unique Vision of the World

Wayang kulit, the shadow theater of Bali, is one of the longest running theatrical spectacles the world has known. For centuries it has survived changes in politics, ideology and fashion — continually renewing itself and providing the Balinese with a unique vision of the world and of themselves.

The elements of the performance are simplicity itself: a white screen, a flame, music, and flat puppets that move and tell a story. Balinese audiences delight in seeing their favorite characters in familiar predicaments. There is the braggart caught in his own lies, the old fool who isn't so foolish, the invincible hero who needs to be rescued, the gods needing help from humans, and of course the beautiful princess — abducted, rescued and stolen back again.

The shadow puppets are made of rawhide, carved and perforated to create lacy patterns of light and dark. The puppets and screen are flat, but when all elements of a performance are in place — flickering firelight, gamelan music, voice and movement — they take on an unearthly dimension.

The characters are all recognizable at a glance by their headdresses, costumes and facial characteristics. There are two main types — *alus* and *kasar. Alus* means refined and controlled. *Kasar* is vulgar and quick to anger. *Alus* is not necessarily good, nor *kasar* bad; what is admired is the right combination of attributes at the right place and time.

A performance is usually a kind of offering that marks the completion of a ceremony. The occasion could be a wedding, a funeral, or any other major event in the life of the individual or community. In urban areas, a performance may be two hours long. In rural areas, expectations are greater and work schedules more flexible, so a performance is likely to begin after 10 pm and last three to five hours. Farmers often go directly from the performance to the fields.

Most puppeteers or *dalangs* in Bali specialize in *wayang parwa* stories from the *Maha-bharata* myth cycle about two families in conflict over succession to the throne. Although each side has valid claims, one operates from greed and self-interest, while the other is more altruistic. The five Pandawa brothers struggle to assert their best qualities, pitted against the 100 Korawas, who lust for power.

An apprentice *dalang* will spend years following his father or teacher from one performance to another. Gradually his understanding of composition, rhetoric and humor become instinctive. He is expected to improvise in several languages, to give convincing and inventive explanations of local customs and events, and to be adept in the use of proverbs and slapstick comedy.

The performance

The shadow play group usually arrives several hours before the performance. As they chat with their host and exchange gossip, the *dalang* will be listening for ways to adapt the story for his audience. He never announces which story he is going to perform, reserving the right to change his mind.

In a given performance, 30 to 60 puppets are used. While the musicians play the overture, the *dalang* makes his selection. Antagonists are placed to his left, protagonists to his right. Major characters are placed closest to the *kayon* — the "tree of life" puppet that marks the beginning and end of major scenes. The shadows are purposely indistinct at this point, symbolizing that the creation of the story has begun, but that like a child in the womb, no one knows what it is going to be.

There is singing as each character is presented. The first scene is the meeting scene, where problems central to tonight's episode are introduced. It is entirely in Kawi, the ancient language of poetry, religion and theater. Then there is a sound like someone clearing his throat, followed by a slow, deliberate laugh. A hush settles over the audience as a large figure moves ponderously across the screen, and bows — this is Tualen, and for the first time, Balinese is spoken.

Tualen is one of four *penasar* — advisors and servants to the king, and interpreters for the audience. They are the only puppets with lips — when the *dalang* pulls a string attached to their jaw, it looks as if they are talking.

During the initial scene it might be revealed that an army is gathering to attack; that someone is missing, kidnapped, or stuck in a dream; that a rare object is needed to complete a ceremony, or that everyone is invited to a marriage contest. There are hundreds of possible openings. They all end with a decision to solve the problem.

In pursuit of their goal, they might journey through a forest filled with dangerous animals, visit a hermit in his cave, enlist the help of an ally, climb mountains or cross an ocean. There will be a meeting between the two sides, ending with sharp words and a battle. There might be a romantic interlude as one of the Pandawas and a beautiful enemy princess fall in love.

Ultimately, fighting ensues and magical weapons fill the air. Eagles fight snakes. Fire fights rain. Ogres change shapes, fly, and become invisible. The penasars are everywhere — fighting, arguing, joking, dodging weapons and providing a commentary which gives the musicians a chance to rest.

The *dalang* works furiously. His assistants try to second guess him and hand him the right puppet when he needs it. The musicians pay close attention, emphasizing each arrow shot with a resounding chord. The audience cheers, laughs and groans, gripping each other in anticipation of what is to follow.

When the *dalang* feels the audience is satisfied, he will play a rousing battle scene ending in victory for the right side. This is not so much the ultimate triumph of good over evil as the re-establishment of a balance between the two. The clowns have a last word, then the *kayon* appears at the center of the screen, and the *dalang* utters the words: "Though the fighting is over, the stories go on forever. We apologize for stopping so soon."

— Larry Reed

AMIR SIDHARTA

Left: *Flickering shadows transport the audience to another world.* **Right:** *The* dalang *or puppeteer is actor, playwright and stage director all in one.*

FOOD

Everyday Fare and Ritual Feasts

Ngajeng! or *Makan!* (meaning "Eat!" in Balinese and Indonesian respectively) are expressions one often hears when passing people in Bali as they are eating. In fact, this is *not* an invitation to join the meal, but rather an apology for eating when the passerby is not. It is a reflection of a strong sense of community found in Bali, and of the great cultural importance attached to food and eating.

Basic ingredients

The staple food of Bali is white, polished rice. Nowadays cooked rice (*nasi*) is of the fast-growing "green-revolution" variety found everywhere in Asia. The traditional Balinese rice (*beras Bali*) tastes better, but is restricted to a few areas and is now mainly used as a ritual food. Other, less frequently grown varieties, are red rice (*beras barak*), black rice (*ketan injin*), sticky rice (*ketan*) and a type of dry rice (*padi gaga*) grown in the mountains. Rice consumption averages 0.5 kilo per day.

Many local vegetables grow in a semi-wild state. These include the leaves of several trees and shrubs, varieties of beans (including soybeans), water spinach (*kangkung*), the bulbs and leaves of the cassava plant, sweet potatoes, maize, etc. The flower and trunk of the banana tree, young jackfruits (*nangka*), breadfruits (*sukun, timbul*) and papayas may also be cooked as vegetables. Foreign vegetables such as cabbage and tomatoes are now commonly found also.

Though they form a major part of the diet, vegetables are considered low-status; high status foods are rice and meat. Because it is expensive, however, meat is reserved for ritual occasions. Surprisingly, fish plays a relatively minor role as a source of protein. Though the seas surrounding Bali are rich, the Balinese are not avid fishermen, as the sea is considered dangerous and impure.

The distinctive flavor of Balinese cuisine derives from a *sambal* condiment and spice mixtures. A standard mixture will include shallots, garlic, ginger, turmeric, galangal, cardamom and red peppers ground together in varying proportions depending on the recipe. A distinctive flavor is also imparted by strong-smelling shrimp paste (*trasi*) and chopped *cekuh* root.

The usual drink served with Balinese food is water or tea. Apart from this, there are

three traditional alcoholic drinks — drops of which are sprinkled onto the earth during rituals to appease the *bhuta* or negative forces. *Tuak* (or *sajeng*) is a mild beer made from the juice of palm flowers. The flower is tapped in the afternoon, the juice collected overnight in a suspended container, and the next morning it is fermented and ready to drink.

Arak or *sajeng rateng* ("straight *sajeng*") is a 60 to 100 proof liquor distilled from palm or rice wine. It is basically colorless, but may have a slight tint from the addition of ginger, ginseng, turmeric or cloves. *Brem* is a sweet, mildly fermented wine made from red or white sticky rice. Yeast is added to the cooked rice, which is wrapped and after about a week liquid squeezed from it is ready to drink.

Everyday fare

Upon waking around 5 or 6 each morning, the typical Balinese woman goes to the kitchen to boil water for the morning coffee and cook rice and other dishes for the day. Cooking is done only once and the food is then eaten cold throughout the day. Breakfast in most cases consists only of coffee and fried bananas or rice cookies. Some will eat small portions of rice with vegetables, often bought in a nearby *warung*.

When the woman has finished cooking, she will prepare a number of small banana leaf mats on which she places rice and other foods. These are then offered to the gods — placed in the house shrines, on the ground by the entrance gateway and in front of all buildings in the compound. Only after this has been done can the main meal of the day commence, usually at about 11 am. A smaller evening meal is had between 5 and 7 pm, just before or after dark.

It is quite unusual for a family to sit and eat together — in sharp contrast to ritual meals, which stress togetherness. Everyday meals are taken in private; one goes into the kitchen, takes what is there and retreats to a quiet place to eat alone, more or less in a hurry, with the right hand. Nothing is drunk with meals; afterward there is lukewarm tea or plain water to rinse the mouth and hand.

Everyday meals consist of rice, one or two vegetable dishes, *sambal*, peanuts, grated coconut with turmeric and spices, and perhaps a small piece of fried fish bought in a nearby *warung*. Usually the same meal is eaten several times, and in general there is not much variation from day to day.

Vegetables are cooked with coconut and spices and served dry or with plenty of broth.

Cooked maize with grated coconut and sugar, boiled sweet potatoes, fried bananas and rice cookies are popular snacks. *Rujak*, a plate of raw fruits mixed with lots of chillies, shrimp paste and/or palm sugar is also popular.

Ritual feasts

Special ritual foods are prepared for each ceremony by the family or community involved. Villagers contribute materials and labor, and the dishes are prepared in the temple's own kitchen. Usually there is a strict division of labor. Men slaughter and butcher the pigs, mix the spices, grate the coconuts, and prepare the *sate* (meat skewers) and other dishes such as blood soup and pork tartar, usually very early in the morning (between 3 and 5 am). Women cook the rice and prepare vegetable offerings (which may be consumed after their consecration).

Each village or area has its own ritual cooking specialists who direct the work. There is a great deal of local variation in dishes, and people from different regions can spend hours discussing differences in traditional foods. For instance, the ritual meat dishes of Gianyar are said to be "sweet" while those from Karangasam are "hard" or "biting."

— *Danker Schaareman*

Opposite: *Roast suckling pig,* beh guling, *served in a Denpasar night market.* **Above:** *Temple priests eating together during a festival.*

TOURISM

Creating a New Version of Paradise

The island of Bali has long been characterized in the West as the last "paradise" on earth — a traditional society insulated from the modern world and its vicissitudes, whose inhabitants are endowed with exceptional artistic talents and consecrate a considerable amount of time and wealth staging sumptuous ceremonies for their own pleasure and that of their gods — now also for the delectation of foreign visitors.

This image is due in large part of course to the positive effect Bali's manifold charms have on visitors, but we should recognize that it is also the result of certain romantic Western notions about what constitutes a "tropical island paradise" in the first place. Moreover, we need to understand that Bali's development into a popular tourist destination has been the result of specific actions and decisions on the part of governing authorities.

Colonial beginnings

To become an important tourist destination, Bali had to fulfill two conditions. Firstly, an island which had previously been known mainly for the "plunderous salvage" of shipwrecks and "barbarous sacrifice" of widows on the funeral pyre had to instead become an object of curiousity for Westerners in search of the exotic. Secondly, the island had to be made accessible. Barely a decade after the Dutch conquest of the island around the turn of this century, both conditions were met.

It was in 1908, just after the fall of Bali's last raja, that tourism in the Indonesian archipelago had its beginnings. In this year, an official government Tourist Bureau was opened in the colonial capital of Batavia, now Jakarta, with the aim of promoting the Netherlands Indies as a tourist destination. Initially focusing on Java, the Bureau soon extended its scope to Bali — then described in its brochures as the "Gem of the Lesser Sunda Isles."

In 1924, the Royal Packet Navigation Company (KPM) inaugurated a weekly steamship service connecting Bali's north coast port of Buleleng (Singaraja) with Java (Batavia, Surabaya) and Makassar (now Ujung Pandang, on Sulawesi). Shortly thereafter, the KPM agent in Buleleng was appointed as the Tourist Bureau's representative on Bali, and the government began allowing visitors to

use the resthouses or *pasanggrahan* originally designed to accommodate Dutch functionaries on their periodic rounds of the island.

In 1928, the KPM erected the Bali Hotel in Denpasar — the island's first real tourist hostelry — on the very site of the *puputan* massacre and mass suicide of 1906. Following this, the KPM also upgraded the *pasanggrahan* at Kintamani, which from then on hosted tourists who came to enjoy the spectacular panoramas around Lake Batur.

Early visitors to Bali sometimes arrived aboard a cruiser that berthed at Padangbai for one or two days, but more often aboard the weekly KPM steamship via Buleleng. Passengers on this ship usually disembarked on Friday morning and departed aboard the same boat on Sunday evening, giving them just enough time to make a quick round of the island by motorcar. The number of people visiting Bali in this way each year increased steadily, from several hundred in the late 1920s to several thousand during the 1930s.

With the landing of Japanese troops at Sanur in 1942, tourism in Bali came to an abrupt halt, and recovery after the war was slow. In fact, right up until the late 1960s, Balinese tourism was severely hampered by the rudimentary state of the island's infrastructure and by unsettling political events in the nation's capital. Yet President Sukarno adopted Bali as his favorite retreat (his mother was Balinese) and made it a showplace for state guests. Eager to use the fame of the island to attract foreign tourists, he undertook construction of a new international airport in Tuban and the prestigious Bali Beach Hotel in Sanur — the latter financed with Japanese war reparation funds. Opened in 1966, the Bali Beach remains a major landmark and the tallest building on Bali.

The master plan

When General Suharto became President of the Republic in 1967, his New Order government rapidly moved to re-open Indonesia to the West. This move coincided with a period of high growth in international tourism, and from this time onward tourism expanded rapidly in Bali.

This development was the direct result of a decision made by the government in their First Five-Year Development Plan (Repelita I, 1969-74), primarily in order to address a pressing national balance of payments deficit. Bali's prestigious image, formed during the prewar years, meant that the island naturally became the focus of tourism development in Indonesia.

Accordingly, the government heeded the advice of the World Bank and commissioned a team of French experts to draw up a Master Plan for the Development of Tourism

Opposite: *Culture shock, a group of Italian tourists on Bali.* **Below:** *A luxury hotel in Sanur.*

AMIR SIDHARTA

in Bali. Their report, published in 1971 and revised in 1974 by the World Bank, proposed the construction of a new 425-hectare tourist resort at Nusa Dua and a network of roads linking major attractions on the island.

With the Master Plan's official promulgation by Presidential Decision in 1972, tourism was ranked second only to agriculture in economic priority in the province. Thereafter the number of tourists visiting Bali each year grew dramatically, from fewer than 30,000 in the late 1960s to over a million by the early 1990s. And these figures do not even take into account the steadily increasing numbers of Indonesians visiting Bali — estimated at around 500,000 in 1991.

During the same period, total hotel capacity increased from less than 500 rooms to over 25,000 — about half of them in larger hotels concentrated around Nusa Dua and Sanur. The Nusa Dua project, in particular, was supported by a substantial loan from the International Development Association, budgetary allocations from the government, and access to cheap credit from state banks.

The Master Plan was designed to attract tourists in the upper-income range who were expected to stay at luxury hotels. But it turned out that a considerable proportion of visitors were not of the target group but comprised young, low-cost travelers staying in small homestays and budget accommodations. As the Balinese have been quick to adapt to this unexpected clientele — for years derogatorily described as "hippies" — new resorts have sprung up at places like Kuta, Ubud, Lovina and Candi Dasa. Whereas the large hotels are owned and operated for the most part by non-Balinese companies, many of them foreign, the smaller tourist accommodations and related services in these areas are mostly Balinese-owned, with close links to the local economy.

This rather neat division between luxury and budget tourist areas is rapidly changing. In 1988, alleging the pressure of demand, the governor designated 15 tourist areas around the island, thus in effect lifting the regional restrictions imposed by the Master Plan, which had prohibited the building of large hotels outside of Nusa Dua, Sanur and Kuta. Currently there is a frenzy of investment and development all over the island by Balinese as well as outside interests.

Tourism: bane or boon?

One significant result of all this has been spectacular economic growth on Bali, so that the province now has one of the highest average income levels in all of Indonesia, with more automobiles per capita in Denpasar than in the nation's capital. Another highly visible result has been the ever-accelerating physical transformation of the island — as more and more hotels, restaurants and souvenir shops dot the landscape.

Not all the changes have been positive, of course. While the resorts employ local staff, they are mostly low-skilled, and many of the tourist dollars end up in Jakarta or overseas. Land prices have soared in many areas, and rural Balinese have often sold their lands to investors below market values. Agricultural output is falling, as more and more farm land is given over to tourism developments, and environmentalists warn that if the present pace continues the island will face critical shortages of water on top of already serious problems of erosion and pollution.

More difficult to assess, however, is the impact of tourism on Balinese society and culture, and opinions on this subject are as contradictory as they are passionate. Many foreign visitors, after only a day or two on the island, are quick to assure you that Bali is finished — almost. The Balinese, so the story goes, have been thoroughly corrupted by tourist dollars and the entire island is up for sale. Authentic traditions are being packaged to conform to tourist expectations, legendary Balinese artistry is being harnessed to create souvenir trinkets, and age-old religious ceremonies are being turned into hotel floor shows. In short, tourism is engulfing Bali, and the island's culture cannot survive much longer. So hurry up and see what you can — next year may be too late.

Other observers, who deem themselves better informed, will counter that this kind of apocalyptic attitude is neither very accurate nor even very new. Travel narratives penned during the 1930s tell a similar tale, they say — these authors having already persuaded themselves that they were witnessing the swan-song of Bali's traditional culture, while in fact that culture is as vibrant as ever, with tourism now sparking a cultural renaissance of sorts by providing the Balinese with much-needed economic outlets for their considerable artistic talents.

This view is reinforced, in turn, by deeply-rooted assumptions about the resilience of Balinese culture. Indeed, the Balinese have been universally praised for their ability to borrow foreign influences that suit them while maintaining their own unique identity. Witness, for example, the blend of Hindu-Javanese and indigenous ideas that inspire current Balinese religious practices. Today, so the argument goes, the Balinese are coping with the tourist invasion of their island by taking advantage of their culture's appeal without sacrificing their basic values on the altar of monetary profit.

What the Balinese think

Faced with such contradictory statements by foreigners, it is interesting to examine how the Balinese themselves feel about the tourist "invasion." To tell the truth, the Balinese did not really have a say in the decision of the central government to trade on their island's charms in order to refill the coffers of the state, and they were never consulted about the Master Plan. Presented with a fait accompli, they attempted to appropriate tourism in order to reap its economic benefits. In 1971, Balinese authorities proclaimed their own conception of the kind of tourism they deemed suitable to their island — namely a "Cultural Tourism" (*Pariwisata Budaya*) that is respectful of the values and artistic traditions which brought fame to the island in the first place.

From the start, the Balinese have evinced an ambivalent attitude towards tourism, which they perceived as being at once filled with the promise of prosperity and yet fraught with danger. The foreign invasion was seen to contain the threat of "cultural pollution" which might destroy those very traditions which provided Bali's main attraction for tourists.

By official accounts, Cultural Tourism has achieved its mission, reviving Balinese interest in their traditions while reinforcing a sense of cultural identity. In actual fact, Balinese culture has neither been "destroyed" nor "revived" by tourism, and tourism should not even been seen as an "external force" striking Bali from the outside. Over the years tourism has instead become an integral part of Balinese society and economy. Even more important, morever, is the fact that tourism is only one of many factors bringing about rapid change on the island. Other equally important ones are mass education, mass media and rising expectations among the young.

In effect, a new Balinese culture and identity is now emerging that is an amalgamation of all sorts of influences, from inside Bali as well as from the outside. The major contribution of foreigners has perhaps been to make the Balinese aware of the fact that they are the lucky owners of something precious and perishable called "culture." Yet they are also increasingly viewing this heritage as something that is detachable from themselves — something that can be photographed, staged, promoted, reproduced and sold.

— *Michel Picard*

Opposite: *A Balinese view of foreigners in Bali. "President Reagan Visits Bali" by I Made Budi.*

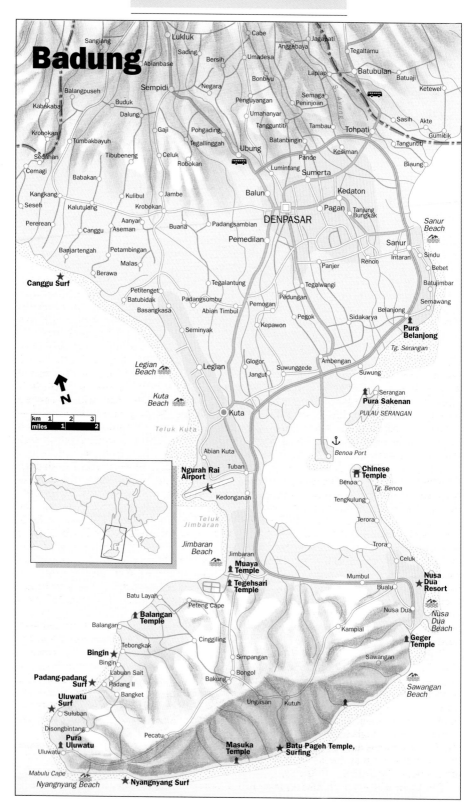

Badung

Sangiang
Lukluk
Cabe
Jagapati
Anggebaya
Tegaltamu
Sading
Umadesa
Batubulan
Batuaji
Abianbase
Bersih
Ketewel
Balangpuseh
Bonblyu
Laplap
Sempidi
Negara
Semaga
Peninjoan
Buduk
Penguyangan
Sasih
Akte
Kabakaba
Dalung
Umahanyar
Gumicik
Krokoan
Gaji
Pohgading
Tangguntiti
Tambau
Tohpati
Tanguntiti
Tumbakbayuh
Tegallinggah
Batanbingin
Kesiman
Sedahan
Tibubeneng
Celuk
Ubung
Pande
Biaung
Cemagi
Robokan
Lumintang
Sumerta
Babakan
Balun
Kedaton
Kangkang
Kulibul
Jambe
Pagan
Tanjung Bungkak
Seseh
Kalutulang
Krobokan
DENPASAR
Sanur Beach
Pererean
Aanyar
Buana
Padangsambian
Sanur
Canggu
Aseman
Pemedilan
Sindu
Banjartengah
Petambingan
Renon
Intaran
Bebet
Malas
Panjer
Batujimbar
Berawa
Tegalantung
Tegalwangi
Semawang
Canggu Surf
Petitenget
Padangsumbu
Pedungan
Belanjong
Batubidak
Pemogan
Pegok
Sidakarya
Pura Belanjong
Basangkasa
Abian Timbul
Kepawon
Tg. Serangan
Seminyak
Legian Beach
Glogor
Suwunggede
Ambengan
Serangan
Kuta Beach
Legian
Jangut
Suwung
Pura Sakenan
PULAU SERANGAN
Kuta
Teluk Kuta
Abian Kuta
Tuban
Benoa Port
Ngurah Rai Airport
Chinese Temple
Kedonganan
Benoa
Tg. Benoa
Tengkulung
Teluk Jimbaran
Terora
Jimbaran Beach
Jimbaran
Trora
Muaya Temple
Celuk
Tegehsari Temple
Mumbul
Nusa Dua Resort
Batu Layah
Bualu
Peteng Cape
Nusa Dua
Balangan Temple
Cinggiling
Kampial
Nusa Dua Beach
Balangan
Tebongkak
Geger Temple
Bingin
Simpangan
Sawangan
Bingin
Labuan Sait
Padang-padang Surf
Padang II
Bakung
Bongol
Sawangan Beach
Uluwatu Surf
Bangket
Ungasan
Kutuh
Suluban
Disongbintang
Pecatu
Pura Uluwatu
Uluwatu
Masuka Temple
Batu Pageh Temple, Surfing
Mabulu Cape
Nyangnyang Beach
★ **Nyangnyang Surf**

km 1   2   3
miles 1   2

PART II

The South: Badung Regency

Badung, the southernmost regency of Bali, is the most heavily populated area of the island — with an average density of more than 1,000 persons per square km. Partly this is because Denpasar, the island's capital and principal metropolis is here. Also, Bali's major tourist resorts are all in Badung, and the tourist boom of the past two decades has fueled a rapid economic expansion and population influx to this traditional southern court center.

Extending north-south from the lofty central volcanic ridge of the island to the the rich rice-growing plains around Denpasar, the regency of Badung is geographically defined by a distributory network of rivers and streams fed from the Plaga rain-catchment area in the north. The clubfoot-shaped Bukit Peninsula in the far south stands apart — its limestone formations, thin topsoil and lack of water make it poor and sparsely populated.

Ill-favored as it is, the Bukit peninsula nevertheless demarcates the Benoa bay and harbor area through which southern Bali traditionally maintained contacts with the outside world. Ships coming from the Bali Strait would sail along the white beaches of the western shore, round the inhospitable cliffs of the Bukit, and anchor in the reef-sheltered cove behind Kuta. Alluvium now clogs up the back channel to Kuta, but a land bridge has been built out into the bay to create the new port of Benoa here. Having reverted to marshlands, the coast is now being developed into fish ponds.

Badung's historical role is due to its pivotal position, allowing control over the three major elements of Balinese economic life: irrigation, rice and the sea. Indianization took place early here, as evidenced by the *Prasasti Blanjong* inscription, dating from the 10th century. Besides Bugis settlements, there are also Chinese tombs and dances named after the Chinese — such as the famed *baris cina* of Semawang and Renon.

The town of Denpasar, also known as Badung, did not enter the limelight until the last century. The early island kingdoms were all farther east, in Gianyar and Klungkung. But soon after the Javanese conquest of the 14th century, western princes arose and for a time Mengwi held sway over the whole of western Bali. After the 18th century, as foreign merchants and warships became more intrusive, power shifted to the sea. This was an historic opportunity for Badung's Pemecutan clan, who defeated Mengwi in 1891.

Pemecutan's rule was short-lived. The Dutch were at this time expanding their territories, and having subdued northern Bali in the mid-19th century, they pushed their claims of suzerainty south with increasing confidence. Many pretexts were used — rights of trade, recognition of the Dutch crown and flag, ritual suicide of widows (suttee). One eventually drew blood.

It started as a common event — a ship ran aground on the reef off Sanur. The Chinese crew survived, but the cargoes disappeared. The Dutch demanded reparations but the raja refused and two years later, in 1906, Dutch troops landed at Sanur. The king chose death over surrender. Dressed in white loincloths, row after row of kris and spear-wielding Balinese hurled themselves into the Dutch gunfire. For them, this was an honorable road to Indra's heaven, abode of fallen warriors.

Its palaces destroyed, its king and warriors dead, Badung surrendered. From the ruins of the palace, a young boy was saved — the last survivor of the proud royal house of Pemecutan. Today, the royal line continues. On July 15th, 1989, the boy's grandson was installed as the new *Cokorda* or King of Pemecutan. The new king is a businessman, his palace a hotel.

— *Jean Couteau*

Overleaf: *A dramatic sunset, for which Badung's beaches are justly renowned. By Made Sudana.*

DENPASAR

'Village-City' with a Regal History

Denpasar is a "village-city" with an aristocratic past. Born from the ashes of the defeated Pemecutan court following the *puputan* massacre of 1906, Denpasar became a sleepy administrative outpost during Dutch times. Since independence, and especially after it was made the capital of Bali in 1958, it has been transformed into a bustling city of some 300,000 souls that provides administrative, commercial and educational services not only to booming Bali, but to much of eastern Indonesia as well. Denpasar is the most dynamic city east of Surabaya, and arguably the richest in the country — there are more vehicles per capita here than in Jakarta.

New city, old villages

Originally a market town — its name literally means "east of the market" — Denpasar has far outgrown its former boundaries, once defined by the Pemecutan, Jero Kuta and Satriya palaces and the brahmanical houses of Tegal, Tampakwangsul and Gemeh. Spurred in all directions by population pressures and motorized transport, urban growth is little by little enveloping the neighboring villages and obliterating the surrounding ricefields, leaving a new urban landscape in its wake — housing estates in the midst of ricefields and ricefields in the middle of the city.

To the east, urbanisation spills across the Ayung River into the village of Batubulan, famous for its *barong* dances, where the conservatory of dance has recently been relocated. To the south, it reaches to Sanur and even to Kuta, while the Bukit itself is now subjected to a frenzy of land speculation. To the west, it sprawls as far as Kapal, whose beautiful temple now has to be seen above the din and dust of suburban traffic.

This unchecked growth has swallowed up many old villages of the plain, yet in many ways they remain as they were — their architecture focused around open courtyards, they have intact their intricate temples and collective *banjars*. The power structure itself, although adapting to new urban tasks and occupations, has also not changed much. Local *satriyas,* be they hotel managers or civil servants, remain princes — they still have control of land and territorial temples and may mobilize their "subjects" for ceremonies. Local brahmans are even more powerful —

MADE ARTHA

continuing to provide ritual services for their followers and occupying some of the best positions in the new Bali. Thus Denpasar is a showcase of Balinese social resiliency — still "Bali" and worth a visit for its gates, its shrines and its royal mansions.

But Denpasar is nevertheless a modern city. Shops, roads and markets have conquered the wet ricefield areas allowed to be leased and sold by village communities. Here, urbanization has taken on the same features found elsewhere in Indonesia — rows of gaudily-painted shops in the business districts; pretty villas along the "protokol" streets; narrow alleys, small compounds and tiny houses in the residential areas.

Experiment in integration

This new urban space continues to welcome waves of new immigrants — Balinese as well as non-Balinese. As such, it represents an experiment in national integration. Inland Balinese indeed make up the majority of the population. The northerners and southern princes and brahmans were here first. Early beneficiaries of a colonial education, they took over the professions and the main administrative positions and constitute, together with the local nobility, the core of the native bourgeoisie. Their villas — with their roof temples, neo-classical columns and Spanish balconies — are the modern "palaces" of Bali.

More recently, a new Balinese population has settled here, attracted by jobs as teachers, students, nurses, traders, etc. Strangers among the local "villagers," these Balinese are the creators of a new urban landscape and architecture. Instead of setting up traditional compounds with their numerous buildings and shrines, they build detached houses with a single multi-purpose shrine. In religious matters, they are transients — retaining ritual membership in their village of origin, praying to gods and ancestors from a distance through the medium of the new shrine. They return home for major ceremonies, to renew themselves at the magical and social sources of their village of origin.

Apart from the Balinese majority, there are several non-indigenous minorities in Denpasar, comprising a quarter of the total population. Muslim Bugis came to Bali as mercenaries as early as the 18th century. They have their own "*banjar*" in the village of Kepaon, where they live alongside the Balinese, speaking their language and inter-marrying with them. Old men of Pemecutan will show you a "Bugis" shrine in a small temple near the family cremation site.

The Chinese came early as traders for the local princes. They integrated easily, blending their Chinese and Balinese ancestry. They also have a shrine, the Ratu Subandar or "merchant king's" shrine up in Batur, next to the shrines of Balinese ancestral gods. New Chinese, often Christians, have arrived, attracted by the booming economy of Bali.

There are also Arabs and Indian Moslems who came in the thirties as textile traders and have since become one of the most prosperous local communities. They live in the heart of the city, in the Kampung Arab area, where they have a mosque.

Most migrants, however, are Javanese and Madurese, known collectively as "*jawa*." They fill the ranks of the civil service and the military (Sanglah and Kayumas areas) as well as the working classes, skilled and unskilled (Pekambingan, Kayumas, "Kampung Jawa" areas). New actors on the Balinese social stage, they introduce new habits — food-selling, peddling, etc. They are also builders of new housing: shacks and tiny houses that bring Denpasar into line with other cityscapes of modern Indonesia.

MADE ARTHA

Opposite: *Looking west along Jalan Gajah Mada, Denpasar's main street.* **Right:** *The Catuh Mukha or "four-faced" statue of Bhatara Guru (Siwa) overlooks the city's main square.*

Thus Denpasar is very much a place where the theme of nation-building is played out. It brings together within earshot of one another the high priest's mantra, the muezzin's call, and the parson's prayer. "Eka Wakya, Bhinna Srutti" — "The Verbs are One, the Scriptures are Many" — so goes the local saying. Balinese tolerance within a national tolerance.

Balinese city, Indonesian nation

Nation-building is also very much a Balinese concern. It is "Indonesia" and "development" overtaking Bali. Denpasar is the center from which the national language, *Bahasa Indonesia*, is spreading to other parts of the island. One speaks Indonesian here interspersed with Balinese words. Through Denpasar, Bali is surrendering its most potent cultural force: its language.

Denpasar is also the breeding ground for a revamped traditional culture. It is here that the concepts of Balinese Hinduism are being re-Indianized by the Parisada Hindu Dharma (Religious Council of Hinduism), beyond the maze of Bali's old *lontars* and oral traditions. The Supreme God, Widhi, here assumes precedence, relegating the ancestors to minor functions. New prayers are taught (*Tri Sandhya*) and new government priests officiate, called from Denpasar to the villages for the rites of officialdom and for inter-caste rituals. Reversing the old village-based trend,

Denpasar is also home to the New Arts. New dances and music are created and taught, spreading into the villages from the city.

Last, but not least, Denpasar is the home of a new breed of Balinese. Born to the sounds of a new music, raised in a world of new wishes and desires, taught in the words of a new national language and culture, the young of Denpasar are Jakarta-looking rather than Bali-oriented. Their thoughts take form in a world of Kuta discos and lavish Sanur villas. They are the avant-garde of a new, Westernized Indonesia. Resilience, renewal and decadence — Denpasar will in any case be the stage for a new Bali.

Denpasar sights

As a microcosm both of modern Bali and of modern Indonesia, Denpasar is easier to understand than to see. Nevertheless, it awaits the intelligent traveler who wants to learn about the future as well as the past, and who wishes to take home more than just a few images. So forget your lens for awhile. Forget the traditional village Bali; have a look at the new urban Bali.

In the very heart of Denpasar, just behind the main artery of the city, Jalan Gajah Mada, one can see many traditional compounds, with their gates, shrines and pavilions, in among the multi-storey Chinese shopfronts. Shrines dwarfed by parabolic TV antennas? Gods of the past versus gods of the future?

RIO HELMI

For a more typical look at Denpasar's villages, a drive through the streets of the "villages" of Kedaton, Sumerta, and particularly Kesiman will do. **Kesiman** has some of the best examples of the simple, yet attractive Badung brick-style. Alas, dying witness to a passing grandeur, the Badung brick-style is disappearing, replaced by the new baroque of the Gianyar-style, and the ugliness of reinforced concrete.

Of the temples, the most ancient is **Pura Maospahit**, right in the middle of the city on the road to Tabanan. It dates back to the Javanization of Bali in the 14th century. No less interesting, although more recent, are the temples of the royal families: **Pura Kesiman** with its beautiful split gate, **Pura Satria** and its lively bird market, and **Pura Nambang Badung** near the princely compounds of Pemecutan and Pemedilan.

A "modern" temple is also worth a visit — the **Pura Jagatnatha**, right on the central square of the city next to the museum. Built as a "world" (*jagat*) temple, its tallest building is a big *padmasana* "lotus-throne" shrine that symbolizes the world as the seat of *Parama-Siwa,* the "Supreme Siwa." Modern Hindu intellectuals meet there for full-moon religious readings — a barometer of Bali's new monotheism.

Among the palaces, the most typical is the **Jero Kuta**, which still has all the functional structures of a traditional princely compound. The **Pemecutan Palace** has been transformed into a hotel. The **Kesiman Palace**, a private mansion, houses the most elaborate family temple.

For a look at examples of traditional Balinese architecture, one might visit the **Bali Museum**, right on Taman Puputan square. The good, yet ill-presented collections are kept in buildings illustrative of the Tabanan, Karangasem and Badung styles.

New architectural landmarks

For a look at modern Bali, go first to Taman Puputan square. Facing the museum and the Jagatnatha Temple one sees the heavy-set, new military headquarters. On the far right, the Balinese **Catur Mukha** "God of the Four Directions" gazes impassively through one of its four faces at the statue of the fallen heroes of the *puputan*. The Javanese-pendopo-styled governor's residence closes the inventory of power symbols in the center of town. "Chinese" Denpasar and the main markets are a few blocks away, on Jl. Gajah Mada, Jl. Thamrin and Jl. Hasanuddin.

For modern Balinese architecture, do not miss the new administrative complex in **Renon**. It is a landmark made to stay, a projection of Balinese architects into their own future. Go also to the **Werdhi Budaya Art Center**. New shrine of the island's culture, it hosts a museum of the Balinese arts as well as stages for dance and theater. On its monumental Ksira Arnawa stage are held equally monumental displays of modern Balinese choreography. For the local color, definitely don't miss the **Pasar Malam Pekambingan** night and food market.

— Jean Couteau

Left: *A procession to the temple in the heart of the city.* **Above:** *The baroque outer facade of the Werdhi Budaya Art Center.* **Right:** *Young princes lead the inaugural procession of the new Cokorda Pemecutan, crowned on July 15th, 1989.*

SANUR

Black & White Mischief in Paradise

The black and white checkered cloth — standard of Bali's netherworld — is nowhere more aptly hung than on the ancient coral statues and shrines of Bali's largest traditional village: Sanur. This was Bali's first beach resort — a place of remarkable contrasts.

Sanur today is a golden mile of Baliesque hotels that has attracted millions of paradise-seeking globetrotters. And yet, within the very grounds of the 11-storey Hotel Bali Beach, a war-reparation gift from the Japanese, nestles the sacred and spikey temple of Ratu Ayu of Singgi, the much feared spirit consort of Sanur's fabled Black Barong.

Sanur is famous throughout Bali for its sorcery. Black and white magic pervades the coconut groves of the resort hotels like an invisible chess game. And yet the community is modern and prosperous.

Sanur is one of the few remaining *brahman kuasa* villages in Bali — controlled by members of the priestly caste — and boasts among its charms some of the handsomest processions on the island, Bali's only all-female kris dance, the island's oldest stone inscription, and the hotel world's most beautiful tropical garden. Even the souvenirs sold on the beach — beautifully crafted kites and toy outriggers — are a cut above those found on the rest of the island.

Traditional Sanur

Just a stone's throw from any of Sanur's beachside hotels lies one of a string of very ancient temples. Characterized by low coral-walled enclosures sheltering platform altars, this style of temple is peculiar to the white sand stretch of Sanur coast, from Sanur harbor in the north to Mertasari Beach in the south. Inside, they are decorated with fanciful fans of coral and rough-hewn statuary, often ghoulishly painted but always wrapped in a checkered sarong.

The rites performed at the anniversary celebrations of these temples are both weird and wonderful — the celebrants often dancing with effigies strapped to their hips, while the priests are prone to wild outbursts, launching themselves spread-eagled onto a platform of offerings and racing entranced pell-mell into the sea.

The Sanur area, with traditional Intaran at its heart, has evidently been settled since ancient times. The **Prasasti Belanjong**, an inscribed pillar here dated A.D. 913, is Bali's earliest dated artifact — now kept in a temple in Belanjong village in the south of Sanur. It tells of King Sri Kesari Warmadewa of the Sailendra Dynasty in Java, who came to Bali to teach Mahayana Buddhism and then founded a monastery here. One may presume that a fairly civilized community then existed — the Sailendra kings having built Borobudur in Central Java at about this time.

It is interesting that the village square of Intaran is almost identical to that of Songan village on the crater lake of Mt. Batur — particularly the location and size of the *bale agung*, the *wantilan* community hall and associated buildings. The priests of Sanur-Intaran are often mentioned in historical chronicles dating from Bali's "Golden Age" — the 13th to the 16th centuries. It was not until the

Right: *Parasailing on Sanur Beach.* **Opposite:** *A* melasti *procession to the sea. Within a few minutes' walk of Sanur's luxury hotels, the traditional life of the villages carries on as before.*

early 19th century, however, that the king of the Pemecutan court in Denpasar saw fit to place his *satriya* princelings outside the village's medieval core.

Before that, Sanur consisted of brahman *griya* (mansions) in Intaran and several attendant communities — the brahman *banjar* of **Anggarkasih**, the fishing village of **Belong** (which still holds a yearly *baris gede* warrior dance at the Pura Dalem Kedewatan temple near the Hotel Bali Beach), and the village of **Taman**, whose Brahmans have traditionally served as the region's chief administrator or *perbekel*. Taman is also home to an electric barong troupe complete with an impish *telek* escort, a *pas de deux* by the freaky *jauk* brothers and a spine-tingling last act featuring the evil witch Rangda — all amidst fluttering *poleng* checkered banners.

Westerners in Sanur

It was in the mid-19th century that Sanur was first recorded by Europeans as more than just a dot on the map. Mads Lange, a Kuta-based Danish trader, at this time mentions the special relationship that the *perbekel* of Sanur enjoyed with his great friend the king of Kesiman, Cokorda Sakti.

In a less flattering light, it was also a *perbekel* of Sanur who turned a blind eye to the landing of Dutch troops here in 1906 on their way to the massacre of the royal house of Pemecutan — one of the most ignoble days in Dutch colonial history. The full story has been immortalized by 1930s Sanur habituée Vicki Baum in her book, *A Tale of Bali*.

The BBC has a film of a Sanur trance medium "possessed" by the spirit of a beer-swilling English sea captain (possibly from one of the merchant vessels which foundered on Sanur's coral reefs) — to whose semi-divine memory a trance *baris*, called Ratu Tuan, is performed by the Semawang Banjar. The costume: Chinese *kung-fu* pyjamas of black and white checkered cloth.

The first half of the 20th century also saw Sanur's emergence as prime real estate for the Bali-besotted. Beach bungalows in what Miguel Covarrubias referred to as, "the malarial swamps of Sanur," were built by, among others, Dr. Jack Mershon and his choreographer wife Katharane (inventor, with Walter Spies, of the very checkered *kecak* dance), writer Vicki Baum, anthropologist Jane Belo (author of *Trance in Bali*); and art-collector Neuhaus, who was killed by a stray bullet during a skirmish between local guerillas and Japanese occupation forces in 1943, while playing bridge on the verandah of his home — site of the present-day Hotel Sindhu Beach.

These early "Baliphiles" hosted a steady stream of celebrity visitors to the island during the 1930s, including Charlie Chaplin, Barbara Hutton, Doris Duke and Harold Nicholson. It was probably more from the

SARITA NEWSON

an and Bali's finest art collection within the grounds of the dream he founded — Batujimbar Estates — now home to the world-weary and the grand.

Sanur designs its future

At about the same time, two Sanur brahmans were leaving their mark on the community. The first, high priest Pedanda Gede Sidemen, was entering the twilight of a prolific career which spanned 70 years as south Bali's most significant temple architect, healer and classical scholar. His life, and the pride he brought to his native Sanur, were to inspire a generation of Sanur brahmans who may otherwise have contemplated abandoning their Vedic scriptures for a life on the juice blender.

The second, Ida Bagus Berata — nephew of Pedanda Sidemen — insisted during his tenure as mayor of Sanur from 1968 to 1986 that the area should be economically as well as culturally autonomous. To that end, Ratu Perbekel, as he was affectionately known, established a village-run cooperative that to this day operates a beach market, a restaurant, a car-wash and service station, and owns land in Kuta and Denpasar. This strident new economic approach provided a friendly environment for the establishment of many other Sanur-based tourist businesses.

By the 1980s the writing was on the wall — Sanur's bread and butter (but not its lifeblood, its culture) was mass tourism. The brahmans of Intaran are now hotel-owners, their "serfs" are building contractors and roomboys, and the farmers of the area have become taxi drivers and art shop owners. Beachside there is no land left, and the ribbon of "Bali Baroque" palace development thickens along the highway. Sanur's brahman priests are met at dawn by convoys of limousines — their schedules of incantations and blessings as busy as those of any senior statesman or tycoon. The mega-Tuans of yesterday are gone and forgotten; the new generation of rich and famous are obsessed more with diet and the ragtrade than with skullduggery and *gamelan* galas. But late at night, when the cash-registers are asleep under their *batik* cosies and the beepers are turned off, Ratu Ayu steals from her throne into the night, to a temple near you . . . Sanur's checkeredness is not a thing of the past.

— *Made Wijaya*

travel reports of these sophisticates than from the movie with a sarong-draped Dorothy Lamour that Bali traces its fame abroad.

Bali's most famous expatriate of this era, artist-writer-musician Walter Spies, was a frequent visitor to the shores of Sanur, but it is to one particular visit that we may trace his aversion for coastal Bali. It was the day of a lunar eclipse and the birthday of Spies' young nephew who was visiting him in Bali. A Balinese soothsayer warned the boy not to go near the water that day, but he defied the warning and swam in Sanur, where he was taken by a shark. A weird coincidence: the Balinese symbol for an eclipse is the giant-toothed mouth of the demon spirit Kala Rauh devouring the moon goddess.

Modern times

Not long after Indonesia proclaimed independence in 1945, Sanur witnessed the beginnings of an expatriate building boom led by Belgian painter Le Mayeur, whose former studio home on the beach north of the Hotel Bali Beach is now a museum. Le Mayeur's heavenly courtyard was the inspiration for his breasty, nymph-filled paintings.

Australian artists Ian Fairweather and Donald Friend, whose marvelous books and paintings have inspired a generation of Australians, also chose picturesque Sanur for their Bali retreats. Donald Friend lived here in imperial splendor with an in-house *gamel-*

Above: *A replica of Goa Gajah in Sanur's Bali Hyatt swimming pool.* **Opposite:** *The evil witch Rangda makes an appearance at Pura Sakenan.*

SERANGAN ISLAND

Important Temple on 'Turtle Island'

Serangan is a small island lying just off Bali's southern coast near Sanur. It has an area of only 180 acres and a population of about 2,500, and is known principally for its turtles and its important Sakenan Temple.

Serangan is too dry for wet rice farming, but its residents grow corn, maize, peanuts and beans. Some islanders earn a living making shell trinkets to sell to the tourists who come here in ever increasing numbers. But the trade in another distinctive item is even more crucial to the local economy.

The sea turtles which give Serangan its popular name are not found swimming picturesquely under ocean cliffs — here they are caught and sold as food. People in the Denpasar area are fond of turtle meat, especially on festival days. Serangan residents make a living capturing and wholesaling the creatures, also buying them from Muslim fishermen from islands to the east.

The turtles are kept live in bamboo sheds on the sandy beach around **Dukuh**, the island's main village on the north coast. Here they are fed with fresh leaves and sold to buyers from Denpasar, who will eventually prepare the turtle meat in dishes like *saté* and *lawar*, a kind of tartare or raw meat dish.

There is also a turtle-egg hatchery on the island. The most popular edible species is the green turtle *(Chelonia mydas)*, which swims ashore to lay eggs in a shallow pit in the sand before returning to the sea. It is at this moment that villagers catch the turtles effortlessly and in large numbers, just by turning them on their backs. The eggs are considered a great delicacy, and are dug up immediately. Not surprisingly, the green turtle is now threatened with extinction and the World Wildlife Fund has consequently appealed to the government to put a stop to the slaughter.

Manis Kuningan festival

The best day to visit Serangan is on the holy day Manis Kuningan in the 210-day Balinese calendar. On this day, the famous **Sakenan Temple** celebrates the anniversary of its founding by Mpu Kuturan, which according to the *Prasasti Belanjong* inscription occurred during the 10th century. The Sakenan complex consists of two *pura* on the north coast of the island just west of Dukuh.

The festival lasts for two days, beginning on the last day of Kuningan *wuku* or week and ending on the first day of Langkir *wuku*. The ferry from Suwung, normally serving the odd tourist or a few villagers coming from Serangan to do their marketing, is at this time chock-a-block with thousands of worshippers in all their colorful finery. They queue up on the dike of a canal meandering through the mangroves to board a ferry which takes them straight to the temple.

Inside the first *pura* there is only a single shrine, in the form of a *tugu* or obelisk. This is the seat of Çri Çedana or Dewi Sri, the goddess of prosperity and welfare. In the second and larger part of Pura Sakenan there are typical Balinese-style shrines for the *prasanak*, relatives of Sri who come to visit the temple on its anniversary day.

On arrival, worshippers pray at the shrine of Dewi Sri to ask her for a prosperous year in the fields or in business. But it is obvious that this day is most prosperous for the ferry men, who earn a lot more money than usual.

— *Nyoman Oka*

GARRETT KAM

KUTA AND LEGIAN

'Beach Blanket Babylon' of the East

Kuta/Legian beach is living proof that one man's hell is another man's paradise. This bustling beach resort has in the short space of just two decades spontaneously burst onto center stage in the local tourist scene. It is here that many visitors form their first (if not only) impressions of what Bali is all about. Many are shocked and immediately flee in search of the "real Bali" (a mythological destination somewhere near Ubud).

The truth is, nevertheless, that certain souls positively thrive in this labyrinth of boogie bars, beach bungalows, cassette shops and honky tonks — all part of the Kuta lifestyle. What then is the magic that has transformed this sleepy fishing village overnight into an overcrowded tourist Mecca — with no end in sight to its haphazard expansion?

Before tourism came to the area, Kuta was one of the poorest places on Bali —

plagued by poor soils, endemic malaria and a surf-wracked beach that provides little protection for shipping. In the early days, it nevertheless served as a port for the powerful southern Balinese kingdom of Badung, whose capital lay in what is now Denpasar.

Rice, slaves and booty

Though Bali was never very trade-oriented, it did supply neighboring islands with several commodities — mainly rice, and notably slaves. Also, the booty salvaged from shipwrecks provided an occasional bonanza for the hardy inhabitants of this coastal outpost.

After an earlier Dutch trading post had been abandoned as commercially unviable (even the illegal trade in slaves proved disappointing), there arrived in Kuta a remarkable Dane mounted on a proud stallion, the likes of which the Balinese had never seen. Mads Lange, as he was called, had the audacity to march straight to the palace of the *raja* of Badung and demand an audience.

Despite his bravado, Lange had in fact recently been a victim of his own intrigues on the neighboring island of Lombok, where he had aided the wrong *raja* in a war and lost all. As fate would have it, Lange not only survived his move to Bali, but prospered — building here an extensive new trading post, coconut oil factory and luxurious residence stocked with wines and other delicacies.

Within the walls of his fabled Kuta resi-

AMIR SIDHARTA

dence, Lange wined and dined a succession of visiting scholars, adventurers, princes and colonial officials. During the tumultuous 1840s, moreover, he repeatedly played a critical role in mediating between the Balinese rulers and the Dutch. Today, his grave can be seen in a Chinese cemetery at the center of Kuta, not far from a Buddhist temple and the crumbling remains of his once-regal house.

A tourist caravansary

It took a young Californian surfer and his wife to first notice Kuta's tourism potential. The year was 1936. Robert and Louise Koke decided to leave Hollywood and start a small hotel in Bali. They describe their discovery of Kuta as follows: "The next day we cycled . . . to the South Seas picture beach we had been hoping to find. It was Kuta ... the broad, white sand beach curved away for miles, huge breakers spreading on clean sand."

The hotel they founded was called the Kuta Beach Hotel, naturally. It was a modest establishment but things went reasonably well in spite of an occasional malaria attack and a run-in with a young and fiery American of British birth by the name of Ketut Tantri, who managed to stir up controversy wherever she went during her 20-odd years in Indonesia.

After the War, tourism in Bali all but disappeared. And when the first tourists began to trickle back during the 1960s, Kuta was all but forgotten. Suddenly and without warning, however, a new kind of visitor began to frequent the island during the 1970s, and their preferred abode in Bali was Kuta Beach.

Nobody quite knew what to make of the first long-haired, bare-footed travelers who stopped here on their way from India to Australia — nobody, that is, except for the enterprising few in Kuta who quickly threw up rooms behind their houses and began cooking banana pancakes for this nomadic tribe.

The main attraction here was and still is one of the best beaches in Asia — and the trickle of cosmic surfers and space age crusaders in search of paradise, mystical union, and good times soon turned into a torrent, as tales of Bali spread like wildfire on the travelers' grapevine. Stories of a place where one could live out extravagant dreams on one of the world's most exotic tropical islands — for just a few dollars a day — seemed too good to be true.

Within the space of a few years, Kuta's empty beaches and back lanes began to fill up with homestays, restaurants and shops. Most visitors stayed on as long as the money lasted, and many concocted elaborate business schemes that would enable them to come back, investing their last dollars in

Opposite: *The Bali Barrel Surf Team of Kuta.*
Below: *Kuta's famous technicolor sunset has always been one of its top drawing-cards.*

MADE ARTHA

handicrafts and antiques before leaving.

In Kuta and Legian, the clothing or "rag trade" developed rapidly. Fortunes have been made and a handful of young enterpreneurs who began by selling batiks out of their backpacks have made it big. With the new affluence has came a lifestyle of flashy villas and sultry tropical evenings beneath moonlit palms.

By the end of the 1970s, nobody knew quite what was going on. Up-scale tourists were mixing in increasing numbers in among the "hippie travelers" and deluxe bungalow hotels were popping up between US$2 a night homestays. With them came the uncontrolled proliferation of shops and bars and tourist touts lurking on every street corner. By the 1980s, Kuta was no longer an underground secret.

Kuta's reincarnation

Many changes, good and bad, have come to Kuta over the past several years. These range from traffic jams and pollution to excellent food, great shopping and a vibrant nightlife. Australians once dominated the scene, but today Kuta is truly international — the spectrum of visitors ranging from macho Brazilian surfers to prim Japanese secretaries. Tourism, however, is the common denominator for everything that happens here.

There has been an equally rapid rise in domestic tourism, with western tourists and their curious ways becoming an attraction for Indonesian visitors from the neighboring island of Java. Large numbers of out-islanders have also settled here, opening businesses or simply hanging out in this Indonesian version of a gold-rush boom town. At times, one has the impression that the local Balinese have become a minority in their own community.

For many, this litany of change reads as an indictment of yet another paradise lost. Certainly for those of us who knew Kuta in an earlier, more innocent state, the new Kuta is often difficult to accept. But what of the local Balinese — what do they think of all this? The most common answer is that despite the changes, the Balinese community remains strong, if wary. The traditional ceremonies are still being held, so there is as yet no need to worry, they feel. One need only witness the powerful *calonarang* dance in Kuta beneath a full moon to understand this. While we despair the loss of Kuta's village past, we cannot condemn all that is new. In fact, goods and services have improved and Kuta enjoys a standard of living higher than almost anywhere else in Indonesia.

Above all, though, Kuta/Legian beach has become a major cross-cultural international meeting spot with few peers. Love it or leave it, only one thing is sure — the old Kuta has passed away and nobody knows what the future may bring.

— *Bruce Carpenter*

KUTA TOUR

'The Scene': Hot Days, Steamy Nights

As the clock strikes midnight, I find myself sitting upstairs in the legendary **Made's Warung**, oldest and most famous of Kuta's many street-side cafes. Nursing a gin and tonic, I slip into a near trance as the "beautiful people" of Kuta swirl about me.

On the table to my left, a sensuous lady proudly announces that she shared a glass of champagne with David Bowie the night before at the Oberoi. "Sting is coming soon, too — he's having a concert atop Gunung Agung to save the forests." Just beyond her a corpulent businessman grins with delight, surrounded by a bevy of Jakartan beauties. A bald-headed chap cruises the floor below in T-shirt and black knickers.

Soon, Made's begins to close up. Last drinks down the hatch and a final scan of the crowd to see who's about and what's happening. It's disco night tonight, but they start up late, so for the next hour or so it's on to Legian's **New Goa** for further "warming up."

Unlike up-scale Sanur and Nusa Dua, Kuta's clubs are free-wheeling places with no dress code. They are of two types: cavernous halls like **Peanuts** and **The Spotlight** with air-conditioning and flashing lights, and *al fresco* beachside patios like **Gado-Gado** or **Double Six**, where you can dance until the wee hours with the moon and palms overhead.

The day after

Mornings start late in Kuta — especially if you went to bed with a hangover at 5 am. Fortunately, strong cappucinos and aspirin are always available at **Benny's**. If you're a people-watcher, keep your eyes open at all times. One favorite game is to guess where all the people come from and what they're doing in Bali. It's easy to distinguish the leathery-skinned oldtimers from pale-faced tenderfoots, and with experience one develops a sixth sense for more subtle differences.

The first order of business is to go shopping. Considering the number and variety of shops in Kuta, this is a daunting task. You can start with the street vendors and small shops — if you dare — but don't be surprised if you later find what you've just bought for half the price in a fancy shop. *Batik* shirts, rattan bags, and other treasures from around the archipelago should be tops on your list.

When you're broke or have had enough of the street life, take a stroll to the beach. If you feel lithe and beautiful, you might want to join the g-string crowd at the **Blue Ocean**, where the revelers you met the previous night will be playing paddle-ball. The surfing is great here and the sunsets magnificent. As for the hawkers — don't let them get you uptight. A little humor and a firm "NO" is all you need. Before getting a massage, make sure you fix the price. Tell her to lay off the coconut oil unless you want to feel like greasy fried rice garnished with sand afterwards.

After a shower and a change, it's time to eat. There's at least one restaurant in Kuta specializing in every major cuisine in the world. Then it's back to Made's and the clubs for another nocturnal round. If you love it enough, you may decide to contract a house, start a business, and become a confirmed Kuta expatriate.

— Bruce Carpenter

AMIR SIDHARTA

Above, left: *The cavernous Peanuts Club disco in Kuta.* **Right:** *Legendary Made's Warung, the place to see and be seen in Kuta Beach.*

BEACHCOMBING

A Naturalist's Guide to Surf, Sand and Sea

Virtually all visitors to Bali spend some time at the beach — wandering along baking strips of sand watching bathers, surfers and sun worshippers, or even lying prone absorbing the sun's UV rays (something the Balinese wouldn't think of doing!). Few visitors, however, appreciate the natural interest that is all around them as they stroll toward the sunset, moan under a masseuses' fingers or paddle in the shallows. For those who feel a bit bored with normal beach activities, the following is a brief guide to beach combing from a naturalist's point of view.

The cool, early morning when the disco crowd is still in bed is a good time to look for interesting items washed up during the night. This is also when Bali's feral dogs congregate on the beach awaiting the first life-sustaining offerings of rice from the faithful. The dogs' games, fights and amours are typical of wild carnivores and the leaders, wimps and sneaks can all be identified.

Time and the tides

The beachcomber's most important tool is a tide table — distributed free by surf shops such as Tubes, on Poppies Lane II in Kuta. These let you identify the rewarding periods of relatively low water, when surfers mope about wondering what to do or watch surfing videos but beachcombers are out in force.

The most common beachcombing activity is shell collecting, and a wonderful variety can be found here — we have found 30 different species along Kuta Beach and nearly 50 at Sanur. Empty shells washed up on the beach may have been tumbling around in the water for a long time but many are still beautifully glossy.

The shells offered for sale in street stalls and by wandering vendors are in very good condition because they have been collected live in other parts of Indonesia (those from around Bali were sold long ago). Some of the larger shells are protected by law and the clams are now also protected by international convention. Customs will not be pleased to find clam shells among your souvenirs.

The beaches of Bali show considerable variation, and one of the most obvious is in the sand itself. Around Kuta the sand is a mixture of coral and shell fragments mixed with grey volcanic ash washed down from the

A. J. WHITTEN

mountains by the rivers. At Nusa Dua and Sanur it is a pale golden color without any ash, and many sand particles are quite large.

A closer look reveals that many of the larger particles are rounded tetrahedrons with four evenly-spaced points. These are skeletons of single-celled marine animals called foraminiferans. A little way offshore they can be found in huge numbers attached to various aquatic plants, where they filter small organic particles out of the water. The skeletons of these "forams" (as they are

known to the cognoscenti) do not pack closely even when wet, and this is why walking along the upper levels of Sanur Beach is so tiring and motorcycling is impossible, whereas Kuta with its hard packed, small-particle sand is a jogger's and motorcyclist's dream.

Kuta Beach

The striking thing about the sea at Kuta is its energy — the waves break close to shore and there is a long tidal reach, so the shore is heavily scoured. Few organisms can cope with the heavy surges of water. But wander along Kuta Beach at low tide and you'll notice what look like the five-pad footprints of a large dog, but not arranged in tracks. Brush away the sand and just beneath the surface you will find Sand Dollars (*Echinodiscus bisperforatus*), relatives of the sea urchins. Their flat shape offers minimal resistance to the moving water and hundreds can be found in a short walk.

Another conspicuous creature is the abundant *kremis* shell (*Donax cuneata*), only about 1 cm long and in various colors: gold, purple, white and red. The waves uncover these bivalves when they are just below the sand but their white "foot" drags them into the sand again, sharp end first, leaving the flattened end topmost. At the end of the day, when bodies beautiful and otherwise have retired to the showers and bars, the beach masseuses can be found collecting the

kremis. They're good to eat, if fiddly, and the water they are boiled in makes a good soup. Much less abundant is the so-called "common" Olive Shell (*Oliva oliva*) which is about 2 cm long and has a shiny, brown-patterned shell. This moves just below the sand's surface and its winding tracks are quite conspicuous as it searches for and eats the *kremis*.

When the tide recedes, tiny Bubbler Crabs (*Scopimera*) emerge from their burrows, as many as 100 per square meter. They feed on minute organic particles in the sand, rolling the processed sand away from their holes in roughly concentric circles around the burrow entrance. When the tide creeps up again the sand is covered with these tiny balls. As the water reaches their burrows, the crabs busily push small domes of sand over the entrances, sealing the air in against the rising tide.

Much larger burrows found higher up the beach belong to Ghost Crabs (*Oxypode*) which venture onto the beach foraging for organic goodies at the water's edge.

Two aquatic crabs may nibble at your toes while paddling — the small (less than 5 cm) Moon Crab (*Matuta lunaris*) with broad paddles at the tip of its legs, and the larger Flower Crab (*Portunus pelagicus*) with long arms and paddles on only the last pair of legs. These paddles are used both for swimming and for digging just below the sand surface, where they generally hide during the day. Both have long and very sharp spines jutting outward from the sides of their bodies. They feed on small fish, shellfish and worms.

Their empty shells can often be found

Opposite: *A bubbler crab* (Scopimera) *emerges from the entrance of its burrow amid sand balls of its own making.* **Above, left:** *A starfish* (Echinaster) *with two shortened legs in the process of regenerating.* **Above, right:** *Aster typicus, along with other starfish, should not be handled, or dried and taken as souvenirs.*

stranded on the beach, but these are usually moulted skins rather than the remains of dead animals.

Kuta is also the best tourist beach to see seabirds. Black, angular-winged Greater Frigates (obtusely named *Fregata minor*) soar effortlessly on unmoving wings in groups of up to 20 individuals. Small white terns dance above the water, picking up unwary fishes, while greyish Brown Boobies (*Sula leucogaster*) sometimes fly in a very determined manner parallel to the coast.

Sanur Beach

The waves at Sanur break over a reef crest several hundred meters from the shore. As a result, only small and gentle waves reach the beach, and this protected lagoon is a very rewarding area biologically.

Between the beach and the reef are some of the best seagrass meadows a casual visitor is likely to see, and it is worthwhile idling a while in this area. Seagrass is thought of as a weed, since the commonest encounter with it is when the broken or rotting leaves get caught in your hair while swimming. Indeed, staff of the large hotels can be seen at dawn busily sweeping this natural frass into holes or trucking it away lest sensitive visitors feel their idyllic beach is despoiled. The seagrass meadows can be explored either by walking around wearing sneakers at low tide when the water reaches only slightly over the ankles, or by snorkeling at high water.

There are at least five species of seagrass present, with the most abundant, *Enhalus acoroides*, having broad, strap-like leaves and black hairy rootstocks. These roots would once have been eaten by dugongs or sea cows which doubtless swam slowly across this lagoon in former times. The meadows are highly dynamic but much of the growth in the system is actually in the thin carpet of fine and fuzzy algae and other organisms growing on the plants' leaves, which are grazed by fishes, molluscs and other animals. Don't forget to look for the living "forams" on and around the bottom of the seagrass stems and among the various types of algae which grow in the vicinity.

Most of the animals in the seagrass meadows are grazers feeding on the algae rather than the seagrass itself. More or less the only animal that eats seagrass leaves is the Green Turtle (*Chelonia mydas*) which still visits Sanur to feed, but no longer to lay eggs.

Also among the seagrass you will find numbers of large, knobbly starfish (*Protoreaster nodosus*), occuring in a variety of colors — orange with red knobs, blue with green, grey with pink, and so on. A smaller and less robust species is *Aster typicus*, an enormous mating orgy of which we once found unnoticed by others just in front of the Hyatt Hotel. A third species, *Culcita schmidmeliana,* is rounded and has five sides rather than arms,

A. J. WHITTEN

and looks like a discolored cauliflower.

It is not uncommon while walking around at low tide to see dense clumps of small (5-10 cm) black-lined catfish (*Plotosus lineatus)* which swim so close to one another that one could be excused for thinking at first that the black mass was a single organism, and it may be that potential predators are similarly duped. Each clump seems to have individuals of one size that may have come from the same mass of eggs.

The black sea urchin *Diadema setosum* is a realtively common sight with its long, slender spines which enter human feet with ease, but then break off and resist removal to the accompaniment of great pain. They do not, however, attack and a close look reveals beautifully delicate spines with a very bright red ring around the upward-facing anus and the adjacent bright blue genitals. In polluted waters these grazing animals form dense plagues, and it is more thanks to the strong current and a natural restorative proclivity than environmental awareness that Sanur's reefs and meadows are as fine as they are and that these urchins occur at such relatively low densities.

Urchins and cucumbers

You might occasionally see a Banded Sea Snake (*Laticauda colubrina*) in the meadows; although its venom is highly toxic, it is reluctant to bite unless unbearably provoked. A beast which can be mistaken for a snake by the naïve beachcomber is the wierd sea cucumber *Synapta maculata*. This, too, is long (up to 2.5 m) thin, striped and lurks among the seagrass, but it is limpid, ribbed and has a feathery mouth that protrudes from its head (they only way to tell which end is which). Other common sea cucumbers are the black *Holothuria atra* to which grains of sand adhere, and *Stichopus variegata* which looks for all the world like a freshly-baked loaf of wholemeal bread.

Back at the water's edge, particularly on weekend afternoons, one can see people bent double, sprinkling rice water onto the wet sand, staring earnestly at it, and occasionally grabbing at something with thumb and forefinger. A slow, steady pull reveals a 10-20 cm ragworm (*Perinereis*), much prized as bait by weekend fishermen. These secretive animals can also be tempted to the surface with delicacies such as soggy bread, fish soup or very dilute shrimp paste.

The more time one spends at the beach the more one sees. Get out there and explore, but please leave live shells and other animals where you find them!

—*Tony and Jane Whitten*

Opposite: *The sea cucumber Opheodesoma feeds on detritus amid the seagrass.* **Below:** *Some of the up to 50 species of shell which can be found on Bali's beaches.*

JIMBARAN & BUKIT BADUNG

Surf-Wracked Shores of Southern Bali

The first thing which strikes the visitor to Bukit Badung, the bulbous peninsula at Bali's southernmost tip, is that the landscape is totally different from the rest of the island. Most of Bali is volcanic — rich soils watered year-round by run-off from mountain lakes and streams, which support a lush, tropical vegetation. In contrast, the Bukit is a non-volcanic limestone plateau which has its own unique ecology.

The so-called "hill" — for that is what "Bukit" means — has an ecosystem characterized by its lack of surface water. The soil lies on a base of cracked and porous limestone, and any rain which does fall quickly seeps through fissures to a very low water table. The area is thus ill-suited to agriculture during the dry season, when the scrubby vegetation looks more Mediterranean than tropical. During the rainy season, however, the area's vegetation becomes quite lush and crops of soybeans, sorghum, cashew nuts, manioc, beans of various sorts and even corn, flourish.

The plateau which constitutes most of the peninsula rises abruptly to about 200 m above sea level, and is ringed on all sides by steep cliffs. It is connected to the rest of Bali by a narrow isthmus, upon which lies the village of Jimbaran. Many lovely beaches line the shores of the peninsula and the isthmus, although access is often difficult. The biggest and best-known beach is just beyond the airport, on the western side of the Jimbaran isthmus. More secluded and equally beautiful sands are found further to the south, at the foot of steep cliffs along the western and southern shores of the Bukit plateau.

The whole area has a host of natural attractions for those willing to invest the time to explore. Grand, grey-white cliffs overlook long, white rollers — world famous among surfers. Graceful boats sway at anchor in tranquil Jimbaran bay. The quiet and empty bush areas of the elevated plateau are ideal for experienced hikers (though few good maps of the area are available). The region also boasts places of cultural significance, the most renowned being Uluwatu Temple (Pura Luhur Uluwatu).

A glimpse of the past

The Bukit bears witness to a long history. There are limestone caves all over the area, and evidence of prehistoric human occupation have been found in Gua Selonding. Before Uluwatu became a Hindu temple, it was the site of worship for more ancient cults. The foundation of the temple itself is dated by Balinese tradition to the 11th century.

The poverty of the soil and its geographical isolation have shaped the social landscape of Bukit Badung. There was never any wet-rice farming and other crops and cattle-breeding did not suffice to feed the population. So those who could not subsist through farming, cattle-raising and crafts, looked to the sea for salt, lime and fish. Others migrated to rice-growing areas. Old men of Sukawati still talk of Bukit peddlars exchanging betel lime and salt for gleaning and accommodation rights. Bukit Badung is also known as a region where the overlords of Mengwi and Badung banished malcontents and defaulting debtors. Nowadays the population is growing, the region having become a major focal point of Bali's relentless tourism boom.

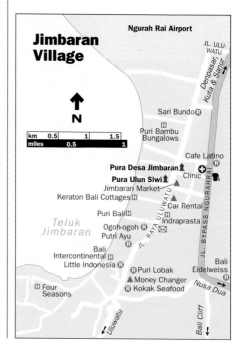

Jimbaran

Jimbaran as an administrative entity forms a part of Kuta, and encompasses the area just south of Bali's international airport. Most of Jimbaran's 12,000 inhabitants live in a cluster of traditional *banjar* neighborhoods at the narrowest part of the isthmus, but the Jimbaran area also includes the sparsely populated northwestern corner of the Bukit plateau.

Since the Nusa Dua highway leads visitors through the region along the eastern mudflats and mangrove swamps, the area went almost unnoticed by tourists until a few years ago. There were no hotels or even homestays, no tourist restaurants, no art shops, few artists, and hardly anyone who could speak English. All that is changing rapidly, perhaps more rapidly than some of the local residents would like. Jimbaran's fine beach has now led to the construction of a number of luxury hotels along its edge, and in a few years the area seems destined to become another major resort rivaling Sanur, Kuta and Nusa Dua.

Jimbaran village is unique in that it borders two separate coasts lying less than 2 km apart, each of which has a markedly different geography. To the west is the broad expanse of Jimbaran Bay and the Indian Ocean. To the east is a tidal mudflat enclosing the shallow and sheltered Benoa Harbor. The ecosystems of the two strands, and the occupations of villagers who live on them, differ dramatically.

Salt making and lime production are the principal livelihoods on the eastern side, while fishing is the main industry of the west. The salt is made by sloshing seawater onto the flats, to be dried by the sun. Villagers then rake up the salty dirt and evaporate the solution over wood fires in shallow metal pans. The abundance of coral fragments provide the raw materials for the lime industry. (NOTE: You will have to ask directions if you want to see salt and lime workings, these areas are only accessible via a rabbit's warren of unpaved tracks.)

Jimbaran's lovely western beach is protected from larger waves by a fragmented reef behind which lies shallow water, an ideal anchorage for large fishing boats. However idyllic it may appear during the dry season, the beach is often rather unpleasant from about November through March when high waves assault the shore, and the sand becomes littered with flotsam of every description.

Fishing is the principal activity all along the bay, not only in Jimbaran itself, and in the villages of Kedonganan and Kelan to the north. Kedonganan's catch always surpasses that of Jimbaran. The Kedonganan fishermen — who are mostly Javanese — use large,

Below: *The limestone cliffs of Bukit Badung.*

motorized *prahu* made in Madura to catch enormous quantities of sardines with huge purse seines. They depart in the late afternoon and return just after dawn to sell their catch to wholesalers waiting by the shore with trucks full of ice.

An early morning visit to witness the arrival of the fishing fleet at Kedonganan is a heady experience. Head north from Jimbaran towards the airport and take the first paved road to your left (west) just beyond Jimbaran village's northern boundary. Bear in mind, however, that fishing comes almost to a halt during the rainy season.

In contrast to those in Kedonganan, almost all fishermen in Jimbaran are local Balinese who use *jukung* (small outrigger boats) and fish with gill nets or large round cast nets. The gill nets are set out in the bay in the late afternoon, and the catch is collected early the next morning. During the fishing season there is lots of interesting activity just after sunrise, well worth waking early for. To get to the hub of the activity, follow the unpaved road that leads to the beach from Jimbaran's main crossroads, past Pura Ulun Siwi.

Jimbaran's market is located on the northeast corner of the main crossroads in the village, just across the street from Pura Ulun Siwi. It is the principal trading center for most of the Bukit, as well as for the villages that lie to the north, between Jimbaran and Kuta. There are no crafts sold specifically for tourists, but there is a considerable variety of local products, including baskets and mats produced by the weavers of villages such as Ungasan and Pecatu. There is no special market day. Activity is greatest early in the morning and almost ceases by noon.

Lesser-known temples

Jimbaran has the usual three village temples, the Pura Dalem (called Pura Kahyangan locally), Pura Puseh and Pura Desa. The latter two are combined into one enclosure in Jimbaran, as occurs in many villages. These tend to be overlooked in favor of the more spectacular and better-known Pura Ulun Siwi (alternatively Pura Ulun Swi). But each is interesting in its own right.

Pura Kahyangan lies just to the west of the cemetery, north of the access road to Hotel Puri Bali. The Pura Puseh/Desa is about 50 m northeast of the market. It is interesting to note that the *odalan* or anniversary ceremonies of these three temples, and of Pura Ulun Siwi, all occur within four days of each other, commencing on the third day after Galungan (which is the biggest holy day in the traditional Balinese calendar). Jimbaran becomes a beehive of ritual activity at this time of year.

One of the most important ceremonies in Jimbaran is the exorcistic Barong procession. The Barong is a mythical beast who acts as protector of the village and its people, represented by a mask and costume which is paraded through the area at periodic intervals. Jimbaran's inhabitants spare no expense to support the Barong, making offerings to it, praying, and performing the ritual. Appearances of the Barong in the main street of Jimbaran between Pura Ulun Siwi and the market are always accompanied by the evil witch Rangda and her two cohorts, and by a retinue of about a dozen other dancers. Trance plays an important part in a Barong performance, and the actions of the trance dancers who try to stab Rangda are bizarre and unforgettable to any foreign visitor.

Pura Ulun Siwi

Pura Ulun Siwi (or Ulun Swi) is Jimbaran's best-known "sight" — for the Balinese as well as for tourists. This large temple lies at the northwestern corner of the principal crossroads, across the street from the market. It is unusual for several reasons. Firstly it faces east, rather than south. During prayers, the worshippers face west, rather than to the north, to Gunung Agung, as is the usual prac-

tice. This is attributed to the fact that the temple, once a primitive shrine, became a Hindu-Balinese temple fairly early, in the 11th century. At this time the Javanese holy man who founded the temple, Mpu Kuturan, still followed the custom of his native Java in orienting his temples toward holy Mt. Semeru, in East Java. It was only much later that Gunung Agung became the focus of Balinese Hinduism.

The temple has only two courtyards, instead of the usual three. The spacious interior courtyard measures 66 x 30 meters and is dominated by an enormous eleven-tiered *meru* tower that is more massive than artistic. The temple has been periodically renovated, but remains simple and rustic, lacking the ornate *paras* stone carvings that characterize the temples of Gianyar.

The principal gate, a *kori agung* with wings, is very similar in construction to that of Pura Uluwatu on the Bukit, except that it is made of brick instead of coral stone. There is a close connection between these two temples, and it is said that one should pray at Pura Ulun Siwi before proceeding to Pura Uluwatu.

Ulun Siwi is unusual in yet another way. It is the principal temple in Bali dedicated to the welfare of both wet and dry rice fields, and the spirits which live in the temple are thought to control the mice and insects such as grasshoppers that periodically infest the fields. Farmers and farming groups regularly come to Pura Uluwatu to get water, which they then take back home and sprinkle on their fields either to protect them from these pests or to rid them of those already present.

South to Uluwatu

South of Jimbaran, the road climbs steeply up several switchbacks onto Bukit Badung plateau, offering dramatic panoramas back up the beach to the ricelands and the volcanoes on a clear day.

All around the southern and western edges of the plateau, limestone cliffs tower above a pounding surf 70 meters (250 feet) below. This is where Bali's best surfing is found — particularly famous are the waves at Suluban, Labuhan Sait and Bingin.

The Bukit's most famous landmark is Pura Luhur Uluwatu, an exquisite monument situated on a headland at the westernmost tip of the peninsula. The carvings which decorate the temple are very well preserved in comparison to many of Bali's temples, due to the extremely hard, dark gray coral stone used in its construction.

Uluwatu was reputedly built by the architect-priest Mpu Kuturan around the 11th century as one of the six major *sadkahyangan* territorial temples of the island. The reformer priest, Pedanda Wawu Rauh, rebuilt it in its present state in the 16th century. He is said to have attained his *moksa* (release from earthly desires) here. The temple is home to a small colony of monkeys who have caused some damage to the temple over the years, but still retain their status as sitting tenants.

The temple's structure follows the tripartite pattern of godly, human and demonic courtyards. The outermost entrance is a *candi bentar* split gate shaped as a set of curved Garuda wings, an unusual feature as they are usually left smooth. Inside the temple, a second gate is capped by a monstruous Kala head guardian figure. At the foot of the gate, right and left, are two Ganesh "elephant god" statues.

The temple underwent renovations in the late 19th century, in 1949, and more recently in the 1980s, and some parts are actually as new as they look. Despite the temple's mixture of old and new it is a breathtakingly beautiful spot, especially when the sun begins to set.

— *Fred Eiseman and Jean Couteau*

Opposite: *Pura Luhur Uluwatu perched above the sea, is one of the six important* sadkahyangan *temples on Bali.*

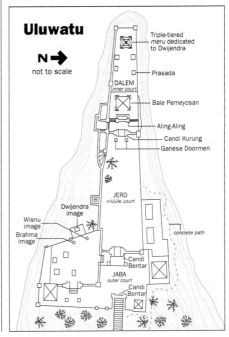

Uluwatu

N➡

not to scale

Triple-tiered meru dedicated to Dwijendra

Prasada

DALEM inner court

Bale Pemeyosan

Aling-Aling

Candi Kurung

Ganesa Doormen

JERO middle court

Dwijendra image

Wisnu image

Brahma image

concrete path

Candi Bentar

JABA outer court

Candi Bentar

NUSA DUA & TANJUNG BENOA

A Well-Manicured Paradise

MADE ARTHA

Nusa Dua and Tanjung Benoa are Bali's modern tourist resorts — a government-run dreamland of coconut palms, white sand beaches and pristine waters located near the island's southernmost tip. Geologically, the area is quite different from the rest of Bali, and even from the rest of the Bukit peninsula upon which it rests.

Instead of rice fields or limestone cliffs, there is sandy soil reaching down to a long, sandy beach protected by a reef. Coconut trees are everywhere — Nusa Dua was once a huge coconut plantation. The climate here is also drier than the rest of Bali, freshened by a mild ocean breeze.

Genesis of a beach resort

Once upon a time, the Balinese giant and master builder Kebo Iwa decided that the Tanjung Benoa marshes should be transformed into ricefields, so he went to the Bukit and picked up two scoops of earth. While shouldering them along the coast, his pole broke, dropping the earth into the sea. Two islets appeared: the **"Nusa Dua."**

The marshes were never to become ricefields; the bay remained a bay with a long cape, Tanjung Benoa, jutting into it. Nevertheless, Kebo Iwa, who created the area, is now engaged in a new venture — luxury hotel development.

Making Nusa Dua into a tourist paradise was a consciously implemented government policy, designed with the help of the World Bank. Two main concepts underly the project: to develop an up-market tourist resort, beautiful, secure, easy of access, with the most modern facilities, while keeping the disruptive impact on the local environment as low as possible.

Bualu was chosen both for its scenic location as well as for its relative isolation from densely populated areas. By 1971, the master plan was ready. Construction began in 1973. The first hotel, the Bualu Club, was complet-

ed in 1979, initially as a training ground for a Tourism and Hotel School (BPLP). Several luxury hotels with over 4,000 rooms have opened since then.

The early days

The project did have its teething pains. Tenants would not leave the land — Balinese custom distinguishes rights over land from rights over trees! And the trees have souls! Fishermen would not leave the beach. And then there were all the temples.

These questions were all eventually settled — tenants got land, fishermen take tourists sailing for a fee, and the temple festivals continue.

The entrance to the complex consists of a tall *candi bentar* split gate. Facing it 200 meters away is a modern-style *candi dwara pala pada* fountain-gate surmounted by a

RIO HELMI

monstruous *kala* head. The outer split gate separates while the inner gate unites. The cosmic complementarity of Bali and tourism in a nutshell.

The hotels are landmarks of the new Balinese architecture. The design committee specified that buildings be no higher than the coconut trees and that their layouts be based on Balinese macro and microcosmic models. Thus, the Club Med has its head in a Padmasana shrine to the northeast and its genitals and bowels in the discotheque (naturally!), with the kitchen to the southwest.

Tanjung Benoa: revamped port

For centuries, the natural means of communication between this area and the rest of Bali was by boat from **Tanjung Benoa**, as this was easier than the overland route via Jimbaran. Tanjung Benoa, which appears isolated at the tip of the peninsula, was in fact a trading port for Badung and the eastern Bukit, with a world outlook extending right across the archipelago. Its population bears traces of this mercantile past. Chinese have lived here for centuries: a "Ratu Cina" shrine in the local temple of death bears witness to their long presence.

Although most families have moved to Denpasar, they still maintain a **Klenteng** temple here, where local fishermen now inquire about the secrets of the stars with a Chinese abbot. The village also has a Bugis quarter, with a small mosque.

Bualu village

Compared to Tanjung Benoa, the village of **Bualu**, where Nusa Dua is situated, was a sleepy village subsisting on copra, fishing and coral collecting. There were two noble houses and no brahmans. As elsewhere in Bali, religion was ever-present.

The area had, and keeps, very special features. Its best-known ritual is an appeasement of the sea, to protect the land from any incursion by the fanged monster lurking beyond the waves — Jero Gede Mecaling — harbinger of death and illness. People present him with offerings in his many shrines along the coast.

The region around Buala is also dotted with sea temples, some within the perimeters of the luxury hotels. And *pengelem* duck sacrifices to the sea are offered under the eyes of passing tourists.

— *Jean Couteau*

Left: An aerial view of Nusa Dua, looking north along the length of Tanjung Benoa, with the peaks of central Bali in the background. **Above, left:** The Chinese temple or klenteng in Tanjung Benoa, evidence of this village's mercantile past. **Below:** Top-end luxury at Nusa Dua's Melia Bali Sol hotel.

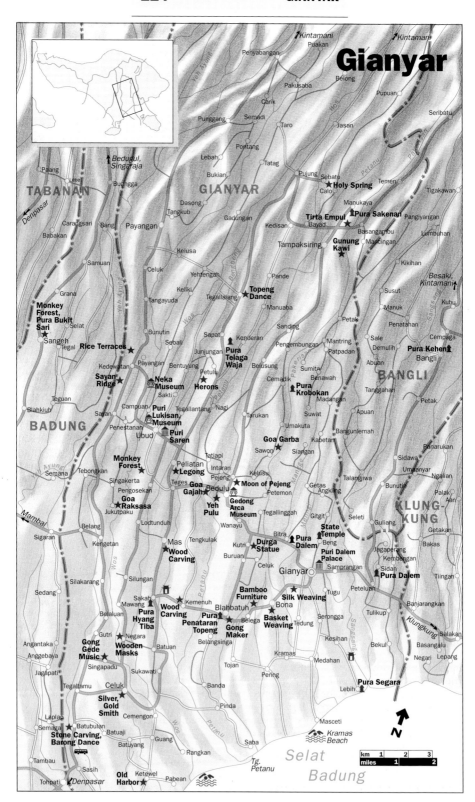

Gianyar

PART III

Central Bali: Gianyar Regency

Gianyar is the very heart of Bali — a modern and prosperous center of the arts with a history dating back a thousand years. Most of the cultural activities relating to tourism on the island — from painting and woodcarving to dance and music — are focused here, as is a broad range of agricultural activities.

Gianyar is the second most densely populated district of Bali (after Badung), with the majority of its 320,000 people relying upon tourism for their income. Nevertheless, the region is quite diverse, economically as well as geographically. The old harbors of Ketewel and Kramas down on the coast are still fishing villages, while up in the mountainous plateau above Ubud, vanilla, coffee and cloves are grown. The rich volcanic soils in between are fed by two of Bali's major rivers — the Ayung and the Petanu — and from these soils grows some of Bali's best rice.

The major tourist area of Gianyar consists of a string of villages along the main road up from Batubulan to Ubud, with each village on the way being famous for a different artistic form. Bali's most famous dancers and best known painters come from this region. Bali's most famous antiquities have also been found in this area, including the 2,000-year-old "Moon of Pejeng" bronze drum, the Goa Gajah hermitage at Bedulu with its elaborate reliefs, and many other remains dating from before the 11th century. These all testify to the strength and continuity of the traditions upon which Bali's modern arts are founded.

Lying at the center of the area in which most Balinese antiquities have been found, the village of Bedulu was the site of an ancient capital of Bali before the Javanese Majapahit kingdom conquered the island in 1343. After the decline of Bedulu, other parts of Gianyar have been important court centers.

When Majapahit established a line of kings in Bali in the 14th century, their first capital was at Samprangan — now a sleepy village just outside of present-day Gianyar Town. Later, in the 18th century, the village of Sukawati established itself as a separate court center and members of the Sukawati royal family settled between the Ayung and Petanu rivers, with branches in Peliatan and Tegallalang up in the mountains.

At the end of the 18th century, the Sukawati dynasty was forced to surrender its control of the area to a new family based in Gianyar to the east. As a result, most of the important districts and villages of Gianyar have members of both the old Sukawati line of Cokordas and the new Gianyar line of Dewas or Anak Agungs, and the history of the 19th century revolved around competition between the two lineages.

In 1884 the royal family of Negara, from the Sukawati line, overthrew the kings of Gianyar and plunged the region into turmoil. The conflict was finally resolved only ten years later, when a prince from Ubud, also of the Sukawati line, took the side of the Gianyar family and suppressed the rebels. There are still other important aristocratic families in Gianyar, however — foremost of which are the Gustis of Blahbatuh, whose palace was a major 19th-century power.

In more recent times, Ubud and Gianyar have been the twin centers of the region. Ubud now has the reputation of being Bali's cultural center, thanks especially to a group of expatriate western artists who made their homes here in the 1930s, but Gianyar has provided most of the political and administrative leadership. Bali's most important politician on the national stage, Anak Agung Gede Agung, diplomat and former foreign minister of Indonesia, is from the Gianyar royal family, and has retired to the palace of Gianyar to serve in the now-ceremonial role of king.

— *Adrian Vickers*

Overleaf: *Elaborate preparations for a* melasti *purification rite in Singapadu, featuring a pair of* barong landung *figures. Photo by Rio Helmi.*

BATUBULAN AND CELUK

Surprising Art and Craft Villages

The neighboring villages of Batubulan, Celuk and Singapadu are the first in a series of surprising art and craft centers that one encounters going north along the main road from Denpasar toward Ubud. These villages have garnered fame for a variety of skills: Batubulan for its *barong* dance and stone carving, Singapadu for its *gong saron* and *gong gede* music, and Celuk for its silver and goldsmithing.

Batubulan: home of the barong

Ten km north of Denpasar, Batubulan is a village known throughout Bali for its ornate door-guardian statues, carved of soft *paras* volcanic tuff. Until these became popular for secular use earlier in this century, the carvings were only used in temples or palaces, but this artform has spread extensively in recent years and is today found in homes and public buildings. **Made Leceg** and **Made Sura**, two of the most famous carvers of the area, continue the legacy of their mentor, the late **Made Loji**. Both have shops on the main road where carvings can be purchased and packed and shipped home.

Batubulan is also home to three famous **Barong Dance** troupes who perform five times a week at 10 am on their own stages before bus-loads of enthralled tourists. The development of these groups parallels that of tourism in Bali, but even so the Batubulan *barong* troupes are relatively young. The first, the Danjalan Barong Group, was established in 1970, while the Tegaltamu and Puri Agung groups were formed later. The three troupes also perform on a large stage that was constructed especially for this purpose in the outer courtyard of Pura Puseh Bendul in 1986.

While in the neighborhood, **Pura Puseh Batubulan** is well worth visiting. Four statues of Vishnu poised on carved pedestals embellished with *Tantri* tales guard the temple. If you care to shop, **Galuh Artshop** on the main road offers an extensive range of Balinese batik and weavings, and **Kadek Nadhi's Antique Store** has many antiques, from krisses and masks to carved doors.

Celuk: jewelry of silver and gold

Although many arts and crafts have prospered in Celuk, the village has evolved into a

RIO HELMI

center for silver and gold smithing. Almost every home in the village contains small scale production facilities fulfilling orders placed by large shops and exporters. Bracelets, rings, earrings and brooches, to name a few of a wide range of products produced here, have started to enter the export market.

The silver and gold craft trade was pioneered by the Beratan clan of smiths (*pande*). Nowadays most Celuk residents, whether or not they are members of the Pande clan, have become gold and silversmiths. **Wayan Kawi** and **Wayan Kardana** are among the better craftsmen.

Along the main road between Batubulan and Celuk you will find about 40 artshops, most of which sell gold and silver jewelry. **Keraton Gold and Silver Collection, Celuk Silver** and **Semadi Gallery** have particularly good selections. Other shops, such as **Wirama Antiques and Modern Art** and **Bali Souvenir**, sell masks, statues, old basketry and textiles, among other things.

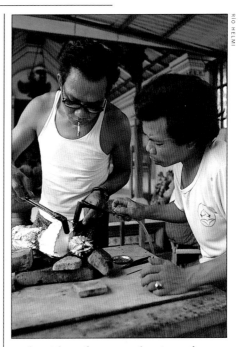

Singapadu: village of the 'twin kings'

The history of the small village of Singapadu, just up the road from Batubulan, goes back to the reign of I Dewa Kaleran, a king of Kalianget who assisted the ruler of Sukawati, I Dewa Agung Anom, to defeat the king of Mengwi with the aid of two powerful krises.

As an expression of gratitude and to strengthen family ties, I Dewa Agung Anom offered his sister to be Dewa Kaleran's bride. Impatient at the long wait for his sister's pregnancy, I Dewa Agung then presented another princess to Dewa Kaleran, this time one who was already pregnant. This princess gave birth to a boy, called I Dewa Agung Api. Meanwhile, Dewa Agung's first wife also became pregnant and gave birth to another son, Dewa Kaleran Sakti. With the birth of both sons, two princes had rights to the throne, and the name *singha-padu* meaning "twin lions" was given to the place.

Some believe that Dewa Kaleran's sacred kris, Sekar Sandat, possesses creative powers and has therefore helped dance, music and carving to flourish in the area. In the past Singapadu was known as a center for dance and music. Unfortunately, these groups have today largely withered away. However, *barong* and *legong* groups continuing the traditions of the past can be found in Banjar Sungguan. At one time these dance groups only entertained locals in temples, but now, they perform for tourists at the large hotels.

Apart from the *gong gede*, a type of *gamelan* which most *banjars* in Singapadu possess, two *banjars,* namely Apuan and Seseh, have an older type of *gamelan* known as the *gong saron*. This is mainly used to accompany death ceremonies, as the tones produced are thought to express sadness and sorrow. The seven-key xylophones of the *gong saron* differ from the 10-key *gangsa* of a typical *gamelan*.

Many well-known dancers have come from Singapadu, such as Wayan Griya, Ketut Rujag, Wayan Kengguh, Made Kerdek and Ni Ketut Senun. Today, there are many good ones left, such as Nyoman Cerita, Ketut Kodi, Ni Nyoman Candri and Ketut Rumita. Made Raos, another prominent dancer, is one of Singapadu's best *barong* (*bapang*) dancers. Another prominent figure in the field of dance, Dr I Made Bandem, Director of STSI (the Academy of Music and Dance) in Denpasar, is also a native of Singapadu.

In the field of *topeng* and *barong* maskmaking, the late Cokorda Oka's mastery has now been handed down to his pupils, I Wayan Tangguh, Cokorda Raka Tisnu and Nyoman Juala. Wayan Pugeg and Ketut Muja also exhibit great talent in carving wood statues.

— *I Made Suradiya*

Opposite: *A Singapadu carver specializing in wooden masks.* **Above:** *Master silversmiths in the village of Celuk.*

SUKAWATI

Ancient Court and Bali's Best *Dalangs*

Conveniently located midway between mountain slopes and the sea on the main road north of Denpasar on the way to Ubud, Sukawati is a modest town of few tourist attractions as such, yet it is rich in cultural traditions and offers much for the interested visitor.

At one time, Sukawati stood with Klungkung as one of the two great *negara* or kingdoms of Bali. From Tegallalang to Ubud to Singapadu, *topeng* mask dancers still interprete the history of the old realm of Sukawati before rapt audiences. Here the arts have remained vital, thanks to royal patronage and commissions from other parts of the island.

'My heart's delight'

Early in the 18th century the Sukawati region, formerly known as Timbul, came under the influence of an evil sorcerer, Ki Balian Batur. His enemies all became violent-ly ill due to his powerful black magic. Seeking to pacify Timbul, the raja of Mengwi, Angelurah Agung, sought help from I Dewa Agung Anom — son of the raja of Klungkung. Together they defeated the sorcerer with magic weapons brought from the court of Klungkung. Ki Balian Batur is still remembered today in the name of the nearby village of Rangkan, which means "place of the evil man." As a token of his gratitude, the raja invited I Dewa Agung Anom to build a palace and live there.

I Dewa Agung Anom dreamed of creating an ideal kingdom based on the example of Majapahit in East Java. From Klungkung he brought attractive men and women who were talented in the arts and representive of the important lineages. Once in Timbul, they built the Pura Penataran Agung as a central shrine and the Puri Goro Gak as a residence for I Dewa Agung Anom and his family.

Lavishly embellished with carvings, the beauty of the great *pura* was enhanced through the addition of fabulous gardens and pools. Every night, the sensuous sounds of the *gamelan* were heard wafting from an enormous *bale* pavilion covered with gold leaf. The marvels of Timbul invariably caused visitors to exclaim "*sukahatiné*" which means "my heart's delight" and gradually the town became known as Sukawati.

Popularly known as Dalem Sukawati, the first raja, I Dewa Agung Anom, enjoyed a

TOM BALLINGER

long reign. Eventually wearying of political life, he retired to meditate in Petemon, near Bedulu. Meanwhile his sons grew fond of gambling and broke up a magic kris belonging to the palace to be made into spurs for fighting cocks. Dalem Sukawati, despairing of his sons' inability to rule, declared that upon his death whichever son would dare to take the deceased Dalem's tongue into his mouth would inherit the kingdom.

Following the Dalem's death, his corpse became so swollen and repulsive that his sons were unwilling to perform the odious chore. This fell to a relative, the raja of Gianyar. Miraculously, when the raja took the hideously protruding tongue into his mouth, the corpse shrank to normal size and emitted a wonderful perfume. This failure of the sons, however, together with the loss of the protective kris, caused the heirs of Dalem Sukawati to be defeated in war by Gianyar, and subsequently the palace was abandoned.

Bali's finest dalangs

Sukawati residents are proud that their town has a complex of temples unrivaled outside of Besakih. Represented here is the complete *sad kayangan* group of six temples symbolizing the sacred mountains of Bali: Pura Desa, Pura Puseh, Pura Dalem, Pura Melanting, Pura Ulun Siwi and Pura Sakti.

The **Pura Penataran Agung** temple at the center of Sukawati is a pilgrimage site for all members of the royal houses of the surrounding areas — Tegallalang, Ubud, Peliatan, Batuan, Mas, Negara and Singapadu. Destroyed in an earthquake in 1917, the temple was rebuilt on a smaller scale, which has in no way affected its importance. Next door to the temple is the **Pura Kawitan Dalem Sukawati** which still boasts panel carvings of *Tantri* tales besides several unusual statues in the outer courtyard.

The massive *candi bentar* gate of the **Pura Desa** on the northeastern corner of the town is a tribute to the continuing excellence of local craftsmen. Also famous throughout Bali are the *tukang wadah* — craftsmen of the great cremation towers required for royal funeral ceremonies, and the *tukang prada* — makers of gold-painted costumes and umbrellas.

Sukawati is best known, however, for its many shadow-puppet masters or *dalang*. As many as 20 of these artists and their troupes are available for hire for ceremonial occasions and they travel all over Bali to perform. The Balinese say that the *dalang* of Sukawati are the best on the island because of many generations of experience.

Two famous *dalangs* live in Banjar Babakan behind the produce market. **I Wayan Wija**, known for his unusual *wayang tantri*, and **I Wayan Nartha**, may both be contacted to commission a shadow play or a special set of puppets. Anyone in the *banjar* can direct you to their houses. Another big-name *dalang* in Sukawati is **Ganjreng**.

A scholar and member of the *sangging* caste of artisans, **I Nyoman Sadia** has turned from his family tradition of stone carving to making fine jewelry. His house and shop are just off the main road at Jl. Sersan Wayan Pugig no 5.

The commercial center of town is the *Pasar Seni* or **Art Market**. With patience and a sense of humor one can find bargains here on everything from woodcarvings to paintings. Along the main road, shops cater to local needs — such as baskets and ceremonial umbrellas. Directly across the road is an open-air produce market. North of this is the present site of the **Puri Agung**, where visitors wishing for an in-depth exploration of the town can overnight.

— Tom Ballinger

AMIR SIDHARTA

Left: *Renowned puppet master I Wayan Wija holding one of his original* Tantri *puppet creations.*
Right: *Entrance to the striking Pelinggih Sunya Loka temple in Sukawati.*

BATUAN

Village of Ancestral Spirits

For over a thousand years Batuan has been a village of artists and craftsmen, old legends and mysterious tales. Batuan's recorded history begins in A.D. 1022, with an inscription that is housed in the main village temple, **Pura Desa Batuan**. The name "Batuan" or "Baturan" mentioned here prompts villagers to joke about being "tough as stone" or "eating rocks" — as *batu* means "stone" in Balinese. But it likely refers to an ancient megalithic tradition in which standing stones served as meeting places and ceremonial sites for the worship of ancestral spirits.

Famous families

Batuan's central location in south Bali is the primary reason for its historical importance. Besides the ancient village temple, there is a temple called **Pura Gede Mecaling** which is said to be on the site of the old palace of the

demon king Jero Gede Mecaling, whose name the Balinese are afraid to even utter. He is supposed to have moved from here to the island of Nusa Penida, where he still resides.

In the 1600s the famous family of Gusti Ngurah Batulepang dominated south Bali, living as prime ministers based in Batuan. They remained prime ministers until the early 1700s, when a branch of the Klungkung royal family was established at nearby Sukawati. At that time the chief centers of the kingdom were Sukawati, Batuan, and the nearby seaside village of Ketewel. Batuan still has ritual links with Ketewel that commemorate that era.

The family of Batulepang scattered to the far corners of Bali in subsequent centuries as the result of a priestly curse, but a small temple for Gusti Batulepang remains on the site of his palace. The Buddhist priests or *pedanda boda* who later made Batuan a great spiritual center built a house, the **Griya Ageng**, on that part of Batulepang's temple where death rituals were once held. They then marshalled powerful Tantric forces here.

Brahman majority

Because Batuan became a center from which Buddhist priests and brahmans spread to the main court centers of south Bali, the village has an unusual preponderance of brahmans. DeZoete and Spies, in their famous book *Dance and Drama in Bali*, describe it as almost entirely a brahman village. This is not really true, but much of the village near the main Denpasar to Ubud road is inhabited by the extended family of the Buddhist Griya Ageng and of a smaller number of Siwa-worshipping brahmans who came later to Batuan. The other main high caste family are the Dewas, related to the Batuan *puri* or extended palace family, who are in turn closely related to the Gianyar royal family. Batuan is unusual in that commoners actually form a minority in the center of the village.

The western area of Batuan, known as Negara, was a separate village and court center in the 19th century. It grew so powerful that it revolted against the main house of Gianyar in 1884, destroying the kingdom and setting south Bali on a path of internal conflict which opened it up to Dutch conquest. In 1900, when the Dutch took over Gianyar, Negara was incorporated within Batuan. Similarly, the adjacent area of Puaya, a

Left: *Statue of the witch Rangda in the Pura Dalem death temple of Batuan.* **Right:** *A ritual cockfight, also in the Pura Dalem.*

famous center for dance and theater ornaments, puppets and other objects made from hide, is regarded as being quite separate.

Dancing ancient tales

The Buddhist brahmans of Batuan, in concert with the famous former king of the village, Anak Agung Gede Oka (1860 - 1947), were responsible for making Batuan the center on Bali for the most courtly and elegant of all Balinese dance forms, the *gambuh*. In all of Bali only two troupes from Batuan still perform this theatrical presentation of tales of ancient princes and princesses.

The first is led by **I Made Jimat**, Bali's most celebrated dancer of modern times, whose genius never fails to leave his audiences breathless. The second consists of the extended family of the greatest dancer of the generation before Jimat — the late I Nyoman Kakul — who passed on the skills and techniques of *gambuh* and of the other important dance forms such as the masked *topeng* plays and the operatic *arja* theater. **Ketut Kantor**, Kakul's son, now leads the troupe.

In his day Kakul was able to call on the mask-making skills of Dewa Putu Kebes, whose *topeng* masks were charged with the spiritual forces of kings and heroes from the Balinese past. Since his death, his son **Dewa Cita** and grandson **Dewa Mandra** have maintained the combination of immaculate skill and divine inspiration which made his work so powerful. A pupil of the family, **Made Regug** of Negara, also upholds the fine carving tradition.

Besides the dances, performed in the central part of the village, Batuan is also famous for its *wayang wong,* masked performances of stories from the *Ramayana.* This is exclusively performed in the *banjar* (hamlet) known as **Den Tiis**.

The 'Batuan style'

From Den Tiis also came the inspiration for the modern Batuan style of painting. In the 1930s, two brothers, **I Ngendon** and **I Patera**, began experimenting painting with ink on paper. The result was powerful black and white images of magic and of Balinese life. The families of these two artists are still influential in the village, and now own the **Artshop Dewata** on the main road leading to Ubud.

Ngendon and Patra originally studied under a traditional painter living to the east of the palace, but from them the painting tradition spread back to the main part of the village where it was enthusiastically embraced by a number of their fellow villagers. The present-day generation of artists includes **Made Tubuh, Wayan Rajin, Ida Bagus Putu Gede** and **Made Buti** who has become famous through his humorous and insightful depictions of tourists in Bali.

— *Adrian Vickers*

MAS

Brahmanical Woodcarving Village

The village of **Mas** lies on the main road, 20 km to the north of Denpasar and 6 km before Ubud, in a hilly countryside covered with ricefields and irrigated year-round by the waters of the Batuan and Sakah rivers.

Today the village appears as a succession of palatial artshops, as Mas has developed into a flourishing center for the woodcarving craft. Indeed, it is difficult to imagine what the village was like before dozens of tourist buses started to drop in everyday. Yet Mas actually played an important role in Balinese history during the 16th century, as it was the place where a great priest from Java, Danghyang Nirartha (also called Dwijendra), had his hermitage (*griya*).

Descendants of the holy priest

The holy man, known locally as Pedanda Sakti Wau Rauh (literally: "The Newly Arrived High Priest") crossed to Bali from Kadiri in east Java after the fall of the powerful Majapahit kingdom, and was invited to Mas by prince Mas Wilis (Tan Kober). Here the pedanda acquired great fame through his teaching, and gathered many disciples. His son by Mas Wilis' daughter is the forebear of one of Bali's four important brahmana clans, which to the present day traces its roots back to the village.

The priest's fame reached the court of Dalem Baturenggong in Gelgel, who, impressed by Danghyang Nirartha's superior wisdom, appointed him the King's counselor and court priest.

Based upon his instructions, many temples were built, especially after his *moksa* (holy death). His belongings — *bajra* (holy bell), black shirt, mattress and staff — are now kept in the Mas *griya,* and the Pura

Right: *A statue of Danghyang Nirartha near the Pura Taman Pule, site of his former hermitage.*
Opposite: *A woodcarving by Ida Bagus Tilem of Mas, one of the village's best-known craftsmen.*

Taman Pule temple was built on the site of the priest's *griya*.

Realm of the blessed craftsmen

The gods are also said to have bestowed talents on two of Mas' houses: the skill of the shadow puppet master to Griya Dauh, and the skill of woodcarving to Griya Danginan. At first, the woodcarvers (*sangging*) were all brahmanas who worked only on ritual or courtly projects. Their disciples (*sisya*) learned the craft from them, and woodcarving skills were transmitted from father to son. The traditional *wayang* style prevailed, featuring religious scenes and characters from the *Ramayana* and *Mahabharata* epics.

During the 1930s, under the influence of Walter Spies and Pita Maha, a new style of woodcarving developed here. The motifs were more realistic, and inspired by everyday scenes featuring humans and animals. Several of these early works may now be seen in Ubud's Puri Lukisan museum.

During this period, woodcarvings began to be appreciated and purchased by foreigners, but only after 1970 did the real boom take place. The first art shops in Mas were those of Ketut Roja (**Siadja & Son**), followed by **Ida Bagus Nyana** and his son **Ida Bagus Tilem**, and **Ida Bagus Taman** (**Adil Artshop**). At first they all produced works of quality in limited quantities, mainly working with locally-available woods. A more abstract

AMIR SIDHARTA

style was later developed by Purna and Nyana, featuring elongated, curved lines and woods such as ebony and sandalwood. Later on, in Pujung and Tegallalang, Cokot began to carve roots into demonic figures.

In recent years, many realistic, brightly painted animals and fruit trees (known here as *pulasan*) have appeared on the market, based on European designs. First created by Togog in Pujung, much of the production is now of questionable quality, but the prices are very low.

Woodcarving shops

Dozens of woodcarving shops now line the main road. The three mentioned above are the famous, as well as **Tantra** and **I. B. Anom** for *topeng* masks.

One can see craftsmen at work in a small workshops in the galleries; the system is paternalistic; the shop owner gives work to his craftsmen according to their skill, the price being settled after the fact based on the final result. They work on the spot or at home. Skill is learned at an early age inside the family; technology is still quite traditional, using various types of axes, chisels and drills made by different local blacksmiths. Prices are very high anyway, especially if you do not come on your own, and always in dollars. They can sometimes handle special orders. Nyoman Tekek Manis recently carved a giant Christ that was placed on the Cengkareng Church altar in Jakarta and inaugurated by Pope John Paul II in 1989.

Located 100 m from the road on the east side, **Pura Taman Pule** does not take its name from the holy *pule* trees growing behind it, but means "Beautiful Garden"; Danghyang Nirartha is said to have planted a purple flowered *tangi* tree in it — still growing behind an altar in the *jaba tengah* (middle court) — from which a golden bud sprouted, which gave the village its name. At the back of the main temple, a *padmasana* surrounded by a pond is said to have been the place of his hermitage. People from all over Bali come to pray there, not only brahmanas, but also commoners of the Pasek Bendesa Mas clan, especially on its five-day *odalan,* falling on Kuningan Day (Saturday).

Dance: shadows of the past

The Wayang Wong Ramayana troupe still alive in Mas is very old. It was revived by Walter Spies — its 22 sacred masks are now kept in the temple. A performance is held on Kuningan eve, and three more on Kuningan day, as ritual contributions (*ayahan*).

Talented *dalangs,* such as I. B. Geriya and I. B. Anom usually perform ritual *wayang lemah* on Kuningan Night in the Taman Pule area; other forms as *topeng drama gong,* dances such as Jangger Pandawa and Kupu-kupu carum (created by Spies) is declining.

— *Agnès Korb*

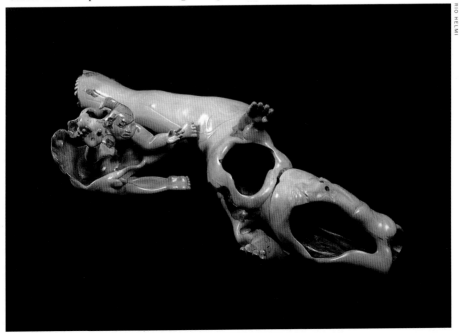

PELIATAN

Home of the Legendary *Legong*

This small village of 6,000 is often over-looked, though it lies just 2 km south of the tourist village of Ubud on the main road. Rich in the arts, and not as full of tourists as Ubud, it is definitely worth a visit — particularly if you are interested in dance and music.

'That which is seen'

The Peliatan court actually preceded the Ubud court. Although the dates are unclear, the 17th century *Babad Dalem Sukawati* (a chronicle of the Sukawati court) recounts an argument between two princes —I Dewa Agung Gede and I Dewa Agung Made — that resulted in two separate courts.

The former ran off to Blahbatuh and the latter to Tegallalang — taking with him a sacred heirloom, the Segara Ngelayang spear that is now kept in the Peliatan palace. I Dewa Agung Made later moved to Peliatan to

be closer to his ancestral home in Sukawati. His children then set up palaces in Ubud, and to this day Ubud royalty still pay homage to their cousins in Peliatan.

Peliatan literally means "that which is seen," and according to some accounts this refers to the fact that Sukawati is within view down the road. Others claim that a former king of Peliatan was given religious instruction here by a priest and was therefore able to "see" the famous temple of Gunung Sari, before it was built. Today, this temple is a favorite with dancers and musicians who come here in search of *taksu* (inspiration).

Bali's most notable legong

Peliatan is best known for its *legong* — a graceful dance performed by two pre-pubescent girls in glittering costumes (see "Balinese Dance," page 44). Indeed, the first Balinese dance troupe to travel abroad was a *legong* group from Peliatan that performed at the Paris Exhibition in 1931 under the leadership of Anak Agung Gede Mandera (affectionately known as "Gung Kak") — a man who excelled in both music and dance. The group's performances created a sensation; it was then, for example, that French actor Antonin Artaud first witnessed the Balinese *barong*. Gung Kak's descendants still carry on the tradition — a 1989 tour to the United States included many of his family members.

Traditions of dance and music in Bali are

passed from teacher to pupil and parent to child. Some teachers become very famous, such as Peliatan's **Gusti Biang Sengog**. A famous dancer in her prime, she was recorded for posterity in the film *Miracle of Bali: Midday Sun* teaching young women who have all become prominent dancers today.

If you like, you can witness Peliatan's young stars in action. To see the tiny *legongs*, travel south from Peliatan to **Teges Kanginan** — this is one of the few places on Bali where the dancers are still trained in the traditional manner. The teacher here, Sang Ayu Ketut Muklin, is from the neighboring village of Pejeng and is of the same age and caliber as Gusti Biang Sengog.

Some of the musicians from the Paris tour are still alive. One is **I Made Lebah**, a master drummer and *ugal* player. His son, **I Wayan Gandra** has followed in his footsteps, and both play in the Gunung Sari group. Lebah is often at home in Banjar Kalah, just off the main curve in the road, while his son lives in the village of Petulu. Also from this area, **I Made Grindem**, who died in 1989, brought the Peliatan style of *gender* playing to a high art form in Teges Kanginan.

Peliatan today boasts 15 *gamelan* groups, including: *gong kebyar, gong semar pegulingan, gong angklung* and *joged bumbung*. Almost every *banjar* owns at least one set of instruments and you can hear the haunting sounds of the *gamelan* in the Peliatan area nearly every night, whether in rehearsal or performance.

In 1987, Peliatan's women's *gamelan*, **Mekar Sari**, was begun under the tutelage of Gung Kak. Now the group performs every Sunday night at 7:30 pm in Banjar Teruna. The dancers are all under 12 years old. The **Gong Kebyar Gunung Sari** also puts on a dazzling show at Pura Dalem Puri in Banjar Tebesaya every Saturday at 7.30 pm. The more lyrical sounds of the **Semar Pegulingan Tirta Sari** (with two different *legongs*) can be heard on Friday night at 7.30 pm at Tebesaya. And every Tuesday at 7:30 pm in Banjar Teges Kawan, the **Gong Kebyar Semara Jati** presents a variety of fine dances and dance dramas.

The traditional and the modern continue to flourish side-by-side here. **Anak Agung Oka Dalem**, one of Gung Kak's children, excels in the kebyar styles which Peliatan put on the map 40 years ago. In 1982, he founded Padma Nara Suara (PANAS for short), a dance group that fuses modern choreography and costuming with traditional Balinese dance movements. One could say that PANAS is the Busby Berkeley of Bali.

Carving and painting

Peliatan is also a village of carvers and painters. Everywhere you go you see orchids, fruits, frogs, ducks and birds being fashioned out of wood. These are all of course for tourists. Two of the more exceptional carvers are **I Wayan Pasti** — whose lifesize horses and dogs will make you do a double-take — and **I Nyoman Togog** (the original "fruit man"), who received a Presidential award in 1985.

I Ketut Madra of Banjar Kalah is an excellent painter in the traditional *wayang* style. He is not a businessman by nature and does not have a gallery, but likes to show his work to visitors and accepts special commissions.

To view the classical painting style of the 1930s, visit any one of the following: **I Gusti Made Kuanji** in Banjar Teruna, **I Nyoman Kuta** in Banjar Tengah and **Ida Bagus Made** in Tebesaya. For an overview of Balinese painting, pop into the **Agung Rai Gallery** on the main road in Peliatan — one of the best collections on the island. If you see something you like, you can probably look up the artist nearby in his home.

— Rucina Ballinger

Left: *Young* legongs *such as these begin to perform at the age of six.* **Right:** *Cok Ratih, once a famous* legong *herself, at her tooth-filling ritual.*

PENGOSEKAN

A Flourishing Community of Art and Soul

Half an hour's walk or a 10-minute drive from central Ubud, due south along the shaded main street of Padangtegal past open rice paddies, art shops and homestays, brings you to the village of **Pengosekan** (pronounced: PongoSAYkan), which despite its small size, has over the past 20 years become a major player on the Balinese art scene.

Although Pengosekan paintings are seldom seen in shops and galleries, and must be hunted down in the village itself, no serious exhibit of Balinese art is complete without a few, and they grace the walls of collectors, museums and palaces around the world (the aristocrats of neighboring Mas were somewhat put out when Queen Elizabeth insisted on being taken to low-caste Pengosekan in search of a painting; the villagers themselves were disappointed that she had forgotten to wear her crown).

Only recently has Pengosekan emerged from a state of semi-isolation, with the bridging of a river which previously could only be forded on precarious stepping stones that washed away with every rainfall. It is perhaps because of this isolation that the artists of Pengosekan have not been followers and imitators, but individualistic pioneers of a new style in Balinese art and life. In 1979 they established the island's first artists' cooperative, exhibiting and selling together and supporting each other with raw materials in the days when the cost of a tube of imported acrylic paint would feed a large family for three weeks. Incorporating elements of traditional Balinese communalism, they called themselves the **Pengosekan Community of Farmers and Artists**.

The cooperative experiment

On my second day in Bali, in 1971, I made the long and tortuous (in those days) *bemo* journey from the coast, hemmed in by chattering market ladies and their produce, and waded calf-deep across the river to Pengosekan. It was the season of the dragonflies, which hovered in their thousands above the rice paddies. Children charged, shouting and laughing in pursuit, trapping them on glue-tipped bamboo whips and threading them on long strings to take home and deepfry as protein-rich snacks. A farmer and his cow, both swollen with a head-to-foot coat of

LORNE BLAIR

glistening mud, laboriously ploughed his field, their enlarged muscles rippling and crackling in a slow, methodical dance of regeneration.

As the earthen walls of the village closed around me, a duck-herd led his flock through shafting rays of evening sunlight. The frantically pumping feet of his platoon (early writers called them "Bali Soldiers") faltered at the sight of so horrific a pink stranger, and their quacking reached an hysterical pitch, but then they swept on past — a relentless wave of dappled brown. I felt a surge of alarm; this was all to good to be true. Beneath the bucolic calm I sensed energies and tensions that no Westerner was equipped to cope with.

I had come armed with only a letter of introduction, given me by a journalist friend in Jakarta with the words: "He's an ex-teacher-turned-artist, and the driving force of the new cooperative. He's a bit of a philosopher and the only person in Pengosekan who speaks any English. You may find him and his village interesting." Quite an understatement — as Pengosekan would become my home, and **Dewa Nyoman Batuan**, my most lasting and stimulating friend in Bali, opening windows for me onto the Balinese way of living and perceiving.

I finally found Dewa Batuan at work on a large canvas of a cosmological *mandala*, with all the levels of existence radiating out from the Hindu trinity at the center. A moon-faced man with lively enquiring eyes, Batuan seemed about my age, though I would later learn that he was almost 10 years my senior. Several other artists continued with their own paintings while he joined me over a glass of potent Balinese coffee. As we talked in broken English and more broken Indonesian, he became animated, often pumping his hands together for emphasis, his face creasing into a broad smile and occasionally escalating to uninhibited laughter at some joke.

The cooperative was still in its first precarious year, and his ambitions for it seemed to me wildly optimistic, but most of his dreams would be realized surprisingly soon. A Westerner was already planning to mount an exhibition of their work in Europe, and a resident Englishman had just asked them to illustrate what would become a charmingly eccentric book of Balinese fables (*The Haughty Toad and Other Tales*, by Victor Mason).

As the moon rose and his friends worked on by lantern light, the conversation became

more metaphysical as he explained the symbolism behind the myths and legends they were painting. One of the painters ambled over to watch another at work and added a few touches of his own. I wondered how a western artist would have reacted to such an intrusion on his creation. In later years I would see this collective approach carried to its logical extreme, with several artists working simultaneously on one large canvas and signing it "Pengosekan Group."

By the mid-70s the cooperative was well established, but still hampered by the river which daunted many would-be visitors, so Batuan moved the whole operation — and his home — across the ford to within 200 yards of Peliatan. Business boomed, and they started painting truly monumental canvasses of pulsating, multi-textured jungles populated by exotic birds of dubious descent. This would become known as the widely imitated "Pengosekan Style," but it was only one of Pengosekan's many new artistic directions.

Eventually, though, they discovered what artists the world over have found: that you cannot live by art alone — a painful fact particularly true in Bali, where sloppy imitations of paintings that should take six months to produce sell for a quarter the normal price;

Opposite: *Dewa Nyoman Batuan telling stories to a group of children during a village temple festival.*
Above: *Naughty detail from a painting by Mokoh.*

and where a talented artist is responsible not only for his own survival, but that of his extended family and community as well.

Then came a visitor who would have a dramatic impact, first on Pengosekan and then on the entire Balinese art world.

The 'Bali-International' craft style

Designer **Linda Garland** — she of the flaming Irish hair and irrepressible creative energy — settled for awhile in the village. Undisputed doyen of a new "Bali-International" style, she would soon be designing living spaces for the rich and famous in the Hamptons, Europe and the Carribean. Pengosekan's only existing handicrafts, other than those produced for the temple and the gods, were baskets somewhat reminiscent of those from the American Southwest, but she suggested one day to Batuan: "Instead of spending months on a single painting, why don't you and the other talented artists do small watercolors and design appropriate wooden frames that your less skilled colleagues can execute and paint?"

That small beginning led to the colorful floral mirror frames, chests, wooden fruits, screens, Kleenex boxes and even toilet seats that can now be seen on every street-corner of Bali and in many western department stores (Pengosekan alone ships out at least one container load every month!).

The new industry brought undreamed of wealth, but it also created jealousies, tensions and financial imbalance. In the mid-80s the cooperative collapsed in acrimony. Those were terrible days for Pengosekan, and I am glad I was away editing *Ring of Fire* at the time. Neighbors stopped speaking, families broke up, stress-related diseases proliferated and at least one talented artist became clinically insane for more than a year. Indeed, it would have destroyed the entire village had their traditional Balinese sense of communalism been less deeply ingrained. Somehow they weathered the storm, and although they now act independently in business, they can again share affably in village affairs and present a genuinely united front at exhibitions. Everyone now agrees that the cooperative's fifteen years laid the groundwork for the future, and that its demise was an essential metamorphosis.

The artists today

Most paintings in Pengosekan today are merely decorative, quickly turned out and lacking that laboriously applied layering of colors and shading which gave the village its fame. But some of the artists remain uncompromised by commercial considerations, devoting six months or more to one canvas. To find these, you must search hard, be fortunate in your timing and prepared to pay, but the hunt can be as rewarding as the acquisition.

Batuan (the artists must forgive my disrespect in using only their last names for clarity and brevity) still lives just east of the bridge near Peliatan. His burgeoning business in wooden fantasies, many of them one-offs — giant painted parasols and carved four-poster beds (Ronnie and Nancy Reagan slept in one during their 1986 visit) — leaves him little time for painting, but he still has the largest cross-section of Pengosekan art on offer. Notable among them are those of his older brother, **Mokoh**, whose subject matter ranges from village scenes to the downright lewd, but all display his unmistakable style and wicked sense of humour. His awkward and seemingly clumsy relative, **Putralaya**, is anything but clumsy in his painting. The most meticulous of all the artists, I have seen him work for more than a year to get one painting of three shells just right. Although he has never put his head underwater, he is best known for his enormous submarine-scapes, which balance vibrant and light-hearted highlights against sinister dark corners dredged from the depths of his unfathomable mind. Unfortunately, Putra invariably falls in love with his latest painting, hiding it away from the eyes of prospective buyers. When an undaunted art lover discovers one of these, Putra puts an exhorbitant price on it in the hopes that the visitor will go away.

Some of the artists have impressive galleries on the road to Padangtegal, but for the best work you must corner them at home.

You might start about a third of the way down the main street at the compound of the brothers **Kobot** and **Barat.**. These are the grand old men of Pengosekan art, with work dating back to the 1930s. Unfortunately, as Kobot is beginning to go blind and Barat has become a temple priest, you may not find any recent examples of their intricately crafted depictions of Hindu deities, but whenever the temple needs a new hanging or banner, it is they who are called upon to paint it.

Just south of them is the house of **Sena**, a contemporary of Mokoh's. He originally

Right: *A painting by Gatra — the "poorest and laziest artist of Pengosekan" — but also, clearly, one of the most talented.*

painted lavish scenes of temple ceremonies and cremations, and still does the occasional one, but is better known as the premier exponent of the "Pengosekan Style." Beyond him and before the big banyan tree, you will find the similarly named **Sana** who belongs to yet a third generation of artists. His temple-dancing frog maidens are as graceful as the gawking western photographers, motorcyclists and surfies are hilarious. His meticulous depictions of erotically entwined princes, princesses and deities make a good purchase for the bedroom wall. It is always a pleasure to visit Mokoh who lives a few houses away from the main street, east of the banyan tree.

For a walk on the darker side, you might look up **Mangku Liyer**, near the gorge to the east (behind Oka's Homestay which is down a path more or less opposite Kobot's house). Not quite sure if he is a healer or a magician, his neighbors jokingly call him *Mangku Leyak* after those magicians who can transmogrify into animals to go out and harm their enemies at night. He makes faithful copies in pen and ink of the magic figures and symbols in his old *lontar* palm-leaf books.

Many other fine and idiosyncratic artists should be mentioned here but cannot. There is one however, whom I can never overlook. Nearing the southern end of the village, in a crumbling compound on the left, lives the poorest and the laziest artist of Pengosekan. **Gatra** produces some of the most remark-able and sought-after of all their paintings — when he can bring himself to work on one. Islands and temples float through a vaporous sky escorted by wispish nymphs, and every rock, hill or tree reveals the dark spirit living within it. They say that whenever he does manage to complete and sell a painting, he disappears for a couple of days to Denpasar to dispose of the proceeds — with the help, I like to believe, of women and wine.

Back home

When I recently returned to Bali after a lengthy exile editing *Ring of Fire*, I took a long, hard look at Pengosekan to decide whether I still wanted to live here. With the tour buses racing along the main street, and with my neighbors' growing commercialism and passion for building cement block monstrosities in the ricefields, I had my doubts. But when Batuan, coming up with a new design idea, pounds his hands together with the same enthusiasm I remember from that first night almost 20 years ago; when Putralaya shuffles his feet uncomfortably and asks US$20,000 for a painting he is not yet ready to part with; and when the entire community bursts into laughter over some raunchy aside at the most solemn moment of a temple ceremony, I know that, although I shall never be one of them, these are my sort of people and Pengosekan is my home.

— *Lorne Blair*

UBUD

A Quiet Village Haven for the Arts

Far from the madding crowds, Ubud has long been a quiet haven for the arts. Set amidst emerald green rice paddies and steep ravines in the stunning central Balinese foothills, some 25 km north of Denpasar, the village was originally an important source of medicinal herbs and plants. "Ubud" in fact derives from the Balinese word for medicine — *ubad.*

It was here that foreign artists such as Walter Spies settled during the 1920s and '30s, transforming the village into a flourishing center for the arts. Artists from all parts of Bali were invited to settle here by the local prince, Cokorda Gede Sukawati, and Ubud's palaces and temples are now adorned by the work of Bali's master artisans as a result. Although the village has experienced a tourist boom in recent years, the casual visitor can still enjoy Ubud's leisurely village lifestyle and atmosphere of creative ferment.

According to an 8th century legend, a Javanese priest named Rsi Markendya came to Bali from Java and meditated in Campuan (*Sangam* in Sanskrit) at the confluence of two streams — an auspicious site for Hindus. He founded the **Gunung Lebah Temple** here, on a narrow platform above the valley floor, where pilgrims seeking peace came to be healed from their worldly cares. You can still get there by following a small road to the Tjetjak Inn on the western outskirts of Ubud, then taking the path down toward the river.

Important 19th century court

In the late 19th century, Ubud became the seat of *punggawa* or feudal lords owing their allegiance to the raja of Gianyar. All were members of the *satriya* family of Sukawati and contributed greatly to the village's fame for the performing and plastic arts. The kingdom of Gianyar was established in the late 18th century and later became the most powerful of the southern states of Bali. And while elsewhere the Dutch conquest had such disastrous consequences for the Balinese royal houses, in Gianyar for the most part the raja and his subjects benefitted from a Dutch administration that brought improved roads, irrigation networks, health care and schools. The period between 1908 and 1930 indeed brought significant changes to the area, and toward the end of the 1930s Ubud was prospering as a budding tourist resort due to the

flowering of the arts here.

In the late 19th century a certain Cokorda Sukawati established himself in Ubud and was instrumental in laying the foundations for the village's fame. The area was at this time bereft of remarkable cultural features. It was in the interest of the Cokorda that various artists and literati sought refuge here from other kingdoms. Ubud slowly accumulated specialists and evolved into a cultural center with resident artists and *lontar* experts.

A prime example is the case of the young I Gusti Nyoman Lempad who, with his father, a noted literati, sought and found refuge in Ubud from the king of Bedulu. In gratitude, the young apprentice sculptor helped to decorate the main **Puri Saren** palace in Ubud and carved statues and ornaments on the main temple (**Pura Puseh**) of the noble family, north of the palace. He also carved the temple of learning (**Pura Saraswati**). His work is still to be seen on location and some of his statues can be admired in Ubud's museum. At an advanced age he turned to pen and ink, working right up until his death in 1978 at the age of 116.

A flowering of the arts

The *punggawa* of Ubud between the World Wars, Cokorda Gede Raka Sukawati, was a member of the Dutch Colonial Government's *volksraad* (People's Council) in Batavia and already interested in the "arts and crafts movement" spreading from Europe to Asia and Japan. He encouraged Walter Spies to settle in Ubud, thus provoking a growing tide of visitors to this enchanting village.

At the turn of the century, painting in Bali was integrated in religious or *adat* ceremonies with the themes being taken from classical Balinese tales that were well-known from *wayang* performances. Inspired by the foreign artists who settled in Ubud, Cokorda Gede Raka Sukawati gradually changed this tradition. The unique mélange of traditional Balinese and modern currents of western artforms that came to be associated with Ubud then took place.

In the late 1920s and early 1930s Ubud became the focal point for foreign artists and other creative people gathering around Spies, a highly gifted and versatile German artist. A

painter and a musician by training, Spies heard of Bali on reading Jaap Kunst's *Music of Bali*, published in 1925, in which the Dutch musicologist praised neighboring Peliatan highly for its *gamelan* orchestra. His work and anecdotes on the island riveted the attention of Spies, who was then director of the sultan of Yogyakarta's European orchestra.

Many other talented foreigners were attracted to Ubud also at this time. Among others, Miguel and Rosa Covarrubias discovered the hitherto unknown beauty of Bali upon viewing Gregor Krause's magnificient photo album, published in 1925. Krause had worked as a doctor in Bali around 1912. After living in Ubud and Sanur, Covarrubias wrote his *Island of Bali,* one of the classics on Bali to this day. Rudolf Bonnet, the Dutch painter, was told of Bali's breathtaking beauty by the etcher and ethnographer Nieuwenkamp in Florence and came here to seek inspiration in the late 1920s. Colin McPhee came to join Spies' experiments and stock-taking of musical traditions, which were at this time very dynamic, with new creations springing up overnight. They worked together with the legendary Anak Agung Gede Mandera of Peliatan. McPhee later published a book on Bali's musical traditions as well as an account of his experiences here, *A House in Bali.*

Ubud rapidly became the village "en vogue" for many of these visitors — an insider tip from the many musicians, painters,

Left: *Well-known Ubud stone carver, Wayan Cemul, fashions whimsical figures out of soft* paras *volcanic stone.* **Right:** *Painting of the Pura Gunung Lebah temple in Campuan by Dutch artist Willem G. Hofker, now in the Neka Museum.*

authors, anthropoligists and avant-garde world travellers who passed this way, especially after Spies settled in Campuan next to Ubud, on what is now the site of the Hotel Tjampuhan.

Spies and Bonnet both encouraged local Balinese artists, each in his own fashion. In 1936 they founded the Pita Maha, an artists' organisation, together with Lempad, Sobrat and I Tegalan, among many other excellent Balinese artists. This association was to guarantee and promote the high artistic standards of its more than 100 members.

Ubud since independence

The Pita Maha movement did survive the vagaries of the Japanese occupation and the Indonesian struggle for Independence. However, Cokorda Gede Agung Sukawati, asssisted by Bonnet, later founded the Palace of Arts Museum (Puri Lukisan Museum) in 1953 to provide a retrospective of local achievements. Balinese artists thus continued to work together, sparking a renewal of artistic activity in the 1950s.

In the early 1950s, Dutch painter Arie Smit founded the Young Painters School of naive painting in Penestanan with Cakra. This style, free of any philosophical or abstract influence, led to relatively uninhibited young school-children using bright chemical colors to produce two-dimensional landscapes depicting daily life. Their work reflects the changing vision and lifestyle of young Balinese during the post-war period.

Han Snel was a young Dutch soldier who left the Dutch Colonial Army and 'vanished' into Bali after his military service. He then found his way up to the hills around Ubud. His work captured the imagination of both foreigners and Balinese alike with its invigorating synthesis of both cultures. Following his marriage to Siti, he built a studio in a secluded spot in Central Ubud. Antonio Blanco, another Western painter, settled with

his Balinese wife and five children on the heights of Campuan, bordering Penestanan. This eccentric even had one of Ubud's first telephones, a link between paradise and the madding crowds abroad.

The tourist boom

In the 1960s and 1970s the hotel and catering industry implanted itself here modestly enough compared to how it had taken firm control of Kuta-Legian, but this idyllic village did nevertheless witness an ever-accelerating flow of visitors who came to delight in the arts and to escape from the daily grind. In short, tourism knocked gently but insistingly on Ubud's door. The advent of mass tourism in the 1980s has provided many young inhabitants of this village with stable employment rather than farming the fertile ricefields in the surrounding hills. Land reform and hereditary laws, in any case, have led to scarcity of arable land.

It is therefore with mixed feelings that the visitor will notice how "business-like" the Ubudians are, although their artistic talents are still being cultivated. But modern times bring progress which is not to be stopped in the name of nostalgia. The inhabitants of Ubud retain their individuality and generosity of spirit through all the changes, which leave the visitor wondering how this charming people can manage to deal with the dizzying alterations in the village structure resulting from the modernization of social, economic and perhaps occasionally spiritual factors. This must be one of the world's most closely guarded secrets, or perhaps it is only that special peace of mind which comes from such a beautiful environment and a mild climate. The unruffled calmness of Ubud has soothed many a visitor, while the extraordinary beauty of the surroundings still inspire the creative to work.

Nowadays you are also able to enjoy the fruits of that extraordinarily prolific period of pre-World War II Ubud in dance, music, painting and sculpture. Dance performances are given daily in at least three places including the main palace. In the meanwhile, ceremonies still abound where you can see various dance or shadow puppet performances or listen to excellent *gamelan* music. Painters and sculptors, writers and creative designers continue to seek abiding inspiration in the quiet stylishness of Ubud, Campuan and nearby Sayan. Gracious Ubud is certainly worth a visit.

— *Kunang Helmi Picard*

UBUD TOUR

On the Gallery and Temple Circuit

It is dawn and Ubud is awakening. The air is fresh, mixed with the heady scent of flowers and the incense of offerings. There are so many ways to spend your day here — visiting galleries and artists' studios, sipping drinks in garden cafes and enjoying long strolls through the countryside. Below we merely mention a few of the "must sees."

The Ubud highlights

No vist to Ubud is complete without a visit to the **Puri Saren** palace at the main cross-roads, with its maze of family compounds and richly carved doorways by Lempad. The royal family temple, **Pura Pamerajaan Sari Cokorda Agung**, is next door — a storage place for the family *pusaka* (regalia).

To the west behind a lotus pond by the **Puri Saraswati** palace (now a hotel), lies the superbly chiseled **Pura Saraswati** temple of learning — a *clin d'oeil* dedicated to Ubud's artistic past. From the crossroads here, walk north to Ubud's "navel" temple, **Pura Puseh**, with its delightful sculptures.

Next stop is the **Puri Lukisan Museum** to enjoy the paintings and sculptures and the peaceful garden. The museum was founded in 1953 by surviving members of Ubud's famed Pita Maha movement. Painted panels that Lempad executed 40 years ago depict the Balinese agrarian cycle.

There are numerous studios and shops in the center of town. Painter **Han Snel** has his up behind the Pura Saraswati. If it's lunchtime, pop into the **Cafe Lotus** for a fresh fettucine and a chocolate cake. Just opposite, check with the **Bina Wisata Tourist Office** about local performances and festivals.

Ubud's best commercial galleries are at the eastern end of town, about a km away. **Munut's Gallery** belongs to a former pupil of Dutch painter Bonnet, and his collection

displays a discerning eye. Suteja Neka, whose father was a painter, is the foremost dealer and collector on Bali — founder of the **Neka Museum**. The most famous artist of Ubud however was Lempad. His great grand-son, Made Tama, now runs the **Lempad Gallery** — ask him to show you some of the master's delicate erotic pen and ink drawings.

Mischievous monkeys

Another of the major "sights" of Ubud is the so-called **Monkey Forest Temple**, 2 km to the south. If for no other reason, stroll down Monkey Forest Road to have a look at all the new shops and restaurants. Before entering the temple itself, however, put away all edibles, eyeglasses, earrings, etc., and hold on tight to your bags. These daring rascals are rapacious thieves and dangerous if provoked. The **Pura Dalem Agung Padangtegal** itself is an extraordinary "temple for the dead," with a covered gate or *candi kurung*.

Having gone east and south, now travel west along the main road across the bridge to Campuan. Up to the left is the gallery of eccentric Filipino-American painter **Antonio Blanco**, with his extravagant nudes and anecdotes. Farther up on the right is the **Neka Museum** — housing the best collection of paintings on the island.

— *Kunang Helmi Picard*

Opposite: *Ubud's Cafe Lotus.* **Right:** *The "lotus throne" of Pura Saraswati, carved by Lempad.*

LIVING IN UBUD

Expat Chic: A Commentary on the Times

The expatriates who lived in Ubud during the 1930s were a handful of patrician, serious-minded people — composers, painters and scholars — whose work helped reveal to the world the beauty and complexity of Balinese culture. The expatriate residents of today are a swarm of hedonists and businessmen — restauranteurs, jewelers and film-makers — rather more into marketing the culture than in understanding it. Nonetheless, standards of cultural chic set over 50 years ago are still being maintained.

Expatriate chic in Ubud began with people like Jane Belo — the American anthropologist and observer of ritual trance — and Walter Spies, the German painter, musician and dilettante par excellence. Spies' charm was legendary, and anyone of any importance who came to Bali in the 1930s came to visit him. His lifestyle was irresistibly chic.

Cokorda Agung Sukawati, Ubud's ruling prince, granted Spies permission to build a house in Campuan. His double-storey villa, with out-buildings and swimming pool later became the Tjampuhan Hotel, and must have been wonderful fifty years ago. Spies had many Balinese dancer and musician friends, and could command astonishing performances to entertain his guests. He and painter Rudolf Bonnet worked closely with local artists and helped them sell their paintings to visitors. Above all, Spies had an impressive knowledge of the culture and geography of Bali, as well as the affection of the local people — he thus made the perfect tour guide.

Spies' example attracted other Europeans to Bali to paint, to compose and to study. Ubud soon became an outpost of artistic and intellectual activity — as well as a glamorous stop on the luxury liner circuit. Cokorda Agung Sukawati was a cosmopolitan man who enjoyed foreign guests and made them welcome in the palace, setting an irreversible precedent for tourism in Ubud.

By the time of the Cokorda's death in 1978, Bali had opened its curly gates to the budget travelers of the world. Young Australians by the thousands helped to make Kuta what it is — whatever it is — today; and a new generation of Kuta expatriates fluttered down to settle around Ubud. They built themselves little bamboo huts out in the ricefields (or next to the cemetery or wherever else the

RIO HELMI

Balinese wouldn't dream of living) and furnished them with *batik* curtains, little cushions and wobbly bamboo furniture.

These expats of the 1970s were back-to-the-earth mystics who wanted nothing more than to become Balinese. They strove to dance like the Balinese, play the *gamelan* like the Balinese, speak Balinese like the Balinese, even get sick like the Balinese (fashionable illnesses were supposed to be caused by black magic). They didn't really try to paint like the Balinese, but they understood, like Spies, that the painting was charming, and marketable.

Who were these new expatriates? Some were artists and scholars. Others were would-be artists and drop-out scholars. The physically and mentally ill also found a haven here: poet-inebriates; convalescents of disease and divorce; the freshly-bereaved or newly-fired — all sorts of people at odds with their fate came to Ubud for a tropico-pastoral lullaby, and many found new vocations.

Some became amateur anthropologists in the emerging field of "Baliology." (Say you are an amateur anthropologist and you get a grant to write a thesis on "Patterns of Courtship in Central Bali" — all you have to do is have lots of dates with Balinese of the sex of your preference and keep a diary. If you can't get dates, you can make a list of a lot of impertinent questions and pay a student to go around the neighborhood collecting the answers. This leaves you plenty of time to set up house, meet friends for lunch at the Cafe Lotus, and research courtship patterns in Candi Dasa.)

Aspiring designer-entrepreneurs also find Bali a creative paradise. It's so easy to realize an idea here. (Say you're suddenly inspired to create a gigantic lily made entirely of wood. All you have to do is roll over and order someone to summon a woodcarver, then tell him, as best you can, that if he can make you a gigantic lily by tomorrow you'll give him a whole dollar. After that it's only a matter of charming the teeth off some millionaire's wife and getting her to order seven hundred of them for her ballroom. Then you close the deal by whispering to her confidentially, "Let's make that prepaid, shall we? You know they're all saving up for their cremations, and it all goes to the gods anyway.")

Meanwhile the Balinese of Ubud themselves were busy imitating Walter Spies —

putting on dance performances and selling paintings to tourists, guiding them around on tours of Bali's beauty spots, dressing them up for the temple and explaining the culture, and basically luring the world to Ubud.

The new expatriates resented this invasion of their world, but (like the Balinese) saw the economic potential in it. By the 1980s the boom was on. Expats upgraded their houses from *lumbung* (rice granaries) to *wantilan* (public halls); and furnishings were the big bamboo sofas and elephantine cushions by Linda Garland. Meanwhile, the Balinese were busily upgrading their houses to look like western tract houses.

Cultural exchanges between East and West continue in Ubud. In the 1930s, composers and choreographers devised systems of notation for *gamelan* and dance. They commissioned new *gamelan* sets, collaborated in new dance forms and made documentary films of ritual dances that have now flown away with the *leyaks*. Expatriate scholars excavated ancient burial grounds and speculated about prehistory. They solicited funds for the restoration of monuments, transcribed classical texts, accumulated archives and founded libraries and museums.

Modern expatriates also make documentaries, study music and dance, and augment their archives. They also teach their Balinese friends (or partners) to make pasta and sorbet and martinis; and help them to develop new skills like silk-screening and shipping.

Whether Ubud is still a center of artistic and intellectual activity is less the issue than whether it can once again become a glamorous stop on the R&R circuit. It would be wrong to deplore the new materialism; Bali turns out to be part of the real world after all. One can only hope that the cultural entrepreneurs will become as epicurean as the cultural sponsors of the '30s were learned.

The recently opened Amandari Hotel just outside of Ubud sets new standards worth studying — its sublime architecture is an indictment of the execrable architecture of other hotels nearly as expensive, and its management philosophy defines high new standards of service.

Development in Ubud is the right of its citizens; but Ubud is no longer the same product it was ten years ago. Funky accommodations and indecisive food are no longer so forgivable, and simply raising the prices will not achieve glamor — it may take some artistic and intellectual activity to do that.

— *Diana Darling*

Left: *A talented, young Italian dancer who lives in Ubud, performing the sacred* gambuh.

DAYTRIPS FROM UBUD

Breathtaking Glimpses of Rural Bali

Ubud's surroundings offer many rewarding walks and excursions up hill and over dale, with breathtaking vistas and many surprising glimpses of rural, unspoilt Bali. What follows is but a short list of suggested itineraries. Many more could easily be added.

Hike 1: The 'high road' to Payangan

This is an easy, half-day hike west of Ubud up along the road through Campuan and over to Payangan. Get an early start at the Campuan bridge and stop in to see the **Pura Gunung Lebah** temple that nestles in the gorge. Rsi Markendya founded it at the confluence of these rivers in the 8th century. Follow the main road up a steep hill past the **Neka Museum** — along the way you have delightful views and a chance to stop in at the studios of famous artists like **Antonio Blanco**, **Tembles** and **Ngurah KK**, to name but a few. Be sure to stop in at the museum, too, to see the works of a veritable Who's Who of Balinese painters, past and present.

After Neka's, the road takes a sharp turn to the left and you'll find **Ulun Ubud Cottages** on your right. Inside, there is a small gallery belonging to Ida Bagus Tilem, Bali's best-known woodcarver. Continuing up the main road, you'll eventually reach the Payangan-Kedewatan T-junction. Turn right, and after a few hundred meters you come to **Payangan Village** on the left, with its extraordinary rice terraces stepping down to the Ayung River below. Look for **Pura Telaga Waja** — a temple with multi-tiered *merus*. Afterwards, travel by bemo back to Ubud.

Hike 2: West to Sayan

This is an exhilarating half or full-day hike through the ricefields west of Ubud, but be prepared for a bit of climbing and bring along your swimsuit. From the Campuan bridge, early in the morning, follow the road up the hill and turn left up a long flight of steps 150 meters after the Hotel Tjampuhan. At the top, follow the path south and west to **Penestanan Village**, where the "Young Artists" — Tagen, Londo, Pugur and Tatra — have their studios. Though each has his own distinctive style, the influence of the surrounding landscapes can be seen in all their works.

Continue on, through ricefields offering spectacular views of distant volcanoes. The

AMIR SIDHARTA

path then dips into a small valley and comes up through a dense bamboo forest, passing through several small villages — as rural and unspoilt as any in Bali. You finally emerge on the main north-south Payangan road just past a *wantilan* community hall.

Cross the road next to the primary school and find a smaller, unpaved track between rows of family compounds. Here, you will be able to cut across to the **Sayan Ridge** where many foreigners have built villas commanding a dramatic view of the Ayung River.

From here, hail a bemo north in the direction of the Payangan and get off at the **Amandari Hotel** on your left. Take the long winding path down to the river to bathe in its refreshing waters. Afterwards, climb up and catch the next bemo back to Ubud. On your way into town, stop for dinner and a drink by the bridge at **Murni's** or **Beggar's Bush**, two of Ubud's notable eateries.

Hike 3: To Petulu — place of herons

This is a fairly easy, half-day hike north and east of Ubud. Start around lunchtime at the main Ubud crossroads in front of the Puri Saren palace, and go north along Jl. Suweta past MM, a snack-bar popular with expats for its *arak*. Next to it is a highly-recommended *jamu* bar serving herbal tonics. The road is paved all the way past the **Pura Puseh** (Ubud's temple of origin, with carvings by Lempad), but the potholes get worse with distance from Ubud.

Continuing straight ahead, the road climbs up to the village of **Bentuyung**, which can be reached in about an hour. On a clear day, you can enjoy spectacular views of Mt Agung. From here, either take a road back south to **Tegallantang** and **Taman** (*banjars* of Ubud), with their important temples nestling in the midst of family compounds at the crossroads, or turn to the right (east) through **Jujungan** to **Petulu** to witness white herons hovering over the village as they alight in lofty trees at sunset. Mention any of the above names, and villagers will point you the way. From Petulu, take a bemo or walk back to Ubud.

Hike 4: 'Sculpted' terraces of Sebatu

This is another spectacular half-day hike to the northeast of Ubud, which can be done all or in parts by car or bemo. From the Kutuh

T-junction at the eastern end of Ubud, head north past the new telephone office along a narrow, paved road that passes through the villages of **Petulu** and **Tegallalang** to **Pujung**, a distance of some 15 km. The road rises gradually, reaching cooler air and passing through verdant ricefields and coconut groves. You will not fail to notice the many assembly-line woodcarvings being produced in small workshops along this road — all sorts of colorful fruit trees and animals. At Pujung, turn right to reach a holy spring at **Sebatu**, 1 km to the east, where you can cool off in deliciously fresh pools. From Pujung, a small but good road to the north continues on up to Kintamani past some of Bali's most dramatic rice terraces.

Hike 5: To the Moon (of Pejeng)

This half-day hike for the hardy takes you east from Ubud across spectacularly hilly country to Pejeng, site of many famous antiquities. Begin at the Kutuh T-junction at Ubud's eastern end, and follow a path beside the pharmacy (*apotik*) due east for a distance of about 5 km, across two lush, steep gorges. The first is formed by the famed Petanu River, which runs south from here to the **Goa Gajah** hermitage. In Pejeng visit the museum and a temple containing a prehistoric bronze drum known as the "Moon of Pejeng" (see "Gianyar Antiquities," page 138).

— *Kunang Helmi Picard*

Left: *Dramatic view of the Ayung River from Sayan Ridge west of Ubud.* **Right:** *Famous "sculpted" rice terraces near Tegallalang and Sebatu, to the northeast of Ubud.*

ANTIQUITIES OF GIANYAR

Ancient Land Between the Rivers

The narrow strip of territory lying between the Petanu and Pakrisan Rivers — extending from Mount Batur in the north to the sea in the south — forms a natural replica of the Hindu-Balinese cosmos. It is no wonder, therefore, that steep ravines, rock riverbeds and cascading streams of this area were the sites of some of the earliest kingdoms and religious settlements on Bali, as evidenced by the great wealth of antiquities found here. The major ones lie along the "Kintamani Tour" route and can be seen in a day, but many more days may easily be devoted to an exploration of the other fascinating sites.

Inscriptions from this area date from the end of the 10th century. In the beginning it was ruled by Hindus and Buddhists — religions probably introduced directly from India. After the end of the 10th century, as the result of a marriage between Balinese Prince Udayana and a Javanese princess, East Javanese cultural influences appeared in Bali, and the language of the inscriptions changed from Old Balinese to Old Javanese. Kings are mentioned in many of these, and there seems to have been a court center located somewhere in the vicinity of Bedulu or Pejeng.

Myths and legends

Numerous myths are connected with this region. Many concern demonic kings who lost their realms as the result of bad marriages or wicked behavior. Their palaces, battlefields and sacred landscapes are often connected with archaeological sites. Such a king was Maya Danawa. His story is told in the 16th century *Kakawin Usana Bali* (a poem on the ancient history of Bali). The center of his realm was Balingkang, close to modern-day Teges or Bedulu.

Maya Danawa was in fact the son of god-dess Dewi Danu of Lake Batur. He defeated many kings in order to extend his realm and the god of the lake, Batara Danu, granted him a boon — he was allowed to take a Chinese Buddhist wife. She did not feel at home in Bali, however, and soon fell ill. Maya Danawa went to the sanctuary of Tolangkir to ask for assistance, but the god did not favor someone with a false religion. Maya Danawa was so angry that he forbade the Hindu gods to be venerated, and dictated that he should be worshipped instead.

After some time his Chinese wife died, and Maya Danawa remained alone in his palace, enriching himself at the expense of his people. Twelve years later he was defeated by the god Indra, who tapped the ground at Manuk Aya (near Tampaksiring), whereupon a magical spring appeared. His warriors drank from it and received great strength. When they killed Maya Danawa, blood spouted from his mouth like a stream of gold, becoming the accursed river Petanu. Those who bathed or drank here encountered misery. The gods then bathed in a spring called Air Empul (now Tirta Empul), and from that time onward, the Hindu religion was restored and good kings reigned over Bali.

One of these kings was the ruler of Bedahulu (Bedulu), who was endowed with great magical powers. He used to sit and meditate, removing his head to reach the beyond. On one such occasion, an unnatural disturbance

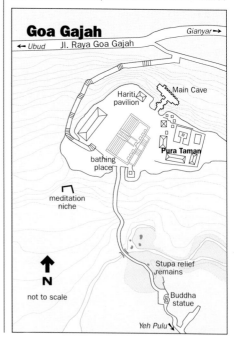

Goa Gajah   *Gianyar* ➤
← *Ubud*   Jl. Raya Goa Gajah

Main Cave

Hariti pavilion

Pura Taman

bathing place

meditation niche

Stupa relief remains

↑
N

not to scale

Buddha statue

Yeh Pulu ↘

Opposite: *Goa Gajah, the "elephant cave," so-called because reliefs carved around its mouth were said at first to resemble an elephant's ears.*

occurred and the king was forced to get a new head quickly. A pig happened by, and its head was taken and placed on the neck of the king. Therefore the king's name became Beda-Hulu ("he whose head is severed"). Some versions state that the king's real head fell to earth where Goa Gajah is now.

The king and his courtiers were ashamed of the pig's head, so they constructed a tower for him to live in. His subjects were not allowed to look up, but had to kneel so as not see the king's head. Somehow this became known in Java and the ruler of Majapahit sent his prime minister, Gajah Mada, to Bali to determine if it were true. By means of a ruse (drinking water from a pitcher with a long spout), the visitor managed to discover the king's secret and caused his downfall.

Another story is that of Kebo Iwa, which literally means bull, but was also the title of a court functionary in ancient Bali. Kebo Iwa was a princely giant in some versions, King Bedahulu's minister in others. He scratched rocks with his fingernails, creating many of the rock-cut monuments and reliefs found here today — for instance, Goa Garba and Yeh Pulu (see below). In some versions, he was killed when invited to the court of Majapahit.

Goa Gajah

The first major site encountered coming from the south or from Ubud, just 2 km east of the Teges intersection, is the complex known as Goa Gajah — the famous "Elephant Cave." It overlooks the Petanu River and consists of a Siwaitic rock-cut cave, a bathing place, a monks' chamber, a number of Buddhist rock-cut stupas and statues, and several foundations. It received its name from the archaeologists who discovered it in 1923, because there is a giant head with floppy ears above the entrance which was at a first glance thought to represent an elephant.

The entrance to the cave itself is 2 m high and 1 m across, with a head sculpted above it that in fact resembles a man with bulging eyes, hairy eyebrows, protruding teeth, and a kind of long moustache. He is surrounded by sculpted ornaments in which little creatures — men, animals and gruesome heads — are depicted. It is as if they refer to a story, but it is not known which tale this could be.

The grotto inside is T-shaped, containing 15 niches hewn out of the cave walls which may have served as benches to sleep on. For this reason, it is thought that the cave once served as a hermitage. A four-armed Ganesa (the elephant-headed son of Siwa) and a set of three *lingga,* each surrounded by eight smaller ones (representing the eight points of the compass and the center), were found at the ends. The cave may date from the second half of the 11th century. There are pavilions to both sides of the entrance, in which ancient statues are placed. One is Hariti, the Buddhist goddess of fertility and protectress

of children.

The bathing spot behind the cave consists of three compartments which were discovered and excavated only in 1954. The central one is small and holy, the left one is for women, and the right one is for men. They are all sunken, flush against a wall, the top of which is level with the courtyard in front of the cave. Each side basin has three statues of women holding urns, from which water pours into them. It seems a statue in the central basin has disappeared.

South of the complex a path leads down to a small stream. On the right are the remains of a hermit's cave with a small pond in front. Past a bridge, the path climbs the opposite slope. The remains of an enormous relief depicting some stupas, once adorning the rock face high above, were found in a ravine on the left. Two meditating Buddhas, probably dating from the 8th century, were found here also. Unfortunately, one was stolen in the late 1980s, and the remaining one is headless. From here a path leads up to the site of Yeh Palu.

Yeh Pulu

A couple of kms to the east, in the direction of Bedulu just off the main road, are the antiquities of Yeh Pulu, dating from the late 14th century. These consist of reliefs cut out of the rock and a sacred well. The reliefs are in a naturalistic style. Horsemen, men carrying animals hanging from a pole, a sitting brahman who holds an offering spoon, sitting women, an ascetic, a man carrying two large pots on a pole over his shoulder, the entrance of a cave or a hut, are among the figures which are depicted. So far, however, nobody knows which story is represented and what is meant by it. Two hundred meters north of Yeh Pulu is another, small bathing place consisting of two basins, with naturalistic reliefs of men cut in niches in the rock at the back.

Southeast of Bedulu, in the village of Kutri, lies the **Pura Pedarman** temple with its famous 2.20 m high stone statue of the six-armed goddess Durga — the spouse of Siwa. She has the outward appearance of a demoness and is killing a demon cursed to take the appearance of a bull. It is said that the statue represents Prince Udayana's Javanese wife, the mother of Airlangga. An oral tale says that Udayana was allowed to marry her provided he did not take other wives, however, he did not keep his promise. The princess became very angry and turned to black magic.

The Moon of Pejeng

The area north of Bedulu, around Pejeng and Intaran, contains many antiquities. The most important is the **Pura Penataran Sasih**, which forms part of a group of three temples. *Sasih* means "moon" and refers to the "Moon of Pejeng" — a giant bronze kettledrum kept high up in a shrine in the temple. It is deco-

Pejeng. It contains several interesting Hindu antiquities, probably dating from the 14th century, which are now placed in shrines.

Two statues, 1.0 m and 0.52 m high, in naturalistic style, are particularly attractive. They each contain four figures. In the taller statue there are dancing demons with bulging eyes, huge teeth and moustaches grouped around a *lingga* in the center. The smaller one represents four gods, each with four arms holding various attributes, corresponding with the four quarters of the compass. Their heads are surrounded by a nimbus. There is also a shrine with a large *lingga*.

In a special pavilion, a 0.75 meter-high stone vessel is venerated. It has reliefs in a naturalistic style, representing a group of gods and demons holding two snakes wound round a cylindrical mountain with trees. Animals and birds fly around it. This represents a story from the *Mahabharata* called the "churning of the ocean" in which gods and demons search for the elixir of life. They do so with a tip of a mountain (Mt Mandara, sometimes also Mt Meru). A snake (in Bali two snakes) is used as a rope. In the beginning nothing happens. Then a magic horse with seven heads, an elephant with two pairs of tusks, a beautiful lady and a jewel emerge and, finally, a vessel with the elixer. This story fits well with the usage of the vessel as a container of holy water. It is dated with a chronogram corresponding with A.D. 1329.

rated with geometric patterns, ogres' heads and stars. According to some stories, it is the ear jewel of Kebo Iwa, others say that it is the chariot wheel of the Moon God which fell in a tree in Pejeng and has been kept in the temple ever since. At first it was bright and shiny, however, a thief tried to steal it and was disturbed by the radiance of the "wheel," so he urinated on the object. As a result, it lost its lustre and turned green. The thief was punished for this deed and died immediately.

Bronze kettledrums have been found all over eastern Indonesia, and in Bali other, smaller drums have been found as well. Even a mould has been excavated, which proves that such drums were manufactured on Bali. Kettledrums date from the bronze age, but it is difficult to determine how old the Pejeng Moon is. They were symbols of prosperity and fertility, and in eastern Indonesia form part of the dowry. Apart from the drum, the temple possesses a number of 11th century stone statues, among them a Siwa and *lingga*.

'Navel of the world'

This area was also once considered the "navel of the world" and there is a temple bearing this name, the **Pura Pusering Jagat** in

Left: *The reliefs at Yeh Pulu.* **Above:** *Six-armed Durga, wife of Siwa, in Kutri.* **Right:** *"Churning the ocean" in the Pusering Jagat temple in Pejeng.*

Another temple in Pejeng, the **Pura Kebo Edan**, possesses the statue of a standing giant 3.60 m tall. He is called Kebo Edan, the Mad One. The figure has a huge penis with four "penis pins" pierced through it right under the glans. The use of such pins to increase a woman's sexual pleasure is an old custom known throughout Southeast Asia. The giant stands in a dancing position and tramples a human figure, its face covered with something which may be a mask, as it is tied with ribbons at the back. The figure may represent a demonic manifestation of Siwa as a dancer. There is another statue representing a fat, crouching demon holding a big skull upside down in front of his chest. The demon is wearing a diadem decorated with small skulls on his curly hair. The style of these statues points to the 13th-14th century.

While in the Pejeng area, stop in also at the **Archaeological Museum**, located just two km north of Bedulu on the main road. Here are displayed quite a number of stone sarcophagi, neolithic axe heads, bronze jewelry and figurines and Chinese ceramics.

Rock-cut caves

Goa Garba lies northeast of Pejeng, on the western side of the Pakrisan. The complex can be entered via steep steps through a gateway at the back of the Pengukur-ukuran temple in the village of Sawah Gunung. One arrives at a hermitage consisting of three caves with slanting roofs. There is an inscription in Kadiri square script in one of these saying "*sri*" — a lucky sign. On the basis of the script, the complex may be dated to the late 11th century. Water basins with spouts are hewn in front of the niches. There are several pedestals with fragments of stone statues and a *lingga*. In the temple above, two stone Ganesas, a *lingga* and a winged stone snake with an inscription dated A.D. 1194 are found.

Krobokan, on the eastern side of the Pakrisan (near the village of Cemadik), dates from the 12th century. Where the waters of the rivers Krobokan and Pakrisan flow together, a 6 m high, oval-shaped niche with the facade of a temple in relief is cut into the rock. It is flanked by a small hermit's cave with a rectangular aperture and a slanting roof.

Mountain of the poet

From Pejeng, the road begins a slow but steady ascent of Mt Batur. About halfway to the top, just near the source of the Pakrisan River, are two sites of great antiquity. The first, near Tampaksiring, is a famous complex of rock-cut monuments dating from the late 11th century and known as **Gunung Kawi** — the "mountain of the poet." The poet in this case is none other than the god Siwa. In the ravines, on both sides of the river, royal tombs, a hermitage and monks' caves have been cut out of solid rock. The main entrance to the site can be reached via a steep footpath

that begins by a large parking lot lined with souvenir stalls on the east side of the road.

As one enters the site, to the left is a rock-cut monument consisting of four facades suggesting the shape of temples. Each is surrounded by an oval-shaped niche about 7 m high. The reliefs are covered with a kind of plaster. On the other side of the ravine are five niches with similar rock-cut facades. In the bases of all these, holes have been made which once contained little stone boxes divided into nine squares, corresponding to the eight quarters of the compass and the center.

The monuments are connected with the youngest son of the powerful East Javanese King Airlangga who lived in the first half of the 11th century, and was of Balinese descent via his father Udayana. Twenty-seven edicts are known to have been issued by him between A.D. 1050 and 1078. The central monument of the five may be devoted to him, because there is an inscription in Kadiri square script at the top reading: "the king monumentalized in Jalu." By Jalu, the name of the site may be meant.

Next to the monuments is a rock-cut monastery complex, consisting of several caves with a free-standing building hewn out of the rock in the center. Characteristic are the large, rectangular apertures and oval-shaped entrances, with overhanging roofs, now overgrown with grass. On the other side of the ravine, to the right of the entrance, another cave has been discovered.

The sacred spring

In an inscription dated A.D. 960 discovered in Pura Sakenan temple in the village of Manuk Aya, mention is made of a double pool dug around a well near the source of the river Pakrisan. The king transformed this into a holy bathing place, called Air Ampul. This is the present-day **Tirta Empul** — one of the most sacred spots on Bali. It lies just north of Tampaksiring along a well-marked road.

The sanctuary consists of an outer courtyard with a basin for public use and a central courtyard with two adjacent, rectangular pools (for those who fought Maya Danawa and were cleansed by the God Indra) containing clear, transparent water — all surrounded by a low wall of recent construction. There are 15 spouts in these pools. The inner court has two pavilions, one of which is for the god Indra (Maya Danawa's adversary), and more than 20 small shrines with newly-carved and freshly-painted wooden doors decorated with reliefs. Among these is one devoted to the rice goddess (Dewi Sri), one to the Lord of Majapahit, and one to Mt Batur.

— *Hedi Hinzler*

Opposite: *The rock-cut* candi *or funerary temples at Gunung Kawi.* **Below:** *The holy spring Tirta Empul, near the source of the sacred River Pakrisan, is a major pilgrimage point.*

AMIR SIDHARTA

GIANYAR TOWN

Royalty and the Sacred Banyan Tree

The *bemo* men on the roads from the south yell "*nyar, nyar, nyar*" in loud nasal tones, delighting in stretching the syllable as long as they can. *Nyar* is short for Gianyar, once a center of royal power, priestly learning and the arts. Today this political and administrative capital has been passed over by the tourist boom, but in one area of creative endeavor it still reigns supreme: Gianyar has Bali's best roast pig or *babi guling*. This most exquisite and festive of Balinese dishes can be had in a number of stalls in the market or near the main square, though everyone you ask has their own favorite and will argue its merits against all comers.

Despite the absence of tourists, the town and its surrounding districts are full of places of interest. This can be a good place to get a feel for Balinese history and culture in a non-touristed atmosphere. The heart of Gianyar is the palace or the *puri*, one of the best preserved of all Bali's royal houses, and home of Anak Agung Gede Agung — heir to the throne of Gianyar, former Foreign Minister, ambassador and a prominent political leader in the 1940s and '50s.

Unfortunately, the splendors of the palace are not open to casual visitors. But from outside the walls, one can appreciate the majesty of an ornamented observation pavilion overlooking the garden near the main crossroads of Gianyar. *Tantri* animal fables are depicted in carvings on the lower part of the outside wall at the crossroads. This palace is also one of the few in Bali to maintain the *waringin* or sacred banyan tree which was the symbol of Balinese and Javanese courts. Gianyar's still stands in the open town square across from the palace, preserving the feel of a 19th century royal town.

The palace of Gianyar was founded in the 18th century, but rebuilt in a more splendid style when the Gianyar dynasty was restored at the end of the 19th. The original palace was said to have been constructed on the site of a priest's house or *griya*. The name "Gianyar" is in fact an abbreviated form of *griya anyar* or "new priest's house."

Just next to the palace is the **Pura Langon**, the "Temple of Beauty," which is the major temple for the extended royal family, and one of the state temples of Gianyar. Further to the west is the **Griya Sidawa**,

home of the major priestly family of the area and one of Bali's most famous centers of learning and priestly tradition.

Other state temples can be found nearby, at Beng and to the south, on the coast at Lebih. The temple at **Beng** is for the descendents of Dewa Manggis, who founded the royal line. At **Lebih**, a few kilometers to the south of the town of Gianyar, is the Pura Segara or "Sea Temple," which is visited in the course of many different festivals that occur all over Gianyar. The temple is situated where the land meets the sea, in sight of the demon's island of Nusa Penida, and is regarded as a "hot spot" — a place where magical forces can be harnessed. Attempts are currently underway to promote this pleasant seaside region as a new beach resort.

On the road going south from the Gianyar town square to Lebih stands a **Chinese temple**, one of only a handful found on Bali. Another, smaller temple can also be seen on the road to the west of Gianyar, just past the village of Kemenuh, hidden below the road in a ravine. Nineteenth century visitors remarked on the strong Chinese presence here, stating that it was once one of the wealthiest states in Bali and a center for trade. The temples recall the strong links that once existed between the community of traders and the royal family of Gianyar who were their patrons. When the palace was rebuilt at the end of the last century, the Chinese community contributed to the work, and many of the buildings show a Chinese style of roofing.

To the west of the town is the adjoining village of **Bitra**. Here, on the southern side of the main road, is the famous Pura Dalem or death temple, beside a river and beneath a spreading banyan tree. Also on the western side of the town are the main centers of silk *ikat* weaving. A number of entrepreneurs have turned their traditional expertise into a thriving industry, and their workshops are open to visitors. The fine silk *ikat* produced here is used not only for the traditional *sarung* but for interior decoration as well.

Southwest of Gianyar lies the former court center of **Kramas**, now known for its dancers, particularly of the operetta *arja*. Kramas is one of many centers of theater and music in Gianyar, lesser known only because it is off the tourist path.

Gianyar town itself is also known for various performing arts, particularly the ever-popular *drama gong,* which is full of romantic plots, slapstick comedy and ribaldry. Kramas was a major power in the area before Gianyar, and its princes are supposedly descended from the great rebel Gusti Agung Maruti, who in the 17th century brought down the kingdom of Gelgel.

Kramas is also near another old mini-kingdom, **Blahbatuh**. The rulers of Blahbatuh were descendents of Gusti Ngurah Jelantik, the prime minister of Gelgel, famous for a military campaign he led against Java in the early 17th century. One of the souvenirs of that expedition was a set of masks which are said to be the prototypes for all Balinese *topeng* dance-drama masks. These are still kept in a temple near the palace of Blahbatuh, the **Pura Penataran Topeng**. In the 19th and early 20th centuries Blahbatuh was home to some of the greatest court dancing in Bali. **Bona**, between Blahbatuh and Gianyar city, is still famous for its dances, especially the fire dance, *sanghyang jaran,* performed regularly for tourists.

On the eastern side of Gianyar lies the village of **Sidan**, just north of the Bangli intersection. Sidan has a famous Pura Dalem which can be viewed from the road, featuring a series of carvings on the outer tower showing the semi-divine hero Bima fighting with the God of Death.

— *Adrian Vickers*

Left: *An early morning encounter with the blade near the* alun alun *in Gianyar town.* **Right:** *A palace doorway bears silent witness to past glory.*

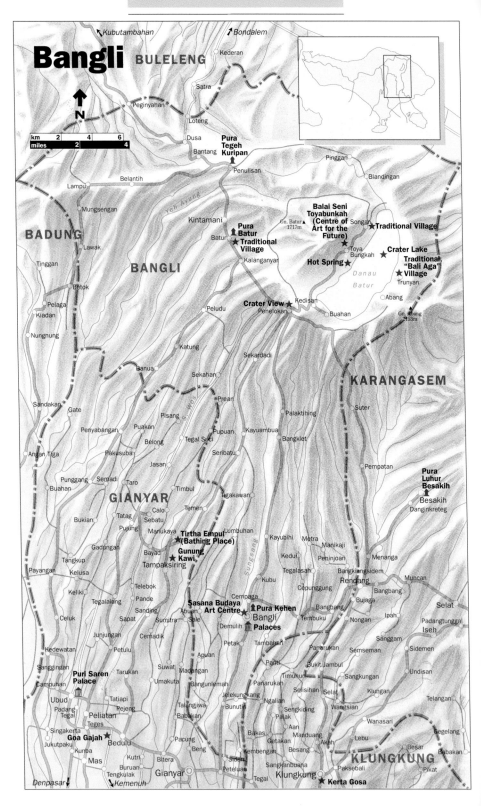

Bangli BULELENG

N

km | 2 | 4 | 6
miles | 2 | | 4

Kubutambahan
Bondalem
Kederan
Satra
Peginyahan
Loteng
Dusa
Bantang
Pura Tegeh Kuripan
Penulisan
Pinggan
Belantih
Blandingan
Lampu
Mungsengan
Balai Seni Toyabunkah (Centre of Art for the Future)
Gn. Batur ▲ 1717m
Songan
Traditional Village
BADUNG
Kintamani
Pura Batur
Traditional Village
Toya Bungkah
Crater Lake
Traditional "Bali Aga" Village
Lawak
Batur
Tinggan
BANGLI
Kalanganyar
Hot Spring
Danau Batur
Trunyan
Betok
Crater View
Kedisan
Abang
Pelaga
Peludu
Penelokan
Buahan
Gn. Abang 2153m
Kiadan
Nungnung
Katung
Sekardadi
Banua
Sekahan
KARANGASEM
Sandakan
Gate
Prean
Palaktihing
Suter
Pisang
Puakan
Pubuan
Kayuambua
Bangklet
Penyabangan
Belong
Tegal Suci
Seribatu
Pempatan
Angan Tiga
Pakusuba
Jasan
Punggang
Semadi
Taro
Timbul
Tigakawan
Pura Luhur Besakih
Buahan
GIANYAR
Calo
Temen
Besakih
Danginkreteg
Bukian
Tatag
Sebatu
Pujung
Manukaya
Lumbuhan
Kayubihi
Metra
Manikaji
Gadungan
Bayad
Tirtha Empul (Bathing Place)
Gunung Kawi
Kedui
Peninjoan
Menanga
Tangkup
Kelusa
Tampaksiring
Kubu
Tegalasah
Bangkiangsidem
Rendang
Muncan
Payangan
Keliki
Telebok
Cempaga
Cepunggung
Bujaga
Bangbang
Tegalalang
Pande
Sanding
Abuan
Sasana Budaya Art Centre
Pura Kehen
Bangbang
Nongan
Ipah
Selat
Celuk
Sapat
Sumitra
Sale
Bangli
Tembuku
Padangtunggal
Iseh
Junjungan
Cemadik
Demulih
Palaces
Petak
Tambahan
Panarukan
Semseman
Sanggam
Sidemen
Kedewatan
Petulu
Apuan
Ponti
Bukit Jambul
Undisan
Sanggingan
Tarukan
Suwat
Madangan
Timuhun
Sangkungan
Campuhan
Puri Saren Palace
Umakuta
Bangunlemah
Panarukan
Selisihan
Selat
Klungan
Telangan
Ubud
Tatiapi
Rejeng
Jelekungkang
Ngalian
Sengkiding
Wangsian
Padang Tegal
Peliatan
Talangjiwa
Babakan
Bunutin
Palak
Wanasari
Teges
Aan
Singakerta
Goa Gajah
Bedulu
Pacung
Bakas
Getakan
Manduang
Lebu
Gegelang
Jukutpaku
Kunba
Beng
Kembengan
Besang
Akah
Besar
Babakan
Mas
Kutri
Buruan
Bitera
Siden
Sangkanbuana
Paksebali
Pikat
Denpasar
Tengkulak
Kemenuh
Gianyar
Peteluan
Tegal
Klungkung
Kerta Gosa
KLUNGKUNG

Yeh Ayung

Sungsang

PART IV

Kintamani and Bangli Regency

The region of Bangli, up in the higher elevations of central-eastern Bali, embraces some of the island's most spectacular scenery. This is a relatively remote region, with a population of only 175,000 — second lowest of Bali's eight regencies after tiny Klungkung.

The overwhelming majority still derive a livelihood from agriculture, growing rice, corn, sweet potatoes, cassava and cabbages on non-irrigated fields, as well as coffee, tobacco, vanilla, citrus, passion fruit and cloves, much of it for export. Tourism is not well-developed here, with the notable exception of Kintamani and other towns up on the crater of Mt Batur, which on account of its breathtaking views has become one of the island's major tourist stops.

The main route through Bangli begins just east of Gianyar, passing through Bangli Town on its way up over Mt Batur via Kintamani, ending on the north coast at Kubutambahan. On the way up, terraced ricefields at first dominate the landscape.

Once past Bangli Town, however, the scenery changes dramatically and temperatures begin to drop. First the road winds through lush groves of giant bamboo which cast an eerie, greenish light. Residents of Bangli regard these as mystically charged. They are also reputed to have been the site of bloody skirmishes between rival princes during pre-colonial times, and more recently provided shelter to Balinese guerillas during the battle for Indonesian independence.

Further north, one arrives at a number of upland villages set amidst black, volcanic soils. The residents of the south refer to these villagers as "mountain people," and although they were once under the sway of the Bangli court, they were less influenced by the Hinduized culture of the south. As a result, they still maintain some archaic religious practices and forms of village organization, like the "Bali Aga" villages further to the north and east.

Approaching the Batur area, swirling mists are likely to obscure the view and increase the chill. For a few moments, while traversing this dramatic landscape of muted colors and indistinct horizons, it is possible to feel that one has crossed over to a different place and time — leaving behind the lush, green picture postcard Bali.

Suddenly, the road crests the hill through a narrow pass, and the famous peak and crater lake of Batur appear. This huge caldera was created when the volcano blew its stack many eons ago, leaving behind a gaping hole that now contains a smaller volcano and a spectacular crater lake.

Amongst the Balinese, Bangli is renowned for its black magic, or "knowledge of the left" as the Balinese put it. This is difficult to verify, as practitioners keep their black arts a secret. More in evidence are the large number of successful trance healers, called *balian*, who follow the "knowledge of the right." Bangli's healers have an island-wide reputation, and one will often see clients arriving from other areas of Bali, bearing offerings dressed in their ceremonial finery.

Bangli was also once a court center. The name comes from "*bang giri*" which means "red forest" or "mountain." It is said that the king of Klungkung told one of his three sons, Dewa Gede Den Bancingah, to go toward the northwest until he reached a red *jarak* forest. There he founded a new kingdom, between the Melangit River and Mt Batur on the site of present-day Bangli Town.

Later, Bangli was defeated by Karangasem and annexed for a time. Until the Dutch came, it was often involved in internecine wars with two neighboring kingdoms, vassals of Klungkung. After 1849, Bangli surrendered to the Dutch and its ruler became a regent.

— *Agnès Korb* and *Linda Connor*

Overleaf: *A stately* baris gede *in the Pura Ulun Danu Batur of Kintamani. Photo by Rio Helmi.*

KINTAMANI

Huge Crater and a Life-giving Lake

The mountainous region around Kintamani, centering around the spectacular volcanic caldera of Mt Batur with its deep crater lake and bubbling hot springs, is rugged with a high and wild beauty. Wonderful mountain air and dizzying views in all directions, as well as several important temples, are what make Kintamani one of the most memorable stops on the Bali tourist itinerary.

A drive-in volcano

Nearing Kintamani, the land rises steadily toward an almost featureless horizon — with only the mountains Gunung Agung and Gunung Abang in view to the east and northeast, respectively. Suddenly, you crest a ridge to find yourself perched on the rim of a vast crater, measuring some 14 km (9 mi) across. Down in the crater sits the blackened cone of Mt Batur, surrounded to one side by the long, blue waters of Lake Batur, and on the other by lava fields and cultivated onion patches.

The great size of the crater implies that Mt Batur was once a much bigger mountain (as big perhaps as Mt Agung) which blew its top thousands of years ago. The volcano is still active — the last serious eruptions occurred between 1965 and 1974, springing from the lower western flank of the mountain and leaving a vast field of black, needle-sharp lava rock. Much of the crater, though, is now being farmed. Although rainfall is slight, farmers irrigate their crops (mostly cabbage and onions) with water from the lake.

Lake Batur, Bali's largest lake, is the source that feeds an underground network of springs throughout the southern-central flanks of the mountain. Homage is paid here to the life-giving grace of the lake at **Pura Ulun Danu Batur**. The original temple is down by the lake, but during the 1920s it was built anew on the western rim of the crater near the town of Kintamani.

Six very old settlements around the lake are called *desa bintang danu* ("stars of the lake"): Songan, Abang, Buahan, Trunyan Kedisan and Batur. People will tell you that these are "Bali Aga" villages, which some people take to mean "original Balinese" while others say it refers to the myth of Markandya, a legendary saint-sage who led several bands of settlers to Bali from Desa

Aga on Gunung Raung in East Java. In any case, the term is in popular use, and there are a number of "Bali Aga" villages throughout the mountains around Kintamani. They are distinguished by their unusual lay-out and the uniformity of the houses — as if they all adhere to a single design. The traditional mountain architecture is very interesting — steep bamboo shingle roof and walls of clay, woven bamboo or wide wooden planks — but in many places this is disappearing as houses are re-built using modern materials.

A paved road follows the crater's rim around its southern and western circumference. From the south, the first stop is **Penelokan**, which means "look-out," and indeed the views from here are stunning. Enterprising people are capitalizing on the panorama, and there are swarms of peddlers and a string of shops, restaurants and small hotels all along the road to Kintamani.

The goddess of the lake

As you go north from Penelokan toward Kintamani, you will soon spot the many *meru* of **Pura Ulun Danu Batur**. This is an imposing complex of nine temples, still undergoing construction. *Ulun danu* means the "head of the lake," and the original site of this temple was at the lake's northeastern corner — the "holiest" quarter, associated with the vitality of the sun as it approaches its zenith. Violent eruptions of the volcano in the 1917

buried much of the area and took the lives of nearly a thousand people. Another serious eruption in 1926 forced the decision to re-build the temple at its present site, high up on the rim of the crater. With help from the Dutch colonial government, the shrines were dismantled and transported across the lava-strewn landscape and up the steep sides of the crater — a staggering task, one imagines, especially without roads or machinery. People from the original village of Batur at the foot of the western flank of the volcano also moved up to the new location (Batur/Kalanganyar) to tend to the temple's maintenance and ceremonies. Lava from the 1917 eruption stopped only a few meters from the village, which somehow encouraged the people to rebuild the village, damaged by ash. The village persists, just beyond the 1965-1974 lava fields.

Ida Batari Dewi Ulun Danu is the goddess of the lake. Myriad springs on the south side of the mountain feed the rich rice-growing districts of Bangli and Gianyar. Tirta Empul in Tampaksiring is one of the springs fed by Lake Batur. The different temples in the complex thus reflect a concern with not only the invisible world, but the world of the living as

Opposite: Sunrise at Penelokan, with Mt Abang in the distance and Lake Batur in the swirling mists below. **Below:** Batur is Bali's largest lake, a vital water catchment that is considered sacred.

SARITA NEWSON

well. The following is a description of the major shrines. Ask someone to point them out to you.

Pura Penataran Agung Batur is the principal temple, with five main courtyards. The dominant shrines are the *merus* — an 11-tiered one for the lake goddess and three 9-tiered ones for the gods of Mt Batur, Mt Agung, and Ida Batara Dalem Waturenggong, the deified king of Gelgel who is said to have ruled from 1460 to 1550. The Chinese-looking shrine to the northwest, with brightly painted statues, is for Ida Ratu Ayu Subandar, the patron saint of commerce. Another important shrine is the 3-tiered *meru* to Ida Ratu Ayu Kentel Gumi, who protects crops from disease.

Penataran Pura Jati is related to the source temple on the western edge of the lake.

Pura Tirta Bungkah is related to the hot springs down by the lake.

Pura Taman Sari and **Pura Tirta Mas Mampeh** are concerned with agriculture.

Pura Sampian Wangi is dedicated to such crafts as weaving, sewing, the making of offerings and ceremonial cakes.

Pura Gunarali is where adolescent boys and girls can invoke help to develop their natural abilities.

Pura Padang Sila consists of forty-five stone shrines for the gods and goddesses of Pura Ulun Danu Batur.

The major *odalan* of the temple, attended by people from all over Bali, occurs sometime in March and runs for 11 days .

Pura Tulukbiu just next to Pura Ulun Danu is another relocated temple. "Tulukbiu" is the old name of Abang, the second highest mountain in Bali at the southern edge of the Batur crater. The original temple was at the summit of Mt. Abang, and is said to have been built by the sage, Mpu Kuturan.

Panoramic frontier town

The village of Batur/Kalanganyar borders the town of **Kintamani**, an administrative center in the district of Bangli. This was formerly a way-station over the mountains that separate Buleleng (the old colonial headquarters of the Dutch) from the rest of Bali. The second hotel built in Bali was in Kintamani — but the place still looks like a frontier town: wooden huts and no-nonsense little cement boxes for the municipal offices. What one notices most is the delicious air and the vistas — the crater to one side and all Bali extending to the sea on the other.

Up the road going north is a market, busy every three days on Hari Paseh in the Balinese calender. This is interesting to visit to see the variety of produce from surrounding moutain farms — oranges, corn, vegetables, fruit and the usual vast array of scented flowers, dried fish, tools, livestock, pots and baskets, plus a big clothing market. You may also see men cuddling big furry Kintamani

ERIC OEY

puppies, highly prized all over Bali.

A temple of ancient kings

A few km past Kintamani on the right is the entrance to the temple **Pura Tegeh Kuripan**, also called **Pura Penulisan**, the highest construction on the island (1,745 m) until a TV tower was installed next door a few years ago. This temple is a powerful place — ancient, royal and remote.

A long steep flight of stairs rises through the eleven terraces of the temple complex. The pyramidal form and the large stones that are still venerated there suggest that this place has been holy for many centuries.

From **Pura Panarajon** on the uppermost terrace, you can sometimes see as far as the north coast of Bali and the mountains of East Java. The proportions of the courtyard and various *bale* are modest, but the atmosphere is heavy with the solitude of hallowed kings. There are many sacred statues — including *lingga* and mysterious fragments housed in the open pavilions. Of particular interest is a royal couple bearing the inscriptions "Anak Wungsu" and "Bhatari Mandul" dated Saka year 999 (A.D. 1077).

Mandul means "childless" and although it is impossible to know who this refers to, one interesting conjecture is that she was the Chinese Buddhist princess Subandar, whose shrine stands in Pura Ulun Danu, and that her barrenness was caused by a curse from a

Siwaite wizard.

From Sukawana, just to the right of the temple's entrance, you can follow a newly paved road that arcs along the northern rim of the crater, offering splendid views of the lava fields below. A steep drop takes you to **Pinggan**, overlooking the crater, and a road is now under construction to connect up with Blandingan and Songan down by the lake.

The more usual approach to the lake is from Penelokan, where a good road descends to the water's edge at Kedisan and heads over to Toyabungkah (Air Panas/Hot Spring). The road to the lake winds down from Penelokan. Men waving and shouting at you at the top of the road are not trying to collect a toll, but want to sell you a boat trip to Trunyan. Best to smile and keep going.

At **Kedisan** at the bottom of the road you have to turn left or right. The road to the left leads to Toyabungkah and Songan. The former is a good place from which to climb the volcano and explore the lake area. To the right, you will soon come to a little port with boat-taxis to Trunyan and points around the lake (see "Kintamani Practicalities," for details).

Of the lake villages, **Trunyan** is surely the most famous, and becoming notorious as a place not to visit after all. The village is virtually inaccessible except by boat, and on arrival the villagers will wade out to meet you and clamor for money. In Trunyan, it's okay to beg, yet the properous residents have re-built their houses in modern materials (cement block and zinc). Traditional architecture is rare.

Still, the place is interesting to some. In the **Pura Gede Pancering Jagat** is a unique, four-meter guardian statue, Da Tonte or Ratu Gede Pancering Jagat, but it is stored out of view in a closed *meru*. The people of Trunyan do not cremate their dead, but place them exposed under a sacred tree by the lakeshore that has the remarkable property of preventing the decomposing corpses from smelling. Tourists are aggressively solicited to visit the graveyard and see for themselves. This is further down from the village itself and you may ask to skip Trunyan and go directly to the gravesite or *kuburan*.

— *Diana Darling*

Opposite: *Looking north to Kintamani from Penelokan.* **Above:** *The market at Kintamani is an important source of produce for all of Bali.*

BANGLI TOWN

A Sleepy District Capital

Bangli is a small, sleepy town lying on the border between central and eastern Bali. It seems at first to contain nothing but concrete buildings and empty streets, which only become crowded on market and festival days. But Bangli is an old city, which may have been founded as early as A.D. 1204, judging from a stele in the famous Pura Kehen temple.

The market lies at the center of the town, partly obscured by shops. On market days, the stalls spill into the street and customers flock here from the surrounding area to buy produce and manufactured goods. Opposite is the bus station, flanked by a row of shops owned by Chinese and Balinese merchants.

For most Balinese, Bangli is in fact the object of some ridicule; when someone says "I come from Bangli," everyone immediately bursts into laughter. The reason is that Bali's only mental hospital is located here — a pleasantly-situated institution with beautiful grounds that was started by the Dutch.

Physically and socially, the town is dominated by the *puri* or palaces of the royal family. The Bangli courts established their independence from Klungkung in the 19th century and played an influential role in Balinese politics through to the post-independence era. Eight royal households spread around the main crossroads. The most prominent is the **Puri Denpasar**, the palace of the last raja of Bangli, who died three decades ago. One of the king's wives, now over 100 years old, still resides here. Much of the palace has been restored by his descendants, and there is now a small hotel in the pavilions run by the raja's grandson. The royal ancestral temple lies just to the north of the crossroads, on the western side. Huge ceremonies are held here, attended by all descendants of the royal house, including many who live in other parts of Indonesia.

Temple of the hearth

One of Bali's most beautiful temples, **Pura Kehen**, stands at the northeastern boundary of the town, seemingly erected in the midst of the forest long before the town itself. Three copper steles testify to its antiquity and importance. The earliest one, in Sanskrit, seems to date to the 9th century and mentions the deity Hyang Api (the "God of Fire"). The second is in old Balinese, and the third is in old Javanese, the latter already mentioning Hyang Kehen and indicating eight villages around Bangli that worship the deity.

The name Kehen is actually a variant of *kuren*, which means "household" or "hearth." The reference to Hyang Api as a symbol of Brahma may mean that there once was a cult to that god here worshipping him with a rite called *homa*, in which offerings are burned on a small hearth. At some point, it seems that Hyang Api became Hyang Kehen — the "God of the Hearth."

Pura Kehen is the state temple of the old kingdom. It is constructed on a number of levels, after the manner of ancient animistic sanctuaries, that are built into the southern slope of a hill — much like Besakih. There are eight terraces: the first five are *jabaan* or outer courtyards, the sixth and seventh ones are lower and upper middle courts or *jaba tengah*, and the eighth one is the sacred, inner *jeroan*. A flight of 38 stairs adorned with *wayang* statues on either side leads to the main entrance, and a frightening *kala*

ERIC OEY

makara demon guardian is carved on the gateway.

In the outer courtyard, a huge old banyan tree with a *kulkul* drum inside can be seen, as well as a flat stone for offerings. The walls are inlaid with Chinese porcelain — a common feature of ancient temples and palaces. The temple has 43 altars, including one 11-roofed *meru* to Hyang Api. Several are dedicated to the ancestors of *sudra* commoner clans such as the Ratu Pasek and Pande — which means that worshippers from all over Bali come to pray here, especially on its *odalan* or anniversary. The huge three-compartment, *padmasana* throne in the northeasternmost corner has beautiful carvings at the back.

Warriors of the mountain

Not far from Pura Kehen, the **Sasana Budaya Art Center** is one of the largest in Bali. Exhibitions and *kecak* or *wayang* performances are held there. In the Bangli area, various types of ritual *baris* dances have developed that are typical of mountain regions, such as the *baris jojor* (eight men in a line with spears), *baris presi* or *tamiang* (eight men in a circle with leather shields) and *baris dadap* (men in pairs with bat-shaped curled shields made from holy dadap

wood). They are performed especially at *odalans*. One of the biggest *gamelan* orchestras in Bali can also be found in the Bangli region. It was captured from the Klungkung dynasty by the Dutch, who gave it to Bangli.

The natural scenery around Bangli is worth admiring. Cool air and quiet paths lead to breathtaking panoramas. About one km west of the town on the road toward Tampaksiring is a huge ravine with springs and a number of bathing pools and irrigation works sponsored by the former mayor of Bangli. Bathers and visitors must descend a long flight of steps to reach the springs, but the beauty of the spot warrants the effort. This is a favorite meeting spot for flirtatious young locals.

Bukit Demulih, literally the "hill of no return," is located farther west, about an hour's walk from Bangli on the southern side of the road. A small temple stands atop the hill, offering a magnificent vista to the west. On the way, in a landscape of bamboo clusters and farmland, there is a holy waterfall.

To the east of Bangli, there is another lovely road meandering through spectacular rice terraces and across deep ravines. It emerges finally on the main road to Besakih, just near Rendang. This road runs just south of the transitional zone between wet-rice and dry-rice cultivation, which form the two main ecological specializations in Bangli.

— Agnès Korb and *Linda Connor*

Left: *An odalan in the famous Pura Kehen temple in Bangli.* **Above:** *Mt Agung from above Bangli Town, showing the area's unique vegetation.*

Klungkung

PART V

Klungkung Regency

This small district in eastern Bali derives its name from the old court town of Klungkung. The name means "beauty" or "happiness" and the town was founded several centuries ago on a site chosen for its many auspicious qualities.

The founding of Klungkung was not as idyllic as the name suggests, however. Prior to 1651 ancestors of the Klungkung kings ruled Bali from their capital at Gelgel, some 5 km to the south. At its height, Gelgel was a great and powerful court, governing a realm that extended to the adjacent islands of Java, Lombok and Sumbawa. In 1651, the prime minister of Gelgel revolted and forced the royal family to flee. Some 30 years later, a young prince chose the present site for a new capital, and a smaller kingdom was born here.

Despite its small size and lack of natural resources compared to the other kingdoms of Bali, Klungkung has always maintained the mystique of being the island's original royal center. The Klungkung royal family is still considered more regal than any other on the island, and up until recent times this meant having exclusive rights to certain ritual status-symbols, such as the 11-tiered cremation towers. In the intricate etiquette of the formal Balinese language, moreover, the Klungkung royalty have the right to speak down, literally, to everyone else.

The people of Klungkung are still extremely proud of this heritage, and uphold a reputation for being more traditional than other Balinese. This is supported by the active role the royal family takes in the life of the area, and by the presence of many famous priestly families in the region, all of whom once participated in the great rituals of the court, and to whom Bali's most famous and venerable *pedanda* priests trace their origin.

The prestige of Klungkung and its illustrious past is such that most Balinese aristocrats trace their ancestry back to Gelgel. Family histories will often tell why their ancestors left the center, and temples in Klungkung still draw people from all over the island for major rituals to celebrate their heritage. Gelgel is full of sites of legendary deeds by ancient kings, ministers and priests.

Perhaps because of its past, Klungkung today seems rather removed from the hustle and bustle of tourist activity. Its main tourist spots are the Kerta Gosa — the famed judgment hall of the former Klungkung palace — and the bat cave temple near Kusamba.

In general, its income derives more from trade than from tourism, since it is a stopping point on the busy inter-island trade route which runs from East Java, via the port of Padangbai, and on to Lombok and eastern Indonesia. A visitor to Klungkung can get a sense of this lively commercial activity from a visit to the city's market — the largest in Bali. Since most of the trade passes along the main road through the town, visitors to Klungkung find the side-roads quiet and serene.

Outside the busy town, Klungkung offers a contrast of landscapes — from the lush hills on the road leading to Besakih temple, to the stark gravel pits to the east, formed when Mt Agung erupted in 1963, its lava flows laying waste to the ricefields of the area. The villages of Klungkung are among the most charming in Bali, and have been major prize winners in the all-Bali "beautiful village" competitions sponsored by the government.

One of the natural highlights of the Klungkung area is the great Unda River just east of the city. Floods and changes in the river's course figure in many episodes of Klungkung's traditional history. Nowadays its caprices are kept in check by a system of dams and man-made dikes, built with the voluntary aid of those who live by the river and are dependent on its waters for their survival.

— *Adrian Vickers*

Overleaf: *Fishermen arrive in* jukung *sailing crafts on the black sand beach at Kusamba, east of Klungkung Town. Photo by Pam Roberson.*

SIGHTS OF KLUNGKUNG

Bali's Most Illustrious Kingdom

The town of Klungkung centers around the **Puri Smarapura** or "Palace of the God of Love" — former home of Bali's most illustrious line of kings. Unfortunately, all that remains now are the great gate and garden, and two pavilions with magnificently painted ceilings. These are the Kerta Gosa Hall of Justice overlooking the town's main intersection, and the larger Bale Kambang or Floating Pavilion just behind it.

The rest of this splendid complex was razed to the ground in 1908, during the royal mass suicide or *puputan* ("ending") against the Dutch invaders. This event removed the last obstacle to Dutch domination of the island. A monument commemorating the *puputan* now stands across the road.

The **Kerta Gosa** was a place for the administration of traditional justice in pre-colonial times by a council consisting of the great king and his priests. The paintings on the ceiling tell of the punishments awaiting evil-doers in hell, and of the delights of the gods in heaven. Different levels and stations in heaven and hell are described through the story of the hero Bima, who journeys to the underworld to save the souls of his parents. These scenes were used to alternately threaten and cajole anyone who appeared before the court.

Like the Sistine Chapel, the Kerta Gosa presents a whole complex of ideas on the workings of fate and the role of the divine in human affairs. The ceilings themselves have been repainted three times in recent memory. The last complete refurbishment occurred in 1960 under the famous artist Pan Seken, although in 1984, weather damage caused a number of panels to be repaired.

The **Bale Kambang** in back is actually rather new, having been added to the complex only in the 1940s. The ceiling was originally painted by Wayan Kayun in 1942, and depicts episodes from the story of the Buddhist king Sutasoma, who defeated his enemies through passive resistance. Also portrayed is the story of the commoner Pan Brayut — a coarse man who received great spiritual blessings.

Palaces and priestly estates

Members of the royal family who survived the massacre of 1908 were exiled to Lombok.

They returned in 1929 and settled in a new palace, the **Puri Agung** to the west of the old site on the other side of the street. Chief among them is Dalem Pamayun, eldest son of the former king, who has become a priest.

To the north of the main crossroads, on the righthand side, is a set of beautiful and important royal temples, with an ancestral shrine dedicated to the great king of Gelgel, Dalem Seganing. Just next to it is the **Pura Taman Sari** or Flower Garden Temple, consisting of a peaceful garden and moat around a main pagoda. In the 19th century, a famous warrior queen of Klungkung meditated and wrote poetry here.

There are many priestly estates in Klungkung with long histories connected with the royal house. The best-known is **Griya Pidada Klungkung**, once home to the chief priests of the court. Another residence with long historical associations is the former palace of **Lebah**, to the east of the city just before the Unda River, now the Ramayana Palace Hotel. Just to the west is the Banjar Pande, the blacksmiths' ward of Klungkung, and the long-established Muslim quarter.

The best time to visit Klungkung is every three days on the Balinese day known as *pasah*, when the **Klungkung Market** is in full swing. The market nestles behind a row of shops to the east of the Kerta Gosa, and although it has lost some of its old atmosphere as a result of being re-housed in a new, multi-storied concrete structure, it offers a full range of local delights, including handmade housewares, baskets, fruits, flowers, vegetables and the like.

For those interested in souvenirs, the row of art shops on the main road in front of the market is well-known to antique collectors. The astute old women who own them have been in business since the 1930s, although age is now thinning their ranks. They all complain, however, that nowadays they can only occasionally find the sort of valuable items which used to routinely fill their shops.

West of the town

To the west of the town of Klungkung, bordering on Gianyar regency, is the fertile district known as **Banjar Angkan**, separated from Klungkung by a spectacular ravine. This once served as a buffer zone between the two frequently warring kingdoms, and changed hands many times during the 18th and 19th centuries. Partly as a result, Banjar Angkan has developed its own unique identity quite apart from the rest of the region.

One of the objects of these frequent wars was the important temple of **Pura Kentel Gumi**, "the Temple of the Congealing Earth" — located on a bend in the main road west of

Opposite: *The Bale Kambang floating pavilion in front of the old palace.* **Below:** *Scene from Klungkung's Kerta Gosa ceiling.*

KAL MULLER

AMIR SIDHARTA

Klungkung. The name of this temple indicates that it was a focal point around which the mystical and political forces of the former kingdoms moved.

Also to the west of Klungkung are the villages of Tiingan and Aan. **Tiingan** is most famous as the village of *gamelan* smiths or *pandé gong,* who have been famous throughout Bali for centuries. **Aan** is best known as the home of a learned high priest, Pedanda Aan, who advises people on the proper procedures for Bali's most important rituals. Between Banjar Angkan and Klungkung lies the village of **Takmung**, which also has many interesting temples, and is known as a center for the Resi Bhujangga sect, who are priestly worshippers of Wisnu.

Bali's original capital

The old court center of **Gelgel** is situated 4 km south of Klungkung town and actually comprises a number of distinct villages, notably Tojan and Kamasan. The entire area is filled with ancient and legendary sites from Bali's "Golden Age" — the 16th and 17th centuries — and this is the area to which all Balinese nobility and just about everyone else on the island trace their ancestry.

The most important site lies at the very heart of Gelgel — the sacred **Pura Jero Agung** or "Great Palace Temple," which stands on the site of the former Gelgel palace. The temple is the ancestral shrine of

the old palace, which was abandoned in the 17th century following a rebellion. Adjacent to it is the **Pura Jero Kapal**, all that remains of the second largest palace in Gelgel — that of the Lord of Kapal.

To the east of the Pura Jero Agung is an ancient temple, the **Pura Dasar** or "base temple." This is the lowland counterpart of Besakih, providing a direct connection with the sacred "mother temple" up on Mt Agung.

The festivals held at Pura Dasar are spectacular, as all members of the royal family join in. It is here that the deified ancestors are worshipped — inside are a number of stones set on a stone throne, archaic symbols of ancestral worship. Nearby is the **Gelgel Mosque**, the oldest on Bali, which was set up to serve the spiritual needs of Muslims who came from Java to serve the king in ancient times.

Further to the east of Gelgel is a large complex of graveyards and temples which are cited in the genealogies of many families from all over Bali. Just north of this is a set of two unusual shrines, the **Pura Dalem Gandamayu**, which was the dwelling of Pedanda Nirartha — Bali's greatest priest and the ancestor of all Siwa brahmans on the island. He established this as a branch of the legendary graveyard of the same name on Java. One of the shrines at Gandamayu is dedicated to the descendants of Nirartha, while the other belongs to the *pande* or blacksmith clan.

The present temple of Gandamayu was restored in the 1970s after being partially destroyed by the 1963 eruption of Mt Agung which devastated the whole area. The adjoining village of **Tangkas** was partially wiped out and many lives were lost, although Tangkas still maintains some of its famous musical traditions, particularly the ancient and rare ensemble called *gong luang*.

To the south of Tangkas, near the coast, is the village of **Jumpai**, which has the reputation of being a powerful center for magic. The benevolent *barong* of Jumpai is famous all over Bali, and there are stories of a powerful magician in the village who meditated and turned aside a lava flow which would have destroyed the village in 1963.

To the south of Gelgel is the pleasant beach of **Klotok**, an area of great importance in Balinese rituals. Processions to Bali's mother temple of Besakih all pay a visit to Klotok to ritually bless their offerings.

Home of traditional painting

The adjoining village of **Kamasan** is a major artistic center, home of traditional Balinese painting. The many forms of painting found today in Bali all derive from the so-called Kamasan or *wayang* style characteristic of this village, in which the figures depicted resemble two-dimensional shadow puppets. The style itself traces back to ancient Java, where similar figures are found on temple reliefs. The amazing thing is that this survives as a living art up until the present day on Bali.

Painters from Kamasan were once sent all over the island in the service of their royal patrons. The painters' ward is *banjar sangging,* but other parts of the village are famous for their crafts as well. Nearby is the *banjar pandé mas,* where gold and silversmiths work. The village also once provided dancers, musicians and puppeteers to the court. Most of these activities have declined in recent years, but they once contributed to a lively creative atmosphere, providing inspiration for local painters.

The presence of *dalang*, or puppeteers, in the village was particularly important. The iconography of the two art forms is the same, as are the stories depicted — great epics like the *Ramayana* and the *Mahabharata*. Scenes portrayed in the flickering shadows of the *wayang* are rendered in reds and ochres and arranged to show the workings of natural and supernatural forces.

Kamasan's foremost artist today is the relatively young Nyoman Mandra (b. 1946), whose work best captures the refinement of the tradition. Mandra heads up a government-sponsored school devoted to ensuring that village children will continue their 500-year-old traditions. Visitors to the school can see how beginners are trained.

Besides Nyoman Mandra there are many other practicing artists here, including Mangku Mura, who has developed his own variation on the Kamasan style, and Ibu Suciarmi, one of the first female painters in what was previously an all-male profession.

Since Kamasan is off the tourist track it is refreshingly free of art shops. Visitors can visit the homes and studios of the artists. Don't be put off by the initial hustle of sellers on the street — it is difficult for these artists to make a living. One compensation for the buyer is that any money spent goes directly to the artists and is not lost on middlemen.

To the magical east

Moving east of Klungkung along the main road, one crosses the Unda River and passes through a number of interesting villages, including Paksabali, Satria and Sampalan.

ADRIAN VICKERS

Above, left: *Ancient ancestral stones placed on a stone "throne" in the Pura Dasar, Gelgel.* **Right:** *Kamasan style painting of Arjuna and the heavenly nymph Suprana by Modara, ca. 1850.*

ERIC OEY

Paksabali is famous for its Dewa Mapalu or Pasraman Dewa festival — the dramatic "clashing" or "meeting of the gods." This is held during the annual Kuningan festival, when idols are borne from the temple aboard palanquins down a steep ravine to the Unda River to be ritually bathed and given offerings. As the palanquin bearers proceed back up to the temple gates, they are possessed by the gods they are carrying and race madly in circles, colliding against each other in an effort to get back into the temple compound.

The adjoining village of **Sampalan** is the home of Bali's foremost traditional architect, Mangku Putu Cedet, who is a builder of fabulous cremation towers and traditional houses. He has traveled all over the world exhibiting his skills, and is thoroughly steeped in the arts of healing and white magic as well. When the royal family of Klungkung holds major ceremonies, it is he who is asked to perform a ritual to prevent it from raining.

An important village further to the east is **Dawan**, home of one of Bali's most famous high priests, Pedanda Gede Keniten. He is directly descended from the court priest of Gelgel and is in great demand for major rituals. Adjoining Dawan is the village of

*Above: The Dewa Mapalu or "clashing of the gods" ritual at Paksabali. **Right:** Goa Lawah, the bat cave. **Opposite:** An aerial view of Kusamba beach, lined with salt pans.*

Besang, famous for its main temple which has an ancient inscription under a giant pagoda. The Dawan area, situated among small hills, is another "hot spot" or center of natural and mystical power on Bali.

Further to the east, the main road meets the coast at the fishing village of **Kusamba**, with its dramatic black sand beaches. For several decades in the late 18th century, the palace of Klungkung was inhabited by a mad king, Dewa Agung Sakti, and Kusamba was the headquarters of his son and rival.

Kusamba was at this time an important port; like Kamasan and Klungkung it was a center for the blacksmith clan, whose skill in the manufacture of weapons was of crucial importance to any ruler. In 1849, when the Dutch conquered north and east Bali, Kusamba was the site of a major battle in which a Dutch general was killed by order of the "virgin queen," Dewa Agung Isteri Kanya.

Not far beyond Kusamba is the famous **Goa Lawah** bat cave temple, one of the state temples of Klungkung. Legend has it that when Klungkung was ruled from Kusamba, a prince of Mengwi sought protection here and entered the bat cave. He was not seen again until he emerged nearly 20 kms to the north, at Pura Besakih. No one has since tried to enter the cave to prove whether it really extends that far — the strong odor of bat droppings is no doubt a major deterrent.

— *Adrian Vickers*

KAL MULLER

PENIDA AND LEMBONGAN

Bali's 'Sister Islands' — Another World

Nusa Penida, Nusa Lembongan and Nusa Ceningan are Bali's three "sister islands" — situated in the deep, whirling straits separating Bali from Lombok. Nusa Ceningan, the smallest of the three, is little more than a tiny rock with a single village that snuggles cosily between the massive highlands of Penida to the east, and the coral beaches of Lembongan to the west. The three islands differ radically from the rest of Bali, consisting of barren limestone highlands covered by cacti and shrubs. Physically, they have much more in common with the southern Bukit Peninsula and the islands to the east of Bali.

An austere physical environment

Water is scarce, so the only crops grown here are maize, cassava, beans and tobacco. It is common in the small villages to see *cacah* — strips of raw cassava drying in the sun before being steamed as a substitute staple for rice.

The islands are very sparsely populated. Nusa Penida (usually called Nusa) has 10 villages scattered along its shores and in the highlands. Access is difficult, as transport is not well-developed and roads in the highlands, winding and uneven, are just beginning to be paved. Everything comes by boat from Bali, including cattle, motorcycles and even bulldozers (which are knocked down, transported and re-assembled).

Houses, built with limestone blocks on the Balinese pattern in the lowlands, are more like Lombok's one-room huts on the plateau. They always include a family shrine (*sanggah*), as most inhabitants are Hindu Balinese. However, in the main town of **Toya Pakeh**, many people call themselves "Muslim Balinese" — by which they mean a mixture of Malay, Sasak, Bugis, and Javanese migrants — settled here for generations. They have their own mosque, and Sasak cloth traders from nearby Lombok live semi-permanently in this *desa Islam*.

Most highland farmers work in terraced dry fields and breed cattle. Cows are brought to market aboard *jukung* to be slaughtered in Denpasar. On the coast, people live by fishing, transporting passengers and goods to and from Bali, and, more recently, by cultivating seaweed. The seaweed — the large, green *kotoni* and the smaller, red *pinusun* — is exported to Hong Kong for use in the cosmetics industry. On shore, one finds coconut and cashew plantations.

Women help their husbands in the fields. They used to spin cotton and weave *cepuk* (rough checkered cloths used for life cycle ceremonies) on backstrap looms, but this has almost disappeared over the last 10 years.

Daily life is hard. Rainwater is collected in huge tanks for supply during the dry season and on the southern cliffs of Penida, a spectacular bamboo stairway has been constructed to gather water from natural springs just above the sea. Electricity is not yet available in the highlands, and education, job and entertainment opportunities are scarce.

The cursed islands

All kinds of appalling myths have always been attached to Nusa Penida, due to its gloomy atmosphere and unrewarding conditions. Black magic is said to flourish here, and Balinese from the mainland are very careful about what they say to Nusa people so as not to offend them. All evil affecting Bali — especially floods and diseases during

MORTON STRANGE

MORTON STRANGE

the dry season — is said to come from Nusa, brought by the giant demon king, Jero Gede Mecaling.

In the Badung and Gianyar regencies, the giant and his troops, who are said to cross the straits and land at Lebih, are met and expelled by means of exorcistic *sanghyang dedari* trance dances.

Formerly, the islands were part of the Klungkung kingdom, which used Nusa as a place of banishment. Therefore, most inhabitants are commoners and only a few bear the noble titles Dewa or Sri.

Visiting the islands

Nusa Penida is the ideal place to get off the beaten track, and to seek quietude and authenticity. The inhabitants here speak Balinese, with a local accent and vocabulary influenced by Sasak, but for them Bali is another world to which they go only from time to time. The form of ceremonies, such as weddings and cremations is similar to those in Bali, but in other ways these islands remind one of Lombok or Sumbawa.

In **Nusa Penida**, there is almost no tourism yet. It is wonderful to walk, ride on *ojek* two-wheeled taxis, or drive through the villages in the highlands and along the shore to experience the island's rough beauty. It is also a rare experience to spend the night in a local home, as people are very friendly.

Several sights are worth visiting, such as **Karang Sari Cave**, the spring at **Sakti** and **Sebuluh Waterfall** near Batu Madeg. The most interesting temple is Ratu Gede Mecaling's **Pura Peed**, 3 km east of Toya Pakeh. In the smaller sanctuary here, a strange tree composed of three entangled

ones grows, and from the trunk a stone mouth of Mecaling's minister protrudes. The temple *odalan* falls on Buda Cemeng Kelawu. Every three years on the fourth full moon (Purnama Kapat), a great festival (*usaba*) is also held, during which pilgrims from all over Bali come to pray at Pura Peed.

The **Gandrung Dance**, performed by two young boys clad in women's attire is still practised in Plilit (Sekartaji) and Cemulik (Sakti) on Kajeng Kliwon, Purnama and Tilem according to the Balinese calendar. It is inspired by a dance of the same name in West Lombok. **Baris Pati** is performed in cemeteries at the time of cremations, in simpler costumes than on Bali. **Baris Gede** is danced at the *odalan* at Batu Ngulapan (Batu Nungul). **Sanghyang Jaran** exorcistic dances are held in times of crisis in Kutampi and Sakti.

Nusa Lembongan is a small island covered with coconut trees, mangrove forests, small farms, and is surrounded by coral reefs. The island is split between two villages, **Jungut Batu** and **Lembongan**. About 75 percent of its population is involved with seaweed farming. The relaxed atmosphere on the island is synchronized with the cycles of the tides. Villagers are seen planting, replanting, and drying the seaweed. Much of this activity takes place on the beach so it is difficult to find an isolated beach for sunbathing.

— *Agnès Korb and Veronica H. Long*

AMIR SIDHARTA

Left: *The southern limestone cliffs of Nusa Penida.* **Above:** *Travel to the "Sister Islands" is by small motorized jukung from Sanur, Padangbai or Kusamba.* **Right:** *A beach on the northern coast of Nusa Penida.*

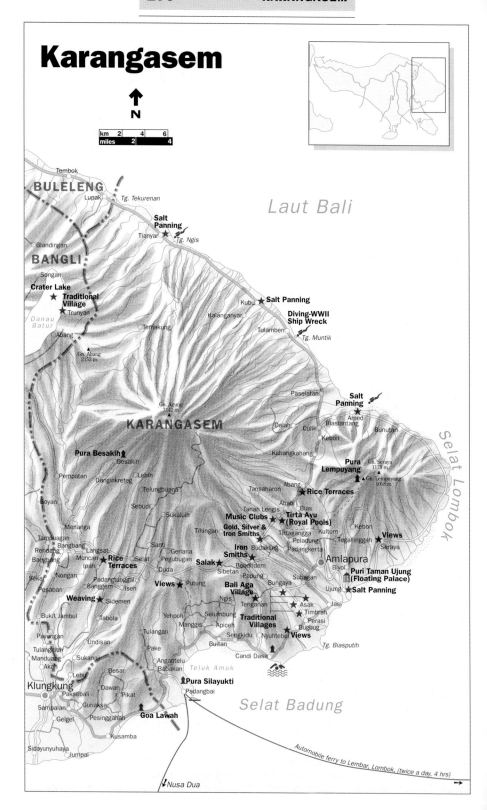

Karangasem

N

| km | 2 | 4 | 6 |
| miles | 2 | 4 |

Tembok

BULELENG

Lupak   Tg. Tekurenan

Laut Bali

Salt Panning

Tianyar   Tg. Ngis

Blandingan

BANGLI

Songan

Crater Lake

★ **Traditional Village**

Trunyan

Danau Batur

Abang

Gn. Abang 2153 m

Temakung

Kubu   ★ **Salt Panning**

Kalanganyar

Diving-WWII Ship Wreck

Tulamben   Tg. Muntik

Gn. Agung 3142 m

KARANGASEM

Paselatan

Salt Panning ★

Amed

Dalah   Blaslantang

Culik   Bunutan

Kebon

Pura Besakih ♦

Besakih

Kahangkahang

Pempatan   Danginkreteg

Lebih

Telungbuana

Pura Lempuyang ★

Gn. Seraya 1128 m

Gn. Lempuyang 1058 m

Abang   ★ **Rice Terraces**

Tansaharon

Ababi   Bias

Sebudi

Sukaluih

Tanah Lengis

Music Clubs ★

Tirta Ayu (Royal Pools) ★

Menanga

Tihingan

Gold, Silver & Iron Smiths ★

Tirtagangga

Kebon

Views

Peladung

Kultom

Tegallinggah ★

Seraya

Tampuagan

Bangbang

Santi

Geriana

Iron Smiths ★

Budakling

Padangkerta

Rendang

Langsat

Muncan ★ **Rice Terraces**

Selat

Pegubugan

Salak ★

Amlapura ●

Bangbang

Ipah

Duda

Sibetan

Bebandem

Biyol.

Sekar

Nongan

Padangtunggal

Putung

Views ★

Bali Aga Village ★

Bungaya

Subagan

Puri Taman Ujung (Floating Palace) 🏛

Pesaban

Banggem

Iseh

Papung

Ujung ★ **Salt Panning**

Weaving ★ Sidemen

Ngis

Tenganan

Asak ★

Jasi

Bukit Jambul

Tabola

Yehpoh   Selumbung

Traditional Villages

Timbrah ★

Perasi

Payungan

Manggis   Apicen

Sengkidu

Bugbug

Tulangan

Buitan

Nyuhtebel **Views** ★

Undisan

Pake

Tg. Biasputih

Tulangkuih

Anggantelu

Candi Dasa

Manduang

Babakan   *Teluk Amuk*

Akah

Lebu

Pura Silayukti ♦

Klungkung

Dawan   Pikat

Padangbai

Pakseban

Gunaksa

Selat Badung

Sambalan

Pesinggahan

Goa Lawah ♦

Gelgel

Sidayunyuhaya   Jumpai

Kusamba

Selat Lombok

Automobile ferry to Lembar, Lombok, (twice a day, 4 hrs)

↓ *Nusa Dua*

PART VI

East Bali: Karangasem

The beautiful eastern regency of Karangasem is truly something special — distinguishing itself in so many ways from the rest of the island. Physically it is dominated by the towering presence of Mt Agung (3142 m), the island's most sacred and highest volcano, whose dramatic foothills and lava flows provide some of the most spectacular landscapes found anywhere in Bali. High up on Mt Agung's southern flanks perches the great "Mother Temple" of Besakih, while to the south and east lie a number of more or less isolated villages that have played a key role in Balinese history.

Culturally, Karangasem is in fact a very conservative area. Here, for example, the use of the various Balinese speech levels is more strictly adhered to and a number of archaic ritual, dance and musical forms have been maintained right up until the present day. The eastern and northern parts of the regency are quite arid, and overall this is a less densely-populated area than southern Bali. In fact, it has many affinities with the drier and more rugged islands of eastern Indonesia — more so than any other part of the island.

For several centuries after the decline of the great Javanese empire of Majapahit, the king of Klungkung just to the west of here was, at least in name, the paramount ruler of Bali. The other Balinese rulers became more and more independent over time, and by the 17th century, Karangasem was able to successfully oppose Klungkung. It subsequently emerged, during the 18th and 19th centuries, as the most powerful kingdom on Bali. Its rulers were particularly influential in northern Bali (Buleleng) and Lombok, and frequently allied themselves with other Balinese rajas in times of war and intrigue.

During the 17th century, Karangasem forces already occupied much of the neighboring island of Lombok, fighting there against Macassarese from Sumbawa and eventually colonizing the western rice-growing areas of the island, with the result that today there are large numbers of Balinese living there who regard Karangasem as their homeland. After the middle of the last century, the tables turned and Karangasem became a vassal of the king of Lombok — himself a Balinese prince from Karangasem.

After Buleleng and Jembrana, which fell into Dutch hands in the middle of the last century, this was the next Balinese kingdom to be conquered by the Dutch when they invaded and "freed" the indigenous Sasak population of Lombok from Balinese rule in 1894.

Altogether Karangasem encompasses an area of 861 sq km, and according to the 1987 census the population numbers around 350,000 souls, meaning that the average population density is about 400 per sq km. Most of the populace, however, lives in central and southern Karangasem, especially around the capital of Amlapura, and population densities here are much higher than the average.

Many areas of Karangasem suffered great devastation as a result of the eruption of Mt Agung in 1963. Traces of this eruption can still be seen today, particularly in the Kubu and Tianyar areas on the northeastern coast. Already very dry, the northeast became all the more so after the eruption. A government project to encourage the planting of *jeruk* (a citrus species) here was not much of a success, but nowadays grapes are very much in vogue, as is cacao. South and southeast of Mt Agung lie the traditional rice-growing areas, with their spectacular terraced and irrigated ricefields. Higher up coffee, cloves and other cash-crops are grown on steep mountain slopes. The coastal areas of Ujung and Seraya to the south, and Amed, Kubu and Tianyar to the north, are the site of traditional fishery and salt-panning communities.

— *Danker Schaareman*

Overleaf: *The majestic "Mother Temple" of Besakih beneath Mt Agung. Photo by Eric Oey.*

A Burgeoning New Beach Resort

Candidasa is a new but rapidly growing beach resort located on the black sand coast of Karangasem Regency. It is the perfect base for explorations of the area, as well as a quieter alternative to the southern tourist centers.

Following the main road from Klungkung, you cross the border into Karangasem shortly after the village of Kusamba and the well-known temple of Goa Lawah. The road continues eastward through coconut groves for several kms before reaching a turn-off. To the right is a road leading to **Padangbai**, a major harbor for ships to Lombok and points east, as well as for smaller boats to Nusa Penida. It is worth the 2 km detour to see the picturesque, semi-circular hills surrounding a sparkling blue bay.

The village itself has several small hotels and restaurants. A famous temple, **Pura Silayukti**, where the Buddhist sage Mpu Kuturan is said to have lived in the 11th century, is also located here. The temple's anniversary is on Wednesday-Kliwon of the week Pahang (consult a Balinese calendar).

Back on the main road, one arrives at the village of **Manggis** a few kms to the east. There is a lovely path from here leading up to nearby **Putung** in the hills overlooking the coast. The path runs through woods and gardens and reaches Putung after a distance of some 5 kms, where one has a splendid view across the sea to the nearby islands.

Another possible sidetrip is from Manggis east along a small road through the isolated villages of **Ngis** and **Selumbung**. The road finally rejoins the main road in **Sengkidu** shortly before Candidasa. It is also possible to continue from Ngis on to Tenganan.

Candidasa town

Continuing east another 7 km, past the villages of Ulakan and Sengkidu, the main road enters **Candidasa** just after the Tenganan turn-off. The name Candidasa was originally applied just to two small temples, one for Siwa and the other for Hariti, that overlook a beautiful palm-fringed lagoon by the beach. Hariti is mainly worshipped by childless parents who pray for children.

Toward the end of the 1970s the first bungalows appeared by the beach here. From 1982 onwards a building frenzy set in, and is still continuing so that new hotels, shops and

restaurants seem to open almost weekly. As a result, Candidasa is now encroaching on the Buitan area to the west — site of several luxurious bungalow-hotels which specialize in snorkeling and diving trips.

Candidasa today is a bustling seaside resort with the full range of hotels, homestays, disco-bars, moneychangers, shops and restaurants. How long the development will continue is an open question, as the beach is eroding quickly and the once-spectacular view across the sacred lagoon to the beach is now blocked by two-storey bungalows.

Dance and music performances for visitors are being developed, but these do not seem to be of high quality. The main attraction of the area is as a base from which to visit the neighboring village of Tenganan, some 5 kms away. Swimming is only more or less possible at high tide. Despite these disadvantages, Candidasa enjoys cool breezes and is a good resting point for trips to the east and north.

Bugbug and environs

Four kms to the northeast of Candidasa lies Bugbug, a sizeable rice-growing and fishing village that is the administrative center for the sub-district. Along the way, the road climbs the unexpectedly steep **Gumang Hill**. There is a beautiful panorama from the top of the sea, the Buhu River, ricefields and Bugbug, with the mountains of Lempuyang and Seraya in the distance. On a very clear day one can see Mt Rinjani on Lombok from here.

Bugbug and the surrounding villages are quite old-fashioned. Apart from the official village head, there is a council of elders responsible for all religious affairs. The elders are not elected, but enter the council on the basis of seniority. Another atypical feature of these villages is communal land tenure, and the presence of associations for unmarried boys and girls which have to fulfill duties in the context of village rituals.

Two rituals are especially important. The first takes place around the full moon of the first Balinese month (between mid-June and mid-July). This ritual worship of the village gods is carried out in the central temple (*pura desa*), and lasts for several days. Most spectacular are the dances by unmarried boys (*abuang taruna*) clad in costumes of white and gold-threaded cloth, with headdresses and *keris*, the traditional weapon.

After the dance there follows the so-called *daratan* in which older men in trance carrying *keris* approach the main shrine of the tem-

ple, to the accompaniment of special music. Three orchestras play simultaneously: the sacred *selunding* (iron metallophones), the *gong desa* with drums and cymbals, and a *gambang* ensemble which has bamboo xylophones and bronze metallophones.

During the same full moon period there are similar rituals in other nearby villages like Asak and Perasi. **Perasi** lies just northeast of Bugbug on the main road, and from its eastern end there is a nice walk through the hills to the beach. Swimming here is hazardous, since the beach is not protected by a reef.

A second major ritual occurs in Bugbug every two years on the full moon of the fourth month (around October). Four villages (Bugbug, Jasi, Bebandem and Ngis) participate in a ritual "war of the gods," which is in fact the enactment of an old legend:

The god of Bugbug had three daughters and one son. One of the daughters was to marry the god of Bebandem but she eloped with the god of Jasi. To appease the former, the god of Bugbug gave his second daughter and son to him, and the third daughter was married off to the god of Ngis. The war is to resolve the dispute, and the ritual battle takes place near the temple on top of Gumang Hill.

— *Danker Schaareman*

Opposite: *An aerial view of the Candidasa lagoon.* **Above:** *A festival atop Bukit Gumang, a sacred hill just to the east of Candidasa.*

TENGANAN

Exclusive Community of God's Chosen

Time is reckoned differently in Tenganan Pegringsingan. Here, each new day begins with 21 deep, throbbing drumbeats and lasts until the same pulsating tones are struck the next morning. Tourists arrive when the sun is at its zenith and the valley is glowing with light. They leave towards evening, when the all-important religious ceremonies commence. A month in Tenganan lasts exactly 30 days. Modifications to the calendar are needed to adjust to the lunar-solar year; altogether 15 days are added every three years.

The ancient, ritualistic Bali Aga ("original Balinese") society of Tenganan has now opened up and become accessible to non-Tenganese — especially since its festivals have been publicized, and since the village itself has become known as a result of its proximity to the new beach resort at Candi Dasa. Gone are the days when it was isolated and difficult of access.

It is said that all footprints of visitors to Tenganan were once literally wiped out once they left. Now the village faces new and different problems. It needs more parking space for the cars, minibuses and limousines that tourism brings, and the art shops which distort the community's divine plan now have to be placed outside the village gates.

Microcosm of the universe

The *desa adat* Tenganan Pegringsingan is a microcosmic reflection of the macrocosm — an *imago mundi*. According to this divine plan, it is arranged systematically both in its delimitation from the outside world, as well as in its separation into distinct private and public areas within the village precincts itself.

The village is laid out in a large rectangle measuring some 500 m by 250 m, encircled by natural boundaries and walls. Three public corridors rise in terrace-like fashion, running along a north-south axis from the sea toward the sacred volcano Gunung Agung. There are six lengthwise rows of compounds; the pairs located in the center and to the west are striking because of their closed housefronts, which resemble palm-leaf covered longhouses.

The buildings and areas for public use are situated on the central axes of the central and western streets. There are a number of walled temple areas, longhouses, smaller pavilions, rice granaries and shrines here, all

KAL MULLER

TOM BALLINGER

of which suggest a strong communal life with pronounced ritual ties. This is where the 300 inhabitants of Tenganan Pegringsingan live.

In the eastern compounds of the *banjar pandé* live those who have been banished from the village, together with those whose customs are more like the majority of Hindu-Javanized Balinese. Labor in the surrounding gardens and communal ricefields behind the hills is performed by them, or by tenant farmers from neighboring villages who receive half of the crop yield. With approximately 1000 hectares of arable land belonging to it, Tenganan is one of the richest land-owning communities in all of Bali.

Divine origins

Unlike other Balinese villages, Tenganan traces its origins and its social institutions back to a written source — a holy book known as the *Usana Bali* (a chronicle of Bali). According to this text, the Tengananese have been chosen by their creator, Batara Indra, to honor his royal descendants through communal offerings and sacrifices. It states, furthermore, that descendants of the original villagers have been chosen to administer the surrounding lands, a consecrated place of devotion and ritual, and to use all available means to keep them pure.

The concept of territorial and bodily purity and integrity plays an exceedingly important role in the village culture. It is reflected not only in many important rituals (purifications and exorcisms), but also in the idea that only if a person is healthy, physically as well as mentally, may he or she take part in rituals. No one with a disability and no outsider can be admitted to the *adat* organizations of the village.

As a result of this divinely ordained scheme, the original layout and social organization of the village may not be changed. Houses, compounds, gardens, village council and youth groups are to be left as the gods have created them. Should anything be changed or taken away, the curse of the gods would fall upon the village and its people would perish. Anyone guilty of not respecting the inherited order is banned from participating in village rites, and thus from sharing in communal property. In the gravest of cases, they are even banished from the village altogether. The *desa adat* is itself regarded as divine and almighty as far as the traditional social order is concerned.

Exclusive membership

It is not surprising that a community regarding itself as divinely blessed would strictly define its own members and place restrictions on outsiders. This exclusivity is

Opposite: The perang pandan *ritual battle in Tenganan.* **Above:** *This swinging ritual, believed to unite sun and earth, may have Vedic antecedents.*

expressed very clearly in the qualifications needed to enter the all-village council or *krama desa*. Only men and women without mental or physical defects who were born and live in Tenganan, having duly passed all ritual stages of initiation by the time they marry, are eligible to join the council. The practice of village endogamy (marrying within the village) also has a restrictive effect. With respect to the *krama desa*, endogamy is an absolute requirement. Men with second wives or wives from outside the village may not become members. The same is true for women who have violated the marriage rules.

Newly-weds take their place at the lowest end of a hierarchical seating in the huge *bale agung* — the forum and sacred meeting pavilion of the village council. With the entrance of a new couple, the parents retire and everyone moves up a step, receiving new ritual responsibilities. The layout of the 50-meter-long hall is eminently suited to the numerous rites that bring together the gods, ancestors and villagers. Here, members of the *krama desa* meet, dressed in ritual clothing, for communal meals with deities and ancestors, whom they worship with prayers, offerings, dances and music. In many cases, youths will take part in the performance of these rituals, either because the girls have been formally invited by the married women to dance before the *bale agung,* or because the village council requires one of the sacred iron *game-*

lan orchestras (*selunding*) maintained by the boys' organizations to be struck.

For such a society to work, a long initiation period is needed, allowing its members to prepare for their complex ritual duties and activities within the village council. When children enter a youth club, between the ages of 6 and 8, they go through a "school of life" in which the behavior required for participation in the *krama desa* is learned, and where the manual skills and esoteric formulas needed for rituals can be practiced.

The three boys' associations of the village are named after the location of their assembly houses, located on three consecutive terraces along the western street. There are also three girls' clubs, with a strict and formal relationship concerning mutual help, exchange of gifts, offerings, meals and entire rituals existing between them. A girl must be at least 7 years of age to join a *sekaha daha* or girls' club, whose meetings are held in the compounds of retired village elders.

Some years ago, the girls would still bring their looms to the meeting houses so they could practice weaving. In the 11th month of the Tenganan year, they had to bring yarn and bast along to their clubhouses to undergo instruction in the exceedingly complex art of double *ikat*. Unfortunately, this custom, so vital to the preservation of the local textile craft, has been abandoned for several years.

The sacred geringsing cloths

Ritual clothing is an indispensable part of the sacred order of Tenganan Pegringsingan. The double *ikat* cloths known as *geringsing* produced here rank among the masterworks of traditional textile art, providing a further sign of the divinely-ordained exclusivity of the society. The cloths are said to have been directly inspired by Batara Indra, the Creator, who was once sitting in a tree enjoying the beauty of the moon and stars. While contemplating the heavens, he decided to teach the women of Tenganan the art of *ikat* patterning. Since then, the community has obeyed a divine commandment to wear *kamben geringsing* or double *ikat* cloths. In this way, the villagers evince purity and the ability to perform rituals — qualities which these clothes protect from harmful outside influences.

Above: *Members of a boys' association in Tenganan wearing the magical* geringsing *cloths that are said to protect the wearer from baleful influences.* **Right:** *Weaving of the* geringsing *is still done on traditional back-strap looms.*

Festival of the swings

Among the most important religious duties of the villagers of Tenganan is the festive reception of gods and ancestors, who from time to time descend to their megalithic thrones and altars in and around the inner village precincts. The presence of deities and ancestors is of great significance, above all during the fifth month of the Tenganan year, Sasih Sambah, for it is then that the universe, the village and the religious community are renewed and given strength through the performance of extensive, solemn rites.

The ceremonies that take place then are reminiscent of old Vedic swinging rites performed during the *mahavrata* winter solstice celebration, which focuses on Indra. The swinging unites sun and earth, and together with textile techniques and recent genetic research, suggests that Tenganan may be connected with an immigration from east or southeast India during Vedic times.

In a legendary account, the people of Tenganan are said to have arrived here while searching for the favorite horse of the king of Bedahulu. Although it was dead when found, the king showed his gratitude by promising to give the searchers all land in the area where the horse's decomposed body could be smelt. So a representative of the court, accompanied by the village head, walked around the huge area which today forms Tenganan, finding that in fact the horse's flesh could still be smelled for quite a distance. After the court officer had departed, the cunning village chief pulled a piece of bad-smelling horse meat from under his waist-band. The remnants of the horse are believed to be scattered around the village as megalithic monuments.

There are other indications, too, that the people of Tenganan have not always lived here. A copper inscription dated A.D. 1040 speaks of a relationship between the powerful governor from Java, a certain Buddhist reformer Mpu Kuturan in Silayukti (near Padangbai), and a nearby village named "Tranganan" that was then on the coast at Candi Dasa and later moved to the interior.

Proof that the villagers of Tenganan moved from the seaside to their present location is provided in the design and placement of the original altars (*sanggah kamulan*) in the house compounds. In other parts of Bali this altar is always built in the corner facing east and toward the mountains. In Tenganan it is placed towards the sea.

When a member of the community of Tenganan dies, his or her body is not cremated. Once the sun is past the zenith, the corpse is carried from the compound to the cemetary. At the grave the body is undressed, then it is returned to Mother Earth (Pertiwi), head seaward and face down.

— Urs Ramseyer

AMLAPURA AREA

Tour of Bali's Fascinating Eastern Tip

Once the seat of the powerful Karangasem court, the district capital of Amlapura at the eastern end of Bali is now a rather sleepy market and administrative town. Formerly known simply as Karangasem, the town was given its present name after the eruption of Mt Agung in 1963 nearly wiped it out; black lava flows can still be seen from the road on the way into town. There are several interesting palaces here, and the surrounding countryside contains superb scenery and some of the most interesting traditional villages in Bali.

The palaces of Karangasem

The main attraction of Amlapura is its several traditional palaces or *puri*. There is a western, a northern, a southern and an eastern *puri* as well as several others — all still occupied by members of the royal family. Of these, only the **Puri Kangin** (the eastern palace)

COURTESY LEIDEN UNIVERSITY LIBRARY

on the main road to the market is easily visited. This is worth a look, as it gives a vivid impression of how local royals used to live. The palace buildings themselves are in fact an eccentric blend of Chinese and European details set in what is essentially a traditional Balinese compound — with several pavilions and rooms surrounded by pools and connected by walkways. The main hall is called the "Balé London" and the furniture curiously bears the crest of the British royal family. One can even rent rooms here — the perfect accommodation for the aspiring aristocrat.

The ruling family of Karangasem traces its ancestry back to the 14th century Hindu-Javanese empire of Majapahit, claiming to be direct descendants of a certain Batan Jeruk who was Prime Minister of Bali during the 16th century. There is also a tale concerning the dynasty's divine origin.

A woman who lived near the palace was once overheard talking to a stranger in her house. When asked who it was, she replied that it was the god of Mt Agung. After some time, the woman became pregnant, and not long afterwards a miraculous fire descended from the mountain to the woman's house. She soon gave birth to a son atop a hill to the east of the town — this son, the "god of the eastern hill," is said to be the founder of the royal Karangasem line.

Karangasem conquered Lombok in the 17th century and in turn became a vassal of the neighboring island in the 18th and 19th centuries. As a result, there are today several Sasak settlements in and around Amlapura, and these have had a significant influence on the culture of the area. Family and trading relations with Lombok still exist until the present day, and intermarriages are common.

When Lombok was occupied by the Dutch in 1894, Karangasem was transferred to Dutch control as well. Nevertheless, the ruler of Karangasem was kept on as "governor" of the region, and his status was confirmed in 1938 when the Balinese kingdoms were granted partial self-rule. After independence in 1945, these princely realms vanished and were replaced by the present-day *kabupaten* or regencies. Until 1979, however, the regent or *bupati* of Karangasem was a prince of the royal house, and was still considered "raja" by most people in the area.

Left: The ruler of Karangasem, I Gusti Bagus Jelantik, with child, ca. 1918. **Right:** Ruins of the magnificent royal pleasure palace at Ujung, with Mt Agung in the distance.

Even today, members of the royal family participate in rituals held in the nearby villages.

Ujung and Mt Seraya

Apart from being a man well-versed in letters, the last king of Karangasem, Anak Agung Anglurah Ketut, was also an assiduous builder of opulent pleasure palaces for his frequent excursions to the countryside with his wives and children. In fact, during his lifetime he built no less than three different "water palaces" — at Ujung, Tirtagangga and Jungutan respectively.

Ujung, 8 km to the southeast of Amlapura, is a small fishing village with distinct Islamic and Hindu-Balinese quarters. The lavish palace complex here — a vast pool bordered by small pavilions with a massive stained-glass and stucco bungalow in the center — was completely destroyed by the eruption of Mt Agung and subsequent earthquakes. Little else but a few sculptures and portals remain, though there are plans afoot to restore the palace to its original condition as a tourist attraction.

Just before Ujung there is road to the left leading toward **Bukit Kangin** ("eastern hill") where there is a panoramic view of the area and a temple dedicated to the founder of the royal dynasty. On the full moon of the fifth month (usually in November) several villages with close ties to the ruling dynasty participate in a festival at this temple.

From the beach at Ujung, a new road climbs up to the village of **Seraya**, perched on the southern flanks of Mt Seraya — Bali's easternmost peak (1175 m). This is one of the most arid areas in Bali, and the road here hugs the hills high above the coast, offering splendid panoramas of the surrounding terrain and across the sea to distant Lombok. From Seraya, the road continues around the mountain and descends gradually on the northern side to the fishing and salt-making village of **Amed**. Though a distance of only about 30 km, the entire drive takes several hours as the road is quite steep and winding.

From Amed one can return to Amlapura or continue along the northern coastal route through the villages of Kubu and Tulamben toward Singaraja. The north coastal region suffered greatly from the eruption of Mt Agung, and was transformed into an arid wasteland with dramatic, black lava flows reaching right down to the sea. Until well into the 1980s the road was not very serviceable, but it is now in very good condition and offers beautiful views of the rugged northern slopes of Mt Agung. There is also excellent diving in the coastal reefs off **Tulamben**, where the sunken wreck of a WW II ship provides a home for a host of colorful marine life.

Refreshing pools at Tirtagangga

The cool, spring-fed pools at Tirtagangga — which literally means "Ganges Water" and

AMIR SIDHARTA

refers to the sacred river of the Hindus — are located some 15 km north of Amlapura along the main road toward Singaraja. A dip in the pools is deliciously refreshing after a long drive, and they are surrounded by a captivating landscape of terraced ricefields. The village itself is small and quiet, and is a good place to pause and rest for several hours or even several days — to take advantage of the many delightful walks from here.

One can stay overnight inside the pool complex itself, known officially as **Tirta Ayu** ("lovely waters"), where a son of the last king of Karangasem operates a small homestay. Another exciting possibility is to stay in a small lodging on a nearby hill with a view over the famous Tirtagangga rice terraces.

Trekking around Tirtagangga

From here there are a number of excellent treks through the surrounding countryside. One of the most spectacular begins to the north in the village of **Tanaharon**, quite high on the slopes of Mt Agung. One may reach it on foot or by car. To get there, follow the main road north from Tirtagangga in the direction of Singaraja for several kilometers, then turn left at **Abang** and follow a small climbing road up to the end. From here one may continue on foot, enjoying the broad panoramas in all directions and the thick, tree-fern vegetation. There is no short-cut back to Tirtagangga, and it is best not to get too far off the main path, as the ravines are quite steep and dangerous.

Another, less taxing trek begins in Ababi, just 2 km north of Tirtagangga on the main road. Turn left in this village and follow the road through Tanah Lengis to Budakling. On foot one can also reach this road by climbing the low hill behind the Tirtagangga spring.

Ababi is an old-fashioned village, and in the fourth Balinese month (around October) a major ritual is held in the village temple — an agricultural ceremony marking the end of the dry season. In **Tanah Lengis**, which is closely linked to Ababi, are several unusual music clubs. One is an *angklung* orchestra and the other is a so-called *cekepung* group.

Cekepung is a form of music known only in Karangasem and on Lombok, from where it originates. It is performed by a group of men. The leader begins by singing a text in Sasak (the language of Lombok); this is then paraphrased by another man in Balinese. After a while the other men join in, and perform a very rhythmic, interlocking song without words — imitating the interplay, rhythm and punctuation of a *gamelan* orchestra with their voices. Villagers drink palm-wine during and in between the singing. Both groups perform commercially, and will sometimes play for visitors in Tirtagangga.

One enters **Budakling** just after crossing a broad river, which is almost completely dry during the dry season. This village is well-known for its Buddhist brahman priests, of whom there are only a dozen or so left in Bali (whereas their Sivaite colleagues number in the hundreds). It is also a famous center for gold and silver smithing. Here are produced jewelry pieces of very high quality, which are occasionally offered for sale in Tirtagangga. It is possible to obtain or order pieces in the village, and Budakling also has several iron-smiths who produce household and agriculture tools.

To go back to Tirtagangga from here, turn left at the first crossroads in Budakling and ask for **Padangkerta**, a few km south on the main Amlapura-Tirtagangga road.

For a longer trip, continue westward to the important market village of **Bebandem**. Entering from this direction, the traveler encounters ironsmiths by the side of the road, who usually work in the mornings on market days (every three days), producing cheap knives, *keris* daggers and cock-fighting

ERIC OEY

Left: *Refreshing pools at Tirtagangga.* **Right:** *Dramatic rice terraces near Abang.*

spurs. There is also an important cattle market here, and once back on the main road one has the choice of going back toward Tirtagangga, south to Candidasa, east to Amlapura or west to Besakih and Rendang.

A walk due east from Tirtagangga through the ricefields brings you to **Pura Lempuyang**, one of the *sad kahyangan* or six main temples of the whole of Bali, perched at the summit of Mt Lempuyang (1058 m). Pass the villages of **Kuhum** and **Tihingtali** and continue on to **Basangalas**. From here, it is a strenuous climb up to the temple. Basangalas can also be reached by car from a turn-off to the north of Tirtagangga at Abang.

A large temple festival takes place at Lempuyang every 210 days on Thursday of the week Dunggulan. Ten days later, on Sunday of the week Kuningan, there are festivals in the temples of origin (*pura puseh*) in many villages around Basangalas, including Lempuyang. These feature fine *rejang* dances by the unmarried girls of the village accompanied by various orchestras.

Traditional villages near Amlapura

The several neighboring villages of Subagan, Jasi, Bungaya, Asak and Timbrah just to the southwest of Amlapura are all very traditional — resembling the archaic Bali Aga village of Tenganan in many ways. Like Tenganan, Asak for instance is a caste-less village.

Bungaya, on the other hand, has groups of brahmana but they do not take part in village rituals.

These villages may be reached quite easily by car or on foot. Coming from Candidasa and Bugbug, turn left at the village of **Perasi** onto a picturesque backroad leading to Bebandem via Timbrah, Asak and Bungaya. Jasi and Subagan lie on the main road between Perasi and Amlapura. There is also a lovely backroad connecting Subagan with the Asak and Bungaya road.

The village of **Jasi**, close to the beach, is well known for its earthenware casks, bowls and pots. They may be purchased locally as well as at the Amlapura and Klungkung markets. **Subagan** has an Islamic quarter that was completely leveled in 1963 when Mt Agung erupted.

Timbrah, **Asak** and **Bungaya** are villages with several fascinating festivals. The biggest and best-known is called *usaba sumbu* — held once a year with certain variations in all three villages (as well as in Perasi, Bugbug and Bebandem). This is an agricultural rite in honor of the rice goddess, Batari Sri, and the god of material wealth, Batara Rambut Sedana as well as the deified ancestors and other village deities. It is held in Bungaya around the full moon of the 12th Balinese month (May or June), in Timbrah during the waning moon of the second month (July or August), and in Asak around the full moon of

the first month (check a Balinese calendar).

Several exquisite dances are performed during the daytime. A *rejang* is performed by unmarried girls, an *abuang* by unmarried boys, and several different groups take part in mock-fight dances called *gebug*. The dancers are beautifully dressed in costly ritual costumes, and the gold headdresses of the girls in Asak and Bungaya are justifiably famous.

The dances are accompanied by some very rare and unusual music. Especially noteworthy is the sacred *selunding* orchestra consisting of iron metallophones that are rarely played, and then only for specific ceremonies. A particular *selunding* in Bungaya, for instance, is only struck once every ten years during a huge temple festival.

In Asak, Timbrah and Bugbug, the *selunding* is played once every year during the *usaba sumbu*. Other interesting festivals are held on Galungan in Timbrah, on Kuningan in Asak and Bungaya, and during the seventh and eighth lunar months (January or February) in Asak and Subagan. New years' festivals (March or April) are worth attending in any of these villages.

Spectacular backroad to Besakih

The backroad leading from Amlapura up to Rendang and thence to Besakih is one of the most scenic in Bali. From Amlapura the first villages passed are Subagan and Bebandem (see above). Shortly after Bebandem there is an intersection, and a turn to the right takes you to the small village of **Jungutan**, site of the third famous Karangasem water palace.

Jungutan is not so much a palace, actually, as a small complex of ponds situated in a quiet and relaxing setting — a nice spot to stop and walk around. Back at the intersection, the road continues west through **Sibetan**, well-known throughout Indonesia for its delicious *salak* — a crisp, tart fruit encased in a rind that has the look and feel of snakeskin. The winding road through Sibetan

is lined by densely-planted salak palms and trucks may be seen loading them for market. These fruits are better here than anywhere else in Indonesia — peel the scaley skin and enjoy the thirst-quenching pulp.

Soon after the *salak* plantations, a road to the left leads a short distance to **Putung,** where there is a small bungalow hotel and restaurant with a view of the coast (see above).

The main road continues on from here to **Duda,** at the foot of Mt Agung. This village holds a large festival in the temple of origin on the full moon of the fourth month (around October). After Duda there is another intersection. The road to the left from here goes through Sidemen to Klungkung. Straight ahead is to Rendang and Besakih.

Sidemen is well worth a visit. The scenery is gorgeous, and traditional varieties of Balinese rice are grown. There is a good homestay with a magnificent view down across a valley of rice terraces to the sea and south Bali. Closeby is a weaving factory where high quality traditional textiles (*endek*) are produced. In Sidemen there are also several places where the costly *kain songket* is woven from silk, with gold and silver threads added to create the patterns.

The road onwards to Rendang leads first through the old village of **Selat**, an area that suffered badly from the eruption of Mt Agung. It is possible to climb the volcano — a sign reading "Gunung Agung, 10 km" marks a turn-off where a road leads a good way up the sacred mountain. Don't attempt the climb unless you are well-prepared and have a guide. If you speak Indonesian, guides are locally available but be sure to bring along food, water and warm clothing for the steep climb to the summit. At 3142 m, this is Bali's highest peak and it gets quite cold. Only to be attempted between July and October.

The village just after Selat, **Padangaji**, is known for its *gambuh* association. *Gambuh* is a classical dance-drama with slow and stately music that is only irregularly performed these days. The road then continues on through **Muncan**, past one of the most exciting ricefield landscapes in Bali. The terraces are at their most spectacular when flooded, just before the young rice is transplanted. Finally at Rendang you arrive at the main Klungkung-Besakih route; a turn to the right will bring you up to Bali's "Mother Temple."

— *Danker Schaareman*

Opposite: *The slow and stately Asak rejang.*
Above: *The Usaba Sumbu festival, also in Asak.*

BESAKIH

Bali's Lofty 'Mother Temple'

Driving up to Besakih from Menanga, the silver-grey cone of Mt Agung looms above, its summit still bare from the ravages of the 1963 eruption. At 3142 meters, this is the highest peak on Bali, and a major locus of divine power in the Balinese cosmos. The huge temple located here, **Pura Besakih**, is the greatest of all Balinese sanctuaries — the most sacred and powerful of the island's innumerable temples. For this reason, it has always been associated also with state power. It lies at an altitude of 900 meters on the southwestern slope of the mountain, offering spectacular views over the whole of southern Bali.

Pura Besakih is not a single temple but a sprawling complex consisting of many separate shrines and compounds, united through ritual and history into a single sanctuary. There are 22 temples in all, spread along parallel ridges over a distance of more than a

kilometer. The highest of these, Pura Pengubengan, lies amidst beautiful groves in a state pine forest. Most of the temples, however, cluster around the main enclosure, Pura Penataran Agung.

In this same area there are many ancestral temples (*pura padharman*) supported by a particular clan group. Four public temples also form a distinct sub-group (*catur lawa* or *catur warga*) and are associated with certain kin groups. Local kin groups of Besakih villagers also have temples here.

It is busy almost every day at Besakih. Balinese often come in order to obtain holy water for ceremonies back in their home villages as a symbol of the god's presence. For most major rituals, the witness of the god of Gunung Agung/Pura Besakih is required. Balinese come to Besakih also at the end of the long series of funeral rites, after the post-cremation purification of the soul has taken place, to ready the soul for enshrinement in the family house temple. In all cases, the worshipper is sure to pay reverence at the triple lotus shrine of the Pura Penataran Agung.

The symbolic center

Pura Penataran Agung, the "Great Temple of State" is the symbolic center of the Besakih complex. Originating probably as a single prehistoric shrine, its six terraces suggest a history of successive enlargements, the latest being in 1962. In all, there are 57 structures in the temple, about half of which are devoted to various deities. A study of these provides a glimpse of important developments in the history of the temple.

The *meru* or pagodas were probably introduced no earlier than the 14th century, whereas the lotus throne (*padmasana)* dates from about the 17th or even 18th century. With the introduction of the *padmasana*, the ritual focus of the temple seems to have shifted from the upper terraces to the second lower terrace. The *padmasana* is now the ritual center of Pura Penataran Agung and of the Besakih complex as a whole.

The three seats in the lotus throne are dedicated to the godhead in his tripartite form as Siwa, Sadasiwa and Paramasiwa or, more commonly in the popular tradition, to Brahma (right), Siwa (center) and Wisnu (left). These deities are associated with the colors red, white and black respectively. Behind the *padmasana* lies the Bale Pasamuhan

Left: *A* baris *dance at Besakih.* **Right:** *The entire complex of 22 temples seen from the air.*

Agung where the gods of the Besakih temples take residence during major rituals.

Of all the present structures in the temple, only one or two predate the great earthquake of 1917. Although visitors are normally not allowed inside the main courtyard, there are several vantage points from where one can get good views of the shrines.

Temple categories

A dual structure underlies the Besakih sanctuary as a whole through a division of the sacred areas into two parts. Pura Penataran Agung is the main temple "above the steps." Its counterpart "below the steps" is **Pura Dalem Puri**, the "Temple of Palace Ancestors." This small but very important temple, associated with an early dynasty of the 12th century, is dedicated to the goddess identified as Batari Durga, goddess of death and of the graveyard, as well as of magic power.

The Hindu Trinity of Brahma, Wisnu and Siwa is the basis of a three-part grouping that links the three largest temples. Pura Penataran Agung, the central temple, honors Siwa; **Pura Dangin Kreteg** ("Temple East of the Bridge") honors Brahma, and **Pura Batu Madeg** ("Temple of the Standing Stone") honors Wisnu. On festival days, banners and hangings in their colors represent these deities. Pura Batu Madeg in particular has a fine row of *meru*.

A five-way grouping links these three temples with two others, each being associated with a cardinal direction and a color. Pura Penataran Agung is at the center. Surrounding it are Pura Gelap (east/white), Pura Dangin Kreteg (south/red), Pura Ulun Kulkul (west/yellow) and Pura Batu Madeg (north/black). This five-way classification, the so-called *panca dewata*, is extremely important in Balinese Hinduism. At Besakih, however, it seems to have been a relatively late development, as it is not mentioned in Besakih's sacred charter, the *Raja Purana*, which probably dates from the 18th century.

The gods descend

The unity of the complex of 22 public temples becomes manifest, above all, in Besakih's great annual festival, the Bhatara Turun Kabeh or "Gods Descend Together" rite. This falls on the full moon of the 10th lunar month (*purnama kadasa*), in March or April. During this month-long festival, the gods of all temples on Bali take up residence in the main shrine at Besakih. Tens of thousands of people from all over the island come to wor-

ship at the triple lotus throne, and solemn rituals are conducted by brahmana high priests.

In terms of numbers of worshippers, the annual ritual at Pura Dalem Puri is also quite remarkable. Within the 24-hour period of this festival, soon after the new moon of the 7th lunar month (around January), vast crowds pay homage here, presenting special offerings with which to insure the well-being of family members whose death rites were completed the previous year.

But these great rituals are only the most important out of a total of more than 70 held regularly at the different temples and shrines at Besakih. Almost every shrine in Pura Penataran Agung, for instance, has its own anniversary, almost all of which are fixed according to the indigenous Balinese *wuku* calendar. The most important festivals, however, follow the lunar calendar. These include rituals conducted by brahmana priests at four of the five main temples, and also a series of agricultural rites culminating in two of Besakih's most interesting ceremonies — the Usaba Buluh and Usaba Ngeed, which center around the **Pura Banua** dedicated to Bhatari Sri, goddess of rice and prosperity. With the exception of the brahmana rituals mentioned above, most ceremonies at Besakih are conducted by Besakih's own *pemangku*.

State and temple

The performance of rituals and the physical maintenance of the temples demand considerable resources, and throughout the temple's history these have been at least partly provided by the state. During pre-colonial times, the relationship between state and temple was expressed in a largely Hindu idiom of religion and statecraft, but in the

Above: *A group of villagers visits Besakih. Most often, Balinese visitors come in order to procure holy water or to prepare a deceased relative's ashes for installation in their house temple.*

course of the 20th century this changed to one couched in legal and constitutional terms.

The earliest history of Besakih consists of legendary accounts that associate the temple with the great priests of the Hindu traditions in Bali, beginning with Rsi Markandeya. In the 15th century two ancient edicts inscribed on wood, now regarded as god-symbols of an important deity of Pura Penataran Agung, indicate heavy state involvement.

The Gelgel and Klungkung dynasties (15th to early 20th centuries) regarded Pura Besakih as the chief temple of the realm, and deified Gelgel rulers are enshrined in a separate temple here, called **Padharman Dalem**.

Through the turmoil and shifting politics of the 19th century, which saw the rise of Dutch power on the island, the temple was seriously neglected. The great earthquake of 1917 completed its destruction, but at the same time galvanized the Balinese, who then rebuilt the temple with Dutch assistance. Control was maintained by the princely houses, who were responsible for rituals and maintenance. After independence, the regional government of Bali took over responsibility. Only in recent years has the Hindu community itself taken on a greater share of the burden involved in the temple's upkeep.

Cosmic rites of purification

The involvement of the Balinese with Pura Besakih is at no time more in evidence than during the great purificatory rites known as Panca Walikrama and Eka Dasa Rudra. Ideally these are held every 10 and 100 years respectively, but in practice they have been irregular. The Panca Walikrama was held in 1933, 1960, 1978 and most recently in 1989.

The Eka Dasa Rudra, greatest of all rituals known in Balinese Hinduism, is an enormous purification rite directed to the entire cosmos, representd by the 11 (*eka dasa*) directions. Rudra is a wrathful form of Siwa, who is to be propitiated. It has been held twice this century, once in 1963, and again in 1979. The Eka Dasa Rudra of 1963, held at a time of great political tensions, was an extraordinary catastrophe, for right in the midst of the month-long festival Mt Agung erupted with violent destructive force for the first time in living memory. Such a strange coincidence prompted various interpretations, the most common being that the deity of the mountain was angry, perhaps over the ritual's timing.

According to certain sacred texts, the rite should be held when the Saka year ends in two zeros. Such was the case in 1979 (Saka 1900), and it was decided to hold the Eka Dasa Rudra once again. The mountain remained calm and hundreds of thousands attended the main day of celebration, including President Suharto. This marked Besakih's new-found status as the paramount Hindu sanctuary not only for Bali, but for all of Indonesia.

— *David Stuart-Fox*

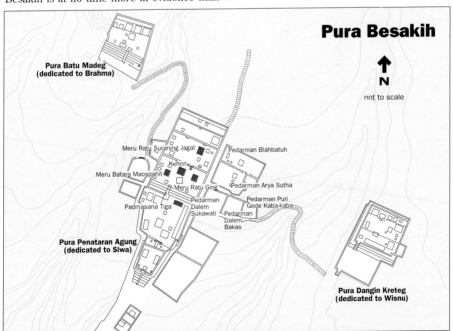

Pura Besakih

N

nnt to scale

Pura Batu Madeg
(dedicated to Brahma)

Meru Ratu Suraning Jagat

Kehon

Meru Batara Maospahit

Meru Ratu Ging

Padmasana Tiga

Pedarman Dalem Sukawati

Pedarman Blahbatuh

Pedarman Arya Sutha

Pedarman Puri Gede Kaba-kaba

Pedarman Dalem Bakas

Pura Penataran Agung
(dedicated to Siwa)

Pura Dangin Kreteg
(dedicated to Wisnu)

PART VII

The North: Buleleng

The important and historic realm of Buleleng is a narrow strip of land running the entire length of the island. Bounded to the north by the Bali Sea, it shares borders with Karangasem to the east and with Jembrana, Tabanan and Bangli to the south. The spectacular chain of volcanoes that stretches right across the island for a distance of some 150 kms forms a natural frontier between Buleleng and all of the southern regencies. These mountains often appear as a distant backdrop, while at other times they seem to gently unfold right down to the coast. Lying between the mountains and the sea, Buleleng is a region of exquisite natural beauty..

In former times, the mountain range hampered contact with the rest of Bali, which in turn gave rise to Buleleng's discrete culture. Buleleng also differs geographically from south Bali: its climate is drier and wet rice cultivation is not as widespread. In the western portion of Buleleng much of Bali's fruit is produced, while the area is also renowned for the cultivation of coffee and cloves.

Buleleng today

The modern administrative unit of Buleleng consists of nine *kecamatan* (sub-districts). It covers almost a third of Bali's total surface area, is more than half again as large as any other *kabupaten,* and has the second largest population (after Badung) — with some 517,000 inhabitants.

In former times, Buleleng was the site of Bali's major port, and was therefore the island's traditional point of contact with the outside world. Even today, there are many Muslims and Chinese here (though there are now many more in Denpasar), and the main city of Singaraja has a feeling that is quite dif-

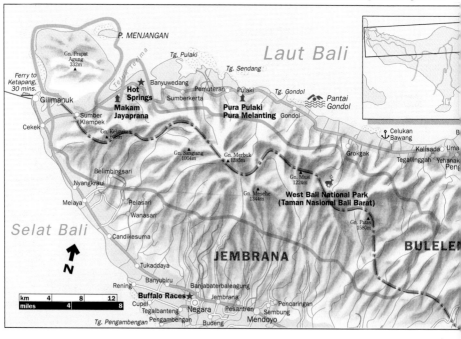

ferent from any other town in Bali.

Since the main harbor was relocated to Benoa in south Bali and especially since the removal of many government offices from Buleleng to the south in recent years, there has been quite an exodus of government employees and skilled workers, and, as a result, a corresponding diminution of the region's influence within Bali. But do not let this situation mislead you — Buleleng was never a sleeping giant, as its vibrant history and rich cultural legacy attest.

Buleleng history and culture

According to local historical texts, Buleleng rose to prominence in the second half of the 17th century under Ki Gusti Ngurah Panji Sakti, founder of the Buleleng dynasty. During his reign Buleleng conquered territory both in Bali and in east Java and became a major power broker in the region. But its glory soon waned under the reign of Panji Sakti's great-grandchildren, whose rivalry enabled the ruler of Karangasem to usurp the throne. In 1823 Buleleng successfully revolted against Karangasem, although its independence was to be short-lived.

The Dutch, eager to establish a foothold in Bali, subjugated Buleleng in 1849, but only after suffering two military defeats at the hands of determined defenders. Even so, sporadic uprisings against the Dutch took place over the next two decades. Ironically, Dutch control of Buleleng brought the region into a position of great power once again, for Singaraja became the center of the Dutch administrative presence in Bali.

Dutch control of north Bali predated their conquest of the south by more than 50 years — consequently the Dutch presence is more in evidence here. Dutch architecture has influenced many buildings constructed during the colonial period, while the character of Buleleng's inhabitants tends to be more egalitarian and direct than that of their southern counterparts.

Culturally, as well, Buleleng has always been a leader. Famed in the traditional arts, Buleleng's dancers, musicians and singers have made a dramatic impact on south Bali in this century. The fast and furious *kebyar* style of music and dance, perfected in the south by Mario, originated in Buleleng. Following the Japanese occupation and the struggle for Indonesian independence, Buleleng's hegemony in the traditional arts began to wane. But as always, Buleleng has succeeded in re-emerging as a leading force, this time in modern expressions of Balinese culture such as the *drama gong* and creative *gamelan* compositions.

— *Raechelle Rubinstein*

Overleaf: *I Gusti Ngurah Ketut Jelantik, ruler of Buleleng (left), and a* pedanda *priest (right), both ca. 1857. Photos courtesy of the KITLV, Leiden.*

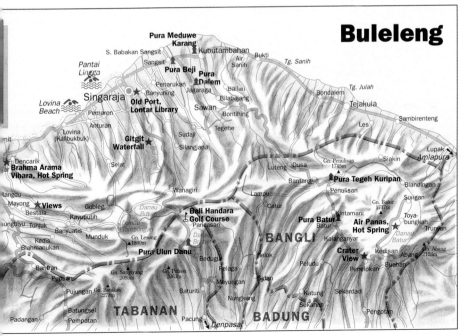

SINGARAJA AREA

An Old Port and a New Resort

Both the beauty and the cultural uniqueness of Buleleng make it rewarding to visit, and tourism continues to increase each year. If you like the sea and are looking for a place that is scenic, quiet, clean and culturally distinctive, include Buleleng on your itinerary.

The following information on the sights of Buleleng is divided into two sections. The first treats sights in and around the capital of Singaraja, located in the central part of Buleleng, and the region to the west. The following section concerns sights in the area to the east of the capital.

Tour of Singaraja

The sights of Singaraja reflect the city's successive historical incarnations — first as a royal court center, then as the center of Dutch commerce and administration on Bali, and now as a modern district capital.

Starting in the western end of the city visit **Pantai Lingga,** just before the Banyuasri bus station. The road to Pantai Lingga ends at Bukit Suci ("sacred hill"), an old Chinese cemetery bordering on the sea. Some of the graves are most unusual, such as that of an illustrious member of the Chinese community. Surrounded by a rail, it is guarded by lions and two life-sized black guards swathed in white turbans and bearing lances. Walk through the cemetery to Pantai Lingga, a swimming spot much favored by locals.

From Pantai Lingga head east to Jl. Dewi Sartika 42. This is the **Pertenunan Berdikari Hand Woven Cloth Factory**, specializing in beautiful replicas of antique Buleleng textiles, many in silk and all highly-priced. Watch thread being spun, cloth being woven, and buy direct from the manufacturer.

East of the main crossroads of the town lies Singaraja's main **Shopping District**. A few shops, such as "Miranda," sell tourist souvenir items, though generally-speaking the shopping is much better in south Bali. Interestingly, however, basic items tend to be cheaper here. The **Buleleng Market** (*pasar*) is down a narrow lane that runs behind a northeast group of buildings. Around dusk this area turns into an animated night market — not to be missed.

From the main shopping district it is just a short drive to the **Old Harbor**. The few old buildings lining the port date from the Dutch

colonial period. Have a look at the gigantic **Yuddha Mandalatama** independence monument with an Indonesian fighter bearing the flag. An unusual sight in the same vicinity is the **Chinese Temple** or *klenteng*, one of the few on Bali and evidence of this community's long presence in the town. While one may not enter the temple, a good view can be gained from within the compound. It houses many exquisite antique pots and cloths.

At the southern end of Singaraja, overlooking the junction of Jl. Ngurah Rai and Jl. Veteran, stands the imposing statue of Singambararaja — a winged lion who gazes imperiously over the city. The name "Singaraja" means "Lion King."

Heading east from here along Jl. Veteran, stop in at No. 22 on the right-hand side. This is the **Gedong Kertya**, a library founded by the Dutch in 1928 for the preservation of *lontar* (palm-leaf) texts collected in Bali and Lombok. A glass display case in the second room contains these traditional manuscripts, as well as several *prasasti* (ancient copper plate inscriptions). You may be fortunate to witness one of the employees copying an old *lontar* onto new palm-leaves, or even see the

now rare art of making *prasi* (drawings on palm-leaf).

Directly behind the Gedong Kertya (entry on the left) is **Puri Kawan** (the "Western Court") — part of the former palace of the king of Singaraja. It is currently the location of **Perusahaan Puri Sinar Nadiputra**, a textile mill where *sarung* are woven.

A few meters to the east is a major crossroads with a market on the southeast corner. To the southwest is the **Sasana Budaya** (the Buleleng Arts Center), and to the northeast lies **Puri Kanginan** (the "Eastern Palace"), formerly part of the Singaraja court and now a private residence.

Two sites to the south of Singaraja, Bratan and Gitgit, are well worth a visit. The village of **Bratan** a few kms away is a center for silversmithing. They make religious items and, less frequently, jewelry. You can watch the craftsmen at work and buy directly from them, or purchase their wares at shops located on the left-hand side of the main road.

If you have private transport, a visit to **Gitgit** is a must. Ten km south of Singaraja, this is the site of Bali's most dramatic waterfall. The road to Gitgit climbs steeply, offering fine views along the way. The waterfall, located about 500 m from the main road, is surrounded by lush vegetation. A fine, cooling mist hangs in the air, providing a refreshing welcome after the walk down. Dip your feet in the rushing river below. A rest area

Left: *A view of the old palace of Buleleng.* **Above:** *An aerial shot of the old harbor area of Singaraja, showing the Chinese temple and a few old Dutch buildings. During the Dutch times, the town was the administrative and commercial center of Bali.*

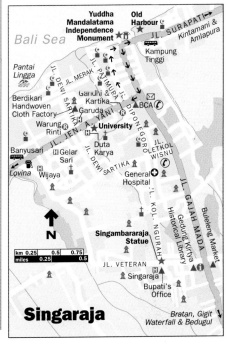

suitable for picnics has been built near the base of the falls.

To the west

The major attractions of western Buleleng are mainly concentrated between Singaraja and the village of Seririt, 21 kms west along the coast, as well as in the hills to the south.

Six km west of Singaraja, the popular new beach resort of **Lovina** is a long stretch of black sand bordering the coastal villages of Anturan, Tukad Mungga, Kalibukbuk, Kaliasem and Temukus. Numerous hotels and restaurants have sprung up here, lining the coast for some 7 km. The pace of life at Lovina reflects the calmness and safety of the sea. This is an excellent spot for swimming and snorkeling, particularly near the reef, and local boats are for hire. The sunsets at Lovina are particularly spectacular.

The name "Lovina" was coined by the last king of Buleleng. A convert to Christianity, he gave the name to a small tract of land that he purchased at Kaliasem, where he built the Tasik Madu ("Sea of Honey") Hotel in the 1960s. The name Lovina signifies the "love" that is contained "in" the heart of all people.

From Temukus it is 3 kms to the twin villages of **Dencarik** and **Banjar**. Pass through Dencarik to the neighboring village of Banjar Tegeha, home of the splendid Buddhist **Brahma Arama Vihara**. This *wihara* is the residence of Bali's only Buddhist monk and it plays a central role in Buddhist religious life and education. Opened in 1971, it replaces another founded in Banjar in 1958. It combines architectural and iconographic elements found throughout the Buddhist world. Quiet, cool, and set high in the hills, it commands a view down to the ocean. For 10 days each April and September the *wihara* is closed to the public while people from around the world assemble here to practice meditation. Visitors are requested to dress in a respectful manner, to speak softly, and to remove their shoes before entering.

Banjar is also the site of the so-called **Air Panas**, a sacred hot-spring. In 1985 the sulphurous spring water was channelled into a public bathing area consisting of 3 pools, set in a tasteful blend of jungle and garden. The water is a pleasant 38° C. There are changing rooms, showers, toilets and a restaurant.

If traveling by public transport, it is easy to reach the *wihara* and Air Panas from the main road. At the entrance to Dencarik and Banjar you can pay a man to take you there by motorbike.

Just 3 km after Banjar lies **Seririt**, the former commercial center of Buleleng. It was devastated by an earthquake in 1976 and was subsequently rebuilt. Seririt does not in itself warrant a visit. However, if you have private transport, there are two scenic drives worth taking that commence there.

Turn south at Seririt and follow the road

AMIR SIDHARTA

as it climbs through the villages of Bubunan, Petemon, Ringdikit and Rangdu. The further one ventures along this road the more impressive the scenery becomes. At Rangdu you may take a right turn at the T-intersection, which leads to Denpasar via Pupuan. Alternatively, you may choose to continue along the road from Rangdu to Mayong, Gunungsari, Banyuatis and Kayuputih. Spectacular views are to be had of rice terraces, coffee and clove plantations, the surrounding hills and, behind, the Buleleng coast. From Kayuputih it is a further 3 km to Munduk, located 1200 m above sea level. Although presently undergoing repair, the road between Kayuputih and Munduk is neither for the faint-of-heart nor for vehicles with bald tires. It comprises a series of narrow hair-pin turns and alternates between asphalt and dirt, with many deep potholes.

From Munduk the road runs atop hills that surround two lakes — **Tamblingan** and **Buyan** (the latter is also visible on the left-hand side of the approach to Singaraja from Bedugul). These lakes were one body of water until a landslide split them in 1818. The road then emerges at Wanagiri near Pancasari, just north of Bedugul.

Seririt to Teluk Terima

After Seririt the road leaves the coast, taking a sharp turn inland — for much of the rest of the journey to the west, the ocean is no longer visible, and the landscape is dominated by the mountains and hills of the south.

The sheltered harbor of **Celukan Bawang**, 16 km west of Seririt, now serves as the port for Buleleng's import and export trade.

Further west, near the village of Banyupoh, experience the delights of **Pantai Gondol**, a superb beach with clean sand and a beautiful coral reef. Pantai Gondol is a marvelous spot for swimming and snorkeling. It is also the site of a fishery research project.

A cluster of temples, the most important and easily accessible of which is **Pura Pulaki**, lies some 30 km past Seririt on the coast. Pura Pulaki is located in unusual terrain — a rock-face rises perpendicularly on the left-hand side of the road while the glimmering ocean laps the right-hand side. Pulaki, the home of monkeys who have a reputation for snatching bags and cameras, has undergone restoration and extension. The temple has a fascinating history that is linked to the legendary personage of Nirartha, a Javanese priest who migrated to Bali in the 16th century. It is told that prior to his arrival,

a village of 8000 people existed here. When Nirartha visited, the village leader requested a boon that Nirartha granted: the entire village was to be given supernatural knowledge that would enable it to attain an immaterial state. The invisible occupants of this village became known as *gamang* or *wong samar* and form the entourage of Goddess Melanting, whose abode is the nearby **Pura Melanting**.

The Balinese in these parts fervently believe in the existence of the *gamang* and routinely make offerings to them. For example, it is held that the entry of *gamang* into one's houseyard is heralded by the howling of dogs. Occasional reports even circulate of the sighting of *gamang* who have momentarily materialized — they are said to have no upper lip and carry a plaited bag over one shoulder.

The final stage of this journey through western Buleleng passes through **Taman Nasional Bali Barat**, the West Bali National Park. Past Labuhan Lalang jetty, boats to Menjangan Island can be hired (see "Bali Barat," page 224).

At Teluk Terima, a short distance down the road, visit **Makam Jayaprana**, the gravesite of Jayaprana. According to Balinese legend, Jayaprana was an orphan who was raised by the ruler of Kalianget village. As an adult he married the lovely Nyoman Layonsari from the neighboring village of Banjar. However, the ruler himself became enamoured of Jayaprana's bride and schemed to kill Jayaprana to have her for himself. He dispatched Jayaprana with an army to contain a band of pirates who he said had arrived in northwestern Bali. On arrival at Teluk Terima the ruler's minister killed and buried Jayaprana. When the ruler asked Layonsari to marry him, however, she chose to remain faithful to her husband and committed suicide.

The temple marking Jayaprana's grave is a long and steep climb but the views from about halfway across to Mt Semeru on Java, to Menjangan Island, and to Gilimanuk at the western tip of Bali, make the effort all worthwhile. The temple, which contains a glass case displaying statues of Jayaprana and Layonsari, is pure kitsch.

— *Raechelle Rubinstein*

Opposite: *A dramatic sunset over Lovina Beach. Having sprung up over the last decade as an "alternative" to Kuta/Legian and Sanur in the south, Lovina is known for its slow pace, serene atmosphere and budget accommodations.*

EASTERN BULELENG

Baroque Temples and Playful Reliefs

East Buleleng is noted for its archaic villages and its unique temple architecture, especially those found around the coastal area from Singaraja to Kubutambahan and the region to the south. Time and again visitors have labelled this style of architecture "baroque" — for so heavily-adorned with reliefs are the temples that it seems no piece of stone has been spared the chisel. Another feature of this style relates to the carving of the heads and hands both of temple statues and of characters in reliefs: they protrude to such a degree that it seems as if the figures lie in wait to pounce upon unsuspecting passers-by.

Singaraja to Air Sanih

Not far from Singaraja are some fine examples of charming old villages set amid lush vegetation — **Sinabun**, **Suwug** and **Sudaji**, reached along a scenic road by turning right at the T-intersection prior to Sangsit.

The best example of Buleleng baroque architecture is encountered at **Pura Beji** in the village of **Sangsit**, 8 km from Singaraja. A small sign on the left-hand side of the road announces the location of the temple. If you subscribe to the view that once you have seen one temple you have seen them all, then cast this misapprehension aside, for Pura Beji is a work of art.

Pura Beji is a *subak* temple, that is, a temple belonging to a rice irrigation association. The path leading to its great, arched entrance is flanked by two serpents. The front of the arch overflows with floral motives interpersed with demon heads. Its reverse is adorned with mask-like heads — some of which have been painted — *garuda* heads, and floral ornamentation. The main shrines have been carved just as elaborately. The beauty of this soft-pink sandstone temple is augmented by the large gnarled frangipani trees growing in its courtyard. Note the faded paintings on two pavilions, clearly the work of mastercraftsmen.

Further examples of old and interesting villages are found not far to the south of Sangsit at Jagaraga, Menyali and Sawan. To get there return to the main road and take the right-hand fork at the next T-intersection.

Jagaraga, the site of fierce fighting between the Dutch and Balinese in the late 1840s, bears no obvious signs of this strug-

RIO HELMI

gle. Visit Jagaraga's **Pura Dalem** on which the foreign presence in Buleleng has been captured with great humor. See, for example, the relief of a European riding in a car held up by a knife-wielding bandit. However, such caricatures are few; this temple is dominated by the terrifying widow-witch Rangda.

From Jagaraga drive through Menyali and follow the road as it climbs to **Sawan**, home of a well-known *gamelan* and iron smith who can be watched at work. Head for the center of Sawan and ask for directions.

Three km past the Jagaraga turn-off is the old village of Kubutambahan, best known for its **Pura Meduwe Karang** temple, which perches high up on the left side of the road. This temple is dedicated to the Lord of Dry Fields; those who cultivate dry fields worship here. The style of this temple, though more restrained than Pura Beji, is impressive.

Three tiers of stone statues which are said to number thirty-four figures from the *Ramayana* are stationed outside the temple. Floral motives predominate within the temple walls. Famous among the reliefs is an old one of a Dutch man riding a bicycle, its back wheel a lotus flower. It is located on the nothern wall of the inner shrine.

Seventeen km from Singaraja is the well-known beach resort of **Air Sanih**. Its main attraction is not its beach but rather a swimming pool located near the beach. Its icy water originates from a spring and is said to

flow at a rate of 800 liters per second. Not as popular with visitors as Lovina, Air Sanih with its accommodation and restaurants is, nevertheless, a good place to recuperate if you are traveling in the area.

Air Sanih to Tejakula

Situated on the coast 7 km east of Air Sanih is the important temple of **Pura Ponjok Batu**. Built atop a hill it affords a fine view of the ocean and some splendid frangipani trees. Cross the road to the small fenced-in shrine that encloses a number of stones. It is said that the 16th century priest Nirartha, drawn to the site by its immense beauty, sat on one of these stones as he composed poetry.

For a change from Hindu Bali visit the "Bali Aga" village of **Sembiran**, 6 km east of Pura Ponjok Batu. A 3 km drive along a steep, narrow winding road brings you into Sembiran. The layout of the village differs from that of predominantly Hindu villages. However, Hindu influence is nowadays visible in the form of temples. The village appears poor with its many mudbrick dwellings roofed with zinc sheets. There are excellent views back to the coast.

Tejakula, 3 km past the Sembiran turn-off, is the last important port of call in east Buleleng. Visit Banjar Pande, the ward of silversmiths, and watch them at work as they produce Balinese religious items and jewelry. Also be sure to see the famous horse bath. To get there, turn south at the T-intersection. This large, elaborate structure with its graceful arches has been turned into a public bathing area.
— *Raechelle Rubinstein*

Opposite and **left:** *The ornately carved gateway of the Pura Beji temple at Sangsit.* **Above:** *A relief on the Pura Meduwe Karang temple in Kubutambahan depicting Dutch artist W.O.J. Nieuwenkamp, who first visited Bali in 1904.* **Overleaf:** *The rice fields near Lukluk village, northwest of Denpasar. By Amir Sidhartha.*

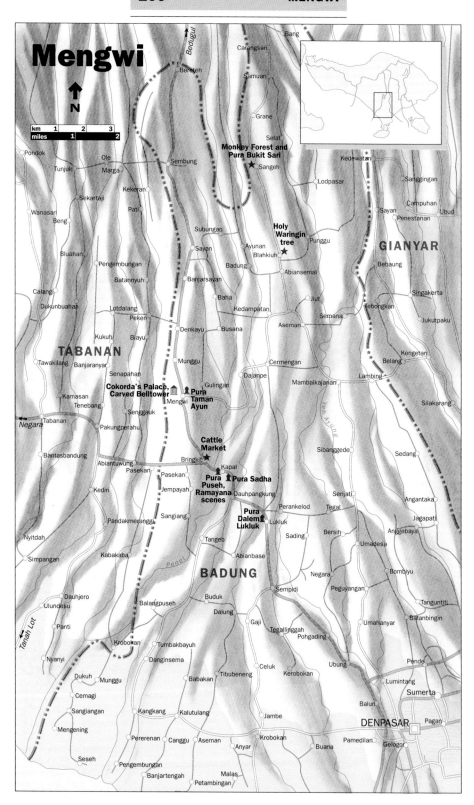

Mengwi

N

| km | 1 | 2 | 3 |
| miles | 1 | | 2 |

Bedugul

Bang

Carangsari

Beréteh

Samuan

Grané

Selat

Monkey Forest and
Pura Bukit Sari

Sangeh

Kedewatan

Lodpasar

Sanggingan

Campuhan

Sayan

Penestanan

Ubud

Pondok

Tunjuk

Ole

Marga

Sembung

Kekeran

Sekartaji

Pati

Wanasari

Beng

Bluahan

Pengembungan

Batannyuh

Calangi

Dukunbuahan

Lotdalang

Peken

Kukuh

Biayu

Subungan

Sayan

Ayunan

Badung

Blahkiuh

Holy
Waringin
tree

Punggu

GIANYAR

Bebaung

Abiansemal

Banjarsayan

Baha

Kedampatan

Singakerta

Jiut

Semana

Tebongkan

Jukutpaku

Denkayu

Busana

Aseman

Kengetan

Belang

TABANAN

Tawakilang

Banjaranyar

Munggu

Cermengan

Lambing

Silakarang

Senapahan

Dajanpe

Mambalkajanan

Cokorda's Palace,
Carved Belltower

Pura
Taman
Ayun

Gulingan

Mengwi

Kamasan

Tenebang

Senggauk

Negara

Tabanan

Pakungperahu

Yeh Ayung

Sibanggede

Sedang

Bantasbandung

Abiantuwung

Pasekan

Bringkit

Cattle
Market

Kapal

Pura Sadha

Angantaka

Pasekan

Serijati

Tegal

Jagapati

Kediri

Jempayah

Pura
Puseh,
Ramayana
scenes

Dauhpangkung

Perankelod

Anggebaya

Pandakmeranggi

Sangiang

Pura
Dalem
Lukluk

Lukluk

Sading

Bersih

Umadesa

Nyitdah

Tangeb

Bombiyu

Simpangan

Kabakaba

Abianbase

Negara

Peguyangan

Dauhjero

Balangpuseh

Buduk

Sempidi

Tanguntiti

Ulundesu

Panti

Dalung

Gaji

Tegallinggah

Umahanyar

Batanbingin

Penet

Pohgading

Krobokan

Tumbakbayuh

Nyanyi

Danginsema

Celuk

Kerobokan

Ubung

Pende

Tanah Lot

Dukuh

Munggu

Babakan

Tibubeneng

Lumintang

Sumerta

Cemagi

Balun

Sangiangan

Kangkang

Kalutulang

Jambe

DENPASAR

Pagan

Mengening

Pererenan

Canggu

Aseman

Krobokan

Pamedilan

Gelogor

Seseh

Anyar

Buaria

Pengembungan

Banjartengah

Malas

Petambingan

BADUNG

Lotdalang

Lambalkajanan

PART VIII

Former Kingdom of Mengwi

The once great realm of Mengwi arose with the weakening of Gelgel in east Bali around 1650. Descendants of a Javanese nobleman opposed the Gelgel ruler and moved to the village of Kapal around 1700. A certain I Gusti Agung Anom then married the daughter of I Gusti Panji Sakti, the mighty ruler of north Bali. He moved to Blayu, near Mengwi, and soon began to expand his territory.

All rulers of Mengwi became engaged in bitter power struggles, not only with the lords and rulers of neighboring realms, but also with members of their own clan. At this time, access to the north coast (via Marga) and to East Java was of great importance, because these areas lay on the vital shipping routes to the Moluccan spice isles. To have access to the southern sea — as antepode of the north — was also convenient for religious reasons. The ashes of the royal dead could be scattered here and purificatory and agricultural rituals could be held on the beaches.

The first ruler of Mengwi made a pilgrimage to Majapahit, land of the Javanese ancestors and of the sacred Mt Semeru. The second ruler did so as well, accompanied by the king of Klungkung. Mengwi and Klungkung remained allies from this time onwards, the ruler of Klungkung being called raja while the ruler of Mengwi was his *patih* (first minister).

In the 18th century, Mengwi expanded to the mountainous north around volcanic Lake Bratan, and to the west and east. Even the southern peninsula came under Mengwi's sway. The rulers mobilized people to construct huge irrigation works and transformed the landscape into a vast ricefield.

As the result of a power struggle, a branch of the family based in Munggu reigned sometime after 1740. Cokorda Munggu then founded a new center, Puri Gede, in the village of Mengwi. He also created a large state temple here, Pura Taman Ayun, and a sea temple, Pura Ulun Siwi, far to the south in Jimbaran.

Between 1740 and 1770, Mengwi thus became a replica of the divine Hindu cosmos. The ancestors and gods lived in the north atop Mt Pengelengan, and holy irrigation water descended from Lake Bratan in the rivers Sungi and Petan. In the south, the demonic forces of the sea were venerated at Ulun Siwi, while at the center of this axis — in Pura Taman Ayun — the rulers themselves were venerated as gods on earth.

A new power struggle around 1780 greatly weakened Mengwi, resulting in a loss of the western and southern villages. From 1829 onwards, I Gusti Agung Nyoman Mayun tried to expand again into Marga (now Tabanan) and Payangan (now Gianyar). These areas were very important since they had rich coffee plantations. Coffee became an important export in the second half of the 19th century, attracting Chinese merchants, and with them came opium. The new ruler also built new temples and created a new axis in his realm — from Pura Panataran Agung in Tiingan, near the coffee plantations in the northeast, to the coastal temple in Seseh in the southwest.

When in 1872 the third powerful ruler of Mengwi, I Gusti Agung Nyoman Mayun, died, the realm began to decay. There were plagues and crop failures, serious conflicts concerning irrigation systems and dams, and family intrigues. Moreover, Mengwi lost the support of Klungkung. In 1891 first Klungkung and then Badung, joined after a while by Tabanan and Bangli, defeated Mengwi. The profitable coffee enterprises, the opium trade and the ricefields were divided among the conquerors. The realm of Mengwi ceased to exist, though the palaces and temples remained.

The Dutch took control of south Bali after 1906 and the former realm was then divided for administrative purposes between the neighboring districts of Tabanan and Badung. However, the inhabitants still feel themselves to be "people from the realm of Mengwi."

— *Hedi Hinzler*

SIGHTS OF MENGWI

The Realm of Royal Architects

The rulers of Mengwi were famous for the temples they built. The oldest of these is **Pura Sada**, a few hundred meters south of the main road in Kapal, about 15 km to the west of Denpasar. The name *sada* may derive from the Old Javanese and Sanskrit term *prasada*, meaning a tower temple. There is indeed a huge shrine in the shape of a tiered tower in the inner court. The local inhabitants call this temple a *candi*, meaning a funerary monument for a deceased king.

According to the chronicles of the rulers of Mengwi, the son of the first Cokorda or Lord of Mengwi, I Gusti Agung Panji, received a shrine in this temple after his death around 1710. The divinity of the temple is Bhatara Jayengrat, the Divine World Conqueror.

At present the complex is venerated and maintained by the people of Kapal, irrespec-

tive of their caste or kin group. It was severely damaged during the earthquake of 1917 and was restored by the Archaeological Survey in 1948-49. The leader of the team of Balinese craftsmen was I Made Nama, and it is said that the construction of the tall tower was quite a challenge for him and his men.

The forecourt of the temple is large and spacious. A big tree grows at the center. The temple complex is surrounded by a wall of red brick constructed in the traditional way, without mortar. By rubbing one stone against the other, a fine powder crumbles from the surface layers. When water is added to it, the stones can be simply stuck together.

A split gateway on the west side leads to the central courtyard. A second, closed gateway with a three-tiered roof on the west gives way to the inner court, in which 16 shrines are to be seen. Right in front of the gateway is the *prasada* and behind it a square pedestal with 54 little stone seats. These are shrines for the *satya*, the servants, and facing them in one shrine together in the south are the three *mekel satya*, their leaders.

The following story is connected with them: A long time ago, when a king of Majapahit in East Java died, he was cremated and his ashes were carried by 54 men towards the sea in a bamboo tower (*bukur*) with a tiered roof. The tower was placed on a little boat (*kapal*), on which were seated the 54 followers (*patih*) of the deceased and three leaders (*mekel*). The boat, however, was stranded at sea.

This episode has been transposed to the temple and is symbolized in the stone tower (*candi*) at the center and in the pedestals with the 54 and 3 stone seats. The tower is, in fact, a replica of the bamboo cremation structure. Close to it, to the south, is a shrine with an 11-tiered roof, called "little garden with a pond" (*taman*). During the temple festival on Tumpek Kuningan, its "water" is used to bathe the god of the tower. This is in fact very convenient, because then a long tour outside the temple to a bathing place is not necessary.

Replicas of mountains which are important for south Bali (Agung, Batur and Batukaru) are found in shrines in the north and the east of the inner court. They are always provided with tiered roofs, called *meru*. The number of tiers should be odd, the highest being 11, which of course is only suit-

AMIR SIDHARTA

Left: *The 11-tiered* meru *of Pura Sadha.* **Right:** *The state temple of Mengwi, Pura Taman Ayun.*

RIO HELMI

able for the most important peak. In this case it represents Mt Agung.

The main purpose of placing a replica of a mountain or lake in a temple is to save the time and effort needed to actually visit them. This is necessary if one needs holy water for a ritual.

There are more shrines in the north and the east devoted to various divine kings, including a *padmasana* seat in which the god Siwa in his manifestation as Surya is venerated, and a little building in which a *barong* mask is kept.

Kapal to Mengwi

Along the northern side of the main road in **Kapal**, a grand *pura puseh* temple has relief panels on its outer wall depicting scenes from the *Ramayana*. The eyes of the monkeys and the demons are painted white, which was the fashion in the '20s and '30s in south Bali. The long *bale gede* pavilion, which is clearly visible from the road, was provided with fresh paint early in 1989. Shiny black-and-white and red-and-white checkered patterns dominate.

The cattle market in **Bringkit** just past Kapal is held once every three days. Here, herds of buffaloes and cows crowd the road and often block traffic along the Denpasar-Tabanan thoroughfare. To watch the traders bargaining over these beasts is as exciting as watching a cockfight in the old days.

The village of **Mengwi**, the former political center of the region, is reached via a turn-off to the right just past Bringkit. Traveling north for 3 km, one soon enters the town, and just west of the main crossroads, the palace of the present Cokorda is to be found. It is surrounded by grey walls and in the northern corner stands a large, square bell-tower with lovely carvings.

A hundred meters east of the crossroads lies the fabulous state temple of Mengwi, **Pura Taman Ayun**. Taman Ayun refers to a huge open space (*ayun*) representing a garden (*taman*). It was constructed under Cokorda Munggu around 1740, and was restored and enlarged in 1937. It "floats," as it were, surrounded by a moat with lotuses. This represents the heavens, where divine nymphs and ancestors relax in floating pavilions and enjoy themselves. At present, one may row round the sanctuary in a little rented boat.

The temple consists of a forecourt, a central court and a spacious inner court. A tall stone gateway with wooden doors leads into it. The inner court has rows of shrines on the north and east sides, and carved stone

pedestals with wooden pavilions to the west. The total number of structures is 27. Apart from the divine ancestor of the dynasty, the mountains so important to Mengwi (Agung, Batur, Batukaru, Pengelengan) are represented here by means of shrines with slender tiered roofs in the north and the east. Replicas of temples founded by the rulers of Mengwi atop these mountains (Pura Pucak) and bordering the sea (Pura Ulun Siwi), and of state temples built by former Mengwi rulers (Pura Sada, Pura Bekak) are to be found as well.

The basement of a pavilion in which the brahman priest prepares holy water during temple festivals (*bale pawedan*) is provided with a relief series on Arjuna, who meditated to receive a grant from the gods and was tested by means of nymphs who tried to seduce him. A recent addition is a colorful painting on the wooden wall of the *bale murda* pavilion. The *barong* from Seseh is displayed here during its visit to the temple a month after Galungan. It represents Siwa's demonic son Kala, who after having stolen the magic elixir (*amreta*), is chased by the host of gods.

Folktales in stone

Continuing east and then north from Mengwi toward the Monkey Forest at Sangeh, one passes along a quiet, beautiful road through the villages of Sibanggede, Abiansemal, Mambal and Blahkiuh. This area is famous for its stone sculptors, and all the temples, *kulkul* towers and palaces along this road are provided with beautiful sculptures, reliefs and stone ornaments.

Many temples in this area were restored or renewed after the earthquake of 1917, and then during the 1930s there was another res-

Above: *The pemangku or resident temple priest of Pura Taman Ayun.* **Right:** *The Monkey Forest at Sangeh. Beware — these rapscallions often steal handbags and jewelry from unsuspecting tourists.*

toration boom. Reliefs with scenes from the *Tantri* stories were favorite subjects. In these stories, which are of Indian origin, animals teach people how to live and about the good and evil they can expect from life, depending on their behavior.

There is the story, for example, of the lion-king of the forest and the bull, the ruler-to-be. They either have a peaceful conversation, face to face, or are engaged in a fight to the death. Then there are the two thoughtful geese holding a pole with a tortoise while flying away to a safe place, and the two jackals devouring an absent-minded tortoise who fell off the pole.

There is the story of the wicked heron Baka, surrounded by the bones of fish he promised to bring to a better lake, but then ate instead. Baka wanted to take a crab also, but this clever creature discovered the wickedness of the heron and pinched its neck off. And there is the story of the grateful crab and the brahman who rescued it. Later the crab rescued the brahman from a wicked bird and snake by pinching their necks off.

A few kms before Sangeh one passes **Blahkiuh**. This village possesses a huge and holy *waringin* tree on the eastern side of the crossroads. In 1989 the temporary stalls of the market at the foot of this tree were replaced by a concrete structure. In order to do this, part of the aerial roots had to be cut, which could only be done by a specialist with enough magic power to protect himself.

The monkey forest temple

In **Sangeh**, 15 km beyond Mengwi, lies the famous Monkey Forest and Pura Bukit Sari temple. This small temple may date from the founding of Mengwi, although it is also said that it existed in the 17th century. There is an old statue here of Garuda, the mount of Wisnu, who is also associated with the search for the magic elixer (*amreta*) to release his parents from their torments in hell.

The temple is surrounded by tall nutmeg trees with greyish-white trunks. These are very rare in Bali, and it is clear that they have been planted deliberately. Many monkeys roam about in the forest. They are quite a nuisance, for they attack visitors and steal their spectacles, jewellery, watches and hand-bags, and make life impossible for souvenir vendors in little shops closeby. It is said that some of Hanoman's monkey troops fell down with the top of Mt Mahameru on Sangeh when he tried to crush the evil demon king Rawana with it.

Far to the north of here on the slopes of Mt Pengelengan, to the east of Lake Bratan, is the **Pura Pucak** or sacred "Peak Temple" of Mengwi. It has various names — Pura Pucak Tiingan, Pura Panataran Agung — and marked the northernmost point of the realm under I Gusti Agung Nyoman Mayun in the first half of the 19th century.

— *Hedi Hinzler*

ERIC OEY

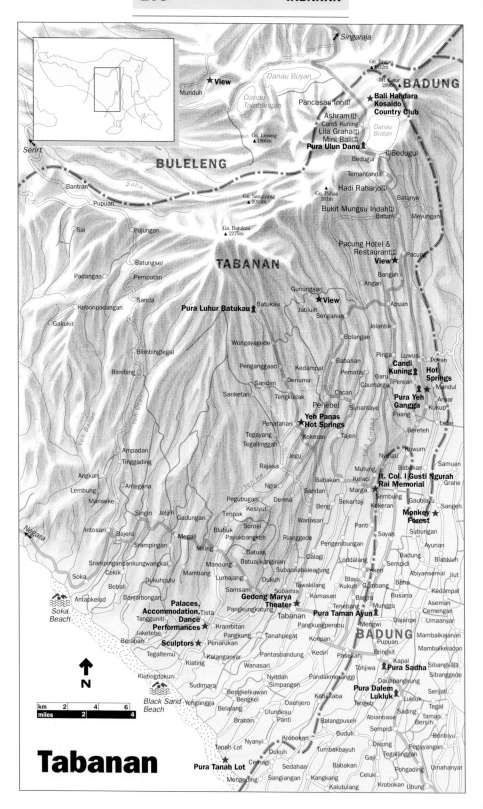

Tabanan

PART IX

Tabanan Regency

Tabanan encompasses a broad range of landscapes — from the lofty peaks in the north, including Mt Batukau and part of Mt Bratan with its dramatic volcanic lake, to the verdant rice plains in the south. Beautiful black sand beaches between Pasut and Klatingdukuh are now being developed for tourism, but apart from the famous seaside temple of Tanah Lot, this is not yet a touristed area.

Many rivers run north to south from the mountains to the sea. The roads follow their courses, with only a few running east to west. The main highway from Java passes through the gently-sloping southern part of Tabanan along the coast. This has turned Tabanan Town into a thriving commercial center.

A steep, winding road leading across to Singaraja on the north coast passes from Beringkit (in Badung) via Perean, Bedugul, Candi Kuning and Baturiti. The mountainous area around Bedugul is cool, misty and rainy. Vegetables, such as carrots, cauliflower, cabbage and maize, as well as many fruits (including apples and even strawberries) grow well here and are sold at the market in Bedugul. It is traditional for travelers to stop here and enjoy the cool mountain air before continuing on their journey.

The fast-flowing rivers have cut steep ravines into soft volcanic rocks overgrown with giant ferns (*pakis*). There are huge boulders in the riverbeds and spectacular waterfalls. The mountain area around Apuan offers fine views. Here one looks down upon innumerable terraces with small rice plots, surrounded by jagged dikes and tiny canals with gurgling water.

There are some archaeological remains in the north. A temple in Perean and a *makara* spout in Candi Kuning date from the first half of the 14th century (1334 and 1339 respectively). Copperplate inscriptions were found in the south in Kediri and Pandak Bandung (1071).

The Balinese believe that the descendants of Arya Kenceng and Arya Belog, who accompanied Patih Gajah Mada during his tour of Bali in the 14th century, settled in Badung and Tabanan. The Tabanan branch of Arya Kenceng's line begins with Arya Tabanan, who lived with 4000 men in the village of Buahan (on the road to Apuan). Arya Belog lived in Kaba-Kaba with 5000 men.

After some time a new and powerful group of descendants of Arya Tabanan settled in the village of Tabanan, which was then called Singasana. They expanded their territory to the northeast (Perean, Pacung) and northwest (Pupuan). In the course of the 18th or at the beginning of the 19th century, a branch of the Tabanan family settled in Krambitan. From the foundation of the realm of Mengwi around 1700 onwards, there were conflicts and battles with Tabanan. Kaba-Kaba became an ally of Mengwi, but never warred with Tabanan.

Soon after the defeat of Mengwi in 1891 by the combined forces of Klungkung, Badung, Tabanan and Bangli, the Dutch began to expand their influence in south and east Bali by intervening in conflicts between the various rulers. This resulted in military annexations. A conflict between Badung and the Dutch over salvage rights for shipwrecks ended in a military expedition, and in September, 1906, Badung fell. The ruler of Tabanan wanted to negotiate with the Dutch. However, he and his son were captured and put in jail, where they committed suicide.

The Dutch soon reorganized Bali into seven sub-departments, with Tabanan as one. In 1929, Bali was redivided into eight realms, ruled by regents chosen from the old royal families. These received the status of "kings" in 1938, but this was only to last a few years. Indonesian independence from Dutch rule brought an end to the active role of royalty.

— *Hedi Hinzler*

Overleaf: *One of Bali's classic sights — sunset at Pura Tanah Lot. Photo by Eric Oey.*

SIGHTS OF TABANAN

From the Mountains to the Sea

Like all old Balinese realms, Tabanan has a mountain-to-the-sea axis — an ordering of the physical landscape that mirrors the ordering of the cosmos, with major points marked by temples. Each former Balinese kingdom thus has six major temples, the so-called *sad kahyangan*, consecrated to the six most significant features of the landscape — the forest, the mountains, the sea, the lakes, the earth and the ricefields. In a similar way, there are six cardinal temples for the whole of Bali. Two of these six are to be found in Tabanan: the seaside sanctuary of Tanah Lot and the ancestral shrine of Pura Luhur high up on Mt Batukau.

Temple in the sea

About 20 km west of Denpasar on the main highway, one arrives at the town of Kediri, where a large sign at the main intersection announces a turn-off to the left toward **Pura Tanah Lot** — the famous seaside temple to the south. *Tanah* means earth and *lot* means south or sea (usually written *lod*) — thus something like "Temple of the Earth in the Sea" is intended. It is actually constructed atop a large, jagged outcropping of rock just off the coast. It is accessible only during low tide. The temple itself is quite modest, consisting of two shrines with tiered roofs (7 and 3), a few small buildings and two pavilions.

Poisonous, black sea snakes live between the rocks and in caves along the coast. They guard the temple, but give the site a reputation of being "dangerous." Nevertheless, many Balinese love to sit on the beach or on a bluff overlooking the temple in the late afternoon, watching the tides change and enjoying the silhouettes of the temple *meru* against the brilliant setting sun.

Like so many other temples in Bali, Tanah Lot is connected with the famous brahman priest, Danghyang Nirartha, who wandered from Java to Bali in the 16th century. On one of his journeys he decided to sleep in this beautiful spot, and then afterwards advised the Balinese to erect a temple here. As mentioned above, this is one of the *sad kahyangan* or six most holy temples for all of Bali as well as for Tabanan district.

On the way back to the Kediri intersection, stop in at the village of **Pejaten**, famous for its pottery. These range from traditional

MADE SUDANA

ERIC OEY

roofing tiles, now painted in bright reds and greens, to replicas of glazed Chinese ceramics. The latter are the result of an initiative taken by Dutch potters during the 1980s. Already in the 1970s a Chinese painter from Tabanan, the late Kay It, introduced the production of terracotta tiles decorated with figures of gods, goddesses and *wayang* heroes in relief. These were mainly used for interior decoration of restaurants and shops in the tourist areas of South Bali.

Tabanan Town

To the west on the main highway, one soon enters the medium sized, bustling town of Tabanan. Though it appears rather non-descript and has not much of a reputation among tourists, the arts are actually well represented here. The town already had skilled woodcarvers at the end of the 19th century, and there were and still are many good *juru basa*, or bards who recite fragments of classic poems (*kakawin*) at festive occasions and during contests of the Bebasan recital clubs.

Bali's most famous dancer, the late I Ketut Marya (pronounced, and frequently written as Mario) is also connected with Tabanan. He was born at the end of the 19th century and died in 1968. Although he was actually born in Denpasar, he was raised in Tabanan under

Left: *Festival day at Tanah Lot.* **Above:** *The* pemangku *of the Tanah Lot temple.*

Anak Agung Ngurah Made Kaleran of the Puri Kaleran palace.

Marya performed as one of the dancers representing the (female) pupils of the witch, Calonarang, with a music club called the Gong Pangkung which was founded in 1900 and became quite famous. The Gong Pangkung, named after a village quarter in Tabanan, also possessed a set of *tingklik* instruments, bamboo replicas of a *gamelan* orchestra.

Marya and his three fellow dancers experimented widely with this orchestra. They traveled and gave *gandrung* (transvestite) performances. They also refined the fast and lively *kebyar* musical style that had been invented in north Bali around 1900. Marya developed a number of new dances for the ensemble. The two most famous are the Trompong Dance, in which the performer crouches and plays the *trompong* (a row of 10 bronze kettledrums) while dancing, and the Kebyar Duduk (sitting *kebyar*), in which he crouches and sinuously flirts with a drummer or another musician while dancing.

In the late 1920s and 1930s, these dances were already well known to tourists. Walter Spies made superb photos of them for the book *Dance and Drama in Bali* which he produced with Beryl de Zoete in 1935-36. Marya was also a teacher of many dancers who would later become famous, in particular I Gusti Ngurah Raka from Batuan. He was a very strict mentor and only accepted the very best pupils. Although he taught them the same dances, he assigned each pupil slightly different movements, to enable him or her to have something characteristic. To remember this dancer and teacher who made Tabanan so famous, the **Gedong Marya Theater** was erected in Tabanan in 1974.

There is also a museum in Tabanan This is the **Subak Museum**, which contains tools and implements connected with ricefield irrigation and agriculture in Bali. It lies just outside of the town on the right-hand side of the main road to Denpasar.

A famous native son

Tabanan also has a modern temple-like memorial, which can be considered a national shrine. It is located in the village of **Marga**, about 15 km northeast of the town, on the spot where lieutenant-colonel I Gusti Ngurah Rai, commander of the nationalist forces fighting the Dutch, was killed with his 94 men on November 20th, 1946. They fought till the death, and their behavior is commonly compared with that of the ruler of Badung and his family in 1906, so that the event is also referred to as a *puputan*.

The heroic death of Ngurah Rai is commemorated not only in this temple, but also in a poem, the *Geguritan Margarana*, written a short time afterwards by a fellow nationalist fighter. His name has also been given to the international airport of Bali. The memorial itself contains a stone tower or *candi* in which a replica of the famous letter containing his refusal to surrender is carved. Placed in rows outside are 94 pointed stone pedestals representing his fellow martyrs.

Rich artistic traditions

Several villages located to the southwest of Tabanan Town are especially rich in dance and art traditions. The village of **Krambitan**, in particular, is noted for its *tektekan* performances. This is in fact not a dance, but a procession of men with giant wooden cow bells with huge clappers around their necks and bamboo split drums. They traditionally marched around the village during an epidemic or great drought to chase away the evil spirits and bring fertility to the area.

There are two palaces here, belonging to a branch of the Tabanan royal family. Since 1972, the Puri Anyar has been holding "Palace Nights" for tourists, with a *tektekan* group from nearby Panarukan and a performance of the dramatic *calonarang* trance play. One can commission a private perfor-

mance with dinner by candlelight within the palace precincts, and both palaces are also renting rooms to tourists.

In the nearby village of **Tista**, just one km to the west of Krambitan, special versions of the *legong kraton* dance, called *leko* or *adar,* are performed. This is a dramatized version of a classic tale (the *Ramayana* or *Malat*) danced by three young girls — a *condong* (female attendant) and the two *legong* (princesses). They change roles during the performance, but wear the same costumes. The Tista group was founded in 1989 under the guidance of two old dancers from the 1920s.

Two km south of Krambitan, the village of **Panarukan** has many good sculptors — both brahmans and *jaba* (sudras) — working in wood as well as in soft volcanic *paras* stone. The village is also known for its *tektekan*, and for the painter Ajin Ida Putu Cegeg from the Griya Gede, who was a pioneer in the use of modern elements in his works.

Several kms beyond Panarukan, the road ends at a broad, black sand beach by the village of **Klatingdukuh**. This long, deserted strip of paradise is slated for tourist development within the coming years on account of its fine sand, pounding surf and stunning views down the coast in either direction.

Left: *Singasendi carving in the Tabanan palace.*
Above: *A* calonarang *performance in Krambitan.*
Right: *Tiered* merus *at the Mt Batukau temple.*

Temple on high

At the end of a steep road north of Meliling past Wongaya Gede, about halfway up the slopes of towering, 2278 meter-high Mt Batukau, perches the **Pura Luhur** temple — an unusual complex of shrines and a pool set amidst lush, tropical forests. The main enclosure lies at the northern end of the complex, with two smaller temples, Pura Dalem and Pura Panyaum, to the south. A man-made lake to the east completes the "cosmic" design.

This was the state ancestral temple of the Tabanan court, and each of the shrines represents a different dynastic ancestor. Di Made, ruler of Gelgel between about 1665 and 1686, is represented by a shrine with a 7-tiered roof, and Cokorda Tabanan by one with a 3-tiered roof. All of the shrines are very modest, without much ornamentation, which gives a great feeling of unity to the complex.

The nearby pond is fed by the river Aa (pronounced "ehe"). In the center are two pavilions on a little isle, one for the goddess of Lake Tamblingan and one for the Lord of Mt Batukau. The sacred peak thus surrounded by waters can be compared with the mythical Mt Meru where the gods reside, enjoying themselves in floating pavilions.

The area around Batukau is one of great scenic beauty. There is a tiny road leading from Wongaya Gede across steep rice terraces to the village of **Jatiluwih**. On the road south back to Tabanan, stop in to see the Pura Puseh in **Penebel**, which possesses an ancient *lingga* (phallus, symbol of Siwa) with a *yoni* pedestal in a pavilion west of the entrance to the inner court. These are quite common in Java, but rare in Bali.

Antiquities of Tabanan

Only a few other antiquities have been discovered in Tabanan. One lies in **Perean**, west of the main road to Bedugul. This stone shrine, discovered here in 1920, consists of a square basement with panels and a temple body with niches on three sides and an entrance on the fourth — a mock-door with a kind of lock carved in stone. Porcelain plates of various sizes were mounted in the temple body on both sides of these niches and the entrance. The temple now has a thatched roof with 7 tiers.

There are remains here also of three small, ancient buildings. The complex is surrounded by a wall with a split gateway. Inscribed stones discovered nearby bear the dates A.D. 1339 and 1429. East of Perean, on the other side of the road, are hot water springs, the so-called Yeh Gangga ("Waters of the Ganges").

More to the north along this road, in Candi Kuning, a fine spout carved with the head of an elephant-fish (*makara*) was discovered. It dates probably from the 14th-15th century.

— *Hedi Hinzler*

BEDUGUL

Bali's Cool Highland Retreat

High in the central ranges of west Bali, a cool mountain retreat nestles in the crater of an extinct volcano. Here lies placid Lake Bratan, source of life-giving water for the springs, rivers and ricefields below. Verdant tropical rainforests blanket the hills, which at 1400 m above sea level provide temperatures several degrees lower than the plains (11° to 30° C).

Few tourists stop to explore Bedugul and Lake Bratan on journeys to and from the north coast. But this little hideaway is well known to long-term Bali residents for its delightful scenery, spectacular mountain walks and many other recreation opportunities.

The road to Bedugul leads west and north from Denpasar through Mengwi, taking an hour and a half to reach the top. As it winds up the mountain, magnificent views stretch back over the lowlands to the coast and across to the misty peaks of Bali's sleeping volcanoes —

GILLES MASSOT

Agung, Abang and Batur to the east. To the west, deep gorges border tiers of jungle foliage below the hazy peak of Mt. Batukaru.

Near the top of the hill the road suddenly branches to the right, sloping gently down, and a striking new panorama is revealed — sparkling blue waters backed by lush, green hills. Cottages dot the hillside down to the shores of the lake, and a pier provides a mooring for boats of all shapes and sizes.

This is the **Bedugul Hotel**, center for waterskiing, parasailing, canoeing and fishing. Facilities include boat sheds, jumping ramps, slalom and trick waterski equipment. Contact Mr. Wayan Purnayasa owner of the hotel, for information and rental equipment.

The lake goddess presides

On the northeastern shore of the lake, dramatic **Pura Ulun Danu Bratan** projects into the water. This is the temple of the lake goddess who is much revered as a source of fertility. Built by the king of Mengwi in 1633, it consists of four compounds, the two outermost of which are completely surrounded by water.

When the three-tiered Siwaitic *lingga petak* was recently restored, the builders discovered a bubbling spring and a big white stone flanked by two red ones — a phallic *lingga* representing the reproductive power of Siwa as the god of fertility. Towering above this, on a separate islet, is a single shrine of 11 roofs dedicated to Wisnu in his manifestation as the lake goddess Dewi Danu, who protects all living creatures.

The main temple complex on the shore, **Pura Teratai Bang**, is a *pura penataran* or temple of origin. Its many shrines, associated with different aspects of creation, are dominated by a large 7-tiered *meru* dedicated to Brahma. The smaller **Pura Dalem Purwa** is dedicated to Dewi Uma Bhogawati, the goddess of food and drink.

Lush tropical gardens

In 1959, a large expanse of tropical rainforest in the foothills of Bukit Tapak was set aside by the government as the **Kebun Raya Eka Karya Bali** — a botanical garden covering an area of 129.2 hectares. This extensive park is a popular place for weekenders, but during the week it is a haven of peace and solitude.

More than 650 tree species have been recorded in the park, and there are 459 different wild and propagated orchids, includ-

Left: *Pura Ulun Danu Bratan — the temple of the lake goddess.* **Right:** *The Bali Handara Golf Club.*

ing some rare ones collected from the nearby forest. Visitors interested to learn more are welcome to call in at the Information Center, although it pays to take a guide, as the staff do not speak fluent English.

The temperate climate, abundant rainfall and rich volcanic soils make the crater ideal for market gardening. In the early 1970s most local farmers cut out their coffee gardens and started growing vegetables. Now the Bedugul gardens supply the huge Denpasar markets and hotel resorts with fresh cabbages, carrots, onions, strawberries, passion fruit and other fresh fruits and vegetables.

Flower growing has also proved profitable, and *bemo*-loads of freshly cut roses, lilies, gardenias and gladioli are sent southwards at dawn. Nursery gardens and orchid shelters have sprung up all over the valley.

Stop at the **Candi Kuning** produce and plant market to see tier after tier of exotic flowering plants. Women here call out to passers-by in a new language. "Dendrobium? Azalea? You buy orchid, madam?"

Tropical golf and mountain hikes

Some will find this the last word on Bali as a paradise. At the northern end of the Bedugul crater is one of the most beautiful golf courses in the world, designed by famous golf architects Thompson, Wolveridge and Fream. This is the **Bali Handara Country Club**, an 18-hole masterpiece with lush green fairways and the fastest greens you are likely to find anywhere. Trees and beds of colorful flowers line the fairways, and there is a spacious clubhouse, complete with pro shop, sauna and fitness center, and a restaurant. Open to the public except on tournament days, the course is playable all year round, with no problems of advance booking.

For those who enjoy nature more without whacking a little white ball around, there are many delightful bush walks in the vicinity of Bedugul. Guides are available at the Bedugul Hotel. They don't speak much English, but they know every inch of the countryside.

One exhilarating hike takes you to the peak of **Mt Mangu**, on the southeastern side of Lake Bratan. It is a 6 hour walk. At the peak is an ancient temple, Pura Pucak, built by the first raja of Mengwi. The view is spectacular.

Another walk begins at the northernmost end of the botanical gardens. There is a good wide path here, so it is safe without a guide. It leads across the foothills of **Mt Tapak** to the northern end of the valley. The 8 km path emerges in the midst of vegetable gardens to greet the main road at **Pancasari** village.

There is a further walk passing up and behind Mt Tapak through dense jungle to a waterfall on this other side. This is a long and steep climb and should only be ventured with a local guide. So set off early and bring food. Nature lovers will find it well worth the effort.

— *Sarita Newson*

RIO HELMI

PART X

The West: Jembrana

A virgin forest, lair of the ferocious Bali tiger and haunt of highway robbers, stretching from rugged mountain chain to ragged coast — this was Jimbar Wana, the "Great Forest" of the west, known today as Jembrana. More than half of the regency's 842 sq km area is forested, much of the rest is dry, and people from other parts of Bali still consider Jembrana to be only half civilized and not quite Balinese.

A Balinese chronicle accounts for the emptiness of Jembrana in the following way: When the region first came under the authority of the court at Gelgel around 1450, two princes were sent to settle the remote western forests. Gusti Ngurah Pecangakan settled near present-day Negara; Gusti Ngurah Bakungan claimed the area around present-day Gilimanuk. Soon a rivalry developed between the two as to who could develop the

more beautiful and prosperous court.

On one occasion, Bakungan invited his brother to Gilimanuk to attend a lavish court ceremony, and Pecangakan left his horse tied to a tree where a pig had been slaughtered. The unguarded horse broke free and ran home, first rolling in the grass and covering itself in pig's blood. Seeing the horse return riderless and bloody, Pecangakan's wife and family thought he had been killed, and as was the custom they took their own lives to share his fate. Pecangakan returned to a deserted palace and immediately declared war on his brother out of grief and rage.

Whatever the truth of this tale, the two brothers destroyed each other and their kingdoms in the civil war which ensued. All that remains of them today is a small temple, Pura Bakungan, by the side of the main road one km northeast of Cekek. And as a result,

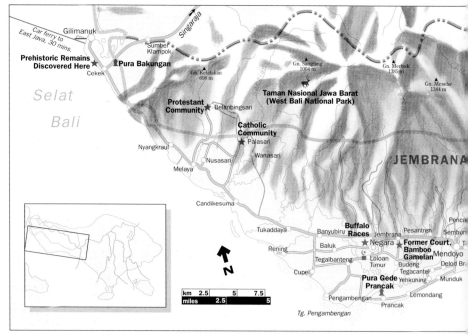

Jembrana remained sparsely populated and barely civilized while the rest of Bali blossomed with court culture. Eventually, a court of sorts developed in the town of Jembrana, which in 1803 moved a few kms west to the town of Negara, the present-day capital.

Who first settled the forbidding Jimbar Wana? The earlist evidence of human habitation on Bali has in fact been discovered at Gilimanuk, near the island's western tip. Not much is known about these prehistoric people.

Later residents came not only from Bali but from other islands also. The Bali Strait bordering Jembrana is notoriously treacherous, and because the Balinese are wary of the sea anyway, parts of the coast were settled by sailors, fishermen and merchants from Java, Madura and Sulawesi. Many of these were Muslims and remained so. One km south of the central market in Negara lies Loloan Timur, a village of Muslim Balinese whose Bugis ancestors migrated here as early as 1653. These villagers have retained elements of Buginese culture, most strikingly the oblong houses built of wood with living quarters on the second floor. Loloan Timur looks unlike any other village on Bali.

Outside influences are thus very much in evidence here. There is one mosque to every five Hindu temples in Jembrana. And Jembrana residents themselves will tell you that prior to the 1920s, many newcomers were people who were politically, economically or legally in trouble in other parts of Indonesia. And after 1920, local transmigration programs encouraged people from the more densely populated areas of Bali to settle in Jembrana.

Most people in Jembrana can tell you where they are originally from, and if you drive up one of the many side roads that snake into the mountains, you will encounter places like Bangsal Gianyar and Bangsal Bangli — entire communities transplanted to Jembrana a generation ago. Some of them had religious motives for coming here. Palasari and Belimbingsari in Melaya district, for example, are the largest Catholic and Protestant communities on Bali. Palasari's handsome Catholic church is the largest in eastern Indonesia.

The regency is today inhabited by only about 210,000 people, and is the least densely populated area of Bali. At least eighty percent make their living by farming, harvesting forest products, or fishing. The Bali tiger was last sighted in the 1930s, and the remaining wilds of Jimbar Wana have been incorporated into the new Bali Barat National Park. Jembrana today is a beautiful agricultural region, with a unique history and character, reflected in the stories, customs and arts of its people.

— *Kate Beddall*

Overleaf: Mekepung, *the fiercely-contested water buffalo races of Jembrana. Photo by Kal Muller.*

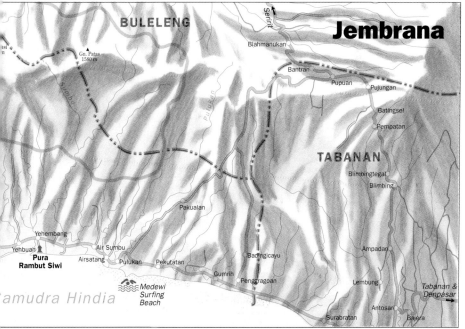

SIGHTS OF JEMBRANA

The Island's Wild West Coast

Jembrana is the area of Bali least visited by tourists. This means that tourist facilities are less developed here than elsewhere, but it also means this is a great place to get off the beaten tourist track. Visitors to Jembrana should not expect to sleep in air-conditioned hotels with hot running water, or to converse in English with every shopkeeper and waiter. It requires some initiative to unearth the treasures which the area has to offer, but most visitors will find it well worth the effort.

Jembrana's main population centers are all found along the 71 kms of road that hug the southwestern coast. You can reach it from Singaraja via the wild, dry forests of the north, or from Denpasar by way of the vast ricefields and brilliant coastline of Tabanan.

The ferry from Java berths at the town of **Gilimanuk** at Jembrana's western tip. To the east, a mountain road winds down from an elevation of 798 m at the Buleleng border to the town of Pekutatan on the main coastal road. Traversing fragrant clove and vanilla plantations that at one point pass through the tangled aerial roots of a giant *bunut* tree, this little-known road offers spectacular views across to Java and is the most scenic way to enter Jembrana.

Three kms west of Pekutatan village, on the left coming from Denpasar, is the entrance to **Medewi Beach** — a black sand beach that is one of the best-kept secrets on Bali, with a pounding surf and a simple accommodation.

Temple of the sacred hair

The most important temple in Jembrana is **Pura Rambut Siwi**, which lies about 20 kms west of the Tabanan border by the village of Yeh Embang. Its entrance is marked by a small shrine at the edge of the road, where Balinese travelers stop briefly to pray for safety in their journey. Two hundred meters from the main road lies the main temple complex, perched on a cliff at the edge of the ocean.

Pura Rambut Siwi is an important monument to the priest Danghyang Nirartha, who came to Bali from Java during the decline of the Majapahit Kingdom in the hopes of fortifying Balinese Hinduism against the spread of Islam occurring elsewhere in the archipelago. Between 1546 and 1550 he traveled through the island teaching and unifying the Hindu

AMIR SIDHARTA

populace. According to legend, he stopped to pray at a village temple at Yeh Embang, and made a gift of his hair to the temple. Since that time it has been known as Rambut Siwi, which means "worship of the hair."

The complex consists of three temple enclosures in a setting of great natural beauty. The first one you encounter as you enter from the main road is the largest and most important, the Pura Luhur where Danghyang Nirartha's hair is kept. A majestic *candi bentar* or split gate on the southern wall of the inner courtyard opens onto the cliff, offering dramatic views of the surf below. Gnarled frangipani trees litter the ground with fragrant blossoms, and incense burns at the feet of moss-covered stone statues swathed in white cloth.

From Pura Luhur you can walk east along the top of the cliff to a winding stone stairway that descends to Pura Penataran, the original temple where Danghyang Nirartha is believed to have prayed. When the Balinese worship at Rambut Siwi they first enter this temple.

Walking back westward along the beach you pass a small shrine at the entrance to a cave in the cliff wall. This cave is said to be the lair of mystical animals — the *duwe* or holy beast of the temple. A well at the mouth of the cave is a source of holy water that is salt free despite its proximity to the ocean. Just beyond the cave, another stairway leads back up to the temple. Perched on the edge of the cliff here is the tiny **Pura Melanting**

where merchants stop to pray for prosperity.

A large open-air performance pavilion and two gazebos set amidst lily ponds to the west of Pura Luhur are excellent places to rest and enjoy a panorama of ricefields and white wave crests curling against the black sand coastline as far as the eye can see.

Continuing west along the main road, another important temple is situated along the coast south of Mendoyo. This is **Pura Gede Prancak**, where Danghyang Nirartha is believed to have first landed. A peaceful shrine of white stone here sits on the banks of the placid Prancak River, which empties into the sea about 100 m south of the temple.

To reach it, turn left off the main road in Tegalcangkring, 8 kms west of Rambut Siwi and follow a narrow backroad one and a half kms to an intersection marked by a monument. Turn right and continue west about 9 kms. The temple is on your right where the road turns south along the Prancak River.

At the time of Danghyang Nirartha's arrival, this area was controlled by the debauched ruler, Gusti Ngurah Rangsasa, who obliged the newcomer to pray in his temple. When the holy priest complied, the temple structures collapsed. Gusti Ngurah Rangsasa then fled and the community rebuilt the temple in honor of Danghyang Nirartha and his teachings.

Tones of the giant bamboo

Jembrana is home to a number of fascinating art forms found nowhere else. By far the most popular and thriving of these is the fabulous **Gamelan Jegog**, a big bamboo orchestra whose deep, resonating tones vibrate through the air almost every night in Jembrana.

Gamelan jegog is an ensemble of fourteen bamboo instruments so big and resonant that their vibrations are felt by the body as much as the ears. The biggest are so tall that musicians have to sit on top of them in order to play them by striking the keys with heavy mallets. These larger instruments play low pitched melodies, while the smaller ones spin out intricately syncopated variations with dazzling precision and speed. The result is a dense, multi-layered fabric of sound, above which a single bamboo flute trills a sweet, sinuous melody.

The most prevalent form of *jegog* today is the awesome **Jegog Mebarung** where two or

Opposite and **above:** *The beautiful surf-swept coast at Yehembang, in Jembrana, is the site of the important temple of Pura Rambut Siwi.*

KAL MULLER

more orchestras perform together. Each plays in turn, pitting their skills against one another in a fierce musical battle. *Jegog mebarung* is an unforgettable event to witness. The instruments sway back and forth, the musicians bob up and down, and the onlookers cheer enthusiastically, occasionally helping the musicians to replace a broken key. The winner is the ensemble that can make itself heard above the frenzy.

Jegogs are also evaluated for their visual appearance. The wooden components of the instruments are all finely carved and brightly painted, with tall ceremonial umbrellas and handsome statues affixed to the big instruments in the back.

Other interesting art forms of the area include the **Jegog Dance**, as unique as the *gamelan* itself; **Pencak Silat**, which is a mixture of choral singing, theater, martial arts and acrobatics, supervised by a sharp-tongued jester named Dag, and a daredevil knife dance called **Cabang**. All of these have roots in the performing arts of Java, Madura, and the Malay world. In recent times, traditional Balinese dances and dramas from the *gamelan gong* repertoire have been set to *jegog* music, and these renditions have become even more popular than the originals.

Kendang Mebarung, a contest of giant drums, shares the competitive spirit of *jegog mebarung*. The contest is between two oversized drums, each 2 to 3 meters in length and one meter in diameter, accompanied by an abbreviated *gamelan angklung* ensemble. When the drums compete, at cremation ceremonies, national holidays, or simply for public entertainment, the drummers play interlocking rhythms that challenge each other's resonance, volume, and rhythmic dexterity.

Another type of ensemble indigenous to Jembrana is the **Bumbung Gebyog**. Eight to twelve lengths of bamboo of varying pitches are struck on the ground in rhythmically intricate, interlocking patterns. Probably the only music in Bali that originated and has remained the preserve of women, *bumbung gebyog* derives from the pounding of newly harvested rice in the *lesung* to remove the husks. Nowadays it is performed on national holidays and at ceremonies related to rice agriculture, usually accompanied by narrative dances or the playful **Ngibing Dance** where spectators may take turns dancing with the dancer.

There are no regularly scheduled performances, so you will have to hunt a little to see any of the above. Of the 46 *jegog* ensembles in Jembrana, the champion today is Jegog Niti Swara in the town of Tegalcangkring. Jegog Suar Agung in Sankar Agung near Negara is also well known for their presenta-

Above: *Rice harvest near Negara.* **Right:** *A view from Lampu Merah at the western tip of Bali, across the narrow straits to the island of Java.*

tion of the new style of *jegog* dance and drama. To see them, it may be necessary to commission a performance.

Contact Ida Bagus Raka Negara in Tegalcangkring for assistance. It costs about $80 to arrange a *jegog* performance, and you should book a few days in advance. *Bumbung gebyog* and *kendang mebarung* are less common today; Ida Bagus Raka Negara can nevertheless help locate or commission one. Another source of information is the Office of Education and Culture (Kantor Pendidikan dan Kebudayaan) in Negara.

Off to the races

The water buffalo races of west Bali, known as **Mekepung** and imported by the local Madurese population, are the most dramatic of Jembrana's events. Throughout the westernmost districts, it is still common to see a team of brawny, grey or pink buffalo pulling wooden carts filled with cacao, coffee or bananas. *Mekepung* began when farmers playfully raced their neighbors in plowing a field or in bringing the harvest home. The races soon became an event in themselves, and the cumbersome *cikar* carts were replaced by light, two-wheeled chariots.

Today, the races are organized by the regional government of Jembrana. All participants are members of a racing club (*sekehe mekepung*) and are divided into two divisions: a Western Block and an Eastern Block, with the Ijo Gading River that bisects Jembrana as the dividing line. These teams compete biannually, in the Regent's Cup Championship on the Sunday before Indonesian Independence Day in August, and the Governor's Cup Championship each September or October.

The buffaloes in each team are ranked prior to the races, and pitted against its counterpart on the other team. Two pairs run at a time, along a circuitous 4 km route. The team with the most winners takes the cup. Apart from this, the only immediate reward for winning is prestige, but owning a prize buffalo does eventually translate into money. A good race animal can fetch almost double the normal price, if its owner is willing to part with it.

If you are in Jembrana between August and October you can find out the time and place of the championships by visiting the Department of Tourism in Negara. You can also see races at other times of the year by commissioning a performance or by attending the rehearsals that take place every other Sunday morning.

To find out about these options, contact the leaders of the *sekehe mekepung*: I Ketut Suelem or I Ketut Dibia in the town of Banyubiru, five kilometers west of Negara, or I Ketut Wenong of Delod Brawah, two kilometers southwest of Tegalcangkring. Rehearsals may be infrequent during the rainy season (November through March).

— *Kate Beddall*

MORTON STRANGE

BALI BARAT

West Bali National Park and Reserve

Much of Bali's natural landscape has been altered by the hand of man. Dense tropical forests that once covered the island have mostly now been cleared; and the land molded into spectacular rice terraces and sprawling village settlements. But on the westernmost tip of the island, extensive montane forests, coastal swamps and marine waters have barely been disturbed by human presence. Today these areas comprise the **Bali Barat (West Bali) National Park**, officially gazetted in 1984 as one of ten national parks in Indonesia.

Several distinct environments are to be found within the park's 76,312 hectares. Forested mountains ranging up to 1500 m stand in the park's central and eastern sectors. Their southern slopes are forested with tropical vegetation that is green year round. The north is much drier than the south, host-ing deciduous forests. Palm savannahs and mangrove swamps are found in the coastal areas. Four nearby islands surrounded by coral reefs are rich in sea and bird life.

The park is home to two rare species of wildlife. The **Bali Starling** (*Leucopsar roth-schildi*), found only in Bali, is a small white bird with black wingtips and a brilliant aqua-blue streak around its eyes. A hundred or so individuals still live in the wild here, mainly on Menjangan Island, and the park is spon-soring a project to train birds donated from zoos around the world for re-release to their natural habitat. The project's training center is located at Tegal Bunder Research Station.

Another rare species is the wild Javan buf-falo (*Bos javanicus*). Only 30 to 40 remain deep inside the park grounds. Other mammals here include *rusa* deer, barking deer, mouse deer, leopard, civets, macaques and several species of monkeys.

The National Park's stated goal is to bal-ance conservation with human needs, now and in the future. Portions of it will be pre-served as a wilderness resource. Other areas bordering on existing human settlements have been designated "buffer zones" and will continue to provide these communities with needed forest resources. Several coconut and eucalyptus plantations will be reconverted to natural habitats. Still other areas are being exploited for timber. The park is also intended for controlled recreational use by Indonesians

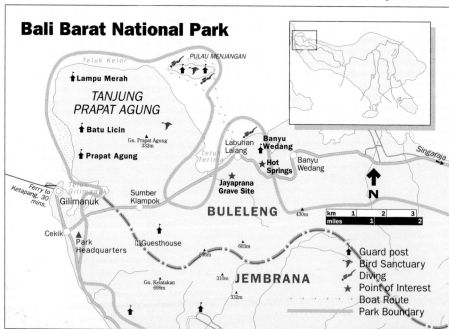

Bali Barat National Park

Teluk Kelor

PULAU MENJANGAN

Lampu Merah

TANJUNG PRAPAT AGUNG

Batu Licin

Gn. Prapat Agung
332m

Prapat Agung

Labuhan Lalang

Banyu Wedang

Teluk Terima

Banyu Wedang

Hot Springs

Singaraja

Ferry to Ketapang, 30 mins.

Teluk Gilimanuk

Gilimanuk

Sumber Klampok

★ **Jayaprana Grave Site**

BULELENG

430m

Cekik

Park Headquarters

Guesthouse

805m

603m

Gn. Kelatakan
698m

310m

JEMBRANA

332m

N

km	1	2	3
miles	1		2

Guard post
Bird Sanctuary
Diving
Point of Interest
Boat Route
Park Boundary

and foreigners alike.

Within the park's boundaries are two well-known tourist sites. The **Banyu Wedang** hot springs are considered to have medicinal properties by those who believe and bathe in them. Also found here is the holy grave of Jayaprana, a nobleman sent on a fatal mission so the king he served might wed his new bride (see page 195).

Hiking in Bali Barat

The best source for information on hikes and facilities is **Park Headquarters** at Cekik, by the intersection of the main roads from Singaraja and Denpasar, just south of Gilimanuk. A small library with exhibits and a knowledgeable staff are available to help you. Since this is a government office, it closes at 3 pm, Monday through Thursday, at noon on Friday, and is closed on Saturday and Sunday.

There are many interesting trails, but to enter Bali Barat you must first obtain a permit and be accompanied by a guide. Permits are available free of charge at Cekik and at Labuhan Lalang, or at the Forestry Department offices (*Departemen Kehutanan*) at Jl. Niti Mandala, Renon in Denpasar (tel: 235679). The cost of a guide is $5 for 1-2 hours.

Shelters are available for overnight stays, but you must provide your own bedding, mosquito protection, food, water and utensils. If you plan to stay overnight, it is best to notify the park staff in advance so that your guide and facilities will be ready when you arrive. If you wish to spend several days exploring the park without camping, you can stay in simple bungalows at Labuhan Lalang, or in hotels in Gilimanuk or Negara.

Diving off Menjangan Island

The most beautiful, unspoiled coral reefs in Bali are located off the coast of **Pulau Menjangan** ("Deer Island"). Comprising hundreds of species of coral, these reefs extend 100 to 150 m from the shore, then drop 40 to 60 m down to the ocean floor. Menjangan and the nearby mainland are excellent places for swimming, snorkeling, and scuba diving. A 45 minute nature walk on Pulau Menjangan, which is uninhabited except for the Java Deer, affords beautiful panoramic views of the mountainous mainland.

To reach Pulau Menjangan, hire a boat at Labuhan Lalang, just opposite the island on the north coast of Bali. The round-trip cost is about $20 for 6 people. Snorkeling and scuba equipment are not available here, but you can organize this through one of the many diving tour operators in Kuta or Sanur (see "Practicalities" for these areas). The boat will stop wherever you want, and the boatmen are experienced guides. It is forbidden to spend the night on Menjangan, but food and simple lodgings are available at Labuhan Lalang.

— *Kate Beddall*

Above: *The best diving in Bali is found off the coast of tiny Menjangan ("Deer") Island.* **Right:** *The rare and beautiful Bali Starling, found only in Bali; just a few hundred survive in the wild.*

Margin tabs (left side):
1 Denpasar
2 Sanur
3 Kuta & Legian
4 Jimbaran
5 Nusa Dua
6 Ubud
7 Kintamani
8 Klungkung
9 Karangasem
10 Buleleng
11 Tabanan

On The Road

TRAVEL ADVISORY, LANGUAGE PRIMER, PRACTICALITIES

The On The Road sections contain all the practical knowledge you need for your journey. The **Travel Advisory** provides useful facts and tips about Indonesia from health precautions to shopping. The **Transportation** section provides an overview of the range of travel options. It is followed by a handy **Language Primer**.

The **Practicalities** sections focus on each destination and have all the local details on transport, accommodations, dining, the arts, trekking, shopping and services, plus maps. Each area is linked to the background articles in the first part of the guide. Easy-to-find margin tabs make cross-referencing simple and fast.

MISS YOUR LOVED ONES BACK HOME?
PUT YOURSELF IN THE PICTURE WITH 001

When you're far away from home, nothing brings you closer to loved ones than a phone call. And it's so easy with 001. Indosat offers International Direct Dial to over 240 countries. Plus, you save 25% during discount hours on weekends*, and around the clock on national holidays and weekends. Call today, and share the good times!

IDD = 001 · COUNTRY CODE · AREA CODE · TELEPHONE NUMBER

From Hotel = HOTEL ACCESS CODE · 001 · COUNTRY CODE · AREA CODE · TELEPHONE NUMBER

001 IDD · NUMBER ONE 〜 INDOSAT

* For information, call 102.

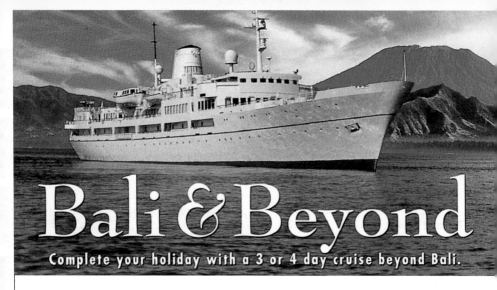

Denpasar 1

Sanur 2

Kuta/Legian 3

Jimbaran 4

Nusa Dua 5

Ubud 6

Kintamani 7

Klungkung 8

Karangasem 9

Buleleng 10

Tabanan 11

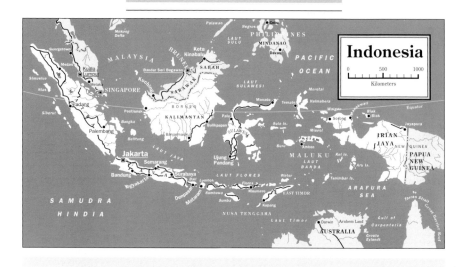

Indonesia At A Glance

The Republic of Indonesia is the world's fourth largest country, with 190 million people. The vast majority (88%) are Muslims, making this the world's largest Islamic country. More than 400 languages are spoken, but Bahasa Indonesia, a variant of Malay, is the national language.

The nation is a republic, headed by a strong President, with a 500-member legislature and a 1,000-member People's Consultative Assembly. There are 27 provinces and special territories. The capital is Jakarta, with 9 million people. The archipelago comprises just over 2 million square km of land. Of 18,508 islands, about 6,000 are named, and 1,000 permanently inhabited.

Indonesia's $175 billion gross national product comes from oil, textiles, lumber, mining, agriculture and manufacturing, and the country's largest trading partner is Japan. Per capita income is $850. Much of the population still makes a living through agriculture, chiefly rice. The unit of currency is the rupiah, which trades at approximately 2,300 to $1 (1996).

Historical overview. The Buddhist Sriwijaya empire, based in southeastern Sumatra, controlled parts of western Indonesia from the 7th to the 13th centuries. The Hindu Majapahit kingdom, based in eastern Java, controlled even more from the 13th to the 16th centuries. Beginning in the mid-13th century, local rulers began converting to Islam.

In the early 17th century the Dutch East India Company (VOC) founded trading settlements and quickly wrested control of the Indies spice trade. The VOC was declared bankrupt in 1799, and a Dutch colonial government was established.

Anti-colonial uprisings began in the the early 20th century, when nationalism movements were founded by various Muslim, communist and student groups. Soekarno, a Dutch-educated nationalist, was jailed by the Dutch in 1930.

Early in 1942, the Dutch Indies were overrun by the Japanese army. Treatment by the occupiers was harsh. When Japan saw her fortunes waning toward the end of the war, Indonesian nationalists were encouraged to organize. On August 17, 1945, Soekarno proclaimed Indonesia's independence.

The Dutch sought a return to colonial rule after the war. Four years of fighting ensued between nationalists and the Dutch, and full independence was achieved in 1949.

During the 1950s and early 1960s, President Soekarno's government moved steadily to the left, alienating western governments. In 1963, Indonesia took control of Irian Jaya and began a period of confrontation with Malaysia.

On September 30, 1965 the army put down an attempted coup attributed to the communist party. Several hundred thousand people were killed as suspected communists.

In the following years, the powers of the presidency gradually shifted away from Soekarno and General Soeharto became president in 1968. His administration has been friendly to Western and Japanese investment and the nation has enjoyed three decades of solid economic

Travel Advisory

TOURIST INFORMATION

Overseas, you can contact the Indonesian embassy or consulate, or one of the following **Indonesia Tourist Promotion Board** offices:

ASEAN & Southeast Asia, 10 Collyer Quay #15–07, Ocean Building, Singapore 0104. ☎ (65) 534-2837, 534-1795, fax: (65) 533-4287.

Australia & New Zealand, Level 10, 5 Elizabeth Street, Sydney NSW 2000, Australia. ☎ (61 2) 233-3630, fax: (61 2) 233-3629, 357-3478.

Europe, Wiesenhuttenstrasse 17, D-6000 Frankfurt/Main 1, Germany. ☎ (49 169) 233-677, fax: (49 169) 230-840.

Japan & Korea, Sankaido Building, 2nd Floor, 1-9-13 Ahasaka, Minatoku, Tokyo 107. ☎ (81 3) 3585-3588, fax: (81 3) 3582-1397.

North America , 3457 Wilshire Boulevard, Los Angeles, CA 90010-2203. ☎ (213) 387-2078, fax: (213) 380-4876.

Taiwan & Hong Kong, 66 Sung Chiang Road, 5th Floor, Taipei, Taiwan. ☎ (886 2) 537-7620. Fax: (886 2) 537-7621.

United Kingdom, Ireland, Benelux & Scandinavia, 3-4 Hanover Street, London W1R 9HH. ☎ (44 171) 493-0334, fax: (44 171) 493-1747.

The **Directorate General of Tourism** in Jakarta has brochures and maps on all Indonesian provinces: Jl. Kramat Raya 81, PO Box 409, Jakarta 10450. ☎ (021) 310-3117/9, fax: (021) 310-1146.

Local government tourism offices, *Dinas Pariwisata*, are generally only good for basic information. More useful assistance is often available from privately run (but government approved) **Tourist Information Services**. Be aware that many offices calling themselves "Tourist Information" are simply travel agents.

The tourist information counter at Ngurah Rai International Airport in Tuban (☎ 751001, ext. 1313) is open 24 hours. Other major offices are:

Badung Government Tourist Office, Jl. Surapati, Denpasar, ☎ 223602, open 8am–2:30pm Mon-Thurs, 7am–11am Fri.

Department of Tourism, Post and Telecommunication Regional Office X, Jl. Raya Puputan, Niti Mandala, Renon, Denpasar 85112, ☎ 225649, 233474, fax: 233475, open 7am–3pm Mon-Thurs, 7am–noon Fri.

Government Tourist Information Center, Mastapa Garden, 2nd Floor, Denpasar, ☎ 751660, ext. 145, open 10am–4pm Mon–Sat.

VISAS

Nationals of the following 45 countries do not need visas, and are granted visa-free entry for 60 days upon arrival.

Argentina	Iceland	Philippines
Australia	Ireland	Saudi Arabia
Austria	Italy	Singapore
Belguim	Japan	South Korea
Brazil	Kuwait	Spain
Brunei	Liechtenstein	Sweden
Canada	Luxembourg	Switzerland
Chile	Malaysia	Taiwan
Denmark	Maldives	Thailand
Egypt	Malta	Turkey
Finland	Mexico	United Arab
France	Monaco	Emirates
Germany	Morocco	United Kingdom
Greece	Netherlands	United States
Hungary	New Zealand	Venezuela
	Norway	

Be sure to check your passport before leaving for Indonesia. You must have at least one empty page to be stamped upon arrival and the passport must be valid for at least six months after the date of arrival. For visa-free entry, you must also have proof of onward journey, either a return or through ticket. Employment is strictly forbidden on tourist visas or visa-free entry.

Visa-free entry to Indonesia cannot be extended beyond two months (60 days) and cannot be converted to any other kind of visa.

A visa is required in advance for all other nationals or arrivals at minor ports.

Upon arrival you will be given a white embarkation/disembarkation card to fill out. Keep this card with your passport as you must present it when leaving the country.

Other Visas

The 2-month, non-extendable tourist pass is the only entry permit that comes without a great deal of paperwork.

A social visa, usually valid for 4–5 weeks, can be extended for up to 3 months, but is difficult to get. You must have a good reason for spending time in Indonesia (relatives, language study), you must have a sponsor who will assume financial responsibility for you. The process can take days or even weeks, and extensions are at the discretion of the immigration office where you apply.

A business visa requires a letter from a company stating that you are performing a needed service for a company in Indonesia. It is valid for up to one year, but you must leave the country every 4 months. This is not intended as an employment visa, but is for investors, consultants, or other business purposes. You are not to earn money in Indonesia on a business visa.

Two other types of passes are available: the temporary residence pass (ITAS) for research, formal study, or employment, and the permanent residence pass (ITAP). Both are difficult to get.

The **Immigration Office** is on Jl. Panjaitan and open 8am–3pm Mon–Fri, ☎ 227828. It can be reached from Sanur by the green *bemo*. Be on your best behavior and dress appropriately.

Customs

Narcotics, firearms and ammunition are strictly prohibited. The standard duty-free allowance is: 2 liters of alcoholic beverages, 200 cigarettes, 50 cigars or 100 grams of tobacco.

There is no restriction on import and export of foreign currencies in cash or travelers checks, but there is an export limit of 50,000 Indonesian rupiah.

All narcotics are illegal in Indonesia. The use, sale or purchase of narcotics results in long prison terms, huge fines and death, in some cases. Once caught, you are immediately placed in detention until trial, and the sentences are stiff, as demonstrated by Westerners currently serving sentences as long as 30 years for possession of marijuana.

WHEN TO TRAVEL

The best time to visit Bali is during the dry season, April to September. Humidity is down and nights can be cool. Australians visit in droves at Christmas and during May–August school holidays. Europeans arrive in July and August. Indonesians come at Christmas/New Years and during the June–July school break. Book well in advance for cheap flights and accommodations during these periods.

FOREIGN CONSULATES IN BALI

The Australian consul in Denpasar also represents citizens of Canada, New Zealand, United Kingdom, and Papua New Guinea. Japan also has full consular services here. All others are consular agents or honorary consuls.

Australia Jl. Prof. Moch. Yamin 51, Renon, Denpasar, ☎ 235092, 235093, fax: 235146.

France Jl. Tambaksari 5, Sanur, ☎ 287383, fax: 287383.

Germany (Honarary) Jl. Pantai Karang 17, Sanur, ☎ 288535, 288826, fax: 288826.

Italy (Honarary) Jl. Cemara, Semawang, Sanur, ☎ 288896, fax: 287642.

Japan Jl. Raya Puputan 1, Denpasar, ☎ 234808, fax: 231308.

Mexico PT. Puri Astina Putra, Jl. Hayam Wuruk 8, PO Box 150, Denpasar, ☎ 223266, 225754, 232680, fax: 237094.

Netherlands Jl. Raya Kuta 99, Kuta, ☎ 751517, fax: 752777.

Norway & Denmark Jl. Jayagiri VIII/10, Denpasar, ☎ 235098, fax: 234834

Sweden & Finland Segara Village Hotel, Jl. Segar Ayu, Sanur, ☎ 288407, fax: 287242.

Switzerland & Austria Swiss Restaurant, Jl. Pura Bagus Teruna (Jl. Rum Jungle), Legian, ☎ 751735, fax: 754457.

United States of America, Jl. Segara Ayu 5, Sanur, ☎ 288478, fax: 287760.

Passport Loss

If you lose your passport, it will be difficult to get new documents to leave the country unless you have the proper official forms from the police. Always keep a photocopy of your passport, visa and driver's license separate from the originals. You can then prove your identity to your consul in Bali in case of theft or loss.

When theft occurs, report to your consulate. Verification of your identity and citizenship takes two or three weeks and involves going to the immigration office in Denpasar.

WHAT TO BRING ALONG

When packing, keep in mind that you will be in the tropics, but that it can get cold in the mountains. Generally, you will want to dress light and wear natural fibers that absorb perspiration. A medium-weight sweater or wind breaker is also a must, as is a sturdy pair of shoes. Suits and ties are almost never worn.

Don't bring too much, as you will be tempted by the great variety of inexpensive clothes available here. Most tourists find a cotton batik shirt more comfortable than what they brought along. If you visit a government office, men should wear long trousers, shoes and a shirt with collar. Women should wear a neat dress, covering knees and shoulders, and shoes.

For those wanting to travel light, a *sarong* purchased upon arrival in Indonesia ($5–10) is one of the most versatile items you could hope for. It serves as a wrap to get to the bath, a beach towel, a waist sash which is required dress for Balinese temples, pajamas, bed sheet, fast drying towel, etc.

Indonesians are renowned for their ability to sleep anytime, anywhere; so they are not likely to understand your desire for peace and quiet at night. Sponge rubber **earplugs** are available from pharmacies in the West or from the in-flight airline toiletry kit. Many consider them the most important 4 grams they carry.

Tiny **padlocks** for use on luggage zippers are a handy deterrent to pilfering hands. Some come with combination locks. **Flashlights** may come in handy, although these can be easily purchased locally.

Bring along some **pre-packaged alcohol towelettes** (swabs). These are handy for disinfecting your hands before eating, or after a trip to the *kamar kecil* (lavatory). Also available at local supermarkets.

In the majority of Indonesian department stores and supermarkets you can find Western toiletries. **Contact lens** supplies for hard and soft lenses are available in major cities. For gas permeable lens wearers it is still necessary to come well-stocked.

Dental floss, tampons, and sanitary napkins are available in Western style grocery stores like Gelael and Hero that are fast becoming common in Indonesian cities. *Kondom* (condoms) are available at all *apotik* (pharmacies). Bring **sunscreen** and **insect repellent**, although these are also available locally.

Passport photos may come in handy for applications/permits (for parks) or even as gifts.

On your travels you will meet people who are kind and helpful, yet you may feel too embarrassed to give money. In this kind of situation a small gift is appropriate. Chocolates, biscuits, pens, stationery from your hotel, even your T-shirt with foreign designs are appreciated.

PLANNING A TRIP TO BALI

While the spiritual heart of Bali lies in the mountains, the tourist heart of the island lies in the south where, the major tourist enclaves of Kuta, Sanur and Nusa Dua are located. This is the focus or at least starting point for almost all visitors, especially those arriving by air.

Those lodging in any of the three above-mentioned areas, find it easy to make day trips to most of the popular tourist destinations, including Gunung Agung and Besakih temple, Kintamani, Singaraja and Lovina, Candidasa, etc. It is also easy to make overnight trips to these destinations or plan a circular route, starting in the south, visiting point of interest over several days and returning to the south for shopping and ultimate air departure.

The ports of Benoa, Batubulan and Padang Bai are launching points for boat journeys to islands east of Bali.

Abundant transportation, numerous tour desks and travel agencies offer overwhelming information and options. It's best to read first, ask questions and then decide what you want to see. Decide whether to drive yourself by car or motocycle, hire a driver, guide or take an organized tour to maximize your experience of Bali.

CLIMATE

The climate in this archipelago on the equator is tropical. In the lowlands, temperatures average between 21°C and 33°C, but in the mountains it can go as low as 5°C. Humidity varies but is always high, between 60% and 100%.

In general, Indonesia experiences two yearly seasons of monsoon winds: the southeast monsoon, bringing dry weather (*musim panas*— dry season), and the northwest monsoon, bringing rain (*musim hujan*—rainy season). Often the changing seasons can bring the time of high waves (*musim ombak*).

The **rainy season** is normally November to April, with a peak around January/February, when it rains for several hours each day. The rain is predictable, however, and always stops for a time, when the sun may come out. Before it rains, the air gets very sticky; afterwards it is refreshingly cool.

The **dry season**, May to October, is a better time to come, and especially June to August. This is the time to climb mountains or visit nature reserves; when wild bulls go in search of water and sea turtles lay eggs more often.

TIME ZONES

Bali is on Central Indonesian Standard Time, the middle of Indonesia's three time zones, which is Greenwich mean time + 8 hours. It is the same time in Bali as Singapore, Hong Kong and western Australia.

MONEY

Prices quoted in this book are intended as a general indication. They are quoted in US dollars because the rupiah is being allowed to devalue slowly, so prices stated in US dollars are more likely to remain accurate.

Standard **currency is** the Indonesian *rupiah*: Notes come in 50,000, 20,000, 10,000, 5,000, 1,000, 500 and 100 denominations. Coins come in denominations of 1,000, 500, 100, 50, 25, 10 and 5 rupiah. Unfortunately, the new coins are very similar in size, so look carefully. Coins below Rp50 are rarely available. In stores small change is often replaced by candies.

Banking

Moneychangers and banks accepting foreign currency are found in most tourist areas. State banks are open from 8-3, Monday to Friday. Private banks open also on Saturday until 11 am. The bank counters at major airports offer competitive rates. Bank lines in town can be long and slow; the best way around it is to arrive promptly at opening time.

Moneychangers in Bali generally give better rates than banks, are much more numerous, and keep more convenient hours.

Get a supply of Rp1,000 and Rp500 notes when you change money, as taxi drivers and vendors often have—or claim to have— no change for big bills. When traveling in the countryside, Rp100 notes are also useful.

Carrying **cash** (US$) can be a handy safety precaution as it is still exchangeable should you lose your passport, but Indonesian banks only accept foreign currency that is crisp and clean.

Major **credit cards** are accepted in a wide variety of shops and hotels. But they often add a 3% surcharge. Most cities have at least one bank at which cash advances can be made— look for Bank Duta, BCA and Danamon. Visa and MasterCard are the most frequently accepted.

There are no exchange controls and excess *rupiah* (bills only) can be freely reconverted at the airport.

Tax, service and tipping

Most larger hotels and restaurants charge 21% tax and service on top of your bill. Tipping is not a custom here, but it is appreciated for special services. Rp500 per bag is considered a good tip for roomboys and porters. Taxi drivers will want to round up to the nearest Rp500 or Rp1,000.

When tipping the driver of your rental car or a *pembantu* (housekeeper) of the house in which you've been a guest, fold the money and give it with the right hand only.

OFFICE HOURS

Many government offices have converted to a five-day work week and are officially open Monday to Friday, 8am to 4pm, but if you want to get anything done, be there by 11am. In large cities most private businesses are open 9am to 5pm. Shops from 9am to 9pm. In smaller towns shops close for a siesta at 1pm and reopen at 6pm.

COMMUNICATIONS

Mail

Indonesia's postal service is reliable, if not terribly fast. *Kilat* express service is only slightly more expensive and much faster. *Kilat khusus* (domestic special delivery) will get there overnight. International express mail gets postcards and letters to North America or Europe in about 7 days from most cities.

Kantor pos (post offices) are found in every little village in Bali, open 8am–2pm every day except Sunday. The main post office in Denpasar (Jl. Raya Puputan, Renon) remains open until 8pm. Most close from noon to 1pm for lunch.

Post offices are often busy and it can be a tedious process to line up at one window for weighing, another window for stamps, etc. Hotels will normally sell stamps and post letters for you, or you can use private postal agents to avoid hassles. Look for the orange *Agen Kantor Pos* (postal agency) signs.

Poste Restante service is usually reliable, but it is advisable to choose more important towns such as Kuta or Ubud. Some post offices ask for ID and may also charge a fee before handing over your letters.

Telephone and Fax

Long distance phone calls, both within Indonesia and international, are handled by satellite. Domestic long distance calls can be dialed from most phones. To dial your own international calls, find an IDD (Internaltion Direct Dial) phone and dial "001" or "008," otherwise you must go via the operator, which is far more expensive.

A magnetic debit (*kartu telpon*) phone card can be purchased at hotels, post offices and many other outlets. This is used on card phones which are increasing in popularity, eliminating the need for small change.

If your hotel has no IDD link you have to go to the main telephone office (*kantor telepon*), use a silver card phone (*kartu telpon*) and pay an uninflated rate or use a private postal and telephone service: *Wartel* (*warung telekommunikasi*/*warpostel*/*warparpostel*. These small "telecom shops" are all over Indonesia and fast becoming the most convenient way to call international (you avoid hotel price hikes). They are often run by well-trained, efficient staff and offer fast IDD services at near standard rates. Open daily from 8am to 10pm or 11pm. Prices per minute are about $2.30 to the Americas and $3.10 to most European countries. Night rates are lower.

International calls via MCI, Sprint, ATT, and the like can be made from IDD phones using the access code for your calling card company. Recently, special telephones have been installed in Indonesia's airports with pre-programmed buttons to connect you via these companies to various countries.

Faxes have become common and can be sent and received at Wartel offices and most main post offices.

Courier Services

Some of the big international courier outfits operate in Indonesia, along with some domestic ones. TNT Express Worldwide and Elteha International are probably the most reliable in Indonesia. Bali offices include:

DHL, Birotika Semesta, Jl. Hayam Wuruk 118, Denpasar, 222526, fax: 234489.

Elteha International Jl. Diponegoro, Komplek Pertokoan Diponegoro Megah, Denpasar ☎ 222889, fax: 235261.

MSA Jl. Hayam Wuruk 128, Denpasar, ☎ 236195, fax: 235025.

Pacific Express Jl. Hang Tuah 3X, Denpasar ☎ 235181, fax: 238062

TNT Express Worldwide Jl. Teuku Umar 88E, Denpasar, ☎ 238043, 222238, fax: 238043.

VIP Jl. Diponegoro B27, Denpasar, ☎ 237343, fax: 236131.

ELECTRICITY

Most of Indonesia has converted to 220 volts and 50 cycles, though a few places are still on the old 110 lines. Ask before you plug in if your are uncertain. Power failures are common in smaller cities and towns. Voltage can fluctuate considerably so use a stabilizer for computers and similar equipment. Plugs are of the European two-pronged variety.

HEALTH

Before You Go

Check with your physician for the latest news on the need for malaria prophylaxis and recommended **vaccinations** before leaving home. Frequently considered vaccines are: Diphtheria, Pertusis and Tetanus (DPT); Measles, Mumps and Rubella (MMR); and oral Polio vaccine. Gamma Globulin every four months for Hepatitis A is recommended. For longer stays many doctors recommend vaccination to protect against Hepatitis B requiring a series of shots over the course of 7 months. Vaccinations for smallpox and cholera are no longer required, except for visitors coming from infected areas. A cholera vaccination is recommended for travel in outlying areas, but it is only 50% effective.

Find out the generic names for whatever prescription medications you are likely to need as most are available in Indonesia but not under the same brand names as they are known at home. Get copies of doctors' prescriptions for the medications you bring into Indonesia to avoid questions at the customs desk. Those who wear spectacles should bring along prescriptions.

Hygiene

Hygeiene cannot be taken for granted in Indonesia. Away from the tourist areas few places have running water or sewerage. Most water comes from wells, and raw sewerage goes into the ground and the rivers. Tap water is not potable and must be boiled.

Most cases of stomach complaints are attributable to your system not being used to the strange foods and stray bacteria. To make sure you do not get something more serious, take the following precautions:

Telephone Codes

From outside Indonesia, the following cities may be reached by dialing 62 (the country code for Indonesia) then the city code, then the number. Within Indonesia, the city code must be preceded by a 0 (zero).

City	Code	City	Code
Ambon	911	Mataram	364
Balikpapan	542	Medan	61
Banda Aceh	651	Merauke	971
Bandar Lampung	721	Metro	725
Bandung	22	Mojokerto	321
Banjarmasin	511	Nusa Dua	361
Banyuwangi	333	Padang	751
Batam	778	Palangkaraya	514
Belawan	619	Palembang	711
Bengkulu	736	Palu	451
Biak	961	Pare-Pare	421
Binjai	619	Pasuruan	343
Blitar	342	Pati	295
Bogor	251	Pekalongan	285
Bojonegoro	353	Pekanbaru	761
Bondowoso	332	Pematang-siantar	622
Bukittinggi	752	Ponorogo	352
Cianjur	263	Pontianak	561
Cilacap	282	Parapat	625
Cipanas	255	Probolinggo	335
Cirebon	231	Purwakarta	264
Cisarua	251	Purwokerto	281
Denpasar	361	Sabang	652
Gadog	251	Salatiga	298
Garut	262	Samarinda	541
Gresik	31	Sekupang	778
Jakarta	21	Semarang	24
Jambi	741	Serang	254
Jember	331	Sibolga	731
Jombang	321	Sidoarjo	319
Kabanjahe	628	Sigli	653
Karawang	267	Situbondo	338
Kebumen	287	Solo	271
Kediri	354	Sorong	951
Kendal	294	Sukabumi	266
Kendari	401	Sumbawa Besar	371
Klaten	272	Sumedang	261
Kota Pinang	624	Surabaya	31
Kotabaru	518	Tangerang	21
Kutacane	629	Tapak Tuan	656
Kuala Simpang	641	Tarakan	551
Kudus	291	Tasikmalaya	265
Kupang	391	Tebing Tinggi Deli	621
Lahat	731	Ternate	921
Lhok Seumawe	645	Tulung Agung	355
Lumajang	334	Ujung Pandang	411
Madiun	351	Wates	274
Magelang	293	Wonosobo	286
Malang	341	Yogyakarta	274
Manado	431		
Manokwari	962		

☛ Never drink unboiled water from a well, tap or *bak mandi* (bath tub). Brush your teeth only with boiled or bottled water, never with water from the tap or *bak mandi*. Bottled water is available everywhere and usually called "Aqua", which is the most popular and reliable brand name.

☛ Ice in Bali is made in government regulated factories and is deemed safe for local immunities. Confirm that the ice is made from boiled water before relaxing with an ice drink.

☛ Plates, glasses and silverware are washed in unboiled water and need to be completely dry before use.

☛ Fruits and vegetables without skins pose a higher risk of contamination. To avoid contamination by food handlers, buy fruits in the market and peel them yourself.

☛ To *mandi* (bathe) two or three times a day is a great way to stay cool and fresh. But be sure to dry yourself off well and you may wish to apply a medicated body powder such as Purol to avoid the nastiness of skin fungus, especially during the rainy season from November to April.

Diarrhea

A likely traveling companion. Called "Bali belly" locally. In addition to the strange food and unfamiliar micro-fauna, diarrhea is often the result of attempting to accomplish too much in one day. Taking it easy can be an effective prevention. Ask around before leaving about what the latest and greatest of the many remedies are and bring some along. Imodium is locally available as are activated carbon tablets (*Norit*) that will absorb the toxins giving you grief.

When it hits, it is usually self-limiting to two or three days. Relax, take it easy and drink lots of fluids, perhaps accompanied by rehydration salts such as Servidrat (local brands are *Oralit* and *Pharolit*). Especially helpful is water from the young coconut (*air kelapa muda*) or strong, unsweetened tea. The former is an especially pure anti-toxin. Get it straight from the coconut without sugar, ice or food color added. When you are ready, bananas, plain rice, crackers, and *bubur* (rice porridge) are a good way to start. Avoid fried, spicy or heavy foods and dairy products for a while. After three days without relief, see a doctor.

Intestinal Parasites

It is estimated that 80 to 90 percent of all people in Indonesia have intestinal parasites and these are easily passed on by food handlers. Prevention is difficult, short of fasting, when away from luxury hotel restaurants and even these are no guarantee. It's best to take care of parasites sooner rather than later, by routinely taking a dose of anti-parasite medicine such as *Kombatrin* (available at all *apotik*) once a month during your stay and again when you get on the plane home.

If you still have problems when you get back, even if only sporadic, have stool and blood tests. Left untreated, parasites can cause serious damage.

Cuts and Scrapes

Your skin will come into contact with more dirt and bacteria than it did back home, so wash your face and hands more often. Cuts should be taken seriously and cleaned with an antiseptic like Betadine solution available from any pharmacy (*apotik*). Once clean, antibiotic powder (*Sulfanilamide*) or ointment, both available locally, should be applied. Cover the cut during the day to keep it clean, but leave it uncovered at night and whenever you are resting so that it can dry. Constant covering will retain moisture in the wound and only encourage an infection. Repeat this ritual after every bath. Areas of redness around the cut indicate infection and a doctor should be consulted. At the first sign of swelling it is advisable to take broad spectrum antibiotics to prevent a really nasty infection.

Mosquito-Borne Diseases

Malaria is very rare in Bali, particularly in the southern tourist areas, but if you're heading beyond the island take a prophylaxis. Mefloquine (Larium) is recommended as it is effective against both Chloroquine- and Fansidar-resistant varieties which are present in Indonesia. Prescription runs from one week before departure through four weeks after leaving the infected area. Malaria symptoms are fever, chills and sweating, headaches, and muscle aches.

The other mosquito concern is **dengue fever**, spread by the morning-biting *Aedes aegypti*, especially during the rainy season. The most effective prevention is not getting bitten (there is no prophylaxis for dengue). Dengue fever symptoms are headache, pain behind the eyes, high fever, muscle and joint pains and rash appearing between the third and fifth days of illness. Within days, the fever subsides and recovery is seldom hampered with complications. The more serious variant, dengue haemorrhagic fever (DHF), which can be fatal, may be the reaction of a secondary infection with remaining immunities following a primary attack.

Cases of **Japanese encephalitis**, a viral infection affecting the brain, have occured recently and are added cause to take protective measures against mosquito bites.

Portable nets (*kelambu*) provide protection at night when sleeping; you can buy these in most general stores for $5. They're a hassle to put up in hotel rooms. Upon request, your room will be sprayed for insects. Be sure this is done long before you are ready to sleep if you want to avoid the smell and inhaling fumes. Aerosols clear out insect intruders, but do not have residual effect.

You can also buy slow-burning mosquito coils (*obat nyamuk bakar*), which last 6–8 hours. Light one before you go out for dinner to drive the critters away. Double Rabbit is one of the more reliable brands. (There are brands which do not contain pyrethum, so are ineffective. An electric (smokeless) version is also available.

Insect repellents and lotions are widely available and supermarkets do sell OFF! Any chemical repellent container deet (diethyl toluamide) should be applied with caution and never to the face. Application to clothing can be more effective. A local non-chemical solution is citronella oil (*minyak gosok, cap tawon*).

AIDS & Hepatitis B

Surprise! **Safe sex** is also a good idea in Indonesia. While AIDS in Indonesia is said to be a foreign problem, foreign experts project it to be one of monumental proportions. Documentation, awareness and education is just beginning. Another area of concern is the Hepatitis B virus which affects liver function and is only sometimes curable and can be fatal. The prevalence of Hepatitis B in Indonesia is the basis for international concern over the ominous possibilities for the spread of HIV virus, which is passed on in the same ways.

Medical Treatment

The Indonesian name for pharmacy is *apotik*; and a hospital is called *rumah sakit*. Smaller villages only have government clinics, called *Puskesmas*, which are not equipped to deal with anything serious.

Fancier hotels often have doctors on call or can recommend one. Misuse of antibiotics is still a concern in Indonesia. They should only be used for bacterial diseases and then for at least 10 to 14 days to prevent developing antibiotic resistant strains of your affliction.

Indonesians don't feel they've had their money's worth from a doctor ($5) without getting an injection or antibiotics. If either is prescribed, be sure it's necessary.

Ensure syringes have never been used before or better yet, buy your own disposable from an *apotik* (pharmacy) and take it to the clinic.

Emergency Medical Assistance

Even in the big cities outside of Jakarta, emergency care leaves much to be desired. Your best bet in the event of a life-threatening emergency or accident is to get on the first plane to Jakarta or Singapore. Contact your embassy or consulate by phone for assistance (see below). Medivac airlifts are very expensive ($26,000) and most embassies will recommend that you buy insurance to cover the cost of this when traveling extensively in Indonesia.

INSURANCE

Check your health insurance before coming to make sure you are covered. Travel insurance should include coverage of a medical evacuation to Singapore and a 24-hour worldwide phone number as well as some extras like luggage loss and trip cancellation.

AEA International Asia Emergency Assistance offers insurance packages for travelers and expatriates living in Asia. This well-respected outfit is considered to have the best response time and operation in Indonesia. AEA maintains 24-hour alarm centers in Jakarta, Bali, Singapore, Sydney, Bangkok, Hong Kong, Seoul, Beijing, and Ho Chi Minh City. Premium for one-year (approx. $125) is available for travelers and covers the cost of medical evacuation to Singapore and repatriation if recommended by the AEA doctor. Contact: **AEA International Pte. Ltd.**,331 North Bridge Road, 17th Floor, Odeon Towers, Singapore 0718. ☎ (65) 338 2311, fax: (65) 338 7611.

In Bali, information, coverage and evacuation is available through the regional representative for AEA, PT Bali Tourist International Assist, Jl. Hayam Wuruk 40/58, Denpasar 80235,☎ 228996 (emergency: 227271/231443), fax: 231442.

International SOS Assistance Asia Pacific Regional Head Office: 10 Anson Road, #21-08/A International Plaza, Singapore 0207. ☎ (65) 221 3981, fax: (65) 226 3937, telex: 24422 SOSAFE. Offers a range of emergency services worldwide. Numerous large corporate clients. Contact them for rates and types of coverage

FOOD AND DRINK

Drink lots of fluids. The equatorial sun takes out a lot from you and dehydration can be a serious problem. Symptoms are infrequent urination, deep yellow/orange urine, headaches.

Tap water in Indonesia is not potable and it should be brought to a full boil for ten minutes before being considered safe. Indonesians are themselves fussy about drinking water, so if you're offered a drink it is almost certainly safe.

Most Indonesians do not feel they have eaten until they have eaten rice. This is accompanied by side dishes, often just a little piece of meat and some vegetables with a spicy sauce. Other common items include *tahu* (tofu), *tempe* (soybean cake) and salted fish. Crispy fried tapioca crackers flavored with prawns and spices (*krupuk*) usually accompany a meal.

No meal is complete without *sambal*—a fiery paste of ground chili peppers with garlic, shallots, sugar, and sometimes soy sauce or fish paste. Fruit, especially pineapple and papaya provide quick relief for a chili-burned mouth.

Cooking styles vary greatly from one region to another. The Sundanese of West Java are fond of raw vegetables, eaten with chili and fermented prawn paste (*lalab/sambal trasi*). Minihasan food in North Sulawesi is very spicy, and includes some interesting specialties: fruit bat wings in coconut milk, *sambal* rat, and dog. In the more isolated parts of the archipelago, the food can be quite plain, and frankly, quite dull.

In most Indonesian restaurants there is a standard menu of *satay* (skewered barbequed meat)—most common are *ayam* (chicken) and *kambing* (goat), *gado-gado* or *pecel* (boiled vegetables with spicy peanut sauce) and *soto* (vegetable soup with or without meat). Also common are Chinese dishes like *bakmie goreng* (fried noodles), *bakmie kuah* (noodle soup) and *cap cay* (stir-fried vegetables).

In most larger towns you can also find a number of Chinese restaurants on the main street. Some have menus with Chinese writing, but usually the cuisine is very much assimilated to local tastes. Standard dishes, in addition to the *bakmie* and *cap cay* mentioned above, are sweet and sour whole fish (*gurame asem manis*), beef with Chinese greens (*kailan/caisim ca sapi*), and prawns sauteed in butter (*udang goreng mentega*).

Indonesian fried chicken (*ayam goreng*) is common and usually very tasty—although the local-grown chicken can be a bit stringy. Then there is the ubiquitous *nasi goreng* (fried rice); the special (istimewa) comes with an egg on top and is often served for breakfast.

There are restaurants everywhere in Indonesia that specialize in food from **Padang**, West Sumatra. This spicy, and very tasty cuisine has a distinctive way of being served. As many as 15-20 different dishes are displayed in the glass case in front of the restaurant. You tell the waiter what you want and he sets a whole stack of the little dishes in front of you. At the end of the meal, you are charged for what you have eaten and any untouched plates are put back in the case.

As tempting as fresh vegetables may be, avoid eating garnishes or raw salads unless the veggies are air-flown/imported.

The beers available in Indonesia are Bintang and Anker, both brewed under Dutch supervision and rather light (perhaps appropriately for the tropics). With electricity such a precious commodity, however, in out-of-the-way places the only way to quaff it cold is to pour it over ice.

Balinese Specialties

Balinese specialties include roast pork (*babi guling*) in which the pork is rubbed with tumeric, stuffed with spices and roasted over a spit, and roast duck (*bebek betutu*), where the duck is stuffed with vegetables and spices, wrapped in banana leaf and either smoked or steamed.

Balinese brews include *tuak* (palm beer), *arak* (palm brandy) and *brem* (sweet rice wine). See pages 80–81.

Fruits

Tropical fruits are plentiful and delicious. Bali is known specifically for *salak* which has a brown snakeskin covering three segments, two of which contain a large brown seed. It tastes like a cross between an apple and a walnut. *Manggis* (mangosteen) is pure heaven hidden within a thick purple-brown cover. The juicy white segments almost melt away. In season November to March.

Warung (Street Stalls)

Restaurant kitchens do not necessarily have healthier food preparation procedures than roadside *warung*. The important thing at a *warung* is to watch and judge whether or not the cooks inspire confidence. *Warung* rarely have a supply of running water, so beware.

The first portion may not fill you up, so a second portion can be ordered by saying *"Tambah separuh"* (add half portion). But only the price is halved. The amount of food is more like three-quarters. Finish off with a banana and say *"Sudah"* (I've had plenty, thank you). The seller will total up the prices of what was served you and ask you how many *krupuk, tempe,* etc. you added; so keep track. The total will come to between Rp500 and Rp2,500 (30¢ to $1.25).

Vegetarianism

Say *"saya tidak makan daging"* (I don't eat meat), *"tidak pakai ayam"* (without chicken) or *"tidak pakai daging"* (without meat). Dietary restrictions are very acceptable and common due to the various religious and spiritual practices involving food. However, finding food that truly has no animal products is a problem. Often meals which appear to be made exclusively of vegetables will have a chunk of beef or chicken in them to add that certain oomph.

SECURITY

Indonesia is a relatively safe place to travel and violent crime is almost unheard of, but petty crime is on the upswing. Pay close attention to your belongings, especially in big cities. Use a small backpack or moneybelt for valuables: shoulderbags can be snatched. Bags have been snatched by thieves on motorbikes, so be vigilant. Be especially wary on crowded *bemos*, buses and trains; this is where **pick-pockets** lurk. They usually work in groups and are very clever at slitting bags and extracting valuables without your noticing anything.

Be sure that the door and windows of your hotel room are locked at night, including those in the bathroom, as thieves are adept at sneaking in while you are asleep. Big hotels have **safety boxes** for valuables. If your hotel does not have such a facility, it is better to carry all the documents along with you. Make sure you have a photocopy of your passport, return plane ticket and travelers' check numbers and keep them separate from the originals.

Don't take valuables to the beach. Period. Bring your camera only if you're not going to swim or if you are in pairs and one can swim while one watches. You can ask other tourists to mind your gear while you swim, but they may decide to leave while you're in the water.

ADDRESSES

The Indonesian spelling of geographical features and villages varies considerably as there is no form of standardization that meets with both popular and official approval. We have seen village names spelled three different ways, all on signboards in front of various government offices. In this guide, we have tried to use the most common spellings.

There are three overlapping and concurrent address systems for any given location: old street name and number, new street name with new numbers, and *kampung* (neighborhood) name with block numbers. Every town now has its street named after the same national heroes, so you will find General Sudirman Street in every city throughout the archipelago.

The names with the new house numbers are the preferred designations for postal purposes. However, when tracking down a hotel address you may find that the old street names, the *kampung* names, or local landmarks more helpful. You will also find number 38 next to number 119 and the streets referred to by different names, such as Jalan Diponegoro (an Indonesian hero), Jalan Abdi Dongo (from local history) or Gajahan Gang II (the *kampung* name and alley number).

Finding Your Way

Westerners are used to finding things using telephone directories, addresses, and maps. But in Indonesia, phone books are incomplete, addresses can be confusing and maps little understood. The way to find something is to ask.

To ask for directions, it's better to have the name of a person and the name of the *kampung*. Thus "Bu Mumi, Banjar Kalah" is a better address for asking directions even though "Jalan Kaliwedas 14" is the mailing address. Knowing the language helps here but is not essential. Immediately clear answers are not common and you should be patient. You are likely to get a simple indication of direction without distance or specific instructions. The assumption is that you will be asking lots of people along the way. Begin by asking three people. Usually two point toward the same general vicinity. Proceed, then ask again.

Maps are useful tools for you, but introducing them into discussions with Indonesians may cause more confusion than clarity. More than likely the north arrow on the map will be turned to real north before a reading. Periplus-Travel Maps provide detailed and accurate maps of all major tourist destinations.

CALENDAR

The Indonesian government sets national holidays every year, both fixed and moveable dates. The fixed national holidays on the Gregorian calendar are the international New Year, Jan. 1; Independence Day, Aug. 17; and Christmas, Dec. 25. The Christian Good Friday, Easter Day, and Ascension Day, the Balinese new year, Nyepi, and the Buddhist Waisak are also legal holidays. These holy days and all the Muslim holy days are based on the moon, so confusion results in attempting to extrapolate several years ahead.

Official Muslim holidays in Indonesia (the dates are for 1996):

Idul Fitri February 21-22. The end of the Muslim fasting month, Ramadan, also called Lebaran. It is very difficult to travel just before and just after Idul Fitri everywhere except Bali, as just about everyone wants to return to their home village to celebrate and then return to their places of work in the cities.

Idul Adha April 29. The day of Abraham's sacrifice and the day that the haji pilgrims circle the Kaaba in Mecca.

Hijryah May 19. The Islamic New Year, when Muhammad traveled from Mecca to Medina.

Maulud Nabi Muhammad SAW July 28. Muhammad's birthday.

Isra Mi'raj Nabi Muhammad SAW. December. 8. When Muhammad ascended to heaven.

Balinese calendar

Bali runs simultaneously on several different calendrical systems, including the Western calendar, a Saka lunar calendar and a 210-day *pawukon* calendar.

The important Balinese holidays include:

Nyepi Balinese New Year is a day of silence and meditation. It falls in March or April each year on the day after the new moon, about the time of the vernal equinox. On Nyepi no physical activity occurs. This means no fire (cooking, electricity), no work, no travel, and no entertainment. Special dispensation is allowed for tourist buses and transportation between the airport and hotels only. Other touring is not allowed. Visitors must stay in their hotels where special permits grant minimal use of lights and minimal activities. Those staying outside hotels or in *losmens* will be required to observe the day of silence. This "silence" is taken seriously and should be respected by visitors.

The day after Nyepi is **Ngembak Nyepi** and

the roads are crowded with people visiting family, friends, temples, dances and drama performances.

Galungan begins on the Wednesday of Dunggulan, the 11th week of 30-week *pawukon* cycle. Pre-Galungan rituals involve offerings of animal sacrifices. One Galungan morning, everyone visits temples carrying colorful offerings.

Kuningan, 10 days after Galungan on the Saturday of Kuningan, the 12th week, marks the end of the celebration. It is a time for family gatherings, prayers and still more offerings as deified ancestors return to heaven.

The last day of the *pawukon* calendar, the Saturday of the Watugunung week, is **Saraswati** Day, when Saraswati, the goddess of knowledge and literature is honored. All books are blessed and no reading or writing is allowed. The next day, the first day of the first *pawukon* week, Sinta, is **Banyupinaruh**, when everyone goes to the beach for cleansing ceremonies.

For 1996–1997, the dates are:
Nyepi March 21, 1996
Galungan July 23, 1996
Kuningan August 2, 1996
Galungan February 19, 1997
Kuningan March 1, 1997
Nyepi April 9, 1997
Galungan September 17, 1997
Kuningan September 27, 1997

Temple Festivals

The temple festivals which are based on the 210-day *pawukon* calendar (*odalan*) last alternatively one day or three days. Some of the major ones are listed by the number and name of the Balinese week, then day of the week:
1. Sinta, Wednesday: Pura Kehen, Bangli
6. Gumbereg, Wed:
      Pura Desa/Puseh, Guang, Sukawati
7. Wariga, Sat: Pura Desa/Puseh, Batuan
11. Dunggulan, Fri: Pura Ulun Siwi, Jimbaran
12. Kuningan, Fri: Pura Taman Pule, Mas
13. Langkir, Wed: Pura Tanah Lot
14. Medangsia Tue: Pura Luwur, Uluwatu
16. Pahang, Wed: Pura Air Jeruk, Sukawati
19. Dwi Tambir: Tue, Pura Dalem Puri, Batuan
21. Matal, Wed: Pura Puseh/Desa, Sukawati
22. Uye, Sat: Pura Puseh/Desa, Gianyar
24. Prangbakat, Wed:
      Pura Rambut Siwi, Jembrana
27. Wayang, Sat:
      Pura Bhatara Ratu Gede, Celuk
29. Dukut, Tue:
      Pura Dalem Batuyang, Batubulan
30. Watugunung, Sat (Saraswati Day):
      Pura Banjar Tengah, Peliatan

The temple festivals based on the lunar calendar (*usaba*) begin on the full moon of the relevant month and last for several days. The major ones are:
April: Pura Besakih

Pura Ulun Danu Batur
October: Pura Besakih
          Pura Ulun Danu Batur
          Tirta Empul (Tampak Siring)

BALINESE CASTES & NAMES

There are four major groups: *brahmana, satriya, wesya,* and *jaba*. The *brahmana* are the priest caste; the *satriya,* the nobility; and the *wesya,* the merchants. Everyone else is *jaba*.

Balinese names are coded to reveal both caste and birth order within the family. Nothing, of course, is simple, especially when considering inter-caste marriages, and there are always exceptions. However, the following are clues to interpreting names:

Ida Bagus (male) and Ida Ayu (female) indicate *brahmana* caste. Gusti is normally used by members of the *wesya* caste, whereas Gusti Agung, Anak Agung, and Cokorda are reserved for the high-ranking members of the *satriya* caste. Desak (female) and Dewa (male) are lower-ranking *satriya*. I (normally male) and Ni (female) are usually used only by the *jaba*.

Wayan, Made, Nyoman, and Ketut mean first-born, second-born, third-born, and fourth-born, respectively. Beginning with the fifth child in the family, the cycle is repeated. Also used similarly to indicate birth order are Putu, Kadek, Koman, and Ketut. Nengah may be used by either the second or third-born child. The birth order names are normally used only by the *jaba* caste, so don't call a member of the *satriya* caste Wayan even if you happen to know that he/she is the oldest in the family!

ETIQUETTE

In the areas of Indonesia most frequented by Europeans, many are familiar with the strange ways of Westerners. But it is best to be aware of how certain aspects of your behavior will be viewed. You will not be able to count on an Indonesian to set you straight when you commit a *faux pas*. They are much too polite. They will stay silent or even reply *tidak apa apa* (no problem) if you ask if you did something wrong. So here are some points to keep in mind:

☛ The left hand is considered unclean as it is used for cleaning oneself in the bathroom. It is inappropriate to use the left hand to eat or to give or receive anything with it. When you do accidentally use your left hand then say *"ma'af, tangan kiri"* (please excuse my left hand).

☛ The head is considered the most sacred part of the body and, hence, the feet the least sacred. Avoid touching people on the head. Go for the elbow instead. Never step over food or expose the sole of your foot toward anyone.

☛ As it is impolite to keep one's head higher than others, it is appropriate to acknowledge the presence of others by stooping (extending the right arm, drooping the right shoulder, and leaning forward) while passing closely by someone who is sitting.

☛ Pointing with the index finger is impolite. Indonesians use their thumbs (palm turned upward, fingers curled in) or open palms instead.

☛ Summoning people by crooking the forefinger is impolite. Rather, wave downward with a flat palm face down.

☛ Alcohol is frowned upon in Islam, so take a look around you and consider taking it easy.

☛ Hands on hips is a sign of superiority or anger.

☛ Indonesians don't blow their noses. Keep a handkerchief handy.

☛ Take off your shoes when you enter someone's house. Often the host will stop you, but you should go through the motions until he does.

☛ Don't drink or eat until invited to, even after food and drinks have been placed in front of you. Sip your drink and don't finish it in one gulp. Never take the last morsels from a common plate.

☛ You will often be invited to eat with the words *makan, makan* ("eat, eat") if you pass somebody who is eating. This is not really an invitation, but simply means "Excuse me as I eat."

☛ If someone prepares a meal or drink for you it is most impolite to refuse.

Some things from the west filter through to Indonesia more effectively than others and stories of "*free sek*" (free sex) made a deep and lasting impression in Indonesia. Expect this topic to appear in lists of questions you will be asked in your cultural exchanges. It is best to explain how things have changed since the 1960s and how we now are stuck with "*saf sek*."

Bali may seem to have been placed here just for you personal enjoyment, but it is not a zoo. Be aware of Balinese sensibilities. Remember the Balinese are offended if the casual visitor does not dress appropriately when entering a temple. A sash over shorts and a T-shirt or a very brief top is not adequate. Have a sarong and sash handy for temple visits and ceremonies, and wear long pants or a skirt and a decent shirt with collar when leaving the beach areas.

Keeping Your Cool

At government offices like immigration or police, talking loudly and forcefully doesn't make things easier. Patience and politeness are virtues that open many doors in Indonesia. Good manners and dress are also to your advantage.

TRAVELING WITH CHILDREN

Luckily for those with children, the Balinese are very gentle and love to have kids around. But you should bring essentials: sunhats, creams, medicines, special foods, and a separate water container for babies to be sure of always having sterile water. Disposable dia-

pers are available in big supermarkets. Nights can sometimes be cool, so remember to bring some warm clothing for your tot. Milk, eggs, fruit which you can peel and porridges are readily available in the supermarkets here. Babysitters are available for a moderate charge at any hotel. An excellent general practitioner and family doctor is Dr. AA Made Djelantik, Jl. Hayum Waruk 190 (Bunderan Renon 101), Denpasar 80235, ☎ 238171. Consultations weekdays. General practitioner and pediatrician Dr. Conny Pangkahila is at Jl. Bypass Ngurah Rai 25X in Sanur (next to Ritra Cargo). Home phone, ☎ 288128; pager ☎ 234139 #302.

ACCOMMODATIONS

Indonesia has an extraordinary range of accommodations, much of it good value. Most cities have a number of hotels offering air-conditioned rooms with TV, minibar, hot water, swimming pool, etc. for $100/night and up. While at the other end of the scale, you can stay in a $2/night losmen room with communal squat toilet (bring your own toilet paper), a tub of water with ladle for a bath, and a bunk with no towel or clean linen (provide your own). And there's just about everything in between: from decrepit colonial hill stations to luxurious new thatched-roof huts in the middle of rice fields.

A hierarchy of lodgings and official terminology has been set by the government. A "hotel" is an up-market establishment catering to businessmen, middle- to upper-class travelers and tourists. A star-rating (one to five stars) is applied according to the range of facilities. Smaller places with no stars and basic facilities are not referred to as hotels but as *losmen* (from the French *logement*), *wisma* (guesthouse) or *penginapan* (accommodation) and cater to the masses and budget tourists.

Prices and quality vary enormously. In the major cities that don't have many tourists, such as Jakarta, Surabaya and Medan, there is little choice in the middle ranges and you have to either pay a lot or settle for a room in a losmen.

In areas where there are a lot of tourists, such as Bali and Yogya, you can get very comfortable and clean rooms with fan or air-conditioning for less than $25 a night. In small towns and remote areas, you don't have much choice and all accommodations tend to be very basic.

It's common to ask to see the room before checking in. Shop around before deciding, particularly if the hotel offers different rooms at different rates. Avoid carpeted rooms, especially without air-conditioning, as usually they are damp and this makes the room smell.

Advance bookings are necessary during peak tourist seasons (July to August, Christmas and New Year and the Muslim Lebaran holiday). Popular resorts are always packed on weekends, and prices often double, so go during the week when it's cheaper and quieter.

In many hotels, discounts of up to 50% from published rates are to be had for the asking, particularly if you have a business card. Booking in advance through travel agencies can also result in a lower rate. Larger hotels always add 21% tax and service to the bill.

Bathroom Etiquette

When staying in *losmen*, particularly when using communal facilities, don't climb in or drop your soap into the tub of water (*bak mandi*). This is for storing clean water. Scoop and pour the water over yourself with the ladle/dipper provided.

If you wish to use the native paper-free cleaning method, after using the toilet, scoop water with your right hand and clean with the left. This is the reason one only eats with the right hand—the left is regarded as unclean. Use soap and a fingernail brush (locals use a rock) for cleaning hands. Pre-packaged alcohol towelettes may make you feel happier about opting for this method. But don't throw the towelettes down the toilet.

Bring along your own towel and soap (although some places provide these if you ask).

Staying in Villages

Officially, the Indonesian government requires that foreign visitors spending the night report to the local police. This is routinely handled by losmen and hotels, who send in a copy of the registration form you fill out when you check in. Where there are no commercial lodgings, you can often rely on local hospitality. But when staying in a private home, keep in mind the need to inform the local authorities. One popular solution is to stay in the home of the local authority, the village head (*kepala desa*).

Carry photocopies of your passport, visa stamp and embarkation card to give to officials when venturing beyond conventional tourist areas. This saves time, and potential hassles, for you and your host.

Villagers in rural Indonesia do not routinely maintain guest rooms. If a cash arrangement has not been prearranged, you should leave a gift appropriate to local needs—biscuits, clothing, cigarettes, or D-cell batteries for radios in remote villages. Note down their address and send prints of the photos you took of them.

SHOPPING

Bali is a shopper's dreamland. The main tourist roads are lined with stores, shops and stalls selling crafts of all types. Lists of local specialties are found in the relevant practicalities sections; below is a general picture of what to look for.

Bargaining

The first price is not the last price in Bali. You should attempt to learn the art of bargaining while you're here. Unless you're buying in a shop or hotel arcade (and often here too), it is expected that you join in. Restaurant meals, items in supermarkets or department stores, and room rates at the larger hotels are generally fixed in price, but nearly everything else is fair game.

First ask the price that the vendor expects and then counter offer. Ask for the "best price" and keep smiling. Your initial offer should be much lower than the price you really want to pay. It is advisable not to seem too eager to buy. Keep a sense of humor about the whole thing. There's no such thing as a "right price." You usually pay more than the locals, but that's the way it is.

Souvenirs

For the widest selection of souvenirs, go to Jl. Legian in Kuta/Legian, Ubud, or the Batubulan Market on the way from Denpasar to Ubud.

Carvings

Mas and Kemenuh are the main spots for polished wood carvings; check with Tilem Gallery in Mas. Batuan is the place for wooden panels. Pujung and Sebatu, to the north of Ubud, specialize in painted carvings and giant statues. For masks, go to Mas, Singapadu, and Batuan.

Traditional Balinese stone carvings made from volcanic pumice (*paras*) are made in Batubulan.

Textiles

Bali is a weaver's dreamland. The *ikat* factories are centered in Gianyar, but Klungkung and Singaraja are also known producers. For the fancier *songket* with gold and silver threads woven into the weft, go to Sideman, Blayu (between Mengwi and Marga), or Singaraja. There are beautiful woven *selendang* (temple sashes) in Batuan, Ubud, and Mengwi, but the exquisite *geringsing* cloth is made only in Tenganan.

Woven textiles from Sumbawa, Sumba, and Sumatra can be found in Kuta and Denpasar.

The batik worn by Balinese and found everywhere is made in Java. When buying, be sure that you're getting real hand-drawn or stamped batik, and not the manufactured "printing" which employs traditional designs on machine-processed fabric. Balinese-made batik is lighter and brighter, much of it on cool "crinkle cotton".

Paintings

Ubud is the mecca of Balinese painting and the surrounding villages of Pengosekan, Penestanan, Sanggingan Peliatan, Mas and Batuan are all lively breeding grounds for the arts. The

Neka Gallery & Museum and the Puri Lukisan, both in Ubud, display some of the best work from around the island. Smaller galleries and art shops in Ubud may be your best bet for reasonably priced local work. You can also visit artists in their homes. For traditional calendar and "wayang-style" paintings, visit Kamasan village near Klungkung.

Antiques

Kuta and Denpasar are hunting grounds for antique dealers on the lookout for keris daggers, ornate beds, palm-leaf books, fabrics, masks, Chinese ceramics, sculpture and primitive statues from all over Indonesia. Be aware that the antique reproduction market is a lucrative one. The best insurance is to shop around until you have a good sense of quality and prices. To export anything older than 25 years old you must have a letter from the Museum Section of the Education and Culture Department.

Jewelry

Celuk, Kamasan (south of Klungkung), and Bratan in Buleleng are the traditional centers for gold and silverwork. The silver is 80%–90% pure. If you don't find anything you like ready-made, then custom-order. For modern designs, go to Kuta. Gold is 22K–24K. Sukawati is the traditional gold working village, or try the gold shops in Denpasar on Jl. Hasanuddin and Jl. Sulawesi. Be sure to bargain.

Beach Vendors

Vendors on the beach, especially Kuta, are obnoxious. Period. They sell everything from "pigs making bacon" to their sisters. They'll drive you nuts with boxes of copy watches and offers for massage, "braid your hair" or "manique" (sic). Good deals on sarongs and bikinis, but you have to bargain hard. Start out at 20% of their asking price and settle at 25–30%. To avoid them, lie on the beach sunbathing and pretend to be asleep, but sometimes, even this doesn't work. Key: Never make eye contact.

Shipping & Freight

Shipping goods home is relatively safe and painless in Bali. Items under one meter long and 10 kg in weight can be sent via most postal agents. All the packing will be done for you at minimal charge, although it's always advisable to keep an eye on how it's done. Buy insurance.

Larger purchases are best sent by air or sea cargo. In Bali, freight forwarders are almost as abundant as watch peddlars. Fowarders will handle the whole process for a price, from packing to customs. Many retailers are also prepared to send goods if purchased in quantity.

Air cargo is charged by the kilogram (10 kg min), and can be costly. Sea cargo (min. one cubic meter) is around $350 to the US or Europe and takes about 60 days. Insure your shipment: sea insurance is about 2.75% of the claimed value.

When shipping cargo, you are responsible for clearing customs back home and for the transportation from the port of entry to your destination. This can cost up to $500 so cargo is only economical for large purchases.

PHOTOGRAPHY

Indonesians generally enjoy being photographed. But, if you are in doubt or the situation seems awkward, it is polite to ask. Some religious activities, cockfighting (which is officially banned), eating, and bathing are inappropriate subjects.

Beware of the strong shadows from the equatorial sun. Late afternoon and, especially, early morning, provide the most pleasing light and the richest colors. The only way to deal with the heavy shadows in midday is to use a fill flash.

The heat and humidity of the tropics is hard on camera equipment. Be particularly careful when moving equipment from an air-conditioned room to the muggy outdoors. Moisture will condense on the inside and outiside of the camera, Wait until it evaporates; don't be tempted to wipe it off. Also, watch the location of your camera bag and film. Temperatures in hot cars or on boats can be searing.

In general, stick with reliable equipment you are familiar with and bring extra batteries.

Photographic Supplies

Some 35mm Fuji and Kodak film is widely available in Indonesia, including color print film from ASA 100 to 400 and Ektachrome and Fujichrome 100 ASA daylight transparency film. In larger towns you can buy Fuji Neopan 100 ASA black-and-white negative film and Fuji Velvia. Kodachrome (with processing included) and medium- and large-format emulsions are available only in Jakarta and Bali.

P.T. Modern Foto is the Fuji agent in Kuta, just opposite the gas station and Gelael Supermarket. It has fresh film and good E-6 processing. For prints, there are many instant mini-labs with while-you-wait service. In Denpasar, Tati Photo on Jl. Sumatra 10, ☎ 226912 or 228337 and Prima Photo on Jl. Gajah Mada 14, ☎ 225005 have a complete range of equipment and supplies.

You can get dressed in traditional Balinese costumes and have your picture taken in front of a kitsch backdrop. It's a one hour service and costs $3–5. For the best backdrops in Denpasar go to Diamond Foto on Jl. Thamrin 5, ☎ 426903 or Jl. Diponogoro 100, Blok A-2, ☎ 262692.

PROTECTED SPECIES

Indonesia is home to more than 500 animal species—more than anywhere else in the world. It also has the greatest number of endangered species in the world. Establishing an effective environmental conservation program is a formidable project. The government with the help of private conversation agencies, such as the World Wide Fund for Nature and the Nature Conservancy, is working to create a viable network of national parks and nature reserves where fragile ecosystems and threatened species can be protected. Two of these national parks, Ujung Kulon in West Java (home to the world's most endangered large mammal, the Javan rhino) and Komodo in the Lesser Sundas (home to the Komodo dragon) have been declared World Heritage Sites by the World Conservation Union.

There are strict laws and severe penalties for trade in endangered species. The appendices of the Convention on International Trade in Endangered Species (CITES) lists more than 200 protected species of Indonesian mammals, birds, reptiles, insects, fish, and mollusks—including orangutan, parrots, cockatoo, crocodiles, tortoises and turtles, birdwing butterflies, and black coral. Visitors should be aware of the fragility of Indonesia's natural environment and not contribute to any further degradation of it.

Balinese Species

Marine turtle meat, specifically the leatherback turtle, is considered a delicacy and one of the traditional dishes of ritual feasts. Leave it for the Balinese. It is illegal to export any products made from marine turtle shells (e.g. jewelry, combs, boxes). Also protected by international convention are clams, Triton's trumpet shells, and the pearly or chambered nautilus shells.

The Bali tiger is confirmed to be extinct. Efforts are on-going through the West Bali National Park to preserve the white, blue-faced Bali starling, which is found only in the wild on Bali and is very seriously endangered.

DANCE & ENTERTAINMENT

Bali has many venues which present a wide variety of dance and drama performances.

For the most traditional ambiance, go to the Ubud-Peliatan area. Here classical dances (legong, topeng, rajapala, gabor and others) are held in princely mansions and neighborhood halls every night. Wayang kulit (shadow puppet) performances are also held on Saturday night. See schedule on page 285.

A fire dance is held on Monday, Wedensday and Friday at 6:30 at Bona, southwest of Gianyar. The Puri Anyar in Krambitan also features traditional dances upon request. Check with your travel agent or with the local tourism office.

Kecak, barong and keris are the most popular dances for tourists. The Art Center shows, at 6:30 pm daily in Denpasar, are the best for kecak while the venues at Singapadu and Batubulan are excellent for barong and keris, both daily from 9:30 am.

Other venues are the La Galleria amphitheater in Nusa Dua, the Sri Wisata Budaya on Jl. Bypass Ngurah Rai and the major hotels. In Kuta, check with the Banjar Pengabetan neighborhood, and in Sanur, stop in at the Penjor, Baris, Canang Sari, Sari Karya, or the Swastika Garden II restaurants for a dinner show.

Bali is also famous for its ceremonial dances. If you have the patience (there is no designated "show-time") and if you are ready to conform to the local rules of dress and behavior, you may well be in for the experience of a lifetime. Ask Balinese friends for advice on attire and proper behavior, and check the Calendar of Events on the Balinese calendar found in every Balinese house. No camera flashes, no shouts, no shorts, and be discrete, please.

The Friday edition of the English-language Jakarta Post newspaper (available in all major tourist spots) has listings of traditional and contomporary music and dance performances in Bali, as well as the week's temple festivals.

ENTRANCE FEES

Almost all temples or tourist attractions levy an entrance fee or ask for a donation. Fees are usually between Rp. 500–Rp. 1,000. A similar amount is fine for a donation. Make sure it is entered into the donation book.

Some self-appointed "guides" are quite knowledgeable and willing to accept whatever you offer. Others may expect some exorbitant fee. If you want their services, it's best to agree on the amount first. Generally $1 for a half-hour escorted tour of a temple is enough.

SPORTS

Surfing

Bali has year-long surf and has become famous as a surfer's paradise. Kuta is the place to start out, as you can rent or buy boards there while scouting out tips on sites and tides. Popular spots, in rough order of difficulty, are Kuta, Legian, Seminyak, Sanur, south of Kuta off the airport reef, Canggu, Lalang Linggih, Medewi, Uluwatu, Padang-padang, and Nusa Lembongan.

For protection from the harsh tropical sun be sure to wear sunscreen and a T-shirt. Tend to coral cuts on feet and fingers immediately and constantly. They take forever to heal.

Refer to Kuta Practicalities (page 273 for surf shops offering equipment, tide tables, etc.)

Scuba-diving and snorkeling

Bali is a great place for snorkeling and scuba-diving. You can dive in the vicinity of Sanur and Nusa Dua, but the most exiting scuba-diving locations are in more remote places. Pulau Menjangan in the west is a favorite, as are Candidasa, Padangbai, Tulamben, and Amed in the east. Other spots are Nusa Penida, Nusa Lembongan, and Lovina. Inquire locally.

The calm waters of the Bali Sea make Singaraja a good site for snorkeling.

Contact, among others: **Bali Marine Sport** Jl. Bypass Ngurah Rai, Belanjong, Sanur, ☎ /fax: 287872. **Baruna** Jl. Bypass Ngurah Rai 300B, Tuban, ☎ 753820, fax: 753809. **Dive & Dive's** Jl. Bypass Ngurah Rai 23, Sanur, ☎ 288052, fax :289309. **Graha Santi** Jl. Danau Poso No 1, Sanur, ☎ /fax: 288714. **Oceana** Jl. Bypass Ngurah Rai 78, Sanur, ☎ 288892, fax: 288652.

Also, contact **Tour Devco** at Benoa harbor, ☎ 720591/771956, fax: 720592, to cross to Nusa Lembongan on a one-day trip for wonderful snorkeling, diving and surfing.

Other Watersports

Some companies have booths at the popular watersports locations. Prices may vary according to the time of year and location. Typical prices: **Banana boat**: $10 per person/round. **Diving**: $45 per person, half a day. **Jet Ski**: $20 for 15 mins. In Nusa Dua, Bedugul and Sanur. **Paddle canoe**: $6 per person/hour. **Parasailing:** $10/round. In Nusa Dua, Bedugul and Sanur. **Rafting**. Rafting has become a popular way to discover the most unknown parts of Bali: its gorges. Try: **Bali Adventure Rafting**, Jl. Tanjung Mekar, Legian Kelod, Kuta ☎ 751292; fax: 262316; **Sobek**, Jl. Tirta Ening No 9, Sanur, ☎ 287059, fax: 289448; **Bali Safari** (Telaga Waja River), Jl. Hayam Wuruk 88A, Denpasar, ☎ 221315, 221316, fax: 232268; **Ayung River Rafting** (Ayung River), Jl. Diponegoro 150B-29, Denpasar, ☎ 238759, 224236, fax: 224236. **Sailing**. You can also charter one of the many outriggers which line the beaches. They charge between $5 - $10/hour according to the beach, and lower rates for longer expeditions. For fishing, diving or sailing trips, many companies now operate from Benoa Harbor. Try : **Bali Camar Yacht Charter** ☎ 720591, 771956, fax 720592; or **Beluga** ☎ 771997, fax: 771967. Up-market hotels also offer yachting trips to neighboring islands. **Snorkeling**: $20 per trip. **Swimming**. For the safest ocean swimming, go to Sanur, Nusa Dua, or Lovina Beach on the north coast. The currents all along the southwest coast (including Kuta and Legian) is extremely strong. Swimming there is at your own risk. Even at waist deep, you can get ripped under. There are no lifeguards on the beach.

The pools at most of the major hotels are open to non-guests for $1–$5. Beluga in Nusa Dua has great pools. Other good public ones include Oongan in Denpasar and Penyu Dewata in Padang Galak near Sanur; all charge $1. Bukit Jati and Samplangan near Gianyar have large public pools which charge a small fee. **Waterskiing**: $20 for 15 mins. In Nusa Dua, Bedugul and Sanur. **Windsurfing**: $15/hour, beginner; $10/hour, experienced.

Biking & Hiking

These are the best ways to get to know the hinterlands of Bali intimately. Beware of sunstroke: start off early in the morning, and avoid the heat of the day. Sunglasses, a hat, sarong and sash are useful, as are a map or a clear geographic notion of your destination. Bottled mineral water is available all over the island.

The best areas for biking and hiking are around Ubud, Kintamani, the back-country of Lovina and Candidasa. Mountain bikes usually cost $1.50–$2 a day, except in Nusa Dua and Sanur where prices are inflated. Always check the bike: brake failure half way down a volcano is no fun. **Bali Adventure**, Jl. Tanjung Mekar, Legian, ☎ 751292, conducts bike tours.

Hiking tour services are available in Kintamani, Candidasa (Tenganan) and Tirta Gangga. Bird watching tours of Ubud are organized by Victor Mason, publican of the Beggar's Bush in Ubud.

Golf

Golf is becoming very popular in Bali. All courses have equipment and caddies.
Bali Handara Kosaido Country Club, village of Pancasari, Bedugul (☎ 228866), nestles in an ancient caldera. An hour from Denpasar, it has an international hotel and restaurant.
Bali Golf and Country Club, Nusa Dua, ☎ 771791. Within walking distance of Nusa Dua's main hotels.
The Grand Bali Beach, Sanur (ex Bali Beach Hotel), ☎ 288511. Has a small 9-hole course, used mostly by hotel guests and Balinese. Also has mini-golf for $2 per hour.

Transportation

GETTING TO INDONESIA

You can fly direct to Indonesia from just about anywhere. Most people traveling from Europe and the US arrive on direct flights to Jakarta, while those coming from Australia usually go first to Bali. The main international entry points are Soekarno-Hatta airport in Jakarta, Ngurah Rai airport in Bali, and Polonia airport in Medan. There are also non-stop flights from several Asian cities, including Singapore, Hong Kong, Taipei, Seoul, Nagoya, Fukuoka and Osaka.

Direct flights connect Bali with many major cities in Asia and Europe. Air fares vary depending on the carrier, the season and the type of ticket purchased. A discount RT fare from the US costs from $1,000–1,200 and from Europe costs $800–1,200; about half that from Australia or East Asian capitals. Garuda Airlines now has a direct flight from Los Angeles that flies non-stop between Honolulu and Denpasar.

An excursion fare return ticket from Singapore to Bali with stops in Jakarta and Yogyakarta, good for a month, is available in Singapore for around $300. Buy through travel agents—check the classified section of the Straits Times for details. **Note**: You need a return or onward ticket to get a visa-free entry upon arrival in Indonesia.

Air tickets from Batam and Bintan are also inexpensive. These Indonesian islands just off the coast of Singapore can be reached via short ferry hops from Singapore's World Trade Center. Ferries to Batam cost $12 single, $17 return and to Bintan $32 single, $45 return. Inquire at travel agents in Singapore for latest fares, then compare with direct Singapore to Bali discount rates.

Garuda offers a visit pass to foreigners purchasing outside of Indonesia. A minimum of three coupons can be purchased for $300. Additional coupons are $100 each, up to 10 coupons. One coupon is valid for one flight and you can not return to a destination already covered. If the flight is not directly to your intended destination, you are charged one coupon per stop. This program is good value for long-haul travel within Indonesia, Medan to Jakarta for instance or Bali to Biak, which otherwise is quite costly.

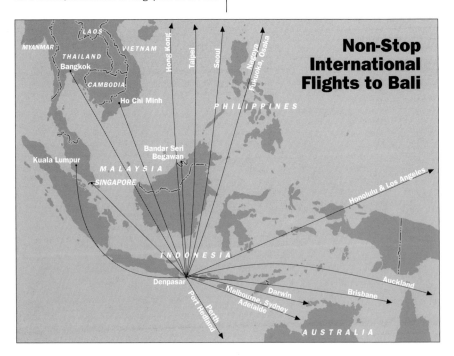

Non-Stop International Flights to Bali

TRAVELING IN INDONESIA

Having arrived in Indonesia, your choices for onward travel depend, as always, on time and money. Travel on Bali ranges from boats, self-drive and chauffeur driven cars, to both slow and fast buses, bicycles and motorbikes. Hiring a car or minibus with or without driver, is one of the most rewarding ways of getting around.

In many ways, Indonesia is an easy place to get around. Indonesians are, as a rule, hospitable, good-humored, and willing to help a lost or confused traveler. The weather is warm, the pace of life relaxed, and the air is rich with the smells of clove cigarettes, the blessed durian fruit and countless other wonders.

However, the nation's transportation infrastructure does not move with the kind of speed and efficiency that Western travelers expect, which often leads to frustration. Bookings are often difficult to make; flights and reservations are sometimes mysteriously canceled.

It is best to adjust your pace to local conditions. What seems like nerve-wracking inefficiency is really so only if one is in a hurry. If you have to be somewhere at a particular time, allow plenty of time to get there. Check and double-check your bookings. Otherwise just go with the flow. You can't just turn off the archipelago's famous *jam karet*—"rubber time"—when it's time to take an airplane and turn it on again when you want to relax. You will get there eventually.

Peak periods around the Christmas/New Year holidays and during the June to August tourist season are the most difficult. It is imperative to book well in advance and reconfirm your bookings at every step along the way. Travel anywhere in Indonesia (except Bali) during the week prior to the Islamic Lebaran holiday is practically impossible. Find a nice spot and sit it out.

The golden rule is: things will sort themselves out. Eventually. Be persistent, of course, but relax and keep your sense of humor. Before you explode, have a cup of sweet coffee or a cool glass of *kelapa muda* (young coconut water). Things might look different.

Planning an Itinerary

The first thing to do is to be easy on yourself and not plan an impossibly tight schedule. Things happen slowly here, so adjust to the pace. Better to spend more time in a few places and see them in a leisurely way, than to end up hot and hassled. You'll see *more* this way.

Wherever you are, keep in mind that the tropical heat takes its toll and you should avoid the midday sun. Get an early start, before the rays become punishing (the tropical light is beautiful at dawn). Retreat to a cool place after lunch and go out again in the afternoon and early evening, when it's much more pleasant.

AIR TRAVEL

The cardinal rule is book early, confirm and reconfirm often. If you are told a flight is fully booked, go to the airport anyway and stand in

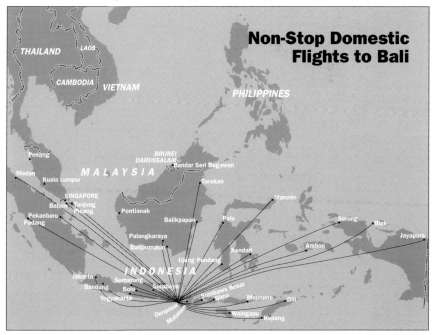

Non-Stop Domestic Flights to Bali

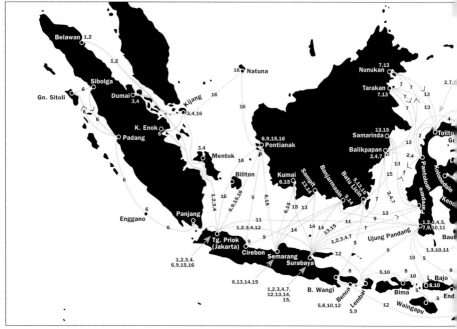

line. While Garuda's booking system is computerized, the other local airlines' are not, and bookings evaporate at the last minute all the time. However it is rare that flights are completely full. Always keep the following points in mind:

✈ It's practically impossible to get a confirmed booking out of a city other than the one you're in. You can buy a ticket and it may say you have a booking, but don't believe it until you reconfirm with the airline in the city of departure.

✈ Reconfirm bookings directly with the airline office in the city of departure between 24 and 72 hours before your flight, particularly during peak tourist seasons and Indonesian holidays. Your seat may be given away if you reconfirm either too early or too late (or not at all).

✈ Make bookings in person, not by phone.

✈ Get written proof or computer printout of bookings. Note the name of the person who gives it to you so you can hold them responsible if your booking "disappears".

✈ Note the computer booking code or PRN (passenger record number). Names have a tendency to go astray or be misspelled. Concrete proof of your booking is essential.

✈ If your name isn't on the computer try looking under your first or middle names as these are frequently mistaken for surnames.

✈ If you are told a flight is full, ask to be put on the waiting list, then go to the airport about two hours before departure and the waiting list. Hang around the desk and be friendly to the staff and you will probably get on the flight. A tip will sometimes, but not always, help.

✈ There are usually alternate ways of getting from point A to B. For example, from Yogyakarta to Bali, if there is no space left on the flights, take a bus to Surakarta (Solo) and fly from there.

✈ Generally, students (12–26 years old) receive a discount of 10%–25% (show an international student ID card), and children between the ages of 2 and 10 pay 50% of the regular fare. Infants not occupying a seat pay 10% of the regular fare. Be sure to ask the airlines or travel agent.

Garuda Indonesia's flagship airline has been in business since 1946. It serves all major cities in Indonesia and at least 38 international destinations. They fly only jets, mainly wide-bodies, and the service is reasonably good.

Merpati A Garuda subsidiary, with a domestic network serving more than 160 airports throughout Indonesia. Merpati (literally "pigeon") flies smaller jets and turboprops (McDonnell Douglas DC-9s, Fokker VFW F-28s) as well as turbo-props (Fokker F-27s, Canadian DeHavilland DHC-6 "Twin-Otters," the Indonesian built Casa Nusantara CN-235s and CN-212s, and Boeing B-737 jets).

Merpati is not known for its punctuality or its service or its safety, but the airline does at least connect towns and villages across the archipelago, in some cases landing on a grass airstrip in a highland village of only 100 people that would take days to reach by any other means. Consider yourself lucky that you can even fly to these places.

Merpati's standard baggage allowance is 20 kg. for economy class, but some of the smaller aircraft permit only 10 kg. (after which excess baggage charges of $1/kg. apply).

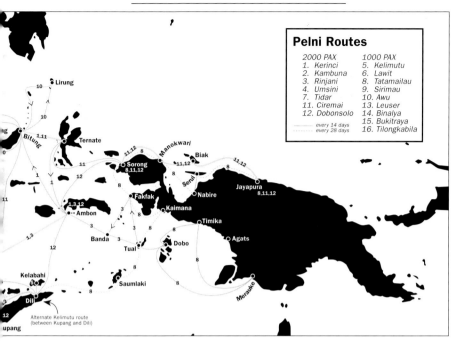

Pelni Routes

2000 PAX	1000 PAX
1. Kerinci	5. Kelimutu
2. Kambuna	6. Lawit
3. Rinjani	8. Tatamailau
4. Umsini	9. Sirimau
7. Tidar	10. Awu
11. Ciremai	13. Leuser
12. Dobonsolo	14. Binalya
	15. Bukitraya
——— every 14 days	16. Tilongkabila
------ every 28 days	

Alternate Kelimutu route
(between Kupang and Dili)

Sempati A privately-owned competitor, with quality service and a growing network inside and outside of Indonesia. Sempati flies new Fokker F-28s and F-100s to several cities in Asia, such as Singapore, Kuala Lumpur, Taipei, and Perth. Domestically it flies between major cities such as Jakarta, Yogyakarta, Surabaya and Denpasar. Sempati has also added destinations previously difficult to reach from Denpasar, such as Balikpapan, Banjarmasin, Tarakan, Palangkaraya, Palu, Padang, and Manado.

Bouraq A small, private company, flying mainly older planes and a few newer B-737s linking secondary cities in Java, Bali, Kalimantan, Nusa Tenggara, Sulawesi, and other remote destinations.

Mandala Operates a few prop planes and B-737s to out-of-the-way airstrips in Sulawesi, Kalimantan and Sumatra.

NOTE: Travel agents often give cheaper fares than airline offices and are easily found. Good for ticketing are **Pacto**, The Grand Bali Beach Hotel, Sanur, ☎ 288247/8, 288511 and **Vayatour**, ☎ 223757.

To and From Bali

Bali's Ngurah Rai airport has daily flights to and from major Indonesian cities, as well as to the islands of eastern Indonesia. Garuda, Merpati, Sempati, Bouraq, and Mandala fly on domestic routes. Many international airlines operate on the island. Almost all the major airlines flying to Bali have an office at The Grand Bali Beach in Sanur or the Wisti Sabha Building at the airport.

Airline Offices

Many airline offices are at The Grand Bali Beach Hotel in Sanur: Air France ☎ 755523. Ansett Australia ☎ 289636. Cathay Pacific ☎ 753942. Continental-Micronesia 287065/287774. Garuda ☎ 288243. Japan Airlines and Japan Asia Airways ☎ 287576/287577. Lufthansa ☎ 286952. MAS ☎ 288716/288511. Qantas ☎ 288331. Sempati Air ☎ 288824. Singapore Airlines ☎ 287940. Thai ☎ 285071/3.

Wisti Sabha Building at the Airport houses: Air New Zealand ☎ 756170/751011 ext. 1116. China Airlines ☎ 754856/757298. EVA Air ☎ 298935. KLM ☎ 756127. Korean Air Lines ☎ 754856/757298, fax: 757275. Royal Brunei ☎ 757292.

Offices in Denpasar: **Garuda** Jl. Melati 61, ☎ 225245 ticketing, hours: 8–4:45 Mon–Sat, 9–1 Sun/national holidays, ☎ 227825/234606 reservations 24-hours. **Merpati** Jl. Melati 51, ☎ 235358 ticketing, hours:7 am–9 pm daily, reservations 24-hours. **Bouraq** Jl. Sudirman 7A ☎ 237420 reservations, hours: 8 am–9 pm. **Sempati** Jl. Diponegoro, Komplek Diponegoro Megah, Blok B/No. 27, ☎ 237343, reservations and ticketing daily, 24-hours.

Departure Tax

Airport tax for departing passengers is Rp. 21,000 for international routes and Rp. 8,800 for domestic flights.

SEA TRAVEL

There is four times as much sea in Indonesia as land and for many centuries transportation among the islands has been principally by boat. Tiny ports are scattered all over the archipelago and the only way to reach many areas is by sea.

To travel by boat you need plenty of time. Most ships are small and are at the mercy of the sea and the seasons. Think of it as a romantic journey and don't be in a hurry.

Pelni (Pelayaran Nasional Indonesia), the national passenger line, has 10 large ships (some 70 ships total) criss-crossing the archipelago carrying up to 1,500 passengers each. These boats travel on fixed schedules and the first and second class cabins are comfortable. Check the route map above for destinations served and contact Pelni's main office for a current schedule.

Many of the older vessels look like floating trash cans, but the new German-built passenger ships are modern and comfortable. Fares are fixed, and there are up to 5 classes, determining how many people share a cabin and kinds of services. Book through travel agents in Bali.

To and from Bali

Java to Bali. If you travel overland from Java, you have to take the ferry. It's a pleasant half-hour trip from Ketapang to Gilimanuk, with many private and state-run services that run continuously at 15–25 minute intervals. Getting on can be a hassle during the Indonesian holidays when you may have to wait several hours: best avoided.

Bali to Lombok. You may also want to venture over to Lombok. Most ferries leave from Padangbai in east Bali; there are ferries daily every two hours beginning at 6 am and the fare is between Rp. 4,800 and Rp. 8,700. The rate for cars is about $25.

A more luxurious alternative on this route is the **Mabua Intan Express**, a 40-meter catamaran that speeds at 60 km/h between Benoa and Lembar, taking just 2 hours. Reclining seats, overhead lockers, a bar and even special facilities for the handicapped make this a luxury affair. There's one catch: in rough weather the cat literally jumps over the waves, causing a lot of upset stomachs.

Departures from Benoa are at 8am and 2.30pm; from Lembar at 11.30am and 5.30pm. There are three classes: Economy Class for $12.50. Emerald Class or Lower Deck costs $17.50 and includes a juice and a coffee. Diamond Class or Upper Deck costs $25 and includes a snack, juice, coffee and transfers at both ends of the line: on Lombok to or from Mataram or Sengiggi; on Bali to or from Nusa Dua, Kuta, Sanur or Denpasar. ☎ 772521

(Benoa harbor, Bali) or ☎ (0364) 37224 (Lembar harbor, Lombok).

OVERLAND TRAVEL

Road conditions in Indonesia have improved dramatically over the past years, but traffic has also increased and driving is a hazardous affair.

Trucks and buses, minivans, swarms of motorcycles piled with goods or carrying a family of four, ox-drawn carts, horse-drawn carts, bicycles, pedicabs (*becak*) and pedestrians of all ages compete in what is at times a crazy battle for tarmac, where the biggest and fastest rule.

Rental cars and motorcycles are available in many major cities, and a number of different types of buses run cheap and regular services.

By Train

Trains are very slow. A first-class Bima night train leaves Jakarta in the late afternoon, reaching Surabaya early the next day. From Surabaya you transfer to a Mutiara train to Banyuwangi on the eastern tip of Java (7 hours) and then take a bus to Denpasar. The whole trip takes 30 hours. It is safe and cheap, at under $40 non-AC, second class.

Night Express Buses—*Bis Malam*

These buses leave in late afternoon and go all night, and often well into the next day. When *bis malam* cross from island to island, they go on the ferry. The fare includes simple meals.

The better buses have a bathroom, loud video and arctic air-conditioning: the other reason you brought a sweater. The key to successful *bis malam* trips is sleep. Choose the best bus available as the price difference is usually not very great and comfort for the long trip is essential.

Most buses have televisions and show videos, often followed by music. You are likely to be the only one who is annoyed by the volume, but a cheerful suggestion that the music be turned off (*dimatikan*) will at least get it turned down to the point where earplugs can block out the rest. There are also karaoke "sing-along" buses—for masochists and anthropologists only.

The seats to avoid are in the very front and the very back. The back seats are raised up over the engine and don't recline, while front row seats give you too intimate a view of what the driver is doing. You can also buy two seats, which will make sure you don't get squashed. The price is cheap enough that most budgets can handle two fares.

On many buses, you can reserve one day ahead. Tickets are sold at the bus terminal or by bus ticket agents and travel services or ask if your hotel or *losmen* can make the bookings for you. There are usually several buses going your way. Shop around to see what you can get.

The trip from Jakarta takes about 27 hours. The night buses leave the Pulo Gadung terminal in Jakarta at 3 pm and arrive in Denpasar (Ubung terminal) at sunset the following day. The one-way fare is about $25 non-AC and $35 AC. Similar AC buses leave for Denpasar from Surabaya's Bungurasih terminal, fare $11; and from Yogyakarta for $20: both one-way.

Local Buses

The major advantages of these rattling buses is that they are extremely cheap, run every few minutes between major towns, and can be picked up at the terminals or any point along their routes. This is also their biggest disadvantage: they stop constantly to pick up passengers.

If you depart from a terminal, find a seat near a window that opens. Try not to share this breeze with passengers behind you; they are likely to have a strong aversion to wind for fear of masuk angin (the wind which enters the body and causes a cold).

The seats are very small, both in terms of leg room and width. You and your bag may take up (and be charged for) two seats. This is fair. But be sure you're not being overcharged. Ask someone what the proper fare is to your destination before getting on. A few words of Indonesian are indispensable for asking directions. People are generally very eager to help you.

Buses depart throughout the day from Ubung terminal in Denpasar for Yogyakarta, Surabaya, Jakarta, and many other destinations. Bus company agents are located on Jl. Hasanuddin in Denpasar. Agung Transport, Jl. Hasanuddin 97, ☎ 222663, has tickets to all destinations.

Express Minibus

Called either mikrolet or travel, these come in two varieties: old and hot (sit by a window and keep it open) and the newer, much revered, L300 van with air-conditioning. Even the L300 gets a lot of engine heat and at midday can still be sauna-like, especially if the air-conditioning is broken and the windows shut.

These 8 to 11 passenger vans connect major cities and deliver you right to your destination. Sometimes they also pick you up. They usually travel during the day, though on longer routes they travel at night like the bis malam. Express minibuses are slightly more expensive than bis malam but more convenient. Buy tickets at the mikrolet/travel office; they do not pick up passengers along the way.

Chartering a Car or Minibus

This can be the best way to handle a land tour as you have the freedom to stop whenever things look interesting and the flexibility to try out some less traveled routes. This can also be an economical alternative if you can fill up a van. The minibus can take up to 7, but you need extra space if you are to be in it for a few days, so 5 passengers is generally maximum.

The quality of both the driver and the vehicle will figure heavily in the pleasure of your trip so don't be shy about checking both out before striking a deal.

Your driver should be responsible and have a personality that won't grate on you in the long haul. If he knows the area you will be seeing and can speak some English, so much the better.

The air-conditioning should work well enough to overcome the midday heat and the vehicle should be clean and comfortable.

Travel agents and services can arrange these charters. For going to and from Bali count on paying between $30–$40 a day for an AC van, excluding fuel. You also pay for fuel, so distance is a major factor. Most of the rest goes to the owner of the vehicle, and only a tiny percentage left for the driver. It is understood that you will pay for the driver's meals and accommodation both while he is with you and on his journey back home. If the driver is good, a tip of Rp 5,000 per day is appropriate.

GETTING AROUND BALI

Taxis

A reliable taxi cooperative operates from the airport with fixed rates to Kuta Beach for Rp 6,500; Legian Rp. 8,500; Sanur Rp15,000; Nusa Dua Rp15,000; Denpasar Rp11,000 and Ubud Rp40,000. Pay at the desk located just outside the terminal near left luggage, and give the coupon to your driver.

If you don't have much luggage, you can walk out of the airport (turn right) to the main road and catch a public bemo minibus to Kuta (Rp500), or Denpasar (Rp800).

Many hotels rent taxis and minibuses with English-speaking driver/guide. Nusa Dua's resort hotels have taxi counters. Expect to pay a minimum of $15 for 2 hours and $40–50 or more for day trips. Rates from Nusa Dua are higher.

The Praja Taxi and Bali Taxi companies have metered vehicles with "set government prices." **Praja** ☎ 289090, **Bali Taxi** ☎ 701111. These AC cabs are blue and yellow or blue and have a taxi sign on the roof. Most drivers are friendly, but usually speak little English. Always insist that the meter be switched on and don't agree to a fixed price. "It's up to you" means it's getting really expensive and possibly nasty. Flag-fall is Rp800, and most trips within Kuta/Legian are around Rp2,000–Rp4,000. If you go from Kuta to Sanur and Ubud, let the car wait and use it for 4–6 hours. The meter fare should be about Rp8,000–Rp10,000/hour.

Due to local monopolies, taxis from outside cannot pick you up at the airport or in Nusa Dua.

Shuttle Buses

A regular shuttle service operates between Ubud, Kuta, Candidasa and various other destinations. For those who want quick fixed-price transportation without the hassles of the local bemo, check with **CV Ganda Sari Transport** on Jl. Legian, Kuta, ☎ 754383; or **Perama Tourist Service** in Kuta, ☎ 751875, 751170. In Ubud try **Cahaya Sakti Utama Tour and Travel**, ☎ 975520.

Private Minibuses

Arguably the best way for small groups to travel around, as these vehicles are generally big and comfortable with large windows for sightseeing. Charters cost between $30 to $40 per day with AC, excluding fuel. Minibuses are widely available on the street. You'll be offered "transport" everywhere you go. These drivers are open to negotiation. To avoid the negotiation process, ask for assistance at your hotel or any one of the abundant travel agent desks.

Public *bemos*

Except on the cross-island routes, public buses are non-existent in Bali. The most efficient form of transport is the *bemos* (minibuses), which are marked on the back fender: "*Angkutan*" (transport) and the name of the area they serve. They ply every major road in Bali at regular intervals. They can also be chartered for almost any kind of trip, or just for the day, by simply asking the driver (see below).

Denpasar has several *bemo* terminals, on the outskirts of the city for destinations beyond. The fares for normal passage (not charter) are listed below. Individual drivers may charge more.

Tegal Terminal to/from
Southwest of Denpasar, serving points south:

Kuta	Rp800	Kerenang	Rp800
Airport	Rp700	Jimbaran	Rp1,200
Nusa Dua	Rp1,500		

Ubung Terminal to/from
Northwest of Denpasar, serving points north and northwest:

Bedugul	Rp2,000	Gilimanuk	Rp3,000
Singaraja	Rp2,000	Kediri	Rp800
Mengwi	Rp800	Tabanan	Rp800

Batubulan terminal to/from
Northeast of Denpasar, serving points east and northeast:

Kereneng	Rp500	Kintamani	Rp1,100
Ubud	Rp800	Klungkung	Rp1,100
Bangli	Rp900	Candidasa	Rp1,500
Amlapura	Rp1,500		

Other routes. There's a direct connection from Sanur to Batubulan, but to go up-country from other southern beaches you must change in Denpasar. From Kuta or Nusa Dua you have to go first to Tegal Terminal (west), hop on a city bemo to Ubung Terminal (northwest) or Batubulan Terminal (northeast) and change again. Each inter-terminal hop will cost you at least Rp600. There are always plenty of touts.

Bemos run between Sangeh (Monkey Forest) and Jl. Kartini in the heart of Denpasar for Rp600. From Suci and Sanglah, in the south of the city, a *bemo* takes you to Benoa harbor for Rp600. On Jl. Gunung Agung (west) a *bemo* goes to Gianyar for Rp600.

Bemo Charters

You can charter any of the public *bemos* that ply Bali's roads for around $20–$25 a day, gasoline included, or for one-way trips to a specific location. These usually cost between $2–10 depending on the distance, the time of day and the amount of business the *bemo* is getting. The more run-down the vehicle, the cheaper it'll be. Bargain hard.

Driving On Your Own

Driving in Bali is not for the faint-hearted. Vehicles and creatures of every size, shape and description charge onto the road out of nowhere. The traffic is horrendous on the main highways. Drive slowly and carefully and beware of the trucks at night. Road construction sites are not marked and few cyclists have reflectors. The condition of road networks has considerably improved in recent years, however, and driving off the beaten track is one of the best ways to discover Bali. Check your fuel gauge regularly as there are few gas stations away from the main roads. Small roadside fuel shops, indicated by a "Premium" sign, sell gasoline for the bit more than the Pertamina stations.

A valid international license is required for driving cars and motorbikes. If you do not have one, you can get a provisional license at the local *Polres* (police headquarters) on the road between Denpasar and Kerobokan. Insurance is not compulsory, but strongly recommended. You can get a policy from most of the rental companies and travel agents.

Renting vehicles is very cheap. Small Suzuki Jimny jeeps and larger Toyota Kijang are available for a daily rate between $20 and $30. Discounts are available during the off-season and for longer periods. Drivers are usually available for an additional $5 a day. Check the condition of the car before signing the contract. Beware: vehicles are usually rented with an empty tank.

There are rental car companies at almost every street corner of the main resorts. More important than the agency you rent from is to check and test-drive the car before renting. A selection: **Bali Happy Rent Car** Jl. Raya Kuta 72X, Kuta, ☎ 751954.
Khairusan Rent Car, Jl. Kartika Plaza, Kuta, ☎ 753608.

Mita Rent Car Jl. Pratama IA, outside Nusa Dua gate, ☎ 771491.

Norman's Car Rental, Jl. Sanur Beh, Sanur, ☎ 288328.

Nusa Dua Rent a Car, Jl. Pantai Mengiat 23, Nusa Dua, ☎ 771905.

Puri Sarana , Jl. Pratama 70, Tanjung Benoa, ☎ 771329.

Putra Intan Rent Car, Jl. Bypass Ngurah Rai (in front of Tragia), Nusa Dua, ☎ 771946.

Toyota Rent a Car & Leasing, Ngurah Rai Airport, ☎ 753744; Jl. Raya Tuban 99X, ☎ 751356; Jl. Bypass Ngurah Rai, ☎ 701747.

Motorbike Hire

Motorcycling used to be the best way to travel on Bali but with the increase in traffic it has lost many of its charms and become increasingly dangerous. Be careful and stick to the back roads.

There are several cooperatives (BAKOR) which rent bikes in Denpasar, Kuta and Sanur, but bike rentals are usually handled through car hire companies or on a person to person basis. The price is usually $5–$7 a day, lowering to $60-$70 a month, including near-useless crash helmet. Check the bike over carefully before renting it—you are likely to be charged for repairs.

Make sure you have the registration papers, in case you are stopped by the police. Also ensure you have good accident insurance covering emergency air transportation home or to Singapore in case of a serious accident. Several tourist casualties occur each month. Insurance sold at time of rental normally covers damages or loss of the bike, with a minimal deductible.

TOURS AND TRAVEL AGENTS

Travel agencies offer a variety of tours with knowledgeable, multilingual guides. A half-day trip to Ubud or Sangeh/Mengwi costs about $7 per person, while a day tour plus lunch and visits to shops and temples, with perhaps a barong dance at Batubulan, should cost $15–$20.

Hiring your own vehicle for a private tour naturally allows you much more flexibility. An AC vehicle with a driver/guide costs anywhere from $30 up to $60 per day, all inclusive. The guides on both types of tours do expect tips, however be aware that they also get a 20–40 percent commission on any of your purchases in the large souvenir shops along the way.

Hotels and travel agents can arrange tours. **BIL** and **Pacto** are highly recommended. The standard tours available are: Bedugul Tour, Denpasar Tour, Karangasem Tour, Kintamani Tour, Monkey Forest Tour, Nusa Penida Sailing, Tanah Lot Tour, Turtle Island Tour, Ubud/Handicraft Tour.

Reputable Tour Agents

Bali Indonesia Ltd (BIL) Travel Desk, Bali

Hyatt Hotel, Sanur, ☎ 288271. 288361; Jl. Danau Tamblingan, ☎ 288463/4.

Bali Sinar Mentari, Jl. WR Supratman 99, ☎ 227879.

Grand Komodo Tours Jl. Bypass Ngurah Rai 9, Sanur, ☎ 288480, fax: 287165.

Jan's Tours Jl. Nusa Indah 62, Denpasar, ☎ 232660, 234930, fax: 231009

KCB Tours & Travel Jl. Imam Bonjol 599, Kuta, ☎ 751517, fax: 752777

Maniara Tours Jl. Bypass Ngurah Rai 88XX, Sanur, ☎ 288821, 288379, fax: 287073

Natrabu Jl. Bypass Ngurah Rai 58X, Sanur, ☎ 288660.

Pacto/AmEx The Grand Bali Beach Hotel, Jl. Bypass Ngurah Rai, Sanur, ☎ 288247 (9 lines), 288511, fax: 288240, 287506.

Satriavi Jl. Danau Tamblingan 27, Sanur, ☎ 287074, fax: 287019

Smailing Tour Jl. Bypass Ngurah Rai 88X, Sanur, ☎ 288738.

Indonesian Language Primer

Personal pronouns
I *saya*
we *kita* (inclusive), *kami* (exclusive)
you *anda* (formal), *saudara* (brother, sister),
  kamu (for friends and children only)
he/she *dia* they *mereka*

Forms of address
Father/Mr *Bapak* ("*Pak*")
Mother/Mrs *Ibu* ("*Bu*")
Elder brother *Abang* ("*Bang*" or "*Bung*")
  Mas (in Java only)
Elder sister *Mbak* (in Java only)
Elder Brother/sister *Kakak* ("*Kak*")
Younger brother/sister *Adik* ("*Dik*")
Note: These terms are used not just within the family, but generally in polite speech.

Basic questions
How? *Bagaimana?*
How much/many? *Berapa?*
What? *Apa?*
What's this? *Apa ini?*
Who? *Siapa?*
Who's that? *Siapa itu?*
What is your name? *Siapa namanya ?*
(Literally: Who is your name?)
When? *Kapan?*
Where? *Di mana?*
Which? *Yang mana?*
Why? *Kenapa? Mengapa?*

Civilities
Welcome *Selamat datang*
Good morning (7–11am) *Selamat pagi*

Good midday (11am–3pm) *Selamat siang*
Good afternoon (3–7pm) *Selamat sore*
Goodnight (after dark) *Selamat malam*
Goodbye (to one leaving) *Selamat jalan*
Goodbye (to one staying) *Selamat tinggal*
Note: *Selamat* is a word from Arabic meaning "May your time (or action) be blessed."
How are you? *Apa kabar?*
I am fine. *Kabar baik.*
Thank you. *Terima kasih.*
You're welcome. *Kembali.*
Same to you. *Sama sama.*
Pardon me *Ma'af*
Excuse me *Permisi*
(when leaving a conversation, etc).

Numbers

1	*satu*	6	*enam*
2	*dua*	7	*tujuh*
3	*tiga*	8	*delapan*
4	*empat*	9	*sembilan*
5	*lima*	10	*sepuluh*
11	*seblas*	100	*seratus*
12	*dua belas*	600	*enam ratus*
13	*tiga belas*	1,000	*seribu*
20	*dua puluh*	3,000	*tiga ribu*
50	*lima puluh*	10,000	*sepuluh ribu*
73	*tujuh puluh tiga*		

1,000,000 *satu juta*
2,000,000 *dua juta*
half *setengah*
first *pertama* third *ketiga*
second *kedua* fourth *ke'empat*

Pronunciation and Grammar

Vowels
a As in father
e Three forms:
  1) Schwa, like the **e**
  2) Like **é** in touché
  3) Short **e**; as in bet
i Usually like long **e** (as in Bali); when bounded by consonants, like short **i** (hit).
o Long **o**, like go
u Long **u**, like you
ai Long **i**, like crime
au Like **ow** in owl

Consonants
c Always like **ch** in church
g Always hard, like **g**uard
h Usually soft, almost unpronounced. It is hard between like vowels, e.g. *mahal* (expensive).
k Like **k** in **k**ind; at end of word, unvoiced stop.
kh Like **k**ind, but harder
r Rolled, like Spanish **r**
ng Soft, like fli**ng**
ngg Hard, like ti**ngl**e
ny Like **ny** in So**ny**a

Grammar
Grammatically, Indonesian is in many ways far simpler than English. There are no articles (a, an, the).
The verb form "to be" is usually not used. There is no ending for plurals; sometimes the word is doubled, but often number comes from context. And Indonesian verbs are not conjugated. Tense is communicated by context or with specific words for time.

Time

minute *menit*	Sunday *Hari Minggu*	
hour *jam*	Monday *Hari Senin*	
(also clock/watch)	Tuesday *Hari Selasa*	
day *hari*	Wednesday *Hari Rabu*	
week *minggu*	Thursday *Hari Kamis*	
month *bulan*	Friday *Hari Jumat*	
year *tahun*	Saturday *Hari Sabtu*	
today *hari ini*	later *nanti*	
tomorrow *besok*	yesterday *kemarin*	

What time is it? *Jam berapa?*
(It is) eight thirty. *Jam setengah sembilan*
  (Literally: "half nine")
How many hours? *Berapa jam?*
When did you arrive? *Kapan datang?*
Four days ago. *Empat hari yang lalu.*
When are you leaving?
  Kapan berangkat?
In a short while. *Sebentar lagi.*

Useful words

yes *ya*   no, not *tidak, bukan*
Note: *Tidak* is used with verbs or adverbs;
bukan with nouns.

and *dan*	better *lebih baik*
with *dengan*	worse *kurang baik*
for *untuk*	this/these *ini*
good *bagus*	that/those *itu*
fine *baik*	same *sama*
more *lebih*	different *lain*
less *kurang*	here *di sini*
from *dari*	there *di sana*
to be *ada*	to be able, can *bisa*
to buy *beli*	correct *betul*
to know *tahu*	wrong *salah*
to get *dapat*	big *besar*
to need *perlu*	small *kecil*
to want *ingin*	pretty *cantik*
to go *pergi*	slow *pelan*
to wait *tunggu*	fast *cepat*
at *di*	stop *berhenti*
to *ke*	old *tua, lama*
if *kalau*	new *baru*
near *dekat*	then *lalu, kemudian*
far *jauh*	only *hanya, saja*
empty *kosong*	crowded, noisy *ramai*

Small talk

Where are you from? *Dari mana?*
I'm from the US. *Saya dari Amerika.*
How old are you? *Umurnya berapa?*
I'm 31 years old.
  Umur saya tiga pulu satu tahun.
Are you married? *Sudah kawin belum?*
Yes, I am. *Yah, sudah.*   Not yet. *Belum.*
Do you have children? *Sudah punya anak?*
What is your religion? *Agama apa?*
Where are you going? *Mau ke mana?*
I'm just taking a walk. *Jalan-jalan saja.*
Please come in. *Silahkan masuk.*
This food is delicious.
  Makanan ini enak sekali.
You are very hospitable.
  Anda sangat ramah tamah.

Hotels

Where's a losmen? *Di mana ada losmen?*
cheap losmen *losmen yang murah*
average losmen *losmen biasa*
very good hotel *hotel cukup baik*
hot water *air panas*
Please take me to... *Tolong antar saya ke...*
Are there any empty rooms?
  Ada kamar kosong?
Sorry there aren't any. *Ma'af, tidak ada.*
How much for one night?
  Berapa untuk satu malam?
One room for two people.
  Dua orang, satu kamar.
I'd like to stay for 3 days.
  Saya mau tinggal tiga hari.
Here's the key to your room.
  Ini kunci kamar.
Please call a taxi. *Tolong panggil taksi.*
Please wash these clothes.
  Tolong cucikan pakaian ini.

Restaurants

to eat *makan*   to drink *minum*
drinking water *air putih, air minum*
Where's a good restaurant?
  Di mana ada rumah makan yang baik?
Let's have lunch. *Mari kita makan siang.*
I want Indonesian food.
  Saya mau makanan Indonesia.
I want coffee, not tea.
  Saya mau kopi, bukan teh.
May I see the menu?
  Boleh saya lihat daftar makanan?
I want to wash my hands.
  Saya mau cuci tangan.
Where is the toilet? *Di mana kamar kecil?*
fish, squid, goat, beef, chicken
  ikan, cumi, kambing, sapi, ayam
salty, sour, sweet, spicy
  asin, asam, manis, pedas

Shopping

I don't understand. *Saya tidak mengerti.*
I can't speak Indonesian.
  Saya tidak bisa bicara Bahasa Indonesia
Please, speak slowly.
  Tolong, berbicara lebih pelan.
I want to buy... *Saya mau beli...*
Where can I buy... *Di mana saya bisa beli...*
How much does this cost? *Berapa harga ini?*
2,500 Rupiah. *Dua ribu, lima ratus rupiah.*
That cannot be true! *Masa!*
That's still a bit expensive. *Masih agak mahal.*

Directions

north *utara*	west *barat*	
south *selatan*	east *timur*	
right *kanan*	left *kiri*	
near *dekat*	far *jauh*	
inside *di dalam*	outside *di luar*	

I am looking for this address.
  Saya cari alamat ini.
How far is it? *Berapa jauh dari sini?*

1 Denpasar PRACTICALITIES

Denpasar is the bustling commercial heart of Bali. Jl. Gajah Mada is the main street, running east-west. It changes names to Jl. Dr. Wahidin to the west and Jl. Surapati to the east. The center of commercial activity is on Jl. Diponegoro and Jl. Teuku Umar.
Prices in US dollars. AC = Air-conditioning. Telephone code is 0361.

TRANSPORTATION

Traffic is heavy and streets are often jammed during peak season. The three-wheeled *bemo* vehicles serve the inner city, while the four-wheeled versions serve the suburban terminals. Fare for a terminal to terminal journey is Rp600.

Bemos can also be chartered for jaunts around town, but we advise you to take the Praja or Bali Taxi metered taxis (see Travel Advisory).

Taxi-bikes (motorbikes with drivers) are also available. You can hire a *dokar* (horse cart), for about Rp1000 per km. However, the best way to get around Denpasar is on foot. The city is relatively small and you'll want to look in the shops anyway.

For **tourist services** see Travel Advisory.

ACCOMMODATIONS

Denpasar has two hotels of historical and cultural note, **Bali Hotel** and the **Pemecutan Palace Hotel**. The rest of the hotels in Denpasar are *losmen*-style, catering mostly to groups and domestic tourists. If you're on a tight budget and travel with a group, these can be a great bargain. During the Indonesian holiday seasons (June through August, Lebaran and Christmas/New Year), the hotels fill up, so make reservations in advance.

Bali Jl. Veteran 3, ☎ 225681/5, fax 235347. 75 rooms. The first hotel on Bali, built by the Dutch in the early 1930s and now part of the Natour chain. Centrally located near the town square, this was where authors Miguel Covarrubias, Colin McPhee and others stayed. It has a good restaurant famous for its *rijsttafel*, and a swimming pool. Many rooms with AC, hot water, phone. $60–$66, suite $102.

Dharmawisata Jl. Imam Bonjol 83, ☎ 222186. 32 rooms. The Indonesian style bathrooms are clean and pleasant. Swimming pool. $5–$8.

Dirgapura Jl. Diponegoro 128, ☎ 226924. 26 rooms. Each room faces the garden. $4.50–$9.

Pemecutan Palace Jl. Thamrin 2, ☎ 423491. 40 rooms. This hotel occupies one side of the Badung palace grounds, and palace life continues around

you. Caged songbirds awaken you in the morning. $23–$27.

Suli Inn Jl. Suli 19. 12 rooms In the up-market part of town. $9 fan, $20 AC/bathtub, incl. breakfast.

Taman Wisata Jl. Nangka 98A, ☎ 236015. 41 rooms. Comfortable and clean. $7 fan, $35 AC.

DINING

Denpasar is a great place for all styles of Indonesian and Chinese food. Prices are very reasonable. Many good restaurants are found on Jl. Teuku Umar, Jl. Sumatra and on Jl. Veteran, near the Satria bird market. Also check out the night markets and food centers.

Ayam Bakar Taliwang Jl. Teuku Umar. Spicy hot Sasak (Lombok) style cuisine. Specialties: *plecing kangkung* (swamp spinach) and grilled chicken.

Bundo Kanduang Jl. Diponegoro 112 A, near Kerta Wijaya shopping center. ☎ 228551. Best Padang food in town: open 24 hrs.

Hong-Kong Restaurant Jl. Gajah Mada 99 ☎ 434845. The local favorite for Chinese food.

Kak Man Jl. Teuku Umar. Authentic Balinese food in a Bali-kitch setting.

Mie Ayam Jakarta Jl. Veteran. Famous for its Chinese *mie* (noodles) and *bakwan* (meatball) soups.

Prambanan Restaurant Jl. Hayam Wuruk 30XX, next to the RRI radio station. ☎ 221909. Great Javanese food in a beautiful wooden building.

Soto Ayam Suroboyo Jl. Veteran, nr Satria bird mkt. Specializes in *soto* chicken soup and other EastJavanese dishes.

Warung Sate Muslim, Jl. Thamrin. Best satay in town.

There are three good restaurants on Jalan Sumatra (near the Corsica newsstand). **Betty** serves Indonesian favorites such as *mie goreng* and frogs legs for a couple of dollars. **Depot 88** has delicious Chinese meat balls and the **Depot Kikel** has good Javanese *soto* soup. For authentic Balinese food, try **Warung Nasi Gemah Ripah** on Jl. Gianyar, near the Sri Partha bank.

Night Markets and Food Centers

For an authentic local experience check out one of Denpasar's night markets (*pasar malam*), where you sit out under the stars and eat at small food stalls. Open from sunset to 10 pm. The biggest is at Kereneng terminal, another is outside the Kumbasari shopping center. The food is mostly Javanese and Balinese.

For the whole range of local food in a cleaner, if less exotic, environment try the food centers, located in the city's supermarkets (see below).

SHOPPING

Denpasar is where Balinese villagers come for all their day-to-day necessities. Most shops close at 1 pm, re-open 6–10 pm.

Markets and Supermarkets

Pasar Badung is Bali's biggest traditional market. Located on the eastern bank of the Badung river, it is in the heart of the city. The first floor has fresh produce, flower offerings and spice vendors. The third floor has textiles, dance costumes and traditional accessories. At Denpasar's supermarkets and department stores prices are fixed and cheap, and quality is high. The six main ones are: Tiara Dewata, Matahari, Libi, Siwa, Kerta Wijaya, and New Dewata Ayu.

Textiles

Modern textiles. Kampung Arab, Jl. Sulawesi; or Toko Yadnya, Jl. Gajah Mada. Tailored clothes at Alus, Jl. Gajah Mada; or Adhie, Jl. Sumatra. **Traditional textiles**. Lestari at the Lokitasari shopping center, Jl. Thamrin, sells traditional *songket* fabric directly from the loom. Danar Hadi, at the same shopping center, sells fashionable batiks from Java. Take a look at Surya Jaya, Jl. Gajah Mada 128, for *ikat*. Kumbasari market, on the west bank of the river, also has a wide variety of *songket* and batik materials.

Handicrafts and Antiques

Pasar Kumbasari and Pasar Badung have all sorts of Balinese crafts for reasonable prices. **Satria Art Market** specializes in handicrafts. Also try the craft shops on Jl. Sulawesi and Jl. Gajah Mada. For genuine antiques, visit **Arts of Asia**, behind Lokitasari shopping center, Jl. Thamrin.

Gold and Silver

Jl. Hasanuddin and Jl. Sulawesi are full of gold shops. Prices are comparable to Singapore or Hong Kong; the gold is 22–24 carat. Check out the Balinese jewelry made of beaten gold on the second floor of Kumbasari market. Mega Artshop, Jl. Gajah Mada 36-38, has silver jewelry.

Coffee

Balinese coffee makes a great souvenir. Toko Bhinneka Jaya, Jl. Gajah Mada 80 (☎ 222053), is the biggest producer and distributor of coffee in Bali. $2.50 per kilo for robusta; $9 per kilo for arabica.

MISCELLANEOUS

Banks. These banks process advances against your credit card for 5% commission. Take your passport. Bank Central Asia (MasterCard), Jl. Hasanuddin 58, ☎ 431010, Bank Duta (Visa), Jl. Hayam Wuruk 165, ☎ 223223.

Cultural Events. The Balinese swarm to Denpasar for cultural attractions, so be prepared to be caught in a big crowd of locals. On the eve of the Nyepi day (Balinese new year), usually in March, hundreds of *ogoh-ogoh* papier machet monsters are carried along the streets of the city. This extraordinary torch-lit cavalcade is reminiscent of a small scale South American carnival.

Bali's annual **arts festival** is held from mid-June to mid-July at the Art Center off Jl. Hayam Wuruk. A month of dance, discussions and exhibitions. The Art Center also holds daily *kecak* dances at 6 pm. *Barong* performances at Kesiman at 9.30 pm.

Beautiful collections of terracotta, carvings, painting and ceremonial costumes are found at the **Bali Museum**, on the eastern side of Puputan Square. Open daily, 8 am–5 pm. Friday til 3 pm. Closed Monday.

Hospital. Sanglah General Hospital, Jl. Kesehatan Selatan 1, Sanglah, Denpasar. Switchboard/Emergency , ☎ 227911/5.

Massage. Masseurs in Denpasar are more professional than those at Kuta. Panti Pijat Canthi, Jl. Hayam Wuruk 20, offers traditional healing and massage for $5 an hour—although the price for tourists might be higher. Open 8 am to 10 pm.

Movies and Nightlife. Wisata cineplex has 5 screens. There's also the Indre theater and the Kumbasari. Check the *Bali Post* for details. The Wisata discotheque is on the top floor of the Kumbasari building. Filled with local youth.

Pharmacy. Apotik Kimia Farma, Jl. Diponegoro 123–125, ☎ 227812.

Photo Processing. Toti Photo at Jl. Sumatra and Fuji Image Plaza at Jl. Thamrin are quite professional. Have your portrait taken wearing a Balinese outfit.

Newspapers. *Bali News* is an English-language supplement twice monthly to *Karya Bakti* newspaper.

Opticians. International Optical, Jl. Gajah Mada 133, ☎ 226294. Lily Kasoem, Jl. Teuku Umar 77XX, ☎ 238405.

Postal services. The central post office is on Jl. Raya Puputan, Renon. Open 8 am–8 pm. Other post offices: Jl. Diponegoro, near Teuku Umar crossroads; Jl. Kamboja, near Kereneng terminal; Jl. Supratman.

Telecommunications (Wartel). The main telecom office is next to the central post office. Open 8 am to 8 pm. Other telecom offices: Jl. Teuku Umar and Jl. Kaliasem, near Puputan square. Smaller *wartels* are scattered across the city.

—updated by Debe Campbell

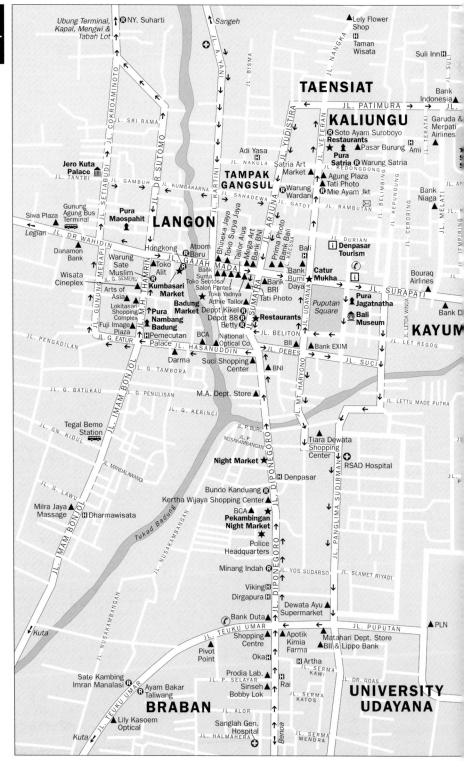

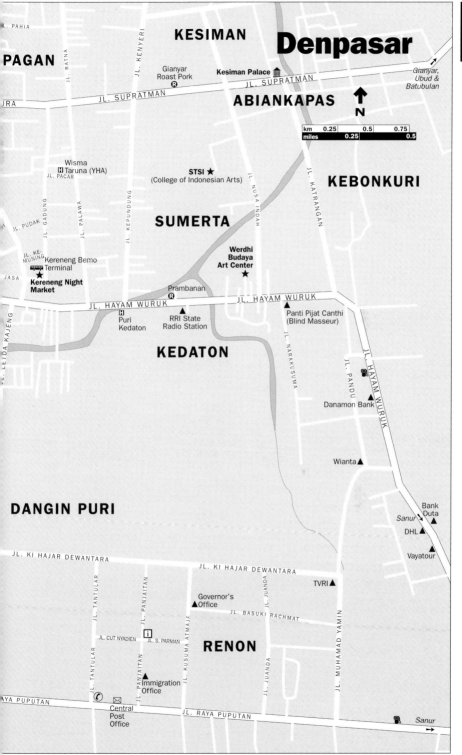

Denpasar

PAHIA

PAGAN

KESIMAN

JL. RATNA

JL. KENYERI

Gianyar
Roast Pork
ⓡ

Kesiman Palace 🏛

JL. SUPRATMAN

JRA

JL. SUPRATMAN

ABIANKAPAS

Gianyar,
Ubud &
Batubulan

N

| km | 0.25 | | 0.5 | 0.75 |
| miles | | 0.25 | | 0.5 |

Wisma
Ⓗ Taruna (YHA)
JL. PACAR

STSI ★
(College of Indonesian Arts)

JL. NUSA INDAH

JL. KATRANGAN

KEBONKURI

JL. KEPUNDUNG

JL. GADUNG

JL. PALAWA

JL. PUDAK

SUMERTA

Werdhi
Budaya
Art Center ★

JL. KE-
MUNING

Kereneng Bemo
🚌 Terminal
★

JASA

Kereneng Night
Market

Prambanan
ⓡ

JL. HAYAM WURUK

JL. HAYAM WURUK

JL. LEIDA KAJENG

Ⓗ
Puri
Kedaton

RRI State
Radio Station ▲

Panti Pijat Canthi
(Blind Masseur)

JL. NARAKUSUMA

KEDATON

JL. PANDU

JL. HAYAM WURUK

🏧
Danamon Bank ▲

Wianta ▲

DANGIN PURI

Sanur

Bank
Duta ▲

DHL ▲

Vayatour

JL. KI HAJAR DEWANTARA

JL. KI HAJAR DEWANTARA

TVRI ▲

JL. TANTULAR

JL. PANJAITAN

Governor's
▲ Office

JL. JUANDA

JL. BASUKI RACHMAT

JL. MUHAMAD YAMIN

JL. CUT NYADIEN

ⓘ
JL. S. PARMAN

JL. KUSUMA ATMAJA

RENON

JL. JUANDA

JL. TANTULAR

JL. PANJAITAN

▲ Immigration
Office

YA PUPUTAN

✆

✉

Central
Post
Office

JL. RAYA PUPUTAN

🅿

Sanur

2

Sanur PRACTICALITIES

Sanur is where Bali's first luxury beach hotel was built over 30 years ago, and has since been the spot for luxurious seaside accommodation. Conveniently located near Denpasar on the main road leading to the east, Sanur is not nearly as frenetic as Kuta, nor as well-mannered as Nusa Dua. Many foreigners have built lavish villas and bungalows here and this is the preferred place for up-market, long-term stays on the island, especially in the Batujimbar and Belanjong areas.

The main attraction here is the white sand beach bordering a reef-sheltered lagoon. The beach stretches south from the The Grand Bali Beach Hotel and ends up in the mangrove marshes opposite Serangan Island. Due to the protection of the lagoon, this beach is one of the safest on the island, and thus perfect for families. There is no surf apart from out on the reef, and one cannot swim at low tide, but at other times this is the best place in Bali for windsurfing and sailing.

Prices in US dollars. AC = Air-conditioning. Telephone code is 0361.

ORIENTATION

Sanur can be divided into several sub-areas: **The Grand Bali Beach Hotel area**. West and south of the hotel, at the point where the black and the white sand beaches meet. This northern section of Sanur is popular with local crowds. **Sindhu** is east of Jl. Bypass Ngurah Rai, and south of Jl. Segara Ayu, extending south to the first stretch of Jl. Danau Tamblingan. This area is classier, with good hotels on the beach, night and art markets, and good restaurants. **Batujimbar**, further south, has few hotels, but is the location of expatriate and Indonesian jet-set society mansions. Exclusive beaches are reached via small lanes.

Semawang stretches south from the Bali Hyatt Hotel to the Sanur Beach Hotel and beyond. It houses both the priciest hotels and restaurants, as well as the red light district.

TRANSPORTATION

Get to Sanur from the airport by **taxi**. Tickets available at the taxi desk, $7. Within Sanur either rent a car or catch one of many public *bemos* that ply Jl. Danau Tamblingan for Rp. 500. These can be chartered for short hops around Sanur ($1-2), and for trips to Denpasar or Kuta ($2-4). Bargain hard. The terminal of the Praja Taxi company is in Sanur, ☎ 289191/289090. Bali Taxi is in Kuta, ☎ 753950.

Biking around Sanur is also fun. At the **Tri Dewi Artshop**, just across from Ronny's Restaurant in Semawang, you can rent a bike for $0.70 per hour or $7 a day; try bargaining. Take the small lanes leading south to the beach temple of Mertasari. Then head for Suwung and hop on a boat to Pulau Serangan.

Sanur is an ideal base for trips to Bali's rice growing heartland and the mountain areas. Rent a self-drive car or a minibus with driver on a daily basis. There are car rental companies on Jl. Bypass Ngurah Rai and on Jl. Danau Tamblingan. Cars and minibuses for hire are found outside all major hotels.

The most reputable self-drive rental agencies are **Avis**, which has desks at the airport (☎ 756141), in the Nusa Dua Beach Hotel (☎ 771210) and the Sheraton Lagoon Nusa Dua (☎ 771327); and **Bali Car Rental** (☎ 288550) on Jl. Bypass Ngurah Rai.

A day-trip in a minibus with a multilingual guide costs around $60–70 including gas, depending on the itinerary. Group tours cost as little as $10–15 for the main tourist destinations. Contact **Pacto** (☎ 288247), **Tunas Indonesia** (☎ 288581), or your hotel travel agent.

ACCOMMODATIONS

The choice of accommodations in Sanur ranges between the superior service and extensive facilities of the larger luxury establishments such as The Grand Bali Beach (formerly Hotel Bali Beach), the Bali Hyatt and the Sanur Beach, or the intimacy and personal attention of smaller bungalow-style hotels.

Make your choice based on location, rather than the number of stars. Some hotels charge no extra cost for two children under 12 years old occupying the same room with parents. Reservations are advisable throughout the year,

Denpasar

Ubud
Sanur Agung
BSB Sanur
Village Club
Pura Dalem
Depot Anda

JL. SANUR

RENON

Golf
Driving
Range

Pura
Buruan

JL. SANUR

Sekar
Tanjung
Antiques

Grand
Komodo

Canangsari

Miranda
Inti Alam
Mirama
Watering
Hole
Pino
Sanur
Paradise

Dinasti
Ananda Hotel & Rest.
Alit Beach Bungalow
Nusa Lembongan tickets/departure
Diwangkara

Money
Changer

Beach Market
Nona
Museum Le Mayeur
Sunrise

Police
Fin Cargo

Grand Bali Beach
Airline Offices

Grand Bali
Beach Golf
Course

Selat
Badung

JL. TUKAD BILOK

JL. DANAU BUYAN

Gelael
Supermarket

Taman Sari
Rani
Sanur Indah
Rafflesia

Sanur
Pharmacy

Bhinneka
Money Changer
Mini
Packing & Shipping
Warung Pojok

US
Consulate

SEGARA AYU

Swiss

Pura
Segara

Bank

ABC

Opal Opulence
Istana Garden
Mango Bar

Sanur Beach Market & Rest.
Segara Village
Borneo
Baruna Beach Inn

JL. TEGEH AGUNG

INTARAN

Sanur Art Market
Warung Sahabat
Abian Srama Inn
Colors of Asia
Oceana Dive
Smailing Tours
Sanur Plaza
Orient Express

Bali
Moon

Sita

Janur
Garden

Kampung Sanur
Swastika I
Sanur Photo
Kalpataharu

Lotus Pond
Imba Leather

Rent Car

SINDHU

Sindhu Beach
Rumors Nightclub

Subec Disco
La Taverna
LG-Sehatku
Sindhu Corner
Gazebo
BSB Respati

Modes Dewi Segara
Money Changer
BSB Irama
Tandjung Sari

Kuri Putih

Levi Photo Center
Bumi Ayu Bungalow

Lenny's Seafood

Ritra Cargo

Bali Artha Expedition

Nuratni Duty Free Shop

Mina Garden
JJ's
Nogo
Kita

Bayu Garden

BSB Besakih
Santrian Beach
Bungalows I

Image Network
Swastika II
Swastika Bungalows
Ramayana

German
Consulate

JL. PANTAI KARANG

Werdhapura

Laghawa
Beach Inn

Mira

Pacto Tours

Tanahmas

Griya Photo
No. 1 Disco
Penjor
Taman Agung

Nanbankan Sushi &
Steakhouse

Eden

Orchid Villa
New Seoul

Cafe Batujimbar
(Jingala Ceramics,
Kika Book Store)
Kul Kul
Sari Karya
Bun Do

Sin Bo Lan

Batujimbar
Estates

JL. BETNGANDANG

JL. KESARI

BATUJIMBAR

Kariya Cargo

BSB Paneeda
View

Telaga Naga

Paon

SIDAKARYA

Chiku Teh
Bali Marine

Bali High
Legong

Bella
Oka's Bar
Nogo
Bali Yobbo

Agung
Warung Jawa Barat
Sativa Sanur Cottages

Bagus

Bali Hyatt

JL. KARANGSARI

JL. DUYUNG

SEMAWANG

Palm Garden

Bali Senia

JL. DANAU POSO

Kesumasari
Villa Kesumasari
Narman's
Pura
Belanjong
Bank

Bar

Abian Boga
Terraza Martini
Bali Marine Sports &
Graha Canti Watersports
Art Market
Santrian Beach Resort
Trattoria Da Marco

Kuta

BELANJONG

Alita
Cemara Beach
Donald's Cafe
& Bakery

JL. MERTASARI

Sanur Beach

Garuda

Pura
Mertasari

Surya Beach

Sanur

km 0.5   1   1.5
miles   0.5   1

N

especially July/Aug. and Dec./Jan. 10%–20% surcharges are added during peak season. At other times, a 10%-20% discount is available upon request at some hotels.

Budget (under $25)

Even budget places in Sanur provide laundry service, though prices are a bit higher than Kuta's flophouse rates; the cheapest rooms are around $7. Most places offer AC, Western toilets, showers, guided tours, and airport transfers.

Rani Jl. Danau Buyan 33,Sindhu, ☎ 288578, 288674. 24 rooms. Opposite the post office. *Losmen*-style rooms are clean and quiet. $9–$27.

Sanur Indah Jl. Danau Buyan,Sindhu, ☎ 288568. 15 rooms. *Losmen*-style hotel. $7 fan only.

Sanur Plaza Jl. Bypass Ngurah Rai, Sindhu, ☎ 288808. 40 rooms. Spacious bungalows with thatched roof and hot water. A pool is available. They also have a family room. $12–$20.

Moderate ($25–$50)

Sanur has great intermediate range hotels, with the only significant difference in price being proximity to and view of the ocean. Most have AC, hot water and private verandah. Prices are subject to 21% tax and service.

Abian Srama Inn Jl. Bypass Ngurah Rai, Sindhu, ☎ 288415, 288792. 47 rooms. Some rooms have hot water. Laundry service and free airport transfers. Rooms can accommodate three. $25–$30.

Baruna Beach Inn Jl. Sindhu 17, Sindhu, ☎ 288546. fax 289629. 8 rooms. Pleasant old bungalows on the beach with lots of character, furnished with antiques and opening onto a courtyard bordering the sea. Cozy, very popular. $35–$40 rooms with fridge. $65 suite. Breakfast, tax and service included. Credit cards not accepted. For longer stays there is a home nearby.

BSB (Bali Sanur Bungalow) Respati Jl. Danau Tamblingan 33, Sindhu, ☎ 288046, fax: 288047. 27 rooms. A narrow row of beachside duplexes $30–$55.

BSB (Bali Sanur Bungalow) Sanur Village Club Jl. Hang Tuah 19, Renon, ☎ 288421/2, fax: 288426. 41 rooms. Right next to the Pura Dalem temple which frequently holds big ceremonies. $40–$50.

Bumi Ayu Bungalow Jl. Bumi Ayu, Batujimbar, ☎ 289101, fax: 28717. 58 rooms. Walking distance to Jl. Danau Tamblingan. $35–$40.

Janur Garden Jl. Bypass Ngurah Rai, Sindhu, ☎ 288155/6, fax: 288144. 42 rooms. Three-story modern hotel patronized by local tourists and businesspeople. The restaurant serves wonderful eafood. $40–$45.

Laghawa Beach Inn Jl. Danau Tamblingan 51, Batujimbar, ☎ 288494, fax 289353. 23 rooms. Simple bungalows in a garden. Fan and AC rooms. Shadow puppet shows on Mon, Wed, Fri. $25–40.

Ramayana Jl. Danau Tamblingan 130, Batujimbar, ☎ 288429, fax: 288674. 22 rooms. Clean with a very attentive, friendly staff. $25–27.

Sanur Agung Jl. Bypass Ngurah Rai, Padang Galak, Renon, 288409, fax: 289575. 17 rooms. On the main highway just north of Sanur. New two-story block of AC rooms. $30–40.

Swastika Bungalows Jl. Danau Tamblingan 128, Batujimbar, ☎ 288693, fax: 287526. 60 rooms. Some spacious rooms. $27 fan, $35 AC.

Taman Agung Beach Inn Jl. Danau Tamblingan 146, Batujimbar, ☎ 289161, 288549, fax: 289161. 24 rooms. One of the best *losmen* in Sanur. Pleasant atmosphere. Five minutes from the beach. $25 fan and hot water; $50 suite.

Villa Kesumasari Jl. Mertasari, Semawang, ☎ 287492, 286591, fax 288876. 21 rooms. Some bungalows have kitchen, fridge, AC, hot water and verandah. Not professionally designed, but reasonably priced. $25–$35. With fan $20–25.

Intermediate ($50–$75)

BSB (Bali Sanur Bungalow) Besakih, Jl. Danau Tamblingan 45, Batujimbar, ☎ 288424, fax: 286059. 50 rooms. Set in a garden leading to the sea. $65–$75.

BSB Paneeda View Jl. Danau Tamblingan, Semawang, ☎ 288425, fax: 286224. 46 rooms. Next to the Bali Hyatt, right on the beach. $60–$75.

Orchid Villa Jl. Danau Tamblingan 79, Batujimbar, ☎ 288334, fax 289162. Three thatched roof bungalows in a small, fabulous compound. Each with own kitchen, living room, dining room, open-air bathroom, garden garage and upstairs verandah overlooking a pond. Can also be rented monthly or annually. $50 fan, $75 AC.

Segara Village Jl. Segara Ayu, Sindhu, ☎ 288407, fax: 287242. 120 rooms. Mini-villages of private bungalows by the sea, built in "rustic Balinese" style (some resemble *lumbung*, Balinese rice granaries). Efficient, friendly staff. Balinese dance classes, children's recreation room, gym, sauna. $65–$135, suite $210.

Sindhu Beach at the beach end of Jl Sindhu. Mailing address: Jl. Danau Tondano 14, Batujimbar, ☎ 288351, fax: 289268. 104 rooms in beachside bungalows. Owned by Natour chain. $40–$100.

First Class ($75–$100)

Santrian Beach Cottages I Jl. Danau Tamblingan, Sindhu, ☎ 288181/4, fax: 288185. 90 rooms. Private cottages on the beach set in a huge garden. $75–$80 standard, $85–90 superior, $95–100 bungalow, $145–$225 suites.

Santrian Beach Resort II Jl. Cemara, Semawang, ☎ 288009, fax: 287101. 131 rooms. An offshoot of the Santrian Beach Cottages. $75–$80 standard, $85–$90 superior, $95–$100 suite/bungalow.

Sativa Sanur Cottages off Jl. Mertasari, Semawang, ☎/fax: 287881. 50 rooms. Shaded by coconut trees, this well-managed hotel is the coziest place to stay in Sanur in this category, but it is away from the beach. The restaurant is excellent. $74–$184.

Luxury ($100 and up)

Most of the hotels in this category have their own beachfront and provide the following facilities: swimming pool(s), bar, restaurants, shops, rooms with private verandah, AC, hot water, fridge, TV/video and telephone. Prices are subject to 21 % tax and service charge. Major credit cards are accepted.

Bali Hyatt Jl. Danau Tamblingan, Semawang, ☎ 288271, fax: 287693. 390 rooms. With thatched-roof and terra-cotta-tiled lobby, open, relaxed feel and magnificently landscaped garden, this is not your typical luxury chain hotel. For years, this has been *the* place to stay in Bali. Renovations completed in 1994 returned it to its classical Balinese roots. Several indoor and outdoor restaurants. Complete sports facilities. One pool has a replica of the famous Goa Gajah—plus waterfall, Jacuzzi and cold dip. $140–$185 superior/deluxe. $165–$185 executive/king. $180–$215 Regency Club. $400–$685 suite.

La Taverna Bali Jl. Danau Tamblingan 39, Sindhu, ☎ 288387, 288497, fax: 287126. 34 rooms. Noted for its unique blend of Mediterranean and Balinese architecture combining thatched roofs and stucco. Tasteful antique-furnished rooms in a tropical garden. The excellent beachside restaurant serves a variety of Italian and Indonesian specialties. $120–$160 standard, $195–$260 suite.

Palm Garden Jl. Kesumasari No 3, Semawang, ☎ 287041, fax: 289571. 23 rooms. All rooms with bathroom and adjoining living room. $100 standard, $200–$300 suite.

Sanur Bali Travelodge Jl. Mertasari, PO Box 9476, Semawang, ☎ 288833, 287301/2, fax: 287303. 194 rooms. Located at the southern end of Sanur's beach strip. $110–$140 for superior to luxury room, $170 beachfront, $350 beachfront suite.

Sanur Beach, PO Box 279 Sanur, Jl. Mertasari, Semawang ☎ 288011, fax: 287566. 425 rooms. This four story block is one of the older beachfront hotels in Sanur, Known for its friendly service. Super deluxe bungalow with marbled bathroom and private pool costs $850. Standard $125–$135. deluxe $145–$170, studio $200–4225, suite $350–$900. Group rates: $85–$95/person. Garuda office on 2nd floor.

Tandjung Sari Jl. Danau Tamblingan, Batujimbar, ☎ 288441, fax: 287930. 26 bungalows. Built in 1962, this remains the top choice for many visitors. Charming decor. tranquil, elegant. The bungalows are reminiscent of those found in the pleasure gardens of the Balinese *rajas*. Caters to a celebrity clientele. The food is highly recommended. $200–$1250 standards, $300–$380 suites.

The Grand Bali Beach (formerly Hotel Bali Beach) Jl. Hang Tuah, ☎ 288511, fax: 287917. 600 rooms. First constructed as a war reparation in 1966 in the classic "Waikiki" high-rise style, the hotel has been fully restored and modernized following a fire which almost destroyed it in 1993. Complete hotel facilities, plus bowling and a 9-hole golf-course. Many airlines which operate in Bali have offices here. $165–$185. Suite $240–$440.

Private Houses. An alternative to standard accommodation is to rent luxury bungalows owned by affluent foreigners. These can work out relatively reasonably, if food and drink are bought at supermarket prices. Prices range from $250/day for a villa for two, to $1,500/day for a two-hectare beachfront estate with 14 staff, an archery range and use of a game fishing boat. For further details, contact: Private Villas Ltd, 2302, HK Diamond Exchange Bldg, 8–10 Duddell St, Central, Hong Kong. ☎ (852) 5251336, fax: (852) 5377181. Bali Land & House, Jl. Raya Seminyak 71, ☎ 753496, 261071, fax: 730824. In Touch, Jl. Raya Seminyak, ☎ 730944, fax: 730683.

DINING

The Bali Hyatt, The Grand Bali Beach and Sanur Beach hotels have a wide variety of restaurants, buffets, and coffee shops. The food is mostly European, but they also offer Indonesian, Chinese and Japanese cuisine.

Restaurants outside the hotels offer a greater variety of food in a broad price range. Most close at 10 pm.

Local Food

The cheapest and most colorful food spot at night is the **Sanur Night Market**, located in the Art Market. The food is spicy, but nothing is cheaper; you can get a *nasi campur* for Rp700. For cheap, but better quality local food—the kind of place where your guides prefer to eat—go to the street restaurants in Sindu, on Jl. Bypass Ngurah Rai between Jl. Segara Ayu and Jl. Sindhu. Try **Haji Imran's** (satay), **Cak Muk** (seafood for $1–$3) or **Depot Robby's** (Chinese).

Warung Jawa Barat, on the corner of Jl. Mertasari and Jl. Kesumasari in Semawang, has a range of Sundanese food from Western Java, such as grilled fish, *karedok* (mixed raw vegetables in coconut sauce) or satay. Prices are good: between $2–$3.

For late-night eaters, Sanur has several moderately priced Padang restaurants open all night. 15–20 spicy dishes are laid out for you to choose from: you pay only for what you eat, so keep track. **Cinto Bundo** is in Batujimbar, whereas **Sari Bundo** and **Murah Meriah** are in Semawang, in the midst of the red-light area.

Co-operatives

There are two village cooperative restaurants in Sanur. Geared to tourists' palates, they have the advantage of being located right on the beach, a privilege denied to their competitors. **Sanur Beach Market**, at the end of Jl. Segara Ayu, is outdoors. Specialities include satay, *nasi* *goreng*, fresh grilled fish, grilled lobster; all reasonably priced. Profits from here and the nearby market go to the Sanur village foundation to run schools, clinics and art classes.

Banjar Restaurant is at the end of Jl.Duyung in Semawang and offers the same range of Indonesian and Chinese food. The association also rents boats for sailing trips on the lagoon.

Simple Restaurants

Sanur's "in" place is the **Batujimbar Cafe** in Batujimbar. Its hanging vines and sturdy furniture gives it the look of a riviera roadside cafe. This is the haunt of the local expat colony, many of whom live in the sumptuous Batujimbar Estates just across the road. The cafe offers light, healthy food with daily specials at reasonable prices. Coffee is a specialty.

Another simple, yet cozy place, is the **Agung Restaurant** just before the Semawang crossroad. For all palates, including Australian, European as well as Japanese, at under $5. A similar place, with music, is the popular **J.J.** on Jl. Tamblingan.

Those looking for American food should try the **Borneo**, conveniently located among the trees of Jl. Sindhu. Open until 11.30 pm.

Luxury Restaurants

Some of the best places for those who want to dine in luxury are found in hotels such as **La Taverna** (good seafood, brick-oven pizza) and **Tandjung Sari**. The latter is famous for its Indonesian *rijsttafel* and its Balinese palace atmosphere. Dine to the strains of a bamboo *tingklink* orchestra while looking out over the sea, or have a drink in the seaside bar. A romantic spot for dinner by moonlight.

A few stylish places can also be found on Jl. Danau Tamblingan, including **Istana Garden** in Sindhu, **Bayu Garden** in Batujimbar and **Lotus Pond**, in Sindhu, which floats on a pond of lotus flowers, is decorated with antiques and serves great fresh pasta. If you want a pleasant Balinese ambiance, try **Kuri Putih**, on Jl. Danau Tamblingan, or **Kul Kul**, further down the road in Batujimbar. All offer similar fare and prices—menus generally feature grilled seafood. Many also stage dance performances and will pick-up services.

Telaga Naga ("Dragon Well"), opposite the Bali Hyatt, has arguably the best Chinese food on Bali in the most exclusive setting: a lotus garden. Great Szechuan food. Try their chicken with dried chili peppers or the roast duck. **Lenny's** on Jl. Bypass Ngurah Rai was the first Chinese restaurant in Sanur. It features good Indonesian/Cantonese style dishes (very fresh vegetables!) at reasonable prices. **Sin Bo Lan**, or SBL, is a favorite of the local Chinese. Tasty spring rolls. **Janur Garden**, Jl. Bypass Ngurah Rai, marvelous squid and shrimps.

Trattoria Da Marco's, in Semawang, claims to serve "the best Italian food on Bali." Their grilled fish, spaghetti carbonara, bean salad and delicious steaks prove it. **Bali Moon** makes marvelous lasagna.

Japanese and Korean

These restaurants cater mostly to the increasing number of Japanese tourists. **Kita** on Jl Danau Tamblingan offers *sukiyaki*, *yakitori* and *tempura*. The **New Seoul** in Batujimbar features all the standard Korean favorites—including *kimchee* and *bulgogi* barbequed beef in sweet soya.

NIGHTLIFE

A quiet family resort, Sanur is not known for its nightlife, but there are four discos. **Subec**, the largest, is popular with the locals. The **No.1** in Batujimbar cater to tourists. The **Banjar**, next to the Bali Hyatt, opens until 2 am. The newest disco, **Scandals**, is at Jl. Sindhu Beach 6, ☎ 288054. Sanur's red light district is Bali's biggest: it is hidden in the alleyways of Semawang and Belanjong.

DANCE PERFORMANCES

Sanur is just a short taxi ride away from Denpasar and Batubulan, where *barong*, *kris*, fire, and *kecak* dance performances are regularly held. Contact a travel agent. Most hotels offer Balinese buffet dinners with dance performance for about $15 a head. A number of restaurants offer similar shows at lower prices. Try: Baris ☎ 288431. Canang Sari ☎ 287027. Penjor ☎ 288226. Sanur Beach Market ☎ 288574. Sari Karya ☎ 288376. Swastika Garden II ☎ 288373.

SHOPPING

Tourist shops line all the main streets of Sanur. Although there is more choice in Kuta and Legian, prices are similar if you bargain well. Otherwise, go to the arcades in the main hotels for high quality goods and no bargaining.

Books. The main hotels and photo centers on Jl. Danau Tamblingan have a range of guides to Bali and Indonesia in English and other languages. Also try Image Network Indonesia (INI) at Jl. Danau Tamblingan 108, Kita Bookshop at Cafe Batujimbar, and Klik Studio, next door, for coffee table books on Indonesia and postcards.

Duty Free. There's a duty free shop on Jl. Bypass Ngurah Rai with the whole range of international goods plus Indonesian luxury items.

Food. Gelael Dewata Supermarket on Jl. Bypass Ngurah Rai is the place for wines, imported cheeses and meats as well as general toiletry items. Many other general stores in Sanur such as Bagus Store and ABC Store offer cold beer and soft drinks at a fraction of hotel prices.

Clothing and Batik. Serasa Batik center on Jl. Bypass Ngurah Rai, Tohpati, west of Sanur, sell a complete range of high quality but expensive batiks. For fancy clothing, Nogo has two shops along Jl. Danau Tamblingan, selling elegant, hand-woven ikat designs. Shoes, handbags and accessories from natural textiles are available at Miranda Inti Alami, Jl. Hang Tuah, across from the entrance to The Grand Bali Beach Hotel. White embroidered dresses are available at Bali High, Jl. Danau Tamblingan at the Jl. Karangsari intersection, and Rafflesia, on Jl. Danau Toba sells leather clothing. Imba Leather sells fashion bags and shoes at Jl. Danau Tamblingan near Jl. Danau Toba . For high fashion or foreign goods, try the major hotel arcades, especially the Sari Bali at Bali Hyatt.

Home Furnishings. For decorative objects go to Bali Curious Goods on Jl. Danau Tamblingan. For creative ceramics, try Cafe Batujimbar's ceramic shop on Jl. Danau Tamblingan or visit the factory outlet across the street in Batujimbar Estate. Pejaten at Griya Market has decorative plates, cups, etc.

Massage. After a long journey around Bali, have a Japanese shiatsu massage at LG Club Sehatku. Sauna, steam, whirlpool, Indonesian herbal *lulur* baths are also available.

Souvenirs. The Sanur Beach Market has a good range of inexpensive gift items. Jl. Danau Tamblingan has dozens of shops selling local handicrafts: textiles, carvings, paintings, leather, and silver goods. Eden has rattan-leather items such as purses and pencil cases. For quality jewelry, go to Opal Opulence on Jl. Danau Toba.

Paintings. For good genuine contemporary painting, go to Wianta's, Jl. Pandu, 300 meters from the Renon junction, on the road to Denpasar.

SERANGAN (TURTLE ISLAND)

The beach at Sanur is lined with outrigger canoes which can be chartered for trips across the lagoon. The standard rate is $15/hour. The fare to Pulau Serangan (famous for its turtle farm) costs $20. Some also sail to Nusa Lembongan and Nusa Penida ($8), but we advise against this often crowded and rather dangerous trip, especially during the rainy season.

Another way to reach Pulau Serangan is to drive or ride to Suwung, 5 km west of Sanur (Semawang). Look for the big sign on Jl. Bypass Ngurah Rai. A shuttle ferry departs from here to cross the 1/2 km channel. Local fare is Rp. 500; more for tourists. You can also charter boats for a return crossing from the ferry co-op, $10. Confirm that both crossings are included in the price.

WATERSPORTS

You can find almost every watersport imaginable here. Most of the facilities are found right on the beach in front of big hotels such as The Grand Bali Beach, Segara Village and the Bali Hyatt.

Sanur offers **diving**, although not the best in Bali. There are several agents that organize trips.

In Sanur, contact Bali Marine Sports (☎ 287872) on Jl. Bypass Ngurah Rai or Baruna Sport which has beach booths in front of The Grand Bali Beach and the Bali Hyatt.

The only operator specializing in **tours to Komodo island** is based in Sanur and has a fully-equipped dive boat running charters on request for a minimum of five passengers. They also organize several one day and charter excursions east of Bali. Grand Komodo Tours, Jl. Bypass Ngurah Rai, Sanur, ☎ 287166, fax: 287165.

Besides the charter services offered by various tour agents, P&O Spice Island Cruises, Jl. Padang Galak 25, Sanur, ☎ 286283, fax 286284, offers 3- and 4-day luxury cruises aboard the 150-passenger Bali Sea Dancer. Departs every Mon and Fri, includes stops on Sumbawa, Komodo and Lombok (with the 4-day trip). Rates, including cabin, food and Komodo tour, start at about $400.

For Jungut Batu on Nusa Lembongan, boats seating 15–30 leave from the beach at the end of Jl. Hang Tuah, next to The Grand Bali Beach Hotel. Departure: 7–8 am. $7 for tourists.

BEACH CEREMONIES

To appreciate the beach from a more Balinese perspective witness the daily ceremonies on the shore: cremations, making of offerings, ritual bathing, among others. Inquire at the beaches and dress appropriately (no swimwear) to attend.

MISCELLANEOUS

Banks. Bank Dagang Negara at Bali Hyatt. Bank Aken on Jl. Sindhu. BDB at intersection of Jl. Bypass Ngurah Rai and Jl. Sindhu. Bank Dagang Negara, Jl. Danau Tamblingan 156, ☎ 288498, 288499. Bank Desa Sanur, Jl. Mertasari in Belanjong. Bank Seripartha, Jl. Danau Tamblingan, south of Image Network.

Money Changers. PT Dewi Segara at Gelael Supermarket, Jl. Bypass Ngurah Rai at Turismo Indonesia, Jl. Danau Tamblingan 85, across from Cafe Batujimbar.

Medical Treatment. If there is no medical service in your hotel, see Dr Anak Agung Made Djelantik at Jl. Hayam Wuruk 190, near the Renon crossroads. ☎ 238171. For a dentist, see Dr. Retno Agung at Jl. Bypass Ngurah Rai close to the intersection with Jl. Danau Buyan. Call ☎ 288501 for an appointment.

Post Offices. Most hotels provide postal services. Post office at Jl. Danau Buyan, open daily 8–2. Closed Sun. There are small post offices next to Sanur Beach Hotel and Cafe Batujimbar. Go to Denpasar's main post office in Renon for full services.

Telecommunications (wartel). Jl. Danau Tamblingan at the corner of Jl. Sindhu, ☎ 287365.

—updated by Debe Campbell

3 Kuta & Legian PRACTICALITIES

INCLUDES SEMINYAK & PETITENGET

The white sands of Kuta are still arguably the best beachfront on Bali. The beach is actually much cleaner than just a few years ago. Kuta is not the fishing village it once was: it now has the feel of a booming Pacific resort and its streets become clogged with tourists and traffic during peak seasons. Legian to the north is a bit quieter, less crowded, and more suitable for longer stays, although in many ways it has become an extension of Kuta. Further north, Seminyak and Petitenget offer more tranquility.

Prices in US dollars. AC = Air-conditioning. Telephone code is 0361.

ORIENTATION

Kuta and Tuban

Kuta proper is the area delineated by Jl. Legian, Jl. Pantai Kuta, Jl. Melasti, the beach front drive and the lanes in between, especially Poppies I and II. Jl. Legian is the commercial hub of Kuta and the stage of many of its restaurants and nightlife. Most of Kuta's big beachfront hotels are in southern Kuta, or Tuban, including the Hotel Patra Jasa Bali, Bintang Bali, Holiday Inn, Kartika Plaza, and Bali Dynasty.

Legian and Seminyak

Legian and Seminyak are northern extensions of Kuta proper along Jl. Legian. Somewhat quieter with cottage-style accommodation, this is where many of the ex-pat designers and long-stay tourists live. The biggest hotels are the Bali Imperial, the Bali Padma and, soon, the Sheraton Beach Legian. There are three ways to reach Legian and Seminyak: through Kuta and Jl. Melasti, then north; from Jl. Imam Bonjol, turn on to Jl. Tanjung Biru and then Jl. Tanjung Mekar at the Pertamina gas station; or from the north via Jl. Kerobokan.

Petitenget and North

Petitenget, Berawa, Canggu, and Seseh are new and quieter continuations of Kuta's beach, easier to reach through Abian Timbul or Denpasar and Kerobokan than through Kuta, as there are no bemos north from Legian. Several large hotels are located in this area: the Bali Oberoi Hotel, the Intan Bali Village and Puri Ratih in Petitenget and the Dewata Beach and Bali Sani Suites in Berawa.

Kuta Beach also extends to the south, beyond the airport to Jimbaran.

TOURIST INFORMATION

For assistance with tours and tickets, and information on events, contact the tourist information offices at Jl. Bakung Sari, Kuta ☎ 751660 ext. 145, Century Plaza Building, Jl. Benesari No. 7, Ground Floor, Legian, ☎ 754090, and the Lifeguard Station, Jl. Pantai Kuta, ☎755660.

TRANSPORTATION

The airport taxi counter is outside customs, near left luggage. The fare is Rp5,000 to Kuta, Rp8,500 to Legian, Rp10,000 to Seminyak, and Rp11,000 to Petitenget. If you want to take a *bemo*, you have to walk out to the main road as far as the impressive white charioteer statue on the corner. From there you can flag down a blue *bemo* van — it will take you down to "*bemo korner*" in Kuta for Rp300.

In Kuta itself, the usual *bemo* fare—to Jl. Kartika Plaza and Tuban to the south or to Jl. Melasti to the north—is only Rp300–Rp500, although the driver may ask for more. There are no *bemos* beyond Legian, so to get further north you'll have to charter: bargain hard.

There are **rent-a-car** and bike agencies on almost every corner in Kuta and "transport?" is an extremely common touts' call. Bargain the price down and check the condition of the vehicle. Suzuki Jimnys are fun for around $25/day. Kijang jeeps go for $25–30/day. Try Bali Happy Rent Car Jl. Raya Kuta 72X, ☎ 751954. Toyota Rent Car, Jl. Raya Airport 99X, Tuban, ☎ 751356. **Motorbikes** rent for around $5/day.

To avoid the hassle of looking for *bemos* or renting a vehicle, use the **shuttle buses** which go to Ubud at 8.30, 10, and 11.30 am, 1, 2.30 and 4 pm and to Candidasa/Padangbai, Kintamani and Lovina at 9.30 am. Contact CV Ganda Sari Transport, Jl. Legian, ☎ 754383 or Perama, Jl. Legian, ☎ 751170.

For renting **mountain bikes**, go to Chi Chat Restaurant on Jl. Bagus Taruna (Jl. Rum Jungle) or to Warung Bambu or Cosmic on Jl. Double Six. The price is $1.50/day or less for longer periods. Always check the bike before riding away.

ACCOMMODATIONS

The Kuta area has thousands of rooms, ranging from tiny $3/night concrete huts in a Balinese family compound to the super-luxurious Imperial Villa at the 5-star Bali Imperial Hotel which has a private swimming pool, Jacuzzi and 2 bedrooms for $2,000/night.

The choice of where to base yourself is relatively easy: if you want action, stay in Kuta; if you want tranquility, try Seminyak; if you want a mix, stay in Legian, and if you want top-end luxury, head for Tuban in the south or Petitenget in the north. Each area has advantages and disadvantages. The main hassle north of Legian is a lack of public transport.

The best way to find a room that suits you is to shop around. If you're in a hurry, you can book through the PHRI Hotel Association at the airport. The recommendations below are designed to give some points of reference. Hotels are often fully booked during the peak season (Christmas/New Year and July/August), so make a reservation for a day or two and look around if the hotel is not to your liking. In the low season most hotels offer discounts of up to 40 %.

For all larger hotels, reservations are a must and surcharges are levied during peak season. In some hotels, two children under 12 sharing their parents' room are allowed free of charge.

Budget (under $25)

There are literally hundreds of *losmen* or homestays scattered about the Kuta and Legian area where rooms rent for as little as $3 a night. The rooms are basic, usually concrete blocks thrown up in a family compound. A breakfast of bananas, black rice pudding and tea is often included.

For a bit more money, $10–$20/night, you can get a larger room or private bungalow with fan near the beach. Rates are negotiable, particularly in the off-season and for longer stays.
Blue Ocean south of Jl. Double Six, Legian. 29 rooms. A popular hangout for locals and surfers, right on the beach in Legian. $9–$10.
Orchid Garden Jl. Pura Bagus Teruna 525, Legian. ☎751802, 752852, fax: 752852. 21 rooms. Clean, caters to groups. $12–$15 fan. $25–$30AC.
Rita's House Gang Poppies I, Kuta. ☎ 751760, 222390, fax 236021. 13 rooms. Very quiet, clean, well kept and friendly place right in the center of Kuta. Rooms with shower and toilet. $4.50–$7 fan. $11–16 AC. Includes good breakfast.
Sorga Beach Inn Gang Menuh, between Jl. Melasti and Jl. Padma, Legian. ☎ 751609. 10 rooms. Near beach. Surfer hangout. Fan only. $8–$10.

Kuta & Legian 3

Yulia Beach Inn Jl. Pantai Kuta 43, Kuta. ☎ 751893, fax: 751055. 48 rooms. One of the original Kuta places near the beach. Five categories of rooms. $3 with shared bath. $12 fan. $30 AC.

Moderate ($20–$50)

Kuta and Legian have a tremendous range of intermediate range accommodations, many offering the same or better facilities than those charging first-class rates. Generally all have AC, swimming pool and hot water. The difference is that these hotels are smaller with fewer sports facilities. Simple breakfast is often included (toast, fruit, tea/coffee). Most rates are subject to 21% tax/service charge.

Asana Santhi Willy Jl. Tegalwangi 18, Kuta. ☎ 751281, fax: 752641. 10 rooms. In the heart of Kuta. Pleasant, newly-renovated with antique furnishings and semi-open bathrooms. Asana Santhi Willy II (14 rooms) next door has large rooms but less character. $30–$35.

Baleka Beach Inn on a small lane between Jl. Padma and Jl. Pura Bagus Teruna, Legian. ☎ 751931, fax: 753796. 45 rooms with a pool. Walking distance from the beach. $30–$35.

Bali Niksoma Beach Cottages Jl. Padma, Legian Kaja. ☎ 751946, fax: 753587. 52 rooms. A quiet beachfront place in Legian. $21–$25 fan, $45–$55 standard, $65–$80 deluxe, $95 suite.

Bruna Beach Inn Jl. Pantai Kuta. ☎ 751565. 36 rooms. Across the road from Kuta beach. Attached or bungalow style, AC and non-AC room. $30–$35. Family room sleeps five $65.

Garden View Cottages Jl. Padma Utara 4, Legian. ☎ 751559, fax: 753265. 56 rooms. Secluded, short walk to the beach. $38–$45.

Kuta Beach Club Jl. Bakung Sari, Kuta. ☎ 751261, fax: 752896. 100 rooms. Bungalows near garden, a calm setting right in central Kuta. Mini tennis, badminton. All rooms w/AC. $38–$42.

Kuta Bungalows Jl. Benesari, Kuta. ☎ 754393/5. 54 rooms. Ten minutes walk to the beach. White brick bungalows with modern bath. $35–$40

Poppies Cottage II Gang Poppies II, Kuta. ☎ 751059, fax: 752364. 4 rooms with fans, showers with hot water and fridges. Clean but no pool. $23–$28. $5 extra for a private kitchen.

Puri Bunga Cottages Jl. Dhyana Pura, Seminyak. ☎ 730939, fax: 730334. 36 rooms. Very nice, intimate, friendly hotel; quiet location, about 300 m from the beach. AC, telephone, radio and TV. Restaurant, pool, travel facilities (minibus, boat tickets to Lombok where the sister hotel is located, diving tours). $30, including American breakfast.

Puri Wisata Bungalows Jl. Raya Seminyak, Seminyak. ☎ 751637, 751855 fax: 753185. 30 rooms. Both AC and fan. Free airport transfers. $25–$50.

Ramayana Seaside Cottages Jl. Bakung Sari, Kuta. ☎ 751864, fax: 751866. 66 rooms. Impressive cottages close to the beach. $40–$60.

Sandi Phala Jl. Kartika Plaza, Tuban. ☎ 753042, fax: 754889. 12 rooms. Two-story bungalows in a big compound with pool and beachfront restaurant. Far from the shops and restaurants but close to the surfing beach. $30–$45

Sari Beach Inn Jl. Padma Utara, Legian. 24 rooms. Small, quiet beachfront hotel. $45–$55.

Sari Uma Cottages Jl. Sarinande 3, Seminyak. ☎/fax: 730496. 13 rooms. On a quiet lane off Jl. Dhyana Pura. 7 two-story bungalows (with kitchen, dining room, and bedrooms) and 6 standard rooms, all with shower, phone, and fan. $30–$40.

Three Brothers Bungalows has three branches. ☎ 751566, fax: 756082. 85 rooms. The first one has old two-story bungalows located on a small lane-off Jl. Legian. Bohemian, but clean; surrounded by tropical gardens. Living room and semi-open baths on the ground floor and bedrooms on the top floor. Fan and hot water. The one at Jl. Dhyana Pura is called **Puri Tjendana**. Located in quiet Seminyak it's only 100 m from the beach. Nice two-story bungalows complete with kitchen set in a big garden. $17–$35, depending on facilities. Coffee and tea included, no breakfast. The one at Jl. Padma has all domestic facilities, except telephone, and caters for long-stay guests. $500 a month.

Intermediate ($50–75)

Most places in this category feature clusters of bungalows by the beach. Recently, however, a number of hotels with larger, two and three story blocks have opened. Most have AC, hot water and upgraded facilities.

Aneka Beach Bungalows Jl. Raya Pantai Kuta, Kuta. ☎ 752066/7, fax: 752892. 59 rooms. New, attractive thatched-roof bungalows. Standard $50–$55, villa $65–$75, suite $70–$250.

Bali Anggrek Inn Jl. Raya Pantai Kuta, Kuta, PO Box 435. ☎ 751265/6, 752833/4, fax: 751766. 151 rooms set in 3 acres of gardens. Standard $57–$64, executive $65–94, suite $165.

Bali Holiday Resort Seminyak PO Box 1045, Kuta. ☎ 7353547, 752055, fax: 730848. 100 rooms. Near the beach with an amazing sunset view. Complete facilities. $55–$80.

Bali Sani Jl. Padma Utara, Legian. ☎ 752314, fax: 752313. 60 rooms. The open-to-the-bedroom bathtubs and closet make this hotel stand out. They also have rooms with "normal" bathrooms. A cozy restaurant overlooks the pool. Friendly staff. Standard $50–$75, cottage $70–$90, villa $80–$100.

Bali Sani Suite Batubelig Beach, Kerobokan, PO Box 3193, Denpasar. ☎ 754050, fax: 754044. 60 rooms. Fine decor, notably Balinese hardwoods, crafted bamboo, traditional textiles and artifacts. Open-air restaurant, a swimming pool and an open-air library overlooking the beach. Standard $50–55, cottage $70–$90, villa, $80–$100.

Bolare Beach Bungalows Jl. Pantai Berawa, Canggu. ☎/fax: 730258. 21 rooms. Small bungalows in a resort setting of lush garden with a pool overlooking the sea. Bungalow $55–$65, suite $70–75.

Legian Garden Cottages Jl.Double Six, Seminyak. ☎ 730876, 730877, fax: 730405. 25 rooms.

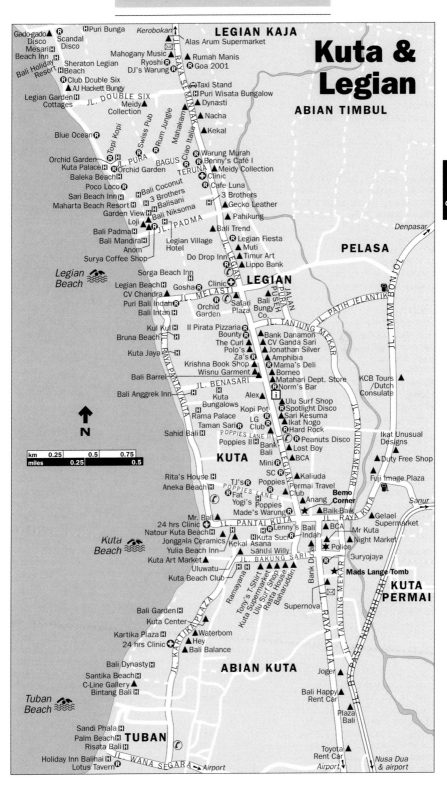

Near trendy Double Six Disco/Restaurant. Convenient for partiers, but noisy. A three minute walk to the beach. Standard $50–$56, suite $80.

Palm Beach Jl. Pantai Banjar Segara, Tuban, PO Box 1037. ☎ 752431, 751661, fax: 752432. 90 rooms. Three minutes to the beach. Two-story hotel with swimming pool. Away from the bustle of Kuta. Standard $50–$60.

Perdana Dadi Jl. Bypass Ngurah Rai 7, Kuta. Reservations: PO Box 1104 Tuban. ☎ 752961/3, fax: 752964. 50 luxury rooms built in traditional Balinese style with modern facilities. Swimming pool with sunken bar in a coconut grove. $60–$85.

Puri Bidadari Cottage Jl. Petitenget, Kerobokan, PO Box 623. ☎/fax 730465. 20 rooms. Typical Balinese thatched roof cottages. Private bath and showers with hot water, AC. Sunny, quiet location in the middle of a rice field with coconut trees. Standard $60, deluxe cottage $85. Price varies seasonally

First Class ($75–$100)

For peace and quiet, stay up at **Bunga Seminyak**, the **Intan Bali Village** or the **Pesona Bali** in Petitenget. All rooms have AC, private bathrooms, and hot water. Rates do not include breakfast or the 21% tax and service charges.

Bali Intan Cottages Jl. Melasti 1, Kuta. ☎ 751770, fax: 751891. 150 rooms. Across the road from the beach. Standard $80–$90, superior $90–$100, cottage $100–$110, suite $180.

Bali Mandira Cottages Jl. Padma, Legian. ☎ 751381, fax: 752377. 120 rooms. Typical Balinese cottages. Conference facilities. Standard $80–$100, suite $135–$150.

Bunga Seminyak Jl. Camplung Tanduk, Seminyak. ☎ 730239, fax: 751239. 12 rooms. Down a narrow lane to this beachfront hotel. Small group of thatched bungalows with complete facilities and antique details. The small pool and Jacuzzi in the garden are private and relaxing. $60–$90. Hotel under renovation in early 1995.

Dewata Beach Hotel Berawa, Canggu. PO Box 271, Denpasar. ☎ 730263, fax: 730290. 168 rooms. Affiliated with Best Western chain. Massive building with complete facilities. Each room has verandah/balcony. Standard or Deluxe $80–$90, suite $130–$160.

Hotel Sahid Bali Jl. Raya Pantai Kuta, Kuta. ☎ 753855, fax: 752019. 171 rooms. Across from the beach. Standard $80–$125, superior $120–$175, suite $175–$625.

Intan Bali Village Spa & Club Jl. Petitenget, Batubelig Beach. ☎730777, fax: 730778. 311 rooms. Past the Oberoi at the quiet, northern end of the beach. Soothing views from the beachfront lobby bar. $80–$95, up to $525 for the presidential suite.

Jayakarta Bali Jl. Pura Bagus Teruna, Legian. ☎ 751433, fax: 752074. 281 rooms. Large two-story block right on the beach. Standard $95–$105, suite $175–$250.

Kul-Kul Jl. Raya Pantai Kuta, Kuta. ☎ 752520, fax: 752519. 77 bungalows. Thatched roof bungalow hotel. Some rooms have open-air bath. Standard $85–$95, bungalow $125–$180, pavilion $350.

Kuta Beach Jl. Pantai Kuta 1, Kuta. PO Box 3393. ☎ 751361, fax: 751362. 137 rooms right on Kuta Beach. All bungalows are Balinese style with modern facilities. Private balcony surrounded by lush green tropical garden. Part of the Natour chain. Recently underwent extensive renovation. Superior $80–$90, bungalow $90–$100, suite $135–$300.

Kuta Jaya Cottage Jl. Raya Pantai Kuta, Kuta. ☎ 752308, fax: 752309. 134 rooms. On the beach, Balinese-style tropical gardens. $80–$95.

Legian Beach Hotel Jl. Melasti, Legian. P.O. Box 3308. ☎ 751711, 755460, fax: 752651, 752652. 190 rooms. Bungalow complex with hotel block on the beach. Hotel wing room $75–$85, bungalow $90–$130, family suite $120–$130, suite $260–$390.

Legong Keraton Beach Cottages Jl. Dewata, Berawa Beach, Canggu, PO Box 617. ☎ 730280, fax: 730285. 20 rooms. Balinese decor. $65–$80.

Poppies Cottages I Gang Poppies I, Jl. Legian, Kuta. ☎ 751059, fax: 752364. 20 rooms. Hands-down favorite of frequent visitors. Well-designed cottages in a beautiful garden with a pool. Refrigerator in every room. Always full: reservations a must. $65–$70. Private cooking facilities $8.

Pesona Bali Jl. Kayu Aya, Petitenget. ☎ 753914, fax: 753915. 69 rooms. Near the beach. All rooms with private balcony, stocked refrigerator. Cottages with cooking facilities. Quiet and remote. Standard $80–$100, deluxe $100–$145, cottage $190–$210, suite $235–$255.

Rama Palace Jl. Raya Pantai Kuta, Kuta. PO Box 293. ☎ 752063/4, 752207/8, fax: 753078. Luxurious resort bungalows and rooms set in a flower garden. Standard $80–$105, superior $100–$125, suite $130–$220.

Risata Bali Resort Jl. Segara, Tuban. PO Box 3207. ☎ 753340, 753349-53, fax: 753354. 154 spacious rooms and suites overlooking gardens. Swimming pool, watersports. Superior $70–$95, deluxe $95–$115, suite $120–160.

Santika Beach Jl. Kartika, Tuban. ☎ 751267-8, fax: 751260. 157 rooms. Three swimming pools, tennis courts, bar and restaurant. Two-bedroom family units face a children's playground. New suite complex has private pool. Convention facilities for 250. Standard $100–$120, deluxe $110–$140, family unit $160–$180, suite $150–$320.

Tjendana Paradise Jl. Dhyana Pura, Seminyak. PO Box 2037. ☎ 730573, fax: 730518. 127 rooms. 4-star hotel built in traditional Balinese style and 250 m from the beach. Two restaurants and bar, gym, swimming pool and sport facilities Conference facilities for 200. Standard $75–$85. Superior $90–$100. Beautiful deluxe suite for $175.

Luxury ($100 and up)

Kuta was not known for its luxury accommodations. The resort began, after all, as a stopover on the hippy trail. However, in the last few years, several exclusive establishments have opened their doors and more are on the way. Rates do not include breakfast or the 21% tax and service charges.

Bali Dynasty Jl. Kartika Plaza, Tuban. ☎ 752403,

fax: 752402. 267 rooms. Managed by the Shangri-la group. Focus on families, one child under age 12 stays free in parents room. Good Cantonese restaurant, disco and games room. Conference facilities. Standard $120, superior $150, family room $150–180, suites $250.

Bali Garden Jl. Kartika Plaza, PO Box 1101, Tuban. ☎ 752725, fax: 753851. 145 rooms and suites in 4-story buildings amid floral gardens. Convenient location: five minute drive from the airport and five minute walk to Kuta. Swimming pool, fitness center and Jacuzzi. Standard $104–$128, suites $180–$280, grand villa $390.

Bali Imperial Jl. Dhyana Pura, Seminyak. ☎ 730730, fax: 730545. 138 rooms. Managed by the famous Imperial Hotel in Tokyo, this hotel offers amazing facilities, great architecture, and a beautifully landscaped garden with access to the beach. $150–$210, suite $270–$360 ($1,000 for the luxurious, 2-bedroom garden suite), villa $400–$700. The Imperial Villa goes for a cool $2,000 per night.

Bali Oberoi Jl. Kayu Aya, Petitenget. ☎ 730361, fax: 730791. 75 cottages and villas. A hotel with style tucked between rice fields and the sea at the northern end of the beach. Coral-rock bungalows are scattered tastefully in the landscaped grounds. Beds are hand carved four-posters and the baths have open-air gardens. Cottage $225–$265, villa $425–$475, villa with pool $600–$850.

Bintang Bali Jl. Kartika Plaza, Tuban. ☎ 753810, 753292/3, fax: 752015, 753288. 400 rooms. Concrete hotel with complete facilities. Beachfront pool, Jacuzzi, gym, tennis court, several restaurants, and conference facilities. No charge for one child under age 12 sharing parents room. Deluxe $140–$150, suite $285–$888.

Bali Padma Hotel Jl. Padma 1, Legian. ☎ 752111, fax: 752140. 400 rooms. Giant beach-front hotel with full amenities. Wooden cottage-style rooms, tropical gardens, huge pool, and an open lounge. Standard $120–$155, chalet $140–$175, suite $185–$1,775.

Holiday Inn Balihai Resort Jl. Wana Segara 33, Tuban 80361. PO Box 2054. ☎ 753035 (12 lines), fax; 752527, 754548. 200 rooms. Right on the beach amid acres of landscaped gardens. Compact and intimate. Ground level suites have outdoor garden bath. Standard $120–$180, family room (max. 5 persons) $200, villa with private pool $290, suite $550.

Hotel Patra Jasa Bali Jl. Kuta Beach, Tuban ☎ 751161, 752810, fax: 752030. 206 rooms. Five minutes from the airport, on the beach. Tennis courts, badminton, watersport facilities, and two pools. Convention facilities for up to 800. Superior $130, deluxe $150, suite $180-$1,000.

Kartika Plaza Beach Jl. Kartika Plaza, Tuban ☎ 751507, fax: 752475, 754585. 380 rooms. Room blocks and beachside bungalows with complete facilities. Conference center for up to 1,000. Standard $125–$135, suite $235–$1,300, bungalows $140–$235.

Puri Ratih Bali Bungalows Jl. Petitenget, Kerobokan. ☎ 751546-8, fax: 751549. 16 bungalows. A member of Pacific Resort Club. Large, lavish beachside bungalows with a kitchen, bedrooms and open-air living room. Tennis court, solarium, two swimming pools, and fitness center. Deluxe $80–$165, suite $225-$250, villa $288–$320.

DINING

Kuta is a great place to eat. New places open almost daily and competition is fierce. Most don't last for long. The ones which do have great food at unbeatable prices. Seafood and Western dishes are your best bets. Or try Mexican, Indian or Japanese. The more well-known places are mentioned below, plus some promising newcomers. Ask around for the latest "in" spots.

Made's Warung on Jl. Pantai Kuta, in the heart of Kuta, (not to be confused with other restaurants of the same name) tops the list of old favorites. A popular hangout and great for people-watching. It also has great food. Specialities include Thai and Vietnamese salads, prawns in chilli sauce, squid fillet, black rice ice cream, fresh and frozen yogurt, fresh fruit juices, and frothy cappucino.

Poppies Restaurant on Gang Poppies I is the other old favorite in downtown Kuta with a rather more up-market atmosphere and menu, though still a bargain. Lamp-lit tables in a cozy garden. Specialities include steak, lobster, shish kebab, and one of the most extensive drink and wine lists on Bali. Advance bookings are an absolute must during the high season as the place is always full (☎ 751059). The same owner has another restaurant offering similar dishes, **Kopi Pot** on Jl. Legian. The second story has a coconut grove view which is now a rarity in Kuta. Try the satay or the baby shark which is not on the menu. Superb desserts. **Goa 2001** on Jl. Raya Seminyak is *the* place to be seen prior to heading for the nightclubs. Spacious, trendy bar and restaurant serving a variety of meat and vegetarian curries. They also have a *sushi* bar.

Breakfast

Zas is famous for its breads and **Mama's Deli** for homemade sausages, both on Jl. Legian, near the junction with Jl. Tanjung Mekar. **Made's Warung** (see above) has a breakfast special that includes fresh fruit juice, eggs, bacon, toast, fresh fruit yoghurt, and cappucino, all for $4.

Coffee

Breakfast, afternoon or after-dinner coffee is a treat at **Benny's Cafe I** and **II**. Number I is on Jl. Pura Bagus Taruna and Jl. Legian Kaja; the new and spacious Number II is on Jl. Dhyana Pura in Seminyak. Service is fast and friendly, food is superb. Pancakes, fruit shakes, ice cream, and a variety of brews: Columbian, Brazilian, Balinese, and Dutch. Try their coffee with *arak* palm liquor.

Desserts

Once again, **Made's Warung** takes the cake with the best desserts in Kuta. Exquisite strawberry pie, cheesecake and chocolate cakes, as well as rum raisin and carrot. **TJ's** (see "Mexican" below) comes in a close second with their "chocolate diablo cake." **Kopi Pot** on Jl. Legian has great lemon meringue pies and black forest gateau.

Indonesian

For a quick and inexpensive lunch, try **Warung Murah** and **Warung DJ's**, both on Jl. Raya Seminyak. Sample their tasty *nasi campur*, a combination plate of five side dishes with rice: all for only 50 cents. For a sampling of typical Indonesian and Chinese dishes try the **Pasar Senggol Night Market** behind the Post Office in Kuta. Open only at night, this is great value for money — good *nasi goreng* for under a dollar and fresh steamed crab for about $3. The small stall called **Ayam Prambanan** has the best fried chicken.

Padang

Everyone's favorite Indonesian regional cuisine is from West Sumatra. For spicy *nasi padang* try **Suryajaya**, next to the police station. Ten different dishes will be served the minute you arrive, all of it fiery hot. You're charged only for what you eat.

Chinese

Golden Lotus at Bali Dynasty Hotel, Jl. Kartika Plaza, has the best Cantonese food in Kuta. **Bali Indah** on Jl Buni Sari and **Lenny's** on Jl. Pantai Kuta (☎ 751121, 752925), **Puri Bali Indah** and **Gosha** both on Jl. Melasti offer first-rate Chinese cuisine and seafood. But everybody's favorite is **Restaurant Mini** on Jl. Legian, about 200 m north of *bemo* corner. Choose your own fresh lobsters, fish, and prawns to be grilled, steamed or stir-fried with vegetables. If you're allergic to MSG, tell them "no Aji-no-moto." **Indah Sari** on Jl. Legian offers the same service in more up-market surroundings with prices to match.

Italian

Italian dishes are now found in almost every restaurant. The newest and best is **La Lucciola** on Kayu Aya Beach, Jl. Oberoi (☎ /fax: 261047). It's worth the drive and is a perfect spot for sunset cocktails. The pool restaurant at **Bali Padma Hotel** and **Fat Yogi's** on Poppies Gang I have the best pizzas in town. **PJ's** at Four Seasons in Jimbaran has the best pizza on the island. **Il Pirata** on Jl. Legian, near Jl. Tanjung Mekar, is a 24-hour pizzaria popular with the late-night crowd. **Club Double Six** on the beach at Jl. Double Six also serves Italian dishes. The restaurant turns into a disco after 11 pm on selected nights. **Lotus Tavern** on Jl. Wana Segara, near the Holiday Inn, has homemade pasta, pizzas as well as fresh seafood cooked over a charcoal grill. **Ciao Italia**, Jl. Pura Bagus Teruna, is a nice place featuring lots of ice creams. **Teraz**, Jl. Legian Kaja 494, ☎ 751790, is a trendy rooftop eatery that visiting stars frequent.

Mexican

Stylish **TJ's** Restaurant, Gang Poppies I, Kuta ☎ 751093, serves the best enchiladas and margaritas this side of the Pacific. The nachos and salsa are great with a cold beer or try a frozen strawberry margarita on a lazy afternoon. A smaller **TJ's** has opened at Jl. Legian, Seminyak, ☎ 730576. **Poco Loco**, on the road between Jl. Padma and Jl. Pura Bagus Teruna has atmosphere, good margaritas and a roving dwarf pouring shots. **Legian Fiesta**, Jl. Legian Kaja 452, (☎ 756062) is a friendly place with good margaritas and an odd but appealing sense of what Mexican food really is. **Santa Fe**, Jl. Dhyana Pura, Seminyak, doesn't have the margaritas down pat but the food is good. **Blue Cactus** at Kul Kul Hotel on Jl. Raya Pantai Kuta, ☎752520, has excellent authentic food and margaritas and is open to the sea breezes.

Indian

The **Bali Oberoi** serves the best Indian food, especially the chicken *tika* and the vegetarian food, for an up-market price. **G&D** (formerly George & Dragon), off Jl. Legian behind the Panin Bank, is one of the few which have a tandoor oven. Delicious tandoori chicken and oven-fresh *naan*. Reasonable prices. **Taj Mahal**, Jl. Oberoi (☎ 753922), serves a limited Indian menu from 6 pm until late.

Swiss

Swiss Restaurant at Jl. Puri Bagus Teruna (☎ 751735) is a meeting place for European hoteliers. The honorary Swiss consulate is next door. The affiliated **Swiss Pub** is on Jl. Legian (☎754719).

Japanese

Bali's most serious Japanese restaurant is the up-market **Yashi** in Hotel Patra Jasa Bali, where Japanese chefs prepare a full range of dishes from *sushi* to *tempura*. At **LG Club**, Jl. Legian, they have the do-it yourself Japanese and Korean buffet, from *shabu-shabu* to *bulgogi*. Fresh *kim-chee*. $6 excluding drinks. **Goa 2001** has a sushi bar, and **Made's Warung** also serves perfect sushi roll, *yakitori* and *sashimi*. **Ryoshi Japanese** Restaurant, Jl. Raya Seminyak 17 (☎ 731152) and at Gelael Top Plaza, Jl. Raya Legian, is air-conditioned and is open until midnight with *sushi, tempura, robata* and *soba* on the menu.

Middle Eastern

Aladdin, off Jl. Raya Seminyak, next to Kaya Gaya shop (☎ 239320), has an excellent tent-draped setting and good *meseh*. It is never busy.

Fast Food

For the hopelessly homesick, Kuta has a complete complement of American fast food outlets:

Burger King, Kentucky Fried Chicken, and Swensen's Ice Cream are all in the Gelael Supermarket on the main road to Denpasar, near the gas station and on Jl. Legian near the Spotlight Disco. Down the road from the former, next to the big duty free store is Pizza Hut, right next to the big duty free shop. Call 751696 for delivery service. For the Big Mac attack, McDonald's sits next to Hard Rock Cafe on Jl. Legian.

MOVIES

Legian Cineplex 21, on Jl. Legian on top of Matahari Department Store, features American movies at 6 and 8:15 pm. For a more Indonesian atmosphere, go to Kuta Theater on Jl. Raya Kuta.

Many restaurants and bars feature after-dinner video and MTV programmes, including: Krakatoa, Jl. Raya Seminyak 56 (☎ 730849); Rum Jungle, Jl. Pura Bagus Teruna (a favorite haunt of old Kuta hands); Bounty, Jl. Legian (very Oz); Norm's, Jl. Legian; Taman Sari, Gang Poppies II; Topi Kopi, Jl. Pura Bagus Teruna, has French TV specials.

NIGHTLIFE

Bars and discos

Kuta and Legian are "party central." Starting at 8 pm, a live band plays reggae music at Baruna, Jl. Pantai Kuta, every Tuesday. Thursday and Saturday night. The action cranks up after dinner in Kuta's many bars, most of them on Jl. Legian. Three of the top watering holes can be visited in organized pub crawls twice a week. Call Peanut's Club (☎ 751920) or Bali-Aussie (☎ 751910) for a pickup. SC (short for "Sari Club"), also on Jl. Legian, is the most crowded spot around—spilling drunken Aussies into the street from 9 pm onwards.

From the bars, proceed to your favorite disco to dance the night away. Most discos charge only for drinks, starting at $1. Two cavernous halls on Jl. Legian, Peanuts and Spotlight feature wide-screen videos, flashing lights and pounding music. Both are packed to the rafters with young tourists and locals after about 10 pm. Crazy House (live band), Rose and Koala Blue are all in the same complex as Peanuts.

Further north at two open-air, beachside discos and restaurants, the crowds are older and rather more hip: Double Six (☎ 730666), Jl. Double Six, is open until dawn and Gado Gado on Jl. Dhyana Pura is open midnight until dawn Fri, Sat, Sun, Tues, and Wed. The ritual is, after dinner at Made's Warung proceed to Goa 2001 (☎/fax 730592) on Jl. Raya Seminyak for a drink or two and then hit one of the discos around midnight. Some new places are trying

to compete with the established venues. Cafe Latino at Jl. Bypass Ngurah Rai on the way to Nusa Dua has an Italian seafood restaurant in the front and an open-air disco at the back, open on Friday. Some big hotels like Bali Dynasty (☎ 752403) and Bintang Bali (☎ 753292) have lively discos too, usually preferred by the local youths wary of mixing with the "Kuta cowboys."

SHOPPING

Kuta is a shopper's paradise. This is partly because it's an important manufacturing center of summer wear, jewelry and decorative handicrafts which are exported all over the world. Most of the goods are designed by young expatriates from Europe, the USA or Japan working through a network of local partners.

The best area for shopping is Jl. Legian, Jl. Bakung Sari, Jl. Melasti and nearby back lanes such as Poppies I and II. Some of the best deals, though, can be made as far away as Seminyak. Before buying, check everything carefully because goods are not returnable. Beware also of "antiques", as most are fakes.

Kuta has also several department stores. On the downmarket side Supernova (☎ 751186), near the post office on Jl. Raya Kuta, offers casual T-shirts, flashy purses and jewelry, while the big Plaza Bali (☎ 753301) on Jl. Raya Kuta is geared to tour groups. Its kiosks have the whole range of Indonesian handicrafts such as batik, ikat textiles, Indonesian designer clothes. The new Matahari department store in central Kuta carries clothing galore.

Clothing

Kuta offers the whole range of clothing prices and styles, from gaudy T-shirts to exclusive designer cloths. Always check the quality of costly items to ensure you don't get export remnants. In small shops, bargain hard. In designer outlets, don't expect more than 10 or 20% discount.

The established manufacturers generally have more than one outlet in Kuta and Legian. Check out Kekal on Jl. Pantai Kuta and Uluwatu on Jl. Bakung Sari for lacy women's wear. Bali Trend on Jl. Legian Kaja has Indonesian designer clothes and accessories. Dodger art shop specializes in T-shirts with Indonesian saying, crafts and oddities you won't find anywhere else.

The Balinese partiality for the shiny and the glittery has inspired flashy sportwear and dazzling footwear, like that found at Meidy Collections on Jl. Double Six and Jl. Legian and Dynasty at Jl. Raya Seminyak 496 (☎ 757149). Muti on Jl. Legian Kaja specializes in flashy footwear at very reasonable prices. Kaya Gaya on Jl. Raya Seminyak has a collection of stylish shoes, bags and jewelry with a strong emphasis on embroidery and beads. It also has antiques. Baik-Baik on Jl. Raya Kuta has colorful cotton print shirts and trendy pants for men. **Mr. Bali** on Jl. Pantai Kuta has fancy shirts, military bermudas and checkered shorts. **Hey**, Jl. Kartika Plaza, features black and white men's shirts, pants and jackets. **Bali Balance**, Jl. Kartika Plaza, has a whole range of cotton pants for men. Many stores are starting to sell childrens' lines as well.

If you're looking for fab surfwear, stop in **Bali Barrel**, Jl. Legian, **Ulu's Surf Shop** or **The Curl** on Jl. Melasti. Get colorful shorts and T-shirts at **Lost Boy** or **Amphibia**, Jl. Legian. The place to buy original design T-shirts is **Tony's** on Jl. Bakung Sari. The big store **Chandra** at Jl. Melasti and **Wisnu Garment** on Jl. Legian also have interesting T-shirt designs at low prices.

Leather Goods

Leather is big business in Bali. Lots of shops, such as **Gecko**, Jl. Legian Kaja, and **Mr Kuta** Jl. Gunung Bayung 8, specialize in leather clothes. Bags, belts and footwear can all be found along Jl. Legian. Some designs incorporate plaited rattan, dubbed "jungle Gucci".

Antiques

You'll find many "antique" stores in Kuta. Be very wary of your Balinese finds: many objects aren't genuine and some may have been stolen. Most genuine antiques have disappeared over the last 15 years, but it's still possible to buy good pieces between 25 and 40 years old from Bali, Java, Kalimantan, and Nusa Tenggara.

Baharrudin on Jl. Bakung Sari specializes in hand dyed *ikat* from Timor, Sumba, Flores, Sawu, and Kalimantan and beads, baskets and curios from various islands. Great *ikat* can also be found at the small **Pahikung Shop** on Jl. Legian Kaja, opposite the Glory Restaurant (it also sells textiles produced by the *pahikung* technique from Sumba). Reasonable prices and nicer than most.

Borneo Art Shop on Jl. Legian makes nifty rattan and leather bags. **Kaliuda Art Shop** on Jl. Legian has a large collection of woodcarvings and *ikats* from Timor, Sumba, and Flores.

Polo on Jl. Legian is the best shop for furniture, ethnic blankets and accessories. **Anang** has a good selection of baskets. There are also great shops along Jl. Raya Seminyak near Jl. Dhyana Pura: **Apo Kayan** at no. 16 displays beautiful but expensive pieces mainly from Kalimantan. Better priced are two places just beyond Jl. Dhyanapura on the left: **Kartika Ria** at no. 61 and **Kutai** at no. 65. Kartika Ria has a wide collection from all over Indonesia, both new and old. Kutai is a small, very down-to-earth place with a neat selection of old and new pieces from Kalimantan and Nusa Tenggara. Unlike most other places, the owners can tell you exact details of the merchandise. Both are very friendly.

Also check out the small shops along Jl. Tanjung Mekar, where copies of colonial and Sino-Javanese furniture is becoming a growing business. **Pelack** on Jl. Bypass Ngurah Rai, near the intersection to Benoa Harbor, has a wide range of beautiful, top quality antique furniture.

Souvenirs & Handicrafts

For bric-a-brac visit the **Kuta Art Market** on Jl. Bakung Sari by the beach, where you can bargain for T-shirts and an endless variety of carved animals, wind chimes, imitation banana trees, shells, and batik. There's a similar market on Jl. Melasti and numerous souvenir stalls along Jl. Raya Kuta. On Jl. Melasti, **Safari Plaza** specializes in beaded apparel and a wide range of carvings, furnishings, and jewelry.

Chandra at Jl. Melasti has a variety of good quality wooden handicrafts such as hanging animals, banana trees, trays etc. If you don't like bargaining, go to **Alex's** in the middle of Jl. Legian for batik, ethnic blankets, medium quality rattan baskets, and an interesting selection of small souvenirs. Also check out **Joger** on Jl. Raya Kuta. They have a lot of interestingly designed pottery, terracotta and wooden artifacts.

For higher quality items, such as *ikat* clothes, cushions and sashes, try **Ikat Nogo** on Jl. Legian or any of the shops mentioned under "Antiques" above. For those in need of ethnic-but-cheap souvenirs, the **Timor Art Shop** at Jl. Legian Kaja 423A has the solution. Starting from about $3 they sell containers, bamboo or rattan statues, *ikat* and other items from Timor, Sumba, Lombok, and Maluku. Nearby, the shop next to the Do Drop Inn sells nice leather goods.

Balinese paintings and carvings are also available in Kuta, but it's best to shop for these in Ubud, Mas and Batuan. To get a look at Indonesian contemporary painting, drop in at **C-Line Gallery** at Jl. Kartika Plaza 33.

Jewelry

All the main hotels have jewelry shops. **Jonathan**, **Mirah** and **Yusuf's** on Jl. Legian are the best places for fashionable designs and quality work. Attractive accessories (bracelets, earrings and broches) can be found in many shops. Try **Kaya Gaya**, on Jl. Raya Seminyak. Seashell jewelry is available in many shops on Jl. Tanjung Mekar. **Ida's Jewelry** on Jl. Pantai Kuta also has a wide range.

Ceramics

Jenggala on Jl. Pantai Kuta, **Rumah Manis** and **Nacha,** both in Seminyak, all have great selections of original wares such as fruit baskets, tea sets, dinner sets and vases. For Lombok pottery, try **Lombok Handicraft Souvenir** on Jl. Bypass Ngurah Rai (near Cafe Latino). There are many similar shops along Jl. By-pass Ngurah Rai.

MISCELLANEOUS

Bungy Jumping. A new adventure to experience. Two new bungy jumping stations opened recently. Facilities in Kuta (Bali Bungy Co., Jl. Pura Puseh, ☎ 752658) and Legian at Club Double Six (☎ 730666), operated by the father of bungy, A.J. Hackett. Cost per jump: $35–$55.

Cassette Tapes. Cassette shops are found all over Kuta. The best selection is at Mahogany in Seminyak. Wana, the owner, is always well informed about latest releases. Some CDs are also available, but tapes are the best buys. Prices here are high.

Duty Free Goods. The Indonesian Biggest Duty-Free Shop is on Jl. Imam Bonjol. You can't miss the big billboards. Sells imported clothes, perfumes, cameras, liquors, etc.

Dance performances. Kuta is not the greatest place to see Balinese dance, although all the main hotels have a Balinese dance dinner. Sri Wisata Budaya on Jl. Bypass Ngurah Rai toward Sanur has daily morning performances of *barong* and *keris* dances. The Pengabetan neighborhood also holds irregular performances.

Film Processing. The Fuji Image Plaza on the main road to Denpasar is the best place for film and processing. Kodak has an outlet in Legian. For camera repairs go to Prima Photo on Jl. Gajah Mada in Denpasar. Instant processing and printing shops are scattered all over Kuta.

Horse Riding. Riding along Seminyak beach at sunset is worth the back pain. Go to Jl. Dhyana Pura and park by the Mesari Hotel (☎ 751852, 751401). About $10/hour is the usual rate. Look for the stable in the small lane starting on Jl. Dhyana Pura leading up to Jl. Legian. The horses are healthy and two ponies plus experienced supervisors are available for children.

Massages. Lots of ladies offer massages on the beach. Although they may not be as good as the ones you can get in Denpasar, most travelers report that it feels good. $3 for a full hour. Massage on Bali has nothing to do with sex. The local euphemism for the latter is "jiggy-jig."

Medical. SOS Natour Clinic at Kuta Beach Hotel, Jl. Pantai Kuta, ☎ 751361.

Money Changers. Easy and fast. Kuta has a great number of banks and money changers. Most money changers are opened daily, mostly until late at night. Rates differ, so shop around.

Post office. The Kuta Post Office is located off Jl. Raya Kuta, open 8–8 daily, except Sunday when it closes at noon. Postal agents (look for the orange sign "approved by the post office") sell stamps, handle shipments and provide courier services. A convenient one is on Jl. Raya Seminyak, south of Jl. Dhyana Pura just south of Alas Arum supermarket.

Supermarkets. Kuta has a big supermarket, Gelael Dewata, located next to the gas station on the road to Denpasar. This is the place for imported foodstuffs, toiletries and drinks at reasonable prices. It also has a newsstand, a bakery and fast food outlets. In Kuta proper, there is the Kuta Supermarket on Jl. Bakung Sari and the Alas Arum Supermarket (☎ 751705, 753133) on Jl. Raya Seminyak with a similar range of items. Service is slow, but the assortment is wide. Also open at night.

Surfing. Kuta and Legian have long been known as surfing areas. The 6 km beach break stretching from Kuta to Petitenget has a range of waves. Kuta reef, further south and 1 km from the beach, can be reached by boat from the Santika Beach Hotel for $20. Get surfing information from the experts at Kuta's surf shops: Bali Barrel, Ulu's Surf Shop and The Surf Shop. The owners are all avid surfers. Talk to them for up-to-the-minute surfing reports. They also have tide charts which are essential for negotiating the tricky currents.

Swimming. The currents at Kuta are extremely strong and the undertow is dangerous. Swimming is at your own risk. There are markers to indicate no-swim areas, but no sea markers to indicate safe distance from the beach. There are life guards at the Kuta Lifesaving Club at the end of Jl. Pantai Kuta, but not along the beach. Drownings are not uncommon.

Waterpark. Bali's first waterpark, Waterbom on Jl. Kartika Plaza, Tuban ☎ 755676/8, is more than a water amusement park for both adults and children with a variety of pools, water "rides", and slides in a beautifully landscaped environment. Plenty of space for swimming, sunbathing, and splashing. Open 9–6.

Telecommunications (*wartel*). Kuta has at least six *wartels* from which you can call directly to most countries around the world. Open daily, 8 am–11 pm. The most convenient ones are: Jl. Legian (between Jl. Padma and Jl. Melasti), ☎ 756868; Jl. Melasti in the Orchid Garden Complex; and Jl. Kartika Plaza. The one in the Peanut Complex on Jl. Legian is no use at night, due to the noise.

An alternative to the *wartel* are the new "business centers" that charge slightly more. Look for the IDD signs. Also popular are Rudi's Business Center, opposite Benny's Café II on Jl. Dhyana Pura in Seminyak and Krakatoa Cafe, Jl. Raya Seminyak 56, ☎ 730824, which operates a business, information and travel center.

—updated by Debe Campbell/Andy Udayana

Jimbaran PRACTICALITIES

4

Located on the isthmus south of Ngurah Rai airport, and a continuation of the white sands of Kuta Beach, Jimbaran bay is one of Bali's most recently developed resort area. Tranquil compared to Kuta, it retains much of its fishing village charm. With its shallow water and lack of sharp corals, Jimbaran is ideal for families. The area also remains free from aggressive vendors. *See map on page 106.*

Prices in US dollars. AC = Air-conditioning. Telephone code is 0361.

TRANSPORTATION

Taxis can be booked at the airport taxi counter, Rp8,500 to Jimbaran and Rp12,000 to the Bali Cliff Resort. The blue *bemo* from Denpasar's Tegal station costs Rp 700. *Bemos* to and from Kuta are Rp 1,000 and require a walk from the end of the airport road. To Sanur, via Tegal and Kereneng stations, Rp 1,700; to the Sentral terminal in Nusa Dua, Rp 500.

ACCOMMODATIONS

Jimbaran and the Bukit Peninsula currently boast some of the most luxurious hotels on Bali. **Bali Cliff Resort,** Ungasan, at the extreme south of the Bukit Peninsula. ☎ 771992, fax: 771993. 200 rooms. Located atop a 100 m cliff overlooking the beach. Complete sport facilities. Breathtaking panorama. $170–$2,000 for the presidential suite. **Bali InterContinental,** Jimbaran. ☎ 701888, fax: 701777. 451 rooms. Every room designed to give clear views of Jimbaran Bay or the surrounding gardens. Superior $185, deluxe $195, Club Intercontinental $215, suites $275–$700. **Four Seasons Resort**, Jl. Jimbaran. ☎ 701010, fax: 701020. Spacious villas comprised of three Balinese-style pavilions, a courtyard and pool; arranged in "villages", each with its own staff and service center. Stunning sunset views. $375–$1,750. **Keraton Bali Cottages** Jl. Majapati. ☎ 701991, fax: 235243. 99 cottages. Two-story AC bungalows in a spacious beachfront, palm-shaded garden. The lobby is designed like a *keraton* (palace). Cottage $110–$160, Suite $290–$450. **Pan Sea Puri Bali** Jl. Uluwatu, Jimbaran. ☎ 701326, fax: 701320. 43 rooms. White brick cottages with thatched roofs, private open-air baths and verandahs. The beach restaurant is a marvelous spot for lunch. Under renovation until December 1995. **Puri Bambu Bungalows** Jl. Pengeracikan, Kedonganan. ☎ 753377, 701468, fax: 753440. 38 rooms. 100 meters from the beach. New bungalows with antique decor. $55–$95. **Puri Indraprastha,** Jl. Uluwatu 28A. ☎ 701552. 11 rooms. The only budget place in the area. Popular

with surfers. Simple rooms with private baths. A pool in the center. $13–$16, including breakfast.

DINING

Jimbaran has yet to experience a restaurant and boutiques boom, but that is beginning to change. **Cafe Latino,** ☎ 701880, Jl. Bypass Ngurah Rai, is well known to Kuta regulars. Italian seafood restaurant in the front with an open-air disco (open on Fridays) at the back. **PJ's** at Four Seasons Resort (☎ 701010) has the best pizza on Bali. Open 11 am–10 pm. **Bali Edelweiss,** Jl. Bypass Nugrah Rai 20 ☎ 772094, serves authentic Austrian cuisine. **Little Indonesia**, Jl. Bukit Permai, offers garden dining and dishes from around the archipelago.

If you wish to "go native," try the stalls near Jimbaran Market or **Sari Bundo**, a good Padang restaurant on Jl. Uluwatu which has spicy Sumatran food for around $3 a dish.

HIKING & WATERSPORTS

If you are a hiker, there's a path running along most of the cliff, passable during the dry season: don't miss the caves of the Balangan area.

For watersports, contact your hotel or a company such as **CV Bukit Kencana Diving Center,** Kawasan Bukit Permai, Jimbaran, ☎ 701070 or **Baruna,** Jl. Bypass Ngurah Rai 300B, ☎ 753820, 751223. Hire fishing boats in the harbor for $12 an hour.

Surfing

The Bukit area south of Jimbaran is sacred to the world's surfers. For tips on the best spots, contact the surf shops in Kuta or just inquire on the beach.

MEDICAL SERVICES

Jimbaran Clinic 24-hour service, Jl. Bypass Ngurah Rai 95XX, Jimbaran, ☎ 701467.

—*updated by Debe Campbell/Andy Udayana*

5 Nusa Dua PRACTICALITIES

INCLUDES TANJUNG BENOA

Nusa Dua's hotels are geared to tourist groups, beach fanatics and international conferences. Each hotel has its own combination of first-class business and resort facilities. Located in a large, landscaped park, the complex also comprises an international convention center, a championship 18-hole golf course, a luxury shopping center, a medical clinic, and an amphitheater for music and dance. More facilites are located in the village of Bualu, just outside the resort.

Prices in US dollars. AC = Air-conditioning. Telephone code is 0361.

TOURIST INFORMATION

Bali Tourism Development Corporation (BTDC) at the center of Nusa Dua complex, ☎ 771010.

TRANSPORTATION

Most hotels have a taxi counter run by a private company or co-operative. Prices are significantly higher (30%) than other resorts, with the drive to the airport costing $10 or more.

Open-topped buses with tropical motifs travel throughout the complex and to Benoa village. The fare is Rp1,000. There are car rental companies at each of the three gates of the Nusa Dua complex, near the Tragia Supermarket and at several hotels. There's also a *bemo* terminal. The fare is between Rp800 and Rp1,000 to Denpasar, and Rp500 to Tanjung Benoa.

One of the main disadvantages in Nusa Dua is the lack of cheap, convenient transportation within the resort, especially between the hotels, the shopping center and the golf course. The distances are too far to walk, the shuttle bus too irregular, and the wait for taxis interminable.

ACCOMMODATIONS

Add 21% to the rates below for tax and service. Up to two children under 12 staying in their parents' room are usually free or half price.
Amanusa PO Box 33, Nusa Dua. ☎ 772333, 771267, fax: 772335, 771266. 35 suites. Commanding views of the golf course and the ocean. Highest standards of luxury. Every suite has a queen-size four poster bed, outdoor patio, and garden shower. Suites $330–$770.
Bali Clarion Suites Jl. Dalem Tarukan 7, Taman Mumbul, PO Box 133, Nusa Dua. ☎ 773808, fax: 773737. 326 suites. Each suite includes living room kitchenette, dining table, sofa bed, terrace or balcony, and large garden. Facilities include 2 tennis courts, gym, swimming pool, meeting facilities,

and shuttle service from hotel to private beach club and Nusa Dua shopping center. $120–$150.
Bali Hilton PO Box 46, Nusa Dua 80361. ☎ 771-102, fax: 771616. 540 rooms. Children's play center, health center, squash and tennis courts, complete watersport facilities. $140–205, suites $425–$2,000.
Bualu Village PO Box 6, Denpasar. ☎ 771310, fax: 771313. 50 rooms. Needs renovations. Free sport activities. PADI-certified diving instructor. The only hotel with a horse and cart available. $69–$112.
Club Méditerranée Nusa Dua, PO Box 7, Lot 6, Nusa Dua ☎ 771521/3, fax: 771853. 350 rooms. One of Le Club's best, housing the usual international facilities and activities. Rates include room, meals and entertainment. $102 (low season), $250 (high season), less for children. Special members' rates.
Grand Hyatt PO Box 53, Nusa Dua. ☎ 771234, fax:772038. 750 rooms. Designed by the architect of the world-famous Hyatt in Waikoloa, Hawai'i, this is one of the most spectacular resort hotels in Southeast Asia. Consists of four Balinese-style villages and five swimming pools. Superior $160–$260, suite $500–$1,535, villa $1,850–$2,100.
Melia Bali PO Box 1048, Tuban. ☎ 771510, 771410, fax: 771360, 771362. 494 rooms. Spanish management and ambience. Lofty, open-air lobby and fountains. Popular with tour groups. Tennis and squash courts, health center with sauna. Superior $176–$198, suite $412–$1,100.
Nusa Dua Beach Hotel PO Box 1028, Denpasar. ☎ 771210, fax: 771229. 380 rooms. Nusa Dua's oldest property, completely renovated in 1995. International standard spa, classes, full gym and squash courts. Conference room for 500. Superior $165, deluxe $185, suite $300–$3,200.
Putri Bali PO Box 1, Denpasar. ☎ 771020, fax: 771139. 384 rooms. Managed by the government; dense tropical grounds. Superior $120–$155, cottages $155–$175, suites $210–$600.
Sheraton Nusa Indah Resort PO Box 36, Nusa Dua. ☎ 771906, fax: 771908. 369 rooms. Views of either the tropical gardens, the pool or the sea. Attached to Bali International Convention Center. Deluxe $180–$210, suites $360–$1,000.
Sheraton Lagoon Nusa Dua Beach PO Box 2044,

Kuta. ☎ 771327/8, fax: 771326. 276 rooms. Surrounded by lush tropical gardens, blue lagoons and cascading waterfalls. Fully equipped health club and tennis courts. Deluxe $210–$300, suites $460–$1,800.

DINING

The Nusa Dua complex has many international restaurants (with international prices) in the five-star hotels. A 7-course French meal at the chic **Semeru Rotisserie** in the Putri Bali costs $45/person. All hotels hold theme buffet dinners featuring Balinese dance for $30–$40/person. The Galleria area offers Chinese, Japanese, European cuisines.

For cheaper food and more natural surroundings, head for the village of Bualu just outside the resort. Outside the main gate to the right is the big **Nusa Dua Grill and Seafood** restaurant. If you like spicy West Sumatran food, try **Mega Meriah Padang** on Jl. Bypass Ngurah Rai. There's also a food center, the **Amanda**, next to the police station, where you can try local delicacies. The best price-quality deal, though, is the **Ulam Restaurant** (☎ 771902, 771590), just outside the gate facing the Hilton. The specialty is grilled fish in banana leaves ($4). It's a favorite haunt of ministers and celebrities. Kuta's popular **Poco Loco** Mexican food has opened a branch at Jl. Pantai Mengiat (☎ 773923).

Finally, if you decide to go native and eat for a dollar, there's a satay stall near the main entrance, or try the *bakso Solo* (meatball soup) at the night market in front of the local movie theater.

Tanjung Benoa

Tanjung Benoa is the natural northern continuation of Nusa Dua, with the white sand beach stretching the length of the coast. It is a booming resort, popular with watersports enthusiasts.

ACCOMMODATIONS

Prices are negotiable at low season. Most hotels can arrange watersports activities.

Budget (under $25)

Rasa Sayang Beach Inn ☎ 771643. 19 rooms. Very simple rooms. $9–$11 fan, $15–$18 AC.
Rasa Dua Jl. Pratama 98, Tanjung Benoa.☎ 771751, fax: 773515. 2 rooms. Two-story bungalows with thatched roofs. Run by a company that rents yachts and a glass bottomed boat. $16–18.

Intermediate ($50–$75)

All rooms have AC, hot water and private bath. Tax and service are included.
Matahari Terbit Bungalows Jl. Pratama, Tanjung Benoa.☎ 771018, fax: 772027. 8 rooms. Rooms overlooking a pool, restaurant in the center. $60.
Puri Joma Bungalows. ☎/fax: 771526. 10 rooms.

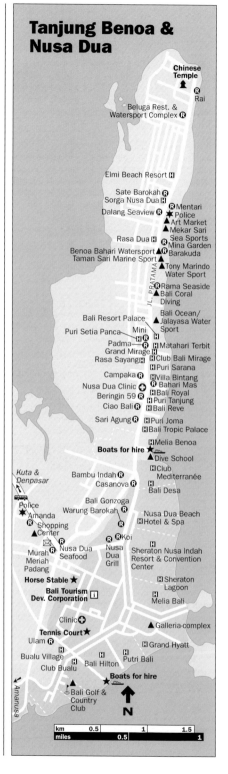

Tanjung Benoa & Nusa Dua

Relaxing beachfront pool and restaurant. $55–$60.

First Class ($75–$100)

All rooms with AC, hot water telephone.

Bali Resort Palace Jl. Pratama, Tanjung Benoa. Reservations: PO Box 39, Nusa Dua 80361. ☎ 772-239, fax: 772237. 186 rooms in two buildings facing each other across the main road. Watersports, pool, jogging track, tennis court, disco. $90–$160.

Club Bali Mirage Jl. Pratama 72, Tanjung Benoa. PO Box 43, Nusa Dua ☎ 772147, fax: 772156. 100 rooms. All inclusive club with rate including room, meals, beverages, entertainment, and non-motorized watersports. Modern facilities and a classical Balinese atmosphere with lush tropical garden. $85/person, twin sharing. Single supplement $25. No children under age 16 allowed.

Luxury ($100 and up)

Bali Royal Jl. Pratama, Tanjung Benoa, Nusa Dua. ☎ 771039, fax:771885. 14 rooms. Set in lush gardens with beachfront pool and restaurant. Some of the bungalows have open-air baths with special tubs. The suites are ocean-view duplexes with private garden. The suites $140–$160, suite $180.

Bali Tropic Palace Jl. Pratama 34, PO Box 41, Tanjung Benoa. ☎ 772130, 772107/9, fax: 772131. 104 rooms. All rooms have private terraces overlooking the sea. Seaside swimming pool with sunken bar. Deluxe $130–$150, suite $250–$350.

Grand Mirage Jl. Pratama 74, Tanjung Benoa. Reservations: PO Box 43, Nusa Dua. ☎ 771888, fax: 772148. 312 rooms. French Thalassotherapy Spa is part of the hotel. 3 restaurants, 3 bars, 2 tennis courts, 1 meeting room, 1 swimming pool. Standard $145, suite $205–$805, villas $505.

DINING

The Tanjung Benoa area has an increasing number of good restaurants. Near the peninsula tip, the sumptuous **Beluga Watersport Complex** is a hull-shaped restaurant renowned for its *rijsttafel*, only $10/person. The beach-side **Rai** restaurant features lobster and fresh fish grilled to perfection. For good Chinese and Japanese food, dine at the **Bali Resort Hotel**. At the southern end, across from Club Med (and a favorite of its staff), is the **Casanova** Italian restaurant. For Indonesian food, **Bambu Indah** has a good reputation among locals. More upscale but excellent quality is **Pasar Senggol**, nightly at Grand Hyatt Bali. For $37, all you can eat of a variety of Indonesian fare from vendor carts and stalls, plus an excellent dance performance.

WATERSPORTS

Facilities are available at reasonable rates in over 10 locations. The following is a rough price guide. Canoes: $8/hour. Deep-sea fishing: $50–$100. Scuba Diving: $34 for certified divers, $55 (boat dive). Snorkeling around Nusa Dua: $10. Day trips to Nusa Penida and Nusa Lembongan: cost $60–$80. Banana boats, waterscooters, waterskiing, jetskis, waverunners, windsurfers, and parasailing are also available.

SHOPPING

Although the Nusa Dua/Tanjung Benoa area does not compare to Kuta or Denpasar for choice, you can find a wide range in a much smaller area. Prices are fair.

Set inside the Nusa Dua resort, the **Galleria Shopping Complex** has textiles and handicrafts, including leather, batik, woodcarving, and paintings. **Keris Gallery** is an up-market department store. There's also a **Duty Free Shop**, a **Tragia** supermarket and several restaurants. The Galleria is, however, a rather sterile environment and devoid of Balinese ambience.

Another shopping area is near the main Tragia supermarket on Jl. Bypass Ngurah Rai. There are a number of leather shops where you can bargain for custom-made leather jackets for as little as $120. Most of the other stuff on sale is the same as that found in all the main tourist areas, minus the chic of some of the Legian and Sanur shops. The Tragia supermarket itself is a good place to buy souvenirs for a fixed, higher price, but minus the hassles.

NIGHTLIFE

Nusa Dua is a resort for short stays, conventioneers and families who generally don't go out. If they do, it's either to Jimbaran or Kuta. There are a few nightspots in the resort, however: **Soarssa Discotheque** at the Bali Resort Palace**,** **Hemingway's Piano Bar** in Tanjung or in Nusa Dua, **Club Tabuh** disco at Nusa Dua Beach Hotel, or **Quinn's Pub** at the Sheraton Lagoon.

For Balinese dance outside the hotel, ask for the Galleria's entertainment program, or better still, try to visit a night rehearsal of a gamelan group in nearby Bualu village.

MISCELLANEOUS

Banks and Money Changers. Both available at Galleria or outside the main gate to Nusa Dua. **Medical Service.** The BTDC Clinic ☎ 772392, across from Nusa Dua Galleria, and the Nusa Dua Clinic ☎ 771324, across from Bali Royal in Tanjung Benoa are both open 24-hours. **Telecommunications.** Wartels are located at the BPLP/STP Hotel & Tourism Institute in Nusa Dua, ☎ 7771165 and behind the Police in Tanjung Benoa, ☎ 773648. Both open 7.30am–10 pm. **Postal Service.** Most hotels will post letters for guests. The Nusa Dua post office is outside the resort's main gate. Hours: Mon–Sat 8am–8pm, Sun 8am–noon, holidays 8am-2pm.

—updated by Debe Campbell

Nusa Dua 5

Ubud PRACTICALITIES

INCLUDES CAMPUAN, PELIATAN, PENGOSEKAN & SAYAN

While it's possible to visit Ubud in just a day, such a short trip would barely touch the surface of this extraordinary village. An interesting melange of rural Balinese life and modern services which co-exist here. Only 45 minutes from Ngurah Rai airport, Ubud is close to many of central Bali's major sights. Despite the fact that visitors may outnumber residents during peak periods, Ubud retains the atmosphere of a small country community and, in contrast to the hussle of Kuta, the pace of life is very relaxed. It's a great place to tour on foot or by bicycle and there's a wide range of facilities for tourists of all budgets, as well as beaches 10 km away. For those who enjoy being close to natural beauty, yet within easy reach of creature comforts, Ubud is ideal.

Prices in US dollars. AC = Air-conditioning. Telephone code is 0361.

ORIENTATION

The main crossroads in front of the Puri Saren palace is the "navel" of Ubud—its cultural and historical focal point. The main street is lined with restaurants, hotels, shops and galleries, stretching all the way from the T-junction at the eastern end of Ubud to the Campuan Bridge in the west. Small lanes lined with homestays, *warungs* and Balinese compounds extend north and south from the main road.

Jl. Wanara Wana, commonly called Monkey Forest Road, branching south from the middle of Ubud is lined with hotels, restaurants, artists' studios, and boutiques for a distance of some 2 km. A parallel road just to the east through Padangtegal is similar, though less congested. Away from these main streets, Ubud is still relatively quiet.

Roads radiate west out of the main town to Campuan and Payangan, south to Pengosekan and east to Goa Gajah. Local *bemos* can be flagged down in the daytime on the main road. Ubud to Campuan, for example, costs Rp500.

TOURIST INFORMATION

For current information on performances, transport schedules, temple festivals, and special activities, inquire at **Bina Wisata Ubud**, next to the village chief's office.

TRANSPORATION

Getting There

Ubud is 45 minutes by car from the airport and southern beach resort areas. Taxis from the airport cost $18 (AC). Look for the booth at the airport: turn right after you leave customs. Alternatively, charter (and bargain for) a *bemo* outside the airport for about $12.

From Denpasar, take a *bemo* from Kereneng Terminal to Batubulan Terminal, then transfer to Ubud (Rp600). Chartering a *bemo* from Denpasar costs about $9. Alternatively, hop on one of the many shuttle buses which depart Kuta for Ubud at 8.30, 10 and 11.30 am, 1, 2.30 and 4pm ($4). Contact Perama Tour, Jl. Legian, Kuta, ☎ 751170.

Getting Around

Although you may choose to rent a mountain bike to save time and effort, it's easy to get around Ubud on foot. Mountain bikes can be rented everywhere for $2/day. Motorbikes (100cc) cost $5.50/day. A Suzuki jeep costs $20 to $30 daily; cheaper by the week or month. Look for signs along all main roads.

Buy shuttle bus tickets to Kuta and Candidasa from many of the travel agencies in town. For a full shuttle schedule, contact Peramaswara Tour & Travel, Jl. Hanoman, ☎ 96316, 974722. Shuttles to Sanur, Kuta and the airport depart at 8.30, 10 and 11.30 am, 12:30, 3.30, 5.30, 6.30, and 7.30 pm. ($2.50). Direct Kuta shuttles depart Ubud the same hours ($3.50). The shuttle to Lombok via Kuta leaves at 6 am ($12.50).

ACCOMMODATIONS

Ubud's accommodations have gone dramatically up-market in recent times—hot water, AC, telephones and even swimming pools are now readily available. Two of Bali's most expensive and exclusive hotels, **Amandari** and **Kupu Kupu Barong**, are also found here.

Decide on the area you want, then look around. Small hotels in the intermediate range line Jl. Raya Ubud and Jl. Wanara Wana (Monkey Forest Road) and offer lovely bungalows set in gardens with swimming pools for $20–$50/ night. Balinese-style homestays provide charming rooms with private bathroom, fan and hot water for $5–$15. Painters, dancers and musicians invite people into their homes to study or just to experience Balinese hospitality. All are easily reached on foot from the town center.

Travel out of Ubud in almost any direction and you'll find little homestays and bungalows tucked in among the ricefields, some with dramatic vistas. If you stay out in the rice paddies, it's handy to take along a mosquito net and flashlight.

Peliatan and Pengosekan, both just south of Ubud, are cheaper and quieter. Penestanan and Campuan to the west are lovely villages. You can see villagers working the fields, the place is lusciously green and small bungalows, shops and restaurants are sprouting up everywhere.

Sayan and Kedewatan, further to the west, offer luxury rooms with great views up to the volcanoes and down the Ayung River to the coast. Saba, on the coast south of Blahbatu, Andong on the road north to Tampaksiring and Goa Gajah also boast hotels for the more affluent traveller.

Most rooms have private bathrooms and rates include breakfast. Budget hotels offer toast, coffee/tea and fruit salad for breakfast.

Budget (under $25)

These are Balinese-style homestays in family compounds or rooms in the paddies built for tourists. Simple and clean, many have attached bathrooms, hot water and fans. A simple breakfast is always included and children are welcome. Homestays are clustered in well defined areas: Jl. Bisma, Jl. Hanoman, Jl. Kajeng, Jl. Wanara Wana (Monkey Forest Road) and Jl. Tebesaya. As there is little difference in the level of comfort, the choice is really between experiencing the intimacy of a family compound or the daily rhythms of the ricefields. For cheaper places and longer stays, look around Peliatan or Penestanan.

Central Ubud and to the West

Ina Inn Jl. Bisma, ☎ 96317. 7 rooms facing the rice paddies. $15–$17 fan.
Kajeng Jl. Kajeng (the lane beside the lotus pond, past Hans Snel), ☎ 975018. 11 rooms. A lovely surprise: facing a huge lilly pond stocked with carp. Overlooks dense foliage. A river roars through the deep ravine nearby. $6.70–$12.
Lecuk Inn, Jl. Kajeng 15, ☎ 96445. 8 comfortable rooms with verandahs, plus 2 with hot water and views across a ravine to ricefields. $10–$20.
Melati Cottages, Penestanan, ☎/fax:975088. 12 isolated bungalows, 150 m along a path from the road (behind Murni's Restaurant). Totally undisturbed ricefield setting. Swimming pool. Rates

aren't fixed and bargaining is the rule. Duplex bungalows about $20, other rooms $25–$30.
Penestanan Bungalows, Jl. Penestanan. ☎ 975604, fax: 288341. 12 rooms. Climb the steep stairs on the left off Jl. Campuan, 100 m past the Campuan bridge and follow the sign. Lovely garden setting with stunning views over the rice paddies. Restaurant, hot water (sometimes) and a swimming pool. Friendly, helpful staff. $20–$25 fan.
Tjetjak Inn Jl. Campuan, by the river on the road to the temple. ☎ 975238, fax: 974467. 10 charming bungalows overlooking Campuan River. Also known as Puri Campuan, it is run by a descendant of Ubud's royal family. No hot water. $10–$12.50. Under complete renovation in 1995.

Monkey Forest Road/Padangtegal

Artini 2 Jl. Hanoman, Padangtegal. ☎ 975689, fax: 975348. 24 rooms set in lush garden with manicured lawns. All rooms with hot water, fan and breakfast. Large pool with restaurant attached. Rooms toward the back are quiet and private. $22–$31.
Loka House Jl. Wanara Wana (Monkey Forest Road). ☎ 975162. 4 rooms rented by a Balinese artist amidst his family compound and gallery. Large enough for families an suitable for long-term stays. $20 including tax and service.
Matahari Jl. Jembawan, behind the post office. 7 rooms near a deep ravine looking out onto a bamboo forest. A Japanese-style hot tub is available for $5/person. Rooms with hot water, $9–$11.
Nick's II Jl. Hanoman 57. ☎ 975526. 5 rooms. Small, quiet establishment. $7–$14.
Pande Permai Jl. Wanara Wana (Monkey Forest Road). ☎ 975436. 16 rooms along the river overlooking tropical forest. Two-story brick and bamboo building. Hot water and fans. $13–$18.

Peliatan/Pengosekan

Bali Breeze Bungalows Jl. Pengosekan. ☎ 975410, fax: 975546. 12 *lumbung*-style bungalows. Bedroom upstairs, toilet and sitting room downstairs. Well designed and managed. A gem! $16–$23.
Ketut Madra Jl. Raya Ubud, Br. Kalah, Peliatan. ☎ 975745. 10 rooms at the end of a lane opening onto the ricefields. Madra is a renaissance man: a renowned painter, a *topeng* dancer and *wayang* afficiando. A favorite of the culture crowd. $9–$11.
Rona Jl. Sukma 23, Desa Tebesaya. ☎ 96229, fax: 975120. 9 clean, comfortable rooms with open-air bathrooms, double beds and mosquito nets. Restaurant attached. Huge library, laundry service, and free luggage storage. $4.50–$9.

Moderate ($25–$50)

This category has the widest selection and the best value. Most hotels have pools and phones. Reservations recommended during the high seasons in July/August and December/January. Rates include breakfast and are subject to 21% tax and service. Rates may vary out of season.

Central Ubud

Nick's Pension & Restaurant Jl. Wanara Wana

Ubud 6

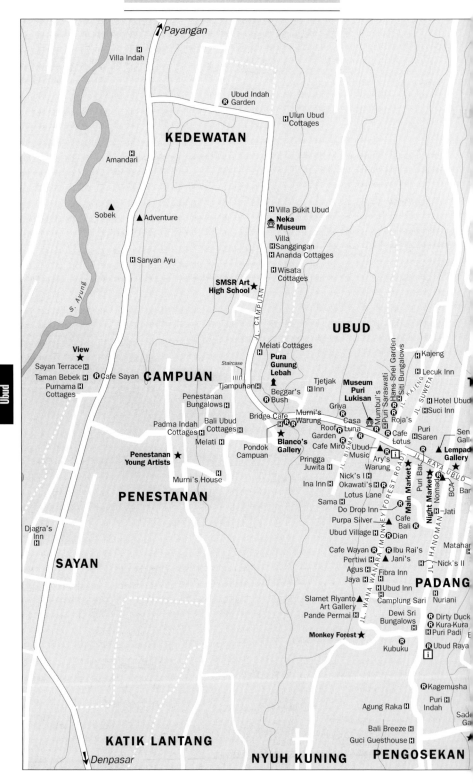

↑ Payangan

Ⓗ Villa Indah

Ubud Indah
Ⓡ Garden

Ⓗ Ulun Ubud
Cottages

KEDEWATAN

Ⓗ Amandari

▲ Sobek

▲ Adventure

Ⓗ Sanyan Ayu

Ⓗ Villa Bukit Ubud
🏛 **Neka Museum**

Villa
Ⓗ Sanggingan
Ⓗ Ananda Cottages

Ⓗ Wisata Cottages

**SMSR Art
High School** ★

S. Ayung

UBUD

Melati Cottages
Ⓗ

**Pura
Gunung
Lebah**

Staircase

View ★
Sayan Terrace Ⓗ
Taman Bebek Ⓗ Ⓡ Cafe Sayan **CAMPUAN**
Purnama Ⓗ
Cottages

Tjampuhan Ⓗ

Penestanan
Bungalows Ⓗ

Bridge Cafe
Padma Indah Ⓗ Bali Ubud
Cottages Ⓗ Cottages Ⓗ
Melati Ⓗ

**Penestanan
Young Artists** ★

PENESTANAN

Pondok
Campuan

Murni's House Ⓗ

Djagra's
Inn
Ⓗ

SAYAN

Tjetjak
Ⓗ Inn

Beggar's
Ⓡ Bush

Griya
Murni's Ⓡ
Ⓗ Ⓡ Ⓡ Warung

**Museum
Puri
Lukisan**

Casa
Ⓡ Roof Ⓡ Luna
Garden Ⓡ

Cafe Miro ★

Pringga
Juwita Ⓗ

Nick's I Ⓗ

Ina Inn Ⓗ Okawati's Ⓗ Ⓡ

Lotus Lane

Sama Ⓗ

Do Drop Inn

Purpa Silver ▲

Ubud Village Ⓗ Ⓗ

Cafe Wayan Ⓡ

Pertiwi Ⓗ Ⓡ ▲

Agus Ⓗ
Jaya Ⓗ Ⓗ

**Blanco's
Gallery** ★

Ⓡ Ⓡ Music

Ⓗ Ⓡ Ⓡ Ⓗ Ⓗ Ⓡ Ⓗ
Mumbul's Ⓗ
Puri Saraswati
Hans Snel Garden
Ⓡ Ⓡ Roja's
Siti Bungalows

Ⓗ Kajeng

Ⓗ Lecuk Inn

Ⓗ Hotel Ubud
Ⓗ Suci Inn

Cafe
Ⓡ Lotus

Ⓡ Ary's
Warung

Ⓡ Ⓗ Ubud
Ⓡ Ⓗ Jani's
Ⓡ Ⓗ Ⓡ Dian

Ⓡ Ibu Rai's

Fibra Inn

Ⓗ Ubud Inn

Ⓡ Camplung Sari

Puri
Ⓗ Saren

Main Market ★

JL. RAYA UBUD

**Lempad
Gallery** ★

Sen
Gall

Puri Bar

Night Market ★

Ⓡ Nomad

Ⓡ Jati

Cafe
Bali Ⓡ

Matahar

Nick's II

PADANG

Nuriani

Dewi Sri
Bungalows

Ⓡ Dirty Duck
Ⓡ Kura-Kura
Ⓗ Puri Padi

Slamet Riyanto ▲
Art Gallery
Pande Permai Ⓗ

Monkey Forest ★

Ⓡ
Kubuku

Ⓡ Ubud Raya
ⓘ

Ⓡ Kagemusha

Puri Ⓗ
Indah

Agung Raka Ⓡ

Bali Breeze Ⓗ
Guci Guesthouse Ⓗ

Sade
Ga

KATIK LANTANG

↓ Denpasar

NYUH KUNING

PENGOSEKAN

6 Ubud

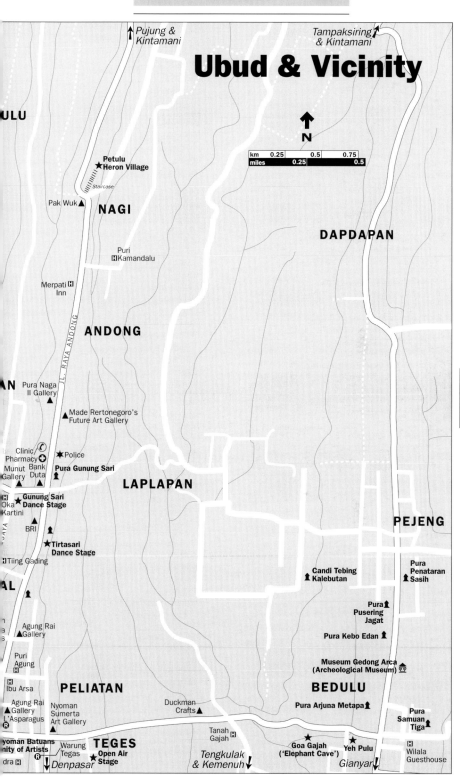

Ubud & Vicinity

ULU

Pujung & Kintamani

Tampaksiring & Kintamani

N

| km | 0.25 | 0.5 | 0.75 |
| miles | 0.25 | | 0.5 |

Petulu
★Heron Village

Staircase

Pak Wuk▲

NAGI

DAPDAPAN

Puri
⊞Kamandalu

Merpati ⊞
Inn

JL. RAYA ANDONG

ANDONG

N

Pura Naga
II Gallery
▲

▲ Made Rertonegoro's
Future Art Gallery

Clinic ⟲
Pharmacy ✚
Munut Bank
Gallery Duta
▲ ⌂

★Police

Pura Gunung Sari

LAPLAPAN

PEJENG

⊞
Oka
Kartini

★Gunung Sari
Dance Stage

⌂
▲ BRI

★Tirtasari
Dance Stage

⊞Tiing Gading

AL

⟲

Pura
Penataran
Sasih

Candi Tebing
Kalebutan

Pura
Pusering
Jagat

Agung Rai
▲Gallery

Pura Kebo Edan

Puri
Agung
⊞

Museum Gedong Arca
(Archeological Museum)

⊞
Ibu Arsa

PELIATAN

BEDULU

Agung Rai
▲Gallery
L'Asparagus
®

Nyoman
Sumerta
Art Gallery

Duckman
Crafts▲

Pura Arjuna Metapa

Pura
Samuan
Tiga

Tanah
Gajah ⊞

yoman Batuans
nity of Artists
®
dra ⊞

Warung
Tegas

TEGES
★Open Air
Stage

Denpasar

Tengkulak
& Kemenuh

Goa Gajah
('Elephant Cave')

Yeh Pulu

Gianyar

⊞
Wilala
Guesthouse

Ubud 6

(Monkey Forest Road). ☎ 975636, 96290. Also accessible through their restaurant on Jl. Bisma. 21 quiet cottages set on a terraced hill and bridging a small stream. $20–$50 per bungalow.

Puri Saraswati Jl. Raya Ubud, adjacent to lotus pond and temple. ☎ 975164. 17 bungalows in a compact garden with free-form swimming pool. The owner, Agung Ari Mas, also has an interest in the Cafe Lotus next door. $17–$37.

Puri Saren Jl. Raya Ubud, center of Ubud at main crossroads. ☎ 975057, fax: 975137. 12 bungalows. Home of Cokorda Agung, head of Ubud's royal family. Set in a palace courtyard decorated with Balinese antiques. Regular dance performances in the spectacular candle-lit outer courtyard. $40.

West of Ubud

Ananda Cottages Jl. Campuan, Campuan. ☎ 975376, fax: 975375. 45 bungalows set in ricefields near the Neka Museum. Ponds stocked with fish provide a tranquil atmosphere. Older clientele, families with children. Swimming pool in the middle of ricefields. $35–$45.

Bali Ubud Jl. Penestanan. ☎ 975058, fax: 287223. In the peace of the rice paddies. 14 rooms in two story bungalows, 2 with AC. Restaurant and a swimming pool. $40–$55 fan, $50–$65 AC, $75–$85 deluxe, $120–$125 suite.

Pringga (Water Garden) Juwita Jl. Bisma. ☎/fax: 975734. 25 rooms in a romantic setting. Ricebarn bungalows literally float in individual pools, all interconnected by a series of bridges. Huge open bathrooms, terracota sculptures and giant bamboo furniture. Swimming pool. Very good and friendly service. $37–$60.

Sayan Terrace Jl. Raya Sayan, Kedewatan. ☎ 975384, fax: 974384. 10 rooms, some with modern conveniences. The newest rooms have teak parquet floors, wrap-around windows, hot water, and great views across the Ayung River. $25–$60.

Ulun Ubud Cottages, Jl. Sanggingan, 1.5 km west of Ubud. PO Box 3, Ubud. ☎ 975024, 975762, fax: 975524. 26 rooms in bungalows strung along a steep descent to the Campuan River. Swimming pool and gigantic outdoor stone chess board. Gallery on premises. $45–$65 standard, $50–$65 studio bungalow, $65–$90 suite, $90–$110 family unit.

Wisata Cottages Jl. Sanggingan, Campuan. ☎/fax: 975017. 23 bungalows on the ridge above the Campuan River. Glorious views. $25–$50.

South of Ubud

Dewi Sri Bungalows Jl. Hanoman, Padangtegal, opposite the Dirty Duck. ☎ 975300, fax: 975777. 18 bungalows. Unusual furniture and artifacts add to the charm. Friendly service and a cozy restaurant by the pool. $25 duplex bungalow with fan, $50 AC.

Garden View Cottages Desa Mas, Banjar Nyuh Kuning. ☎ 974055. 14 rooms facing the rice paddies within sight of the Monkey Forest. Large rooms with ceramic tile floors, mosquito nets, overhead fan, hot water, and huge verandahs. 4 of the units are two-story bungalows with three beds. $25–$30.

Okawati's Jl. Wanara Wana (Monkey Forest Road). PO Box 158. ☎/fax: 975063. 14 rooms with at-

tached bath and fans. Swimming pool and restaurant. A nostalgic favorite. Ibu Okawati opened the first restaurant in Ubud. $27–$50.

Pertiwi Bungalows Jl. Wanara Wana (Monkey Forest Road). PO Box 110, Ubud. ☎ 975236, fax: 975559. 38 large rooms with attached bath, phones and mini-bar. Swimming pool set in spacious grounds; great space for children to play. Deluxe rooms have AC and huge verandahs with luscious, leafy outlook. Good for families. $32–$75.

Ubud Inn Jl. Wanara Wana (Monkey Forest Road). ☎ 975071, 96257, fax: 975188. 34 rooms in a well maintained garden. Clean and serene. Rooms are spacious. Pleasant restaurant adjacent to the swimming pool. $25–$30 fan, $30–$55 AC.

Ubud Village Hotel Jl. Wanara Wana (Monkey Forest Road). ☎ 975571, 974071, fax: 975069. 28 rooms in a garden setting. Standard rooms with fan, attached bath; some AC. Convenient location. Swimming pool. $40–$75.

Intermediate ($50–$75)

These hotels have either individual bungalows or two-story buildings of four units, each with fan or AC and attached bathroom with hot water. Most have swimming pools, restaurants, and pleasant views of gardens, river valleys or rice fields. Some have phones and TV. Major credit cards accepted. Prices include tax and service. Many are located some distance from the center of town, so a car is recommended.

Central Ubud

Siti Bungalows Jl. Kajeng 3. ☎ 975699, fax: 975643. 7 bungalows in a garden with a small swimming pool. Owner and painter, Hans Snel, is a congenial host and raconteur. When not tending to his orchids, he can be found regaling guests at his bar/restaurant. Snel's gallery floats in a lily pond in his lush tropical garden and is reached by stepping stones leading from the bar. $50–$60.

East of Ubud

Bamboo Jl.Raya Ubud, between Padangtegal and Tebesaya. ☎ 975037. A delightful cottage hidden away in it's own private world. A path which clings to the side of a ravine snakes down to the river where a green tiled pool awaits the weary. Pavilions on different levels are enticements to relax in a cocoon of tropical lushness. The spacious bedroom, adjoined by a huge bathroom, opens onto a private terrace. $75.

South of Ubud

Agung Raka Bungalows Jl. Raya Pengosekan. ☎/fax: 975757, fax: 975446. 10 rooms. Bungalows have an open-air living space and bathroom downstairs; upstairs is a bedroom with plaited bamboo walls and a four poster bed. $45–$80. A suite adjoining the pool is $120.

Camplung Sari Hotel Jl. Wanara Wana (Monkey Forest Road). PO Box 87, Ubud. Adjacent to the sanctuary surrounding the Pura Dalem. ☎/fax: 975473.

50 rooms. White ceramic decor. All rooms with AC, bathtubs; some with TV, mini-bar. Swimming pool and restaurant. Caters to groups. $50-$90.

Puri Padi Jl. Hanoman, Padangtegal. ☎ 975010, 975075, fax: 975740. 16 rooms. Great value. Two-story buildings in dressed *paras* stone. Marble floors and rich wood interiors; marble bathroom with glass shower stalls. AC, TV and mini-bar. Swimming pool. Standard $60, deluxe $70–$80.

Tiing Gading Bungalows Jl. Tebesaya, Peliatan. On a 100 m path off the main road. ☎ 96228, fax: 975573. 5 duplex bungalows (10 rooms) scattered in a manicured garden setting. Quiet, serene, enchanting. Lush tropical forest outlook. Swimming pool, restaurant. $60–$65.

North and West of Ubud

Merpati Inn Jl. Raya Andong, 1.5 km to the northeast on the road to Pujung. ☎ 96083, fax: 95862. 21 rooms. Spacious and spotlessly clean. Restaurant, swimming pool and complimentary shuttle service. $58 fan, $69 AC, $125 cottage.

Murni's House Banjar Ubud Kelod, Ubud Heights, on the path leading from the aqueduct. ☎ 975165, fax: 975282. 4 rooms. Suitable for families. Catering from Murni's Warung. $50–$95. A separate two bedroom house at $95.

Puri Tjampuhan Jl. Raya Ubud, Campuan, across the bridge. ☎ 975368/9, fax: 975137. 52 rooms Bungalows in the "royal" style, overlooking the Campuan River and temple. Spring-fed swimming pool and tennis court. Built on the site of Walter Spies' compound in the 1930's. Agung rooms $54–57, Raja rooms $65–$80.

Taman Bebek Desa Sayan Heights. ☎ 975385, fax: 720507. 5 colonial style bungalows with wrap around verandahs. High ceilings, four-poster beds, kitchenette, dining area and large open-air bathroom. Garden views. $70-$90, suite $300.

Villa Bukit Ubud Jl. Raya Sanggingan. PO Box 20, Ubud, behind Neka Museum. ☎ 975371, fax: 975787. 24 rooms. Fantastic views down the Campuan River. Spacious rooms with marble floors, bathtubs, and mini-bars; most have AC. Swimming pool and restaurant. $60-$90. Two bedroom suites with sitting rooms, TV and panoramic views, $230.

First Class ($75–$100)

Padma Indah Cottages Jl. Penestanan. PO Box 190, Ubud. ☎/fax: 975719. 10 rooms. Two-story *lumbung*-style bungalows with marble floors and outdoor bathrooms. Mini-bar and telephone in all rooms. Uninterrupted panorama of rice paddies on the south side. Huge swimming pool. Art gallery attached. $90-$100, family cottage $180.

Puri Indah Villas Jl. Pengosekan. ☎ 975742, fax: 975332. 15 rooms. Set in an enchanting tropical garden beside a small river. Solidly built duplex bungalows with large verandahs and bathrooms. Swimming pool. Superior $75–$185; deluxe $150–$175.

Luxury ($100 and up)

Spacious Balinese inspired bungalows with AC, mini-bar, private pool and balconies overlooking a private garden with a view. Airport transfers are usually included. Major credit cards accepted. Prices quoted include tax and service.

Amandari on Sayan Heights overlooking the Ayung River, about 3 km west of Ubud. ☎ 975333, fax: 975335. 29 private pavilions. Designed by Australian architect Peter Muller to be *the* ultimate hotel in Bali. Each bungalow is nestled in its own private walled compound and several have private swimming pools. Service is exemplary. The restaurant is considered by many to be the best in Bali and is open from 8 am to 10 pm. $330–$770. Definitely worth the splurge.

Bali Spirit Jl. Nyuh Kuning. ☎ 974013, fax: 974012. 20 bungalows, two with kitchens. Tranquil setting above the river, overlooking a local bathing spot. Swimming pool and two outdoor spas with facilities for masseurs and beauty treatments. Ubud's first health spa! Spacious bar with a restaurant serving California-inspired food. $125–$175.

Kupu Kupu Barong Desa Kedewatan, PO Box 7, Ubud, on the road to Payangan, about 4 km northwest of Ubud. ☎ 975478, fax: 975079. 19 bungalows. Dramatic views overlooking the terraced hills above the Ayung River. Two swimming pools, restaurant and tennis court. Does not cater to small children. Deluxe $335, luxury $405, suite $699.

Puri Kamandalu Jl. Tegal Padang, Banjar Nagih. PO Box 77, Ubud. ☎ 975825, fax: 975851. 34 rooms. The newest of the luxury hotels, 2 km northeast of Ubud on the road to Pujung. Spacious rooms with marble floors, detailing in tropical woods and views to the Petanu River. Large free-form swimming pool, two restaurants, conference facilities. Pavilion $175, villa $225, deluxe pavilion $325 with Jacuzzi, $375 with pool, deluxe/royal villa $550.

Tanah Gajah Jl. Raya Goa Gajah. PO Box 71, Tengkulak, near Goa Gajah, 3 km east of Ubud. ☎ 975685/6, 974261, 974259, fax: 975260. 10 rooms. Owned by a famous Jakarta architect, Hadiprana. Extensive grounds laid out with great attention to detail. Restful setting with huge pool, tennis court and small gym. Family room $375, honeymoon suite $250. Prior booking is essential, as this is more a private residence than a hotel.

Villa Indah Kedewatan. PO Box 1, Ubud, 4 km. from Ubud. ☎/fax: 975490. 8 suites in three villas. Each suite has a kitchen and private staff dedicated to serve. Meals prepared to order and served on wrap-around living terrace. Blind masseuse available. A peaceful escape. Airport transfers available. $100–$120, incl. laundry.

DINING

Ubud has an incredible variety of places to eat. The simple *warungs* serving *nasi campur* and satay are still around, but so is everything else. Today Ubud offers a choice ranging from American hamburgers and steaks, country-style Japanese, and sophisticated Italian pastas all the way to haute cuisine with a world-wide acclaim. A few restaurants stand out head and shoulders above the crowd both for the quality and the originality of their food.

Ubud 6

Those on a budget can find the ubiquitous *warungs* and, in the evenings, Pasar Senggol (the *bemo* station masquerading as a night market) comes alive with food stalls and local color. One can always find good *satay ayam* or *soto Madura* here. Be warned! While prices are ridiculously cheap, hygiene is noticeably lacking.

The following is a sampler of the village's better restaurants, listed by area.

Central Ubud

Ary's Warung Jl. Raya Ubud, opposite Pura Pusat. The place to see and be seen. Nostalgic atmosphere with marble-topped tables and sepia-tinted photos. Creative menu with a wide range of appetizers and entrees: potato skins, Waldorf salad, chicken ranchero, and pumpkin pie. Extensive drinks menu, including wine and champagne.

Cafe Lotus Longtime favorite and reigning monarch of eateries. Fabulous location in the center of town adjoining Ubud's beautiful lotus pond. Fresh salads, homemade pasta with imaginative sauces, Indonesian favorites, and divine desserts. Ubud's claim to culinary fame, smoked duck, is available here as either an entree or a pasta dish. Daily specials on the blackboard. In many ways it retains it's status as *the* eatery—an open-air courtyard overlooking a royal temple and its lotus pond is a hard location to beat! Pricey but good.

Cafe Roof Garden Spacious dining area and gentle service. Ketroprak and pesto soup are great; mousse au chocolat or dame blanche to top it off.

Casa Luna Two floors of spacious dining is the new home of an old Ubud stand-by, Lily's. Exotic menu combining old favorites (Jungle Jim chicken and Indian potato *masala*) with new taste treats like *focaccio*, Amalfi tuna salad and paella. Just inside the entry is a bakery with fresh baked breads and cakes, killer desserts and cheeses and smoked salmon—Ubud's first and only deli.

Griya Old stand-by known for its delicious barbecued chicken and tuna fish and zabaglione dessert.

Hans Snel Garden Restaurant On a side lane behind the lotus pond. Offers gracious service and lovely surroundings. Painter Hans Snel and his charming wife Siti often entertain guests. A marriage of Dutch and Balinese cuisine: try the duck cooked in rice wine or the spare-ribs.

Mumbul's An ice cream parlor overlooking a ravine featuring an open-air patio. The obvious place to bring kids as the menu caters to young and old alike. Extensive selection of burgers and Indonesian favorites and a special kids' menu. Top it all off with a hot fudge sundae. The Sunday brunch at $5 is an Ubud institution.

Nomad's Restaurant-cum-bar open until late. Specializes in sizzler steaks. A haunt for nightbirds.

West of Ubud

Amandari, Sayan. ☎ 975333. Arguably the premier restaurant on Bali. Romantically situated overlooking the Ayung River, with superb food and impeccable service. The European menu is the attraction: rack of lamb, breast of duck and seasonal seafood dishes are all acclaimed. The desserts are

divine; the crème brulée and chocolate cake are outstanding. Reservations required. Major credit cards accepted—you'll need one!

Beggar's Bush Campuan, above the bridge. An English pub in Ubud... why not? Icy cold draft beer and a convivial ambience. Victor Mason, historian, birdwatcher supremo, author and raconteur, often entertains the congregation late into the night. Highly original menu with emphasis on surf'n'turf staples.

Bridge Cafe Campuan end of the bridge, clinging to the ravine's edge. Chic interior. Great view but indifferent food.

Cafe Sayan Sayan. Set in a colonial bungalow, it caters to a demanding clientele, many of whom own homes on Sayan Ridge. Continental cuisine.

Kupu Kupu Barong Kedewatan. Fabulous view from the upstairs bar: the perfect place for a romantic sunset cocktail. Unfortunately the food is average.

Murni's Warung An old favorite, on the Ubud side of the Campuan bridge. This is where the eclectic menu mix of American and Balinese favorites started in the late 1970's. The hamburger has stood the test of time and the satay, *gado-gado* and *nasi campur* are still delectable. The lower dining areas offer tranquility, with only the sound of the river to disturb the peace. Good desserts, notably the banana cream pie.

South of Ubud

Cafe Wayan Jl. Wanara Wana (Monkey Forest Road). Delicious food, pleasant surroundings and friendly service. Original salads, pastas and seafood are all good. Try the crepe gypsy or the pasta carbonara. The bakery at the front offers an scruptious selection of cakes and breads.

Dian's Jl. Wanara Wana (Monkey Forest Road). Unpretentious, good Javanese and Chinese food at a modest price. Open late.

Dirty Duck Diner Padangtegal. Offers a highly creative, cheeky menu—try the Pita Hayworth or Tator O'Neal. The speciality is crispy fried duck, a variation of a traditional Javanese recipe. Low tables with cushions create a cosy atmosphere and the food is wholesome. Local ex-pats swear by the salads, pastas and vegetarian dishes. Daily specials and a great selection of desserts.

Do Drop Inn Jl. Dewi Sita, behind the soccer field on Jl. Wanara Wana. Cheap, filling food. An incredible 15-course *rijsttafel* at $5 for two. Many other similar value dishes. The yoghurt and meusli are delicious for breakfast.

Ibu Rai Jl. Wanara Wana (Monkey Forest Road), opposite the soccer field. Superb sea bass with herb sauce at only $2. Satay is an old stand-by. Food uniformly good.

Kagemusha Padangtegal. A traditional Japanese-style inn specializing in home-cooked food. Great *bento* box-lunch as well as *tonkatsu*, *yakitori* and *udon* noodle soups. On a cool evening, the hot sake is fortifying, as is the Japanese green tea, *o-cha*.

Kura-kura Padangtegal. Ubud's first Mexican restaurant. The food is prepared off the premises, but authentic none the less. Lethargic service allows plenty of time to enjoy the margaritas.

L'Asparagus Pengosekan, is claimed by the Ubud Millionaires Club as their clubhouse.

Lotus Lane Jl. Wanara Wana (Monkey Forest Road). Balinese cuisine, fresh seafood, pizza, and homemade pasta. Overlooks the nearby ricefields.

Ubud Raya Padangtegal. Japanese and Javanese specialities. Wholesome food done simply and well. The pumpkin or *miso* soups as starters compliment the *tempura teriyaki* and *sukiyaki* entrees.

Warung Teges Jl. Raya Ubud, as it opens onto fields leading to Mas. Serves either *nasi campur* made with pork or a *nasi ayam* for $1. Clean and simple, a favorite with local taxi drivers.

PERFORMANCES

Dance and/or shadow puppet performances are held every evening in the Ubud area, often in two or more venues. You will be accosted on the street by people hawking tickets no matter where. Admission is normally $2.50. While most performances are within walking distance, transportation must be arranged for those held out of town in places such as Teges or Bona. Ask at your hotel or **Bina Wisata Tourist Information** booth in the center of Ubud for further details. The following was correct at the time of writing, but it is always advisable to confirm:

Sunday. Kecak, Fire and Trance dance, Bona at 7 pm. Women's gamelan, Peliatan, 7.30 pm. Kecak, Padantegal, 7 pm. Wayang Kulit, Ubud, 8 pm.

Monday. Kecak, Bona, 7 pm. Legong Sedap Daya, Ubud Palace, 7.30 pm. Ramayana, Pura Dalem Puri, 8 pm.

Tuesday. Ramayana Ballet, Ubud Palace, 8 pm. Mahabarata dance, Teges, 7.30 pm.

Wednesday. Wayang Kulit, Ubud, 8 pm. Kecak, Bona, 7 pm. Legong, Banjar Tengal, 7 pm.

Thursday. Gabor dance, Ubud Palace, 7.30 pm. Kecak, Puri Agung Peliatan, 7:30 pm. Calonarang, Mawang Village, 7 pm.

Friday. Barong dance, Ubud Palace, 6.30 pm. Legong Tirta Sari, Puri Kaleran Peliatan, 7.30 pm. Kecak, Fire, Trance dance, Pura Dalem Ubud, 7 pm.

Saturday. Legong Binar Maya, Ubud Palace, 7.30 pm. Legong Puri Dalem Puri, Tebesaya, 7.30 pm. Calonarang, Mawang Village, 7 pm.

Village performances can occasionally be commissioned at Teges Kangin. Contact the *kepala desa* (village head) to arrange one of the ancient *legong* dances still performed here. The open-air theater under a huge banyan tree in front of a temple gate, is a spectacular setting for performances created by Indonesian choreographer, Sardono Kusumo. His group has achieved worldwide acclaim and has toured overseas. Many foreigners come to Ubud to study with the group's leader, I Wayan Lantir, or to learn *legong* from the principal dancer, Murni.

MUSEUMS AND GALLERIES

Most museums and galleries open at 8 am and many remain open on demand through the evening.

Agung Rai Museum Pengosekan. This monumental structure houses the private collection of highly regarded collector, **Agung Rai**. See originals by famous painters such as Spies, Bonnet, Hofker, Affandi, and others.

Bamboo Gallery Jl. Raya Ubud, east of Neka. A small air-conditioned gallery tastefully decorated and specializing in contemporary Indonesian art.

Lempad Gallery Jl. Raya Ubud. Home and studio of Bali's most famous artist, Lempad, who died in 1978 at the age of 116. It is run by his great grandchildren. The film *Lempad of Bali* and the gallery are not to be missed.

Munut Gallery On the main road, near the turnoff to Peliatan. Run by I Wayan Munut, a pupil of Rudolf Bonnet. Contemporary Indonesian and Balinese art.

Museum Puri Lukisan. Founded under the auspices the royal family in 1953, the collection represents the evolution of Balinese painting from its inception in the 1930's until the present. Originally catalogued by Rudolf Bonnet, the current trustees have maintained the same standard through a continuous program of acquisitions. Tranquil setting in lovely gardens. Small admission fee. 8 am–4 pm.

Neka Gallery Opposite the post office. Home of Bali's most foremost collector, Suteja Neka.

Neka Museum Sangginan, on the main road 1.5 km west of Ubud. Neka is Ubud's foremost art dealer and patron. Four traditional buildings house Neka's private collection by Bali's most revered artists: Lempad, Spies, Covarrubias, I Bagus Made and Made Wianta. Open 9 am–noon, 2 pm–6 pm.

Seniwati Gallery of Art by Women Jl. Sriwedari 2B, Banjar Taman. Although displaying works by women world-wide, the focus is on female Balinese artists. 8 am–5 pm.

SHOPPING

Ubud offers a surprisingly sophisticated range of shopping opportunities. Take your time and browse in a leisurely fashion.

If you are seriously in the market for paintings, first look in the major galleries to see what is available for how much, then seek out the artists in their own homes. Much of the fun is meeting them and discussing the nature of things over a cup of Balinese coffee. The best known galleries are Neka, Agung Rai, Munut, Rudana, Purpa, and Nyoman Sumertha. Outside Ubud itself, the best painters are found in Pengosekan, Peliatan, Penestanan and Batuan.

A partial list of highly regarded local artists: **Antonio Blanco**, long-term resident and self-styled "Dali of Bali," Campuan. **Ketut Budiyana**, Jl. Hanoman. **Wayan Durus,** classic style, Jl. Tebesaya, Peliatan. **Ngurah K K**, refined "Young Artist" style, Campuan. **Hans Snel**, Dutch painter known for his abstract style, Jl. Kajeng.

Cemul on Jl. Kajeng, has phantasmagoric sculptures by Bali's best known stone carver. **Jani's** on Jl. Wanara Wana (Monkey Forest Road) has a wide range of high quality *ikat* textiles from the archipelago. **Argasoka** specializes in collector's quality Javanese batiks. **Kunang Kunang** has two stores, one near Murni's and the other below the Pura Dalem, offering silver and antiques, clothes, textiles and collectibles. Get great presents for kids at **Adinda**, Jl. Hanoman, and kids' clothes at **Gayatri** in Ubud Kelod. **Purpa Silver** has a range of designer jewelry made on the premises at Jl. Wanara Wana.

Lotus Studio, next to Cafe Lotus, specializes in *ikat* jackets, shirts and designer accessories. At a small jewel of a boutique next to Cafe Wayan you can find pricey but chic clothing and shoes. **Aumsari** at the intersection in Andong is an innovative retailer with a range of quality items.

Wooden handicrafts of all imaginable sizes, shapes and colors are available from **Dewa Windia**, west of the huge banyan tree in Peliatan. If you want to buy at lower prices, head up the hill to Tegallalang and Pujung, northeast of Ubud. A bewildering number of shops along the way, mostly exporters, invite inspection. Don't miss the **Pasar Seni Sukawati**, a handicraft market in the middle of Sukawati, south of Ubud. Masses of stalls offer an endless array of souvenirs at bargain prices.

Ubud Market in the center of town offers the usual selection of T-shirts, shoes, sarongs and cheap, ready-made clothes. Try to time your visit to coincide with the produce market held every three days—great bustle and activity!

Antique teak furniture can be found in the shops along the road to Denpasar: **Mario's** in Batuan and **Puri Sakanan** in Batubulan are two reliable places. Handsome wrought iron furniture and interior pieces are available at **Mondirama** in Andong. This shop also makes stained glass windows to order. **Pak Wuk** on the corner of the turn-off to Petulu makes Balinese ceremonial umbrellas in designer sizes—$125 for a 2-m-wide monster. Perfect for the patio!

The more adventurous can find handicrafts in many of the less visited villages surrounding Ubud. Beautiful beadwork belts, bags and earrings are made in the lanes of Penestanan; batik cushions and bedcovers are sold by Wayan Sulastri in Penestanan Kaja. The woodcarvers of Nyuh Kuning are renowned for their lifelike animals in *waru* wood. Kliki is home to artists specializing in minature watercolors. Giant bamboo furniture abounds in Belaga on the road just before Bona. There are also many woodcarvers on the road between Tengkulak and Kemunuh.

Pondok Bamboo, on the road east of the Monkey Forest, offers an assortment of bamboo musical instruments—*suling* and *tingklik*—as well as the drums and percussion instruments found in the *gamelan* orchestra. Nearby **Kubuku** has a variety of wind chimes for sale: this bohemian Indian restaurant also has two cottages for rent.

Tino's drugstore opposite Mumbul is a minimarket stocked with alcohol, toiletries and foodstuffs. **Ubud Music** next door has a wide selection of cassettes and books. **Ubud Bookshop** next to Ary's sells magazines and newspapers as well as a range of topical books.

ACTIVITIES

Sobek, Jl. Tirta Ening 9, ☎ 287059, operates **white water rafting** trips on the Ayung River, a fabulous ride down dramatic gorges. $33–$43 per person, including all equipment, transfers, guides, and a great lunch. Many agents in Ubud handle bookings. Sobek also organizes jungle treks, mountain biking and river kayaking trips for $50–$65 per person. For other rafting companies operating on the Ayung River, see page 243 of the Travel Advisory.

The **Bali Bird Club** organizes walks around Ubud. Tours are led by Victor Mason, longtime resident and orinthological expert. The $43 price includes lunch, transport, and a copy of Bali Bird Guide. ☎ 975009.

The **Crackpot Batik Workshop** on Jl. Wanara Wana (Monkey Forest Road) allows you to make your own batik T-shirt (or *sarong*, cushion, etc.) using their designs or yours. Kids love it! $7.50–$17.50.

MEDICAL CARE

There's a good 24 hr pharmacy at Andong, 100 m north of the T-junction east of Ubud.

Doctors. Try Dr. Dharma Usada in Ubud, Jl. Abangan, ☎ 975235; open 8am–8pm, Mon–Sat. Dr. Budiana on the main road in Teges; Dr. I Wayan Darwata, general practitioner, 5pm–8 pm, Mon–Sat, Jl. Raya Ubud 14, ☎ 974691.

MISCELLANEOUS

Beauty services. Nur Salon, Jl. Hanoman, provides haircuts, manicures and massages. *Mandi lulur* massages are the rage for local ladies. The blissful float in a hot-water bath fragrant with fresh flowers is heaven.

Meditation. There is a public meditation room in the **Meditation Shop** on Jl. Wanara Wana (Monkey Forest Road). The shop also sells books and tapes on Raj Yoga.

Packing/shipping agents. Abundant in Ubud . Ary's Tourist Service and Nomad's are reliable.

Post office. Jl. Jembawan, opposite Neka Gallery. Open 8am–2pm, Mon–Sat; 8am–11am, Fri. Offers poste restante service.

Telecommunications (*wartel*). Jl. Wanara Wana (Monkey Forest Road), ☎ 975823. Also on Jl. Raya Ubud. There is a **telephone office** in Andong, 100 m north of the T-junction east of Ubud; open 8am–5pm daily, except Sundays. You can also make calls or send faxes from **Ary's Tourist Services** and **Nomad's**, both centrally located on the main road. Local entrepeneurs use Ary's to receive faxes as well: (62 361) 975162.

—updated by Debe Campbell/Andy Udayana

Kintamani PRACTICALITIES

7

Kintamani is great for day trips, trekking or simply for getting away from it all for a few days. At Penelokan you can view the panorama of Mount Batur set in a huge volcanic crater basin. Stop here on the way to Singaraja to climb to peaceful Pura Tegeh Kuripan. Try to arrive at Kintamani in the morning, as it's often overcast in the afternoon, especially during the rainy season.

Prices in US dollars. Telephone code is 0366.

ORIENTATION

There are two possible options for staying near Lake Batur: up on the ridge or down inside the crater. The villages within the crater tend to have a rather unpleasant atmosphere with a lot of people hassling you. The views, however, are stunning. The main reason to spend the night in the crater is to climb Mt. Batur at dawn.

There are several attractions from Penelokan, starting with the view from the crater rim toward Lake Batur. Rim temples include Pura Ulun Danu Batur and Pura Tegeh Kuripan, both on the main road. A visit to the crater might include a boat trip to the trditional village of Trunyan, the lava fields, the hot spring at Toya Bungkah, or climbing Mt. Batur.

The best way to visit the crater is with your own transportation or chartered minibus. Walking is possible, but distances are long and the descent into the crater is very steep. You might want to finish your visit with a dip in the lake. The water at Kedisan is quite clear. Elsewhere, it is being used as a public lavatory.

Penelokan and the crater villages are rather "un-Balinese" with vendors hassling you and people approaching you in the street to book accommodations.

There's a local authority charge of Rp550 per person for any car with tourists crossing into the region, plus Rp250 for the car. A similar fee is charged in Toya Bungkah.

TRANSPORTATION

Kintamani is the end-point of several tour itineraries heading up from the lower rice plain in the south. Most buses come up the good, scenic road via Tampaksiring, with stops on the way at Goa Gajah, Gunung Kawi and Tirta Empul, then going back down through Bangli and Pura Kehen. But there are other interesting routes. One leads from Peliatan in the Ubud area through the wood-carvers' villages of Tegallalang, Pujung and Sebatu. The views along the way are superb. Other roads from Ubud to Kintamani run through Payangan or from Denpasar through the Sangeh monkey forest, Plaga and Lampu, arriving to the north of Kintamani.

Bemos to Kintamani are available from Ubud via Sakah (notable for its huge "Baby" statue). They also run via Tampaksiring and Bangli.

From Denpasar *bemos* leave for Kintamani from the Batubulan terminal until late afternoon. The normal fare from Batubulan is Rp1,500 and from Singaraja Rp3,500. Rent a motorbike or car if you want to explore the great backroads in the Kintamani area.

Shuttle buses which run between Ubud and Singaraja stop in Penelokan. From Ubud $4.50–$7, from Singaraja $9–$11.

Alternatively, you can also join a day tour and ride up in air-conditioned comfort, lunch included. On such tours, however, you will only see the view of Penelokan and then return, missing the caldera and the lake down the Kedisan road.

Charter *bemos* from Penelokan to Kedisan cost Rp5,000; Kedisan to Toya Bungkah Rp500 by *bemo* or Rp5,000–Rp10,000 for charter *bemo*, depending on your bargaining skills.

To Trunyan

Down inside the caldera you can cross to the lake village of Trunyan either from Kedisan or from Toya Bungkah. Be warned that the people here can be quite aggressive and the government has long advised tour operators not to send tourists to Trunyan.

In Toya Bungkah, the normal "tourist" price is $16 (including insurance) for the round trip for a full boat of seven. Don't expect to pay the local price. In Kedisan, the round trip costs about $20 per boat, with a price per person decreasing to $3 per person is the boat is full. If you are tired of bargaining hassles, simply drive or hike around the crater to Trunyan.

Kintamani

7

ACCOMMODATIONS

You have the choice here of being down by the lake in Toya Bungkah or up on the rim of the crater in either Penelokan or Kintamani. Take a sweater, a blanket and sheet if you're staying in a budget *losmen*.

On the Ridge

Gunawan, just outside Penelokan. ☎ 50150. 2 bungalows with private baths. Pleasant and clean with the best views over the crater and lake. $11, including tax and service.

Lakeview Restaurant & Homestay Penelokan. ☎/fax: 51464. 17 rooms. A popular but basic place with a lovely view. Very good food at the restaurant. A tiny room without private bath, $7.50 (WC & *mandi* stalls not too far away). Room with private bath, $15. Room with 4 beds, $30. The superior spacious rooms for two, $26.50. Rooms overpriced but include breakfast.

Miranda Kintamani. ☎ 51096. 6 rooms. Small, older homestay, cheap, clean and friendly. $3. Private bath $5.50, including breakfast.

In the Caldera

Amertha's 5 rooms. Somewhat exposed to wind an dust, but the rooms are very nice with private garden bathrooms. $9, including breakfast, tax and service. Two restaurants attached.

Balai Seni Toya Bungkah "Art Center." 15 rooms. Probably the most comfortable place to stay in Toya Bungkah, but still basic. There are big gardens, a restaurant and a well-stocked library. This is also the location of the World Headquarters for the International Association for Art and Future. This daunting concern was founded by the famed Jakartan idealist and intellectual, Sutan Takdir Alisahbana ("Father of the Indonesian Language"). Standard $9, family bungalow (3 rooms, sleeping 5) $18.

Hotel Puri Berning ☎ 51234, 51235, fax: (0361) 730285. New incongruous block of modern hotel rooms in the shadow of the volcano. International standard. Bungalow $20, standard $35, deluxe, $50, including hot water, breakfast, tax & service.

Nyoman Pagus ☎ 51167. 10 rooms. A popular place and an attractive *warung* restaurant. $5–$11, including simple breakfast.

Siki Inn A great location. $5–$11.

Surya Homestay Kedisan. ☎ 51139. 22 bungalows on the hill. Spacious and clean rooms. $4.50–$7 without hot water, $11 with hot water, including breakfast, tax, and service.

Segara Hotel & Restaurant. Turn left before Kedisan coming from Penelokan. 42 rooms with private bathrooms. Pleasant open-air restaurant, minibus with English-speaking driver for rent. $7 (cold water)– $65 (hot water), depending on the facilities. Hot water rooms over-priced. VIP room has television; bargain for best rate. Breakfast, laundry, tax and service included.

Under the Volcano I Toya Bungkah. ☎ 51166. 12 clean, well-designed rooms with a good dining room. Excellent food. This is the area's most service-minded establishment, run by Nyoman Mawa, who also has a tour service and a shop. $7-$9.

Under the Volcano II Songan. ☎ 51166. 8 rooms. $9–$11 for hot water, including breakfast and tax.

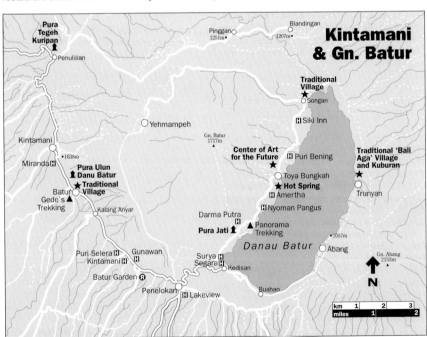

7 Kintamani

Kintamani & Gn. Batur

DINING

The better places are attached to the hotels in Penelokan up on the caldera and down in Toya Bungkah by the hot springs. Penelokan has choices ranging from very simple and cheap places with good local food to big fancy restaurants which cater to tour groups from the expensive hotels on the coast.

The local lake fish is a tasty variety called *be jahir*, available fried or grilled. It's best fried crisp—more of the fish is edible.

A good place for lunch (and one of the few on the rim open for evening meals) is the **Lakeview**. Prices here are moderate, but they are geared up for buffet tour group lunches.

The **Batur Garden Restaurant** has an interesting menu of Chinese and Indonesian dishes, as well as Western bar drinks. Friendly and reasonably priced. Lunch only.

A smaller restaurant, **Gunawan**, is another scenic spot for lunch. Have the Fried Fish a la Batur right on the terrace overlooking the mountains. Prices are reasonable.

Down in the crater at Toya Bungkah, most *losmen* have small restaurants (*warung)*, and new eating places are springing up all the time. Our recommendation is Nyoman Mawa's **Under The Volcano**. His lake fish with homemade *sambal matah* is worth the trip to the mountains alone.

TREKKING AROUND BATUR

If you've always wanted to walk around inside the crater of an active volcano, here's your chance. Mt. Batur is 1,717 m high, but the upper cone itself is only several hundred meters above the level of the lake and can be climbed and descended in a few hours. At the top, there's a warm crust of ground over the cauldron. Be sure to hire a guide, as it can be dangerous.

It's best to start very early in the morning, around 4 am: it's cool and you're likely to see a wonderful sunrise. Your guide will probably find you before you find him. Choose someone friendly who is not charging a ridiculous amount of money: $4–5 is a fair price. Gede at **Gede's Trekking** near Kintamani market is a helpful contact. Another professional trekking guide service is **Panorama Tourist Services**, located near the Toya Bungkah Hot Spring. They also organize other trekking trips in the area.

There are several well-marked approaches to Batur. From Pura Jati, near Kedisan (where a large sign announces "Klim Prom Here—Please Polow Wite Plag"), and from Toya Bungkah where the climb up and back takes about three hours. The latter route is notably easier.

Wear high-top shoes: the slopes are covered with fine dust. Other necessary supplies are drinking water and a snack or two. On reaching the summit your guide will boil some eggs (in the sand) and make coffee. If you're fortunate, a great view stretching all the way to Lombok will be revealed as the sun rises.

Going down is much easier than climbing up and it's possible to take another route down, via the hot spring at Toya Bungkah. Ask your guide to have a car ready to bring you back to the original starting point once you get down. The spring, set in a concrete pool, is not overly spectacular. Entrance is 50¢.

This trip is not recommended during the rainy season (November–April).

There's a good new road that circles the volcano rim from Penulisan east to Pinggan and Blandingan, where it comes to a dead end. Another route is to drive past Toya Bungkah to Songan and follow the sign west to **Air Mampeh**. The road leads to Penelokan through the caldera behind Batur. It is sometimes difficult to pass because of volcanic sand and stones.

—*updated by Debe Campbell/Andy Udayana*

8 Klungkung PRACTICALITIES

INCLUDES THE NUSA ISLANDS

Prices in US dollars. Telephone code is 0366.

Klungkung Town

This former royal capital is one of the busiest towns in eastern Bali and the main transit point for *bemos* and minibuses en route to Pura Besakih and points east—Padangbai, Candidasa and Amlapura. *Bemos* cost around Rp500 from Klungkung to any of these places.

The **Tourist Information Office** on Jl. Diponegoro, ☎ 21448, is open 7am–2.45 pm, Mon–Thurs and until noon on Friday.

Only one hotel can be recommended: **Ramayana Palace Hotel and Restaurant** Jl. Diponegoro. ☎ 21044. 9 rooms; at the eastern end of town. The new rooms are clean and have private showers and sit-down toilets; the ones in the back are simple rooms with shared showers and squat toilets. The restaurant serves Chinese food.$4.50–$9. **Bali Indah** on Jl. Nakula is the only proper restaurant in town. Good cheap Chinese food.

The post office is at Jl. Surapati, ☎ 21010. There is a *wartel* on Jl. Diponegoro, ☎ 21500.

Buy essentials at the **Tragia** supermarket, Jl. Batukaru, ☎ 21997. The only place for souvenirs is Kamasan village, south of Klungkung. Here painters still produce traditional works in the so-called *wayang* style. Ask for Nyoman Mandra, Mangku Mura or any of their pupils.

There's an astonishing view just north of Klungkung at Bukit Jambul, with the **Bukit Jambul Garden Restaurant** at the best spot. $10 for lunch. There are two other restaurants nearby, one of which, **Lembah Arca**, rents two rooms at $4.50/night, including breakfast.

The Nusa Islands

Nusa Penida, Nusa Ceningan and Nusa Lembongan. These three unspoiled islands are southeast of Bali. Boats ply the routes to the islands from Sanur and Benoa (south Bali), Padangbai and Kusamba (east Bali). Most leave by 9–10 am. When travelling from Padangbai, it is advisable to overnight in Candidasa or Padangbai.

There are different take-off points depending on your destination. If you are heading to Jungut Batu on Nusa Lembongan, where most of the *losmen* are, then leave from Sanur, Benoa or Kusamba. If you are going to Toya Pakeh on Nusa Penida, leave from Kusamba or Padangbai.

You will have to wade through the water to get on and off the boat and you may get splashed during the crossing. Pack everything in plastic bags and keep a raincoat or poncho handy.

At certain times of the year the sea can be treacherous, full of strong currents and even whirlpools. Ask locally. During these periods, the voyage is not advisable in a small *jukung* and it's safer to take one of the large excursion boats leaving Benoa. Another problem is pricing: the fare is low for locals, but for tourists it's $7.

BOATS

From Padangbai. Be there early and register on the beachfront east of the main pier. Boats leave from 7–9 am.

From Kusamba. Take small *jukung* on the beach,

Klungkung Town

Besakih

Government Office

Police

Kerta Gosa Museum ▲ Tragia

🚌 Bus Terminal

Tourist Information

"Floating" Palace

JL. DIPONEGORO

ℍ Ramayana

▲ Market

JL. NAKULA

Bali Indah

JL. KECUBUNG

N

| km | 0.25 | 0.5 | 0.75 |
| miles | | 0.25 | 0.5 |

Sideman, Iseh

Amlapura, Padangbai & Candidasa

Gianyar, Denpasar

Klotok

100 m from the market. When local traders book all the boats it's difficult to sail from here.

From Sanur. Boats seating 50 leave from the beach at the end of Jl. Raya Sanur, next to The Grand Bali Beach Hotel and take you to Jungut Batu on Nusa Lembongan in an hour. Departure: 7–8am. Boat with two 80 HP engines, life jackets and radio communication is operated by Yayasan Pembangunan Desa Sanur Kaja.

From Benoa. Join a day-trip tour on a yacht. Contact Bali Camar (☎ 231592), the Bali International Yacht Club (☎ 288391), Bali Adventure Club (☎ 751767), Baruna Watersport (☎ 751223) or any of the companies mentioned in Sanur practicalities. $60–$80, include diving and depend on the condition of the vessel and facilities. **Bali Hai Cruises** (☎ 720331, 771463, fax: 720334) has daily cruises to Nusa Lembongan. The Beach Club Cruise (9am–4.30pm) features swimming and a barbecue lunch at a private club. ($65). On the Reef Cruise (9.30am–4pm) the boat ties up to a pontoon in the bay so passengers can play all day. ($80). **WakaLouka** (☎ 261129, 226695, fax: 261130, 227067) yacht sails to Lembongan daily from Benoa at 9 am, returning at 6 pm. $78, includes buffet lunch and use of WakaNusa Resort facilities. Diving available at $40 per dive.

TRANSPORTATION

Nusa Penida. In Toya Pakeh, take a *bemo* to Sampalan terminal (Rp500) where you can charter another *bemo* for an island tour ($20 unless you are very good at bargaining). To go to Jungut Batu on Nusa Lembongan either charter a *jukung* ($10) or take a public *jukung* (Rp2,000). **Nusa Lembongan**. Hire a trail bike from Jungut Batu for a tour of the island for $7.50/day. The price is high because there are no *bemos*. Cross the new bridge to get to Nusa Ceningan. Bird-watchers should check out the cliffs there.

ACCOMMODATIONS AND DINING

On Nusa Penida there are several beachfront *losmen* with restaurants. There's nothing at all on Nusa Ceningan. There are about 50 rooms and bungalows on Nusa Lembongan, mostly on the northern beach area near Jungut Batu. Try bargaining, especially in the low season. Facilities are limited: there are no phones, but a few people have CB radios that reach Bali. There's no electricity from 7 am to 5 pm and water is scarce. Expect slightly salty showers at the northern end of the beach. There is no money-changer, but there is a health center with two doctors. Nightlife consists of drinking at one of the restaurants open until 11 pm.

Jungut Batu

Agung Bungalows 12 rooms. Rooms and duplex bungalows with thatched roofs. The restaurant here has the best buys; try their daily special. $7 *losmen* room, $14 bungalow.
Baruna Beach Inn 4 rooms. Mini-restaurant, private baths with showers and toilet. $5–$6.
Bunga Lembongan. 4 rooms. Mini-restaurant, private bath with hot water. $7–$9.
Main Ski Inn. 22 rooms. Basic duplex bungalows set in a simple garden close to the beach. Private shower, fan. Restaurant. $9–$11.
Number 7 Losmen. 9 rooms. Private bathroom and shower. Meals available. Quieter than most; located in the village. $4.50–$7, incl. breakfast.
Nusa Indah Bungalows. 4 rooms. Set back from the beach but the rooms still have a beach view. Private baths. Fan on request. $7–$9.
Nusa Lembongan Bungalows 8 rooms. Two-story bungalows with living rooms and spacious bathrooms. Pleasant and clean. $5.50–$7.
Nusa Lembongan Young Bungalows 4 rooms. Near a seaweed farm. Private bathrooms. $4–$5
Puri Nusa Bungalows 10 rooms. Rooms with private bath, shower and tub, fan. $16–$20.
Wayan Tarci Homestay 8 rooms. Two-story bungalows near the beach. Private shower. The restaurant serves mainly Western food. $5–$7.

Lembongan

Backpackers Inn Bungalows 4 rooms. Newer place located in a lush ravine. $8.50.
Mushroom Beach Bungalows 4 rooms. On a bluff with a trail down to the beach. $10.
WakaNusa Resort 10 bungalows. Romantic, luxury bungalows Watersports facilities, village tour and treks. $75–$150.
Wayan Villa Bungalows 5 rooms. Pleasant overlooks a quiet bay. $10.

WATERSPORTS

Most people visit these islands either to surf, scuba dive or snorkel. The snorkeling here is some of the best on Bali. There are three main surf spots all just offshore from Jungut Batu: the playground, the abration and the shipwreck, which has the best breaks. Masks, fins, snorkels and surfboards can all be rented from local residents: snorkeling $10, scuba diving $45. **WakaNusa Resort** has dive masters and offers introductory dives for $20 and dives with equipment for $40 for one dive, $70 for two.

Charter a *jukung* to visit Lembongan, Lombok and Sumbawa. **Island Express Surf Tours** on Nusa Lembongan provides snorkeling and fishing equipment, surfing, and all meals. $380/person/week.

—updated by Andy Udayana

9 Karangasem PRACTICALITIES

INCLUDES CANDIDASA, BALINA BEACH, PADANGBAI & AMLAPURA

Karangasem, Bali's easternmost regency, is also its most beautiful. It has a wide variety of resorts, some of them little-known. Padangbai, where the ferries depart to Lombok; Candidasa on the southern coast; Tulamben and Amed, the divers' hide-outs on the north coast; Tirtagangga, near the cultural heart of the eastern coastal plain, and the more remote areas of Sidemen and Putung. Karangasem is a great area to base yourself for several days of exploration. *See map on page 170.*

Prices in US dollars. AC = Air-conditioning. Telephone code is 0363.

Candidasa

Candidasa is a good place to escape the bustle of Kuta. Accommodations are good and relatively cheap, as is the food. There are no beach vendors and aggressive hawkers are rare. Although the town has tripled in size in recent years, the surrounding area is still serene and very quiet. Everything is oriented along the main street that parallels the beach.

TOURIST INFORMATION

Perama Information Center in the west part of town is helpful. **No Problem International Air Ticketing** can book tickets on Garuda and many international airlines. They also arrange bus travel to Java and eastern Indonesia.

TRANSPORTATION

Public *bemos* run between Batubulan station and Candidasa until dark for Rp1,000 (this is the local price: you may end up paying more). Public *bemos* operate between Candidasa and either Klungkung or Amlapura charging around Rp500.

If you come from Kuta and want to avoid crossing Denpasar, take the direct shuttle bus which departs from Kuta at 9.30 am. Buy tickets at CV Ganda Sari Transport, Jl. Legian, ☎ 754383. From Ubud (next to Nomad Restaurant), take a similar shuttle at 8.15 am or 4 pm, Rp6,000.

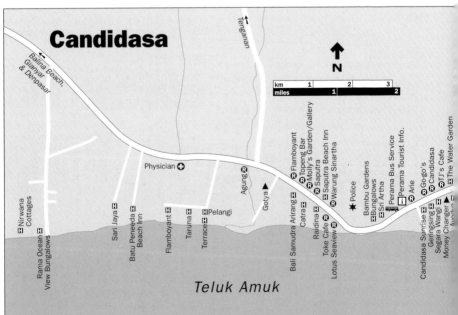

These buses also run the return journey.

The best way to explore the area's back-roads is by car, motorbike or bicycle, all of which can be rentedat several outlets in Candidasa at rates similar to those in Ubud (see Ubud practicalities). Motorbikes with drivers park on the main road at the Tenganan road junction and at the Culik junction to offer lifts to Tenganan and Amed, respectively. The usual fare is Rp500 one way: bargain.

ACCOMMODATIONS

Candidasa boasts all types of accommodations, from simple bamboo cubicles at $5/night to the exclusive $1,200/night villas of the Amankila Hotel. There is little difference, however, between bungalows going for $10 and $20, apart from the distance to the beach, the landscaping and the bathrooms.

Most places offer discounts for stays of more than a week—talk to the management on arrival. Watersports, tours and transportation rentals are often readily arranged. Prices vary according to the season.

Budget (Under $25)

Ampel Bungalow Manggis beach. 15 isolated bungalows. Fishermen work on the nearby beach. Good place to get away from the crowds. Double $9, including breakfast, tax and service.

Bayu Peneeda Beach Inn ☎ 41104. 14 rooms. West of town. Medium-sized twin huts set in a huge tract of land. A large, grassy lawn makes this a fa-

vorite spot for families with kids. Blankets, reading lights and towels are supplied. Some hot water units with fans and screens. $9–$16.

Homestay Pelangi 9 rooms. West of town in a quiet oceanside setting. Private garden. Decent-sized bamboo rooms, bathrooms with open-air garden. The owner, Pak Gelgel, is very friendly. Often bamboo gamelans with flutes lull one to sleep. $7–$9, breakfast included. You can join organized treks to Tenganan via Kestala for as little as $5/person.

Ida Homestay Jl. Raya Candidasa, ☎ 41096. 6 rooms. East of the town on the beach in a beautiful setting. Private thatched bamboo bungalows in a large, grassy coconut grove. These two-story houses have upstairs bedrooms with wide ocean views. Beautiful open-air bathrooms. Carved furniture in some units. No hot water. $9–$23.

Losmen Geringsing 15 rooms. The best bargain in town. This friendly place offers small bamboo and brick bungalows in a banana grove on the beach. One of the few places to have any beach left, though only at low tide. $9–$14, includes breakfast, but not tax and service.

Pandan Bungalows Jl. Raya Candidasa, ☎ 41929. Bamboo bungalows on the beach. Hot water, private bathrooms. Water sport facilities available. $5–$7, including breakfast.

Puri Pundak ☎ 33978. 17 rooms. In the banana groves east of town, near the homes of local fisherman. Large bamboo rooms, Western bathrooms, some with bathtubs. Overlooks the bay. $7–$23.

Moderate ($25–$50)

Bungalows are usually medium-size with verandah and electricity. The higher priced units

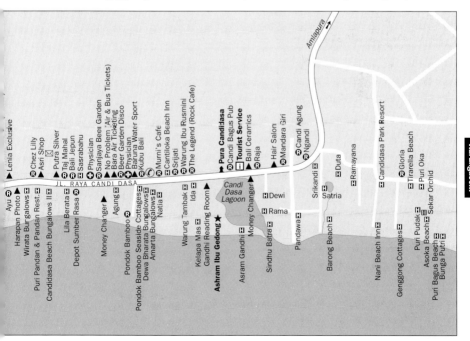

include fan and reading lamp, sometimes AC. No room phones. Restaurant often attached to the hotel. Breakfast always included. The following are highly recommended.

Balina Beach Desa Bunutan, Manggis, Karangasem. ☎ 41002-3, fax: 41001. 41 rooms. West of Candidasa. Six different classes of bungalows, all landscaped and built with an eye to aesthetics and privacy. A bit pricey considering the condition of the buildings. Good restaurant. $30–$60. Suite $100, Continental breakfast included.

Candidasa Sunrise Jl. Raya Candidasa, ☎ 41539, fax: 41538. 18 tastefully designed bungalows using bamboo and traditional Balinese decor. Each has luxury bathroom and a terrace that faces the beach. $22–$27 fan, $35–$45 AC, Continental breakfast included.

Nirwana Cottage Jl. Raya Candidasa. ☎ 41136, fax: 41543. 12 rooms. Small hotel with thatched roof bungalows surrounded by coconut trees and garden. Some fridges. Clean and quiet. Poolside restaurant. $35–$50.

Puri Buitan. Jl. Raya Candidasa. PO Box 344, Buitan ☎ 41021-2, fax: (0361) 223718. 32 rooms. Two-story duplex units with oceanside pool and restaurant. $30–$35 fan, $40–$45 AC, $65–$75 deluxe seaview.

Intermediate ($50–$75)

The Candidasa resort area has a number of good first-class places with more soon to be completed. Most provide spacious rooms, western-style baths with hot water, IDD telephone and AC. The majority are beachfront, have seaside restaurants and safety deposit facilities. Those mentioned here are pleasant and well-managed. Prices do not include 21% tax and service. Most credit cards are accepted. Up to two children sharing the same room with their parents can stay free of charge in some.

Bali Samudra Arirang Hotel ☎ 41795, 41542, fax: 41181. All rooms with balcony, TV, and refrigerator. Fishing, snorkeling and scuba diving can be arranged. $50–$77.

Candidasa Beach Bungalows II ☎41536, fax: 41537. 69 spacious rooms overlooking the sea. A large two-story block of rooms. Swimming pool and open-air bar. Some rooms have refrigerators and TVs. $60–$85. Bungalow $100. Suite $150.

Puri Bagus Beach Hotel Jl. Raya Candidasa. PO Box 129, Amlapura. ☎ 41291/2, fax: 41290. 50 rooms. Clean, spacious bungalows with semi-open bathroom and mini-bar. Pool and restaurant overlooking the ocean. $65–$125. Ocean view/front-room surcharge $10–$15.

The Water Garden ☎41540, fax: 41164. 12 rooms. This hotel venture of TJ's restaurant in Kuta has been designed with their usual attention to detail and quality. Gorgeous bungalows set in a network of cascading streams, pools and elegant gardens. Mountain bikes, hiking maps and information about local events and places of interest available. Swimming pool. $60–$65.

First Class ($75–$100)

Candi Beach Cottage Desa Sengkidu, Kecamatan Manggis. ☎41234, fax: 41111. 64 rooms. Hotel and cottage rooms with satellite TV, mini-bar, verandah. Also has a pool, spa, open water diving school, fitness center, and tennis court. $75–$100.

Rama Ocean View Bungalows Balina. ☎ 33974, fax: 233975. 74 rooms. West of Candidasa, away from the noise and bustle. A beachside enclave with a pool, restaurant, mini-bars, and satellite TV. Fitness center, sauna, tennis court and games rooms. $75–$90. Suite $250–$350.

Luxury ($100 and up)

Amankila Manggis. ☎ 41333, fax: 41555. 35 individual suites, seven of which have their own swimming pool. Located on a seaside hill in the village of Manggis, a few kilometers west of Candidasa proper. Extraordinary luxury. $300 Superior Suite to $1,200 for the Amankila Suite.

Serai Desa Buitan, Manggis. PO Box 13, Karangasem 80871.☎ 41011-2, fax: 41015. 58 rooms. Just west of Candidasa. Secluded beachfront hotel with swimming pool, restaurant. Superior $90, deluxe $105, suite $175.

DINING

Candidasa sprouts new restaurants almost daily, so there are always new places to try out. Menus are similar, so we recommend only those which stand out in some way. The typical menu includes various salads, Indonesian and Chinese dishes, seafood, sandwiches, and desserts. Some add steak, curry, pasta and cakes. Prices are good, averaging $4–$5/person with drinks. Seafood can be a lot more expensive. Most places close by 10 pm. Breakfast and lunch are available everywhere.

Arie Bar and Restaurant Down-to-earth, family-run establishment with a good selection of Balinese, Chinese and Western dishes. Good quality and prices that are hard to beat.

Kubu Bali ☎ 41532. Serves a bit of everything but excels in seafood: grilled, steamed or fried. Their open kitchen is fun to watch. Finish up with a peach melba, chilled fruit or a cognac.

Lotus Sea View Next to Toke cafe. Larger and more formal. But it has great seafood and its location near the water gives it a Venetian flavor.

Pandan Restaurant ☎ 41541 By the beach. Well known for its Balinese buffet of *babi guling* (roast pork), chicken, fish, vegetable, noodles and salads. Experience this feast or sample one of the many other delicious local or Chinese dishes.

Puri Bagus Beach Hotel A good restaurant on the second story overlooking the sea. Great seafood.

Rama Bungalows and Restaurant Has added Swiss dishes such as *Roschti*, *Kartoffel* and *Puffer Mitgemuse* to an already good menu.

TJ's Cafe ☎ 41540. Has the best grilled fish, stuffed baked potatoes and salads around. Elegant open pavilions overlook a carp pond.

9
Karangasem

Toke Cafe Near the bend in the road. Opens to the beach on one side and to the main road on the other. Offers the best combination of Balinese ambience and Western intimacy. Great welcoming drink and good pasta for a couple of dollars.

Warung Ibu Rusmini has the best *nasi campur* (mixed vegetables, tempe and chicken with rice) in town for under $1, plus a range of other simple Indonesian dishes.

SHOPPING

Candidasa is not particularly a place for shopping, but a limited selection of textile bags, *sarongs*, locally designed clothing, and jewelry, as well as other gear is available. The following places are of some interest:

Ratu Oka is a *lontar* palm-leaf artist who works in his small shop next to the Sri Artha Homestay. Traditional *lontar* books are available here for $20.

Bali Ceramics, east of town, has a variety of quality glazed stoneware. Simple bowls, vases, cups, and plates in interesting designs. They also sell shuttle bus tickets to Ubud and Kuta.

It's also worth checking out some of the shops in Tenganan. They offer typical Tenganan *ikat* textiles as well as other traditional textiles. Some are genuine antiques. Most shops also have pandanus baskets in a number of different designs and stories from the Ramayana Hindu epic carved into *lontar* leaves.

NIGHTLIFE & ENTERTAINMENT

Candidasa has entered a new age with the recent advent of discos and nightclubs which seem rather out of place in this once quiet seaside village. **Raja Restaurant** shows video movies nightly. **Go-go's** is a favorite with the younger crowd and has great dance music. But to dance all night long, the only place to go is **Beer Garden Disco**.

There are also traditional music performances and dance at several places. **Candidasa Beach Bungalows II** holds *barong* and *keris* dances in the restaurant upon request for groups, $15 including dinner. **Pandan Harum** stages *legong*, *baris*, and *barong* dances with gamelan orchestra on Tuesday and Friday at 9 pm. Closed during low season. $2.75/person.

ACTIVITIES

Diving

Karangasem has several dive spots not to be missed, namely **Gili Tepekong** (off Padangbai), **Tulamben** (with its ship wreck swarming with marine life), **Amed** (great 40 meter drop-off), and the reefs of **Tianyar**. Scuba diving equipment is available for rent at several diving centers along the main street of Candidasa. Their prices change according to the location. For those near Candidasa and Padangbai, expect to pay $50 for one dive and $55 for two. Contact **Barrakuda Bali Dive** (☎ 41214), **Stingray** (☎ 41063), or **Baruna** through its Denpasar office (☎ 0361/753820).

Snorkeling

Most hotels rent snorkeling gear and can arrange for a *perahu* to take you out to a nearby reef. $15 for a two-hour trip. Same price for sailing.

Cycling

Many places rent bikes. **Kubu Bali** has five and ten-speed mountain bikes. **The Water Garden** has mountain bikes and maps at similar rates. Count on paying Rp5,000 per day.

Hiking

A fine three-hour, 6 km, walk from Candidasa to Tenganan starts just east of Kubu Bali or at Sri Jata Restaurant. Follow the ridge-top trail and drop left into Tenganan just before the fourth major hill. Magnificent views, but start early to avoid the midday heat.

A shorter hike starts at the tip of the headland east of town: walk the hill due northeast down to a long, deserted black sand beach. Other hikes can be organized from Tenganan to Putung or to Bedabudug (Bandem).

MISCELLANEOUS

Candidasa is a small town with few services apart from the hotels and restaurants.

Books Shop near The Water Garden has a good selection.

Doctors. There are two doctors in town. Hours are limited. Inquire about the cost before accepting treatment. Look for the sign opposite Pondok Bambu Seaside Cottages and Restaurant and opposite the Bayu Peneeda Beach Inn. Ask at the big hotels for more information.

Money Changers. Scattered along the main road are numerous money changers.

Necessities. Asri Shop, mid-town, is the official post office and the closest thing to a convenience store in town, selling medicine, foodstuffs, cassettes, and simple clothing, as well as stamps.

Photography. A basic selection of film, 10% above Kuta prices, is available at several places. One-hour film processing is also available.

Telephone Service. The Kubu Bali Restaurant has a *wartel* for telephone service.

Padangbai

Upon arrival at the small beach resort of Padangbai, don't be put off by the busy pier. Padangbai hides great coves and dive spots behind its

Karangasem 9

hills. Quiet Biastugel lies behind a small hill to the west, while Padang Kurungan, or Blue Lagoon, lies to the north, nearer to the accommodations. Rows of colorful outriggers are lined up on the sandy beach, east of the pier. There is a tourist information office at the harbor. Made's Cafe provides diving services at $50 a dive. Only simple accommodations and restaurants are available here.

TRANSPORTATION

Padangbai is a main departure point for Lombok and other islands. A ferry leaves the harbor for Lombok every two hours from 9 am. There are private boats to Nusa Penida for Rp4,000 per person. These only go to Nusa Penida and leave early in the morning. A charter will cost about $7 if you bargain well. To sail directly to Nusa Lembongan you should leave from Sanur.

There are direct buses from Padangbai to Jakarta for Rp100,000. Public *bemos* to Padangbai from Denpasar (via Batubulan and Klungkung) charge Rp2,000 to those who bargain well.

ACCOMMODATIONS

Bungalows are beginning to sprout up in Padangbai. Villagers usually wait for you at the harbor to offer rooms. Prices are still very reasonable. No phones, hot water or AC:

Topi Inn Three-story thatched roof and bamboo-wall inn at the north end of the village. 5 simple rooms on the second story. Mosquito nets, private baths, squat toilets. You can watch the daily life of the villagers from a huge verandah overlooking the beach. A dormitory-studio on the top floor accommodates 10. Sandy floor restaurant. $1.50 for dormitory, $5 for room with private bath, including breakfast.

Rai Beach Inn. Jl. Sila Yukti No. 2, Padang Gai. ☎41385-6. 21 individual rooms and spacious two-story bungalows with thatched roofs. Living room, big open baths on the ground floor, bedroom at the top. Small restaurant. $9–11, including breakfast, excluding tax and service.

DINING

A few small restaurants are scattered around Padangbai. **Topi Inn**'s attractive sandy floor restaurant serves a wide range of food and is famous for its fried fish prepared by the owner herself. **Pantai Ayu Restaurant**, right on the beach, is always full. Chinese and seafood dishes. The pleasant English-speaking manager Ibu Komang presents you with small gifts—a *krupuk udang* to welcome you and a cute outrigger souvenir to take home. She has also a few rooms for rent: $2.50–$10.

Tirtagangga

Tirtagangga is still a small hamlet, quiet by day and even quieter by night—nice place for a few days of hiking and reading with periodic dips in the spring-fed pools. The few places to stay are all quite basic. Reach Tirtagangga from Candidasa by *bemo* via Amlapura for Rp1,000.

ACCOMMODATIONS

Rooms are non-AC, no hot water. Prices include breakfast.

Dhangin Taman Inn.☎ 21055. 9 rooms, two with fan. Adjacent to water palace. Restaurant. English-speaking guide service and shuttle bus to north, east and south Bali and Lombok. $7–$13.50.

Dhangin Taman Inn II. Ababi village. 1 km from Tirtagangga. ☎ 21055. 4 single rooms. A village experience. Book at Dhangin Taman Inn. $5.50.

Kusuma Jaya Inn. ☎ 21250. 12 rooms with wonderful vistas on a steep hill above the pools. Take the steps on the left just past the bridge. The newly renovated rooms are relatively comfortable. Semi-open shower. $7.50–$20.

Prima Bamboo Homestay. ☎ 21316. 9 spacious rooms on the steep hills overlooking beautiful ricefields. 4 rooms have hot water and fan. $16.

Rijasa Homestay and Warung. ☎ 21873. 8 rooms. Facing the water palace. $5.50–$7.

Tirta Ayu Homestay and Restaurant.Taman Tirtagangga, Desa Ababi, Kecamatan Abang. ☎ 21697. 4 rooms in the grounds of the water palace. Medium-sized bungalows with private bathroom. Owned by descendants of the *Raja* who built the palace. $14.

DINING

Kusuma Jaya and **Warung Rijasa** serve Indonesian dishes such as *mie goreng* (fried noodles) or *nasi goreng* (fried rice) for $1. **Warung Tirtawati** has a selection of delicious Indonesian food; their *mie goreng* is a delight, and a bargain at under $1.50. Both **Good Karma** and **Tirta Ayu Homestay** serve a wider selection of Indonesian and Chinese meals.

Several *warung* and restaurants are in a little shopping arcade in front of the water palace. **Gangga Cafe** serves pizza, Indian, vegetarian, and homemade yogurt.

ACTIVITIES

Swimming

Most people visit Tirtagangga to swim in the pools, which are quiet and cool. Also look for the fresh spring by the bridge.

Treks

There are many walks through the rice fields. Ask around or just keep to the wider, well-worn paths. A wonderful cascade of rice terraces and steep hills drop down into Culik just north of Tirtagangga. Trekking guides are available in Tirtagangga. For $30 they will take you to the top of Mt. Agung; $15 to Mt. Lempuyang.

Cycling

This is probably the best area in Bali for biking. There are some steep hills but there are lots of great backroads. Rent a bike elsewhere and either ride it out or bring it on the *bemo*.

Amlapura

Amlapura is not a place where many tourists stay, but you can. *Bemos* run frequently between town and the surrounding areas, as it is a business and market center. *Bemos* to Ujung leave from the terminal east of town. The fare to Denpasar is Rp2,500 and to Singaraja Rp2,000.

ACCOMMODATIONS

With the exception of the Balai Kiran, the accommodations in Amlapura consist of small to medium dorm rooms with small Balinese-style bathrooms, drab colors and small windows.
Homestay Balai Kiran. 4 rooms. A pleasant place to stay. It's clean; located within the grounds of Amlapura's Puri Agung palace. The staff is always helpful. $35–$37. Breakfast and dinner are provided.
Losmen Lahar Mas. Jl. Gatot Subroto 1. ☎ 21345. 20 rooms. A typical Amlapura *losmen*. Some rooms overlook a ricefield. Clean and friendly. $4.50–$6.

DINING

Restaurant Lenny Associated with the Pandan Restaurant in Candidasa, has a wide selection of quality Indonesian and Chinese food.
Warung Manggis Behind the *bemo* center. Excellent Indonesian food. Under $2 a meal.

Tulamben

The village of Tulamben can seem uninviting: the beach is rough black sand and in the dry season the countryside is uniformly brown. But Tulamben's attractions lie beneath the water. The wreck of a World War II Liberty class ship lies 30 m from the beach. It is a magnet for divers. Experts say 400 species of reef fishes live on the wreck, visited by 100 species of open-ocean pelagics. It's not hard to see why this is probably Indonesia's most popular dive spot. Reach Tulamben by *bemo* from Candidasa via Amlapura for Rp1,500. Taxi is Rp25,000 each way.

ACCOMMODATIONS

Ganda Mayu Bungalow and Restaurant Simple beachfront accomodations. Near dive entry point

to wreck site. Bali Coral Dive Center in front of bungalows. $7–$14
Mimpi Resort Sales office: Kawasan Bukit Permai, Jimaran Denpasar 80361 ☎ (0361) 701070, fax: (0361) 701074. 16 new bungalows. Swimming pool, restaurant, and Bukit Kencana Dive Center on beachfront grounds. Fan and AC. $75–$125.
Paradise Palm Beach PO Box 31, Amlapura 80811. ☎ 41032. 22 nice, thatched bungalows, 300 m from dive entry point. Beach restaurant, souvenir shop and Tulamben Dive Center attached. 2 beds & toilet, $11–$16.Two rooms with AC and hot water, $35. Reserve in high season.
Saya Resort 5 AC rooms with mini-bar, hot water, private balconies. Attached restaurant. Snorkeling and dive excursions with hotel's Ena Dive Center. $35–$50, American breakfast included.

DIVING

Tulamben Dive Center, PO Box 31, Amlapura 80811 ☎ 41032; **Bukit Kencana Diving Center,** Kawasan Bukit Permai, Jimbaran 80361, ☎ (0361) 701070, fax: (0361)701074; **Ena Dive Center,** PO Box 3798, Denpasar, ☎ (0361) 287945, 288829, fax: 287945. Prices range from $30 for a one-dive day in Tulamben, to $85 for a two-dive day off Nusa Penida. A two-dive beginners' course costs $60 for two dives, off Tulamben or Cemeluk. Prices include equipment, guides and transport.

Amed

Amed is on the easternmost tip of Bali where some of the island's most idyllic beaches are located. You'll need your own transport to reach these places. A few *warung* are scattered throughout the Amed area. The tidy, new **Amed Cafe** boasts clean "healthy" food, including Indonesian and Australian fare and lunch boxes.
Coral View. New resort with 19 thatched bungalows, swimming pool, bar, and restaurant. Motorboat available for dolphin cruises. All rooms with hot water. Economy with fan $29, Standard with fan $40, AC $52, Suite $104.
Good Karma Dusun Selang, Amed. 10 bamboo bungalows right on the beach. $9–$11.
Hidden Paradise Cottages Lipah, Bunutan, Abang, Amed, ☎ (0361) 431273, fax: (0363) 21044, (0361) 423820. 16 rooms. Hot water, fan and AC. Complete facilities: pool, bicycles and watersports. $35–$87, including American breakfast.
Kusumajaya Beach Inn Jemuluk village, 12 km from Amlapura. ☎ 21250. 12 rooms. On a steep hill above the pool with wonderful vistas. Beautiful sunrises and sunsets. Take the steep steps on the left past the bridge. $13–$16, incl. breakfast.
Vienna Beach Bungalows PO Box 112, Lipah, Amed. 12 bungalows. Watersports facilities: diving, snorkeling, fishing, sailing. $11–$21, incl. breakfast.

—updated by Debe Campbell

10 Buleleng PRACTICALITIES

INCLUDES SINGARAJA, LOVINA BEACH AND AIR SANEH

While it is possible to make a day-trip to the north coast, it's a very long drive and you really need to stay longer to see the area. Best to base yourself in the Lovina resort area, with its many hotels and restaurants. Besides Lovina, both Singaraja and Air Sanih have accommodations. *See map on p. 190-191.*

Prices in US dollars. AC = Air-conditioning. Telephone code is 0362.

Singaraja

Bali's administrative center during the Dutch times, Singaraja is now way behind Denpasar in terms of development. It is, on the other hand, a more pleasant place to visit, with a flavor somewhat more Islamic than Hindu. There are no traffic jams nor pollution and everything is conveniently located on one main street, Jl. Jen. A. Yani.

TRANSPORTATION

Singaraja can easily be reached from the east, west and south. From Denpasar, it takes two to three hours by car via Bedugul. The official *bemo* fare is Rp3,000. Another road, still more breathtaking, runs through Tabanan, Pupuan and

Seririt, for a Rp3,800 fare. All *bemos* leave from the Ubung terminal in Denpasar.

There are two terminals in Singaraja: Banyusari and Kampung Tinggi, with *bemos* running between them for Rp300. *Bemos* from Denpasar and Gilimanuk arrive at Banyusari while those from Amlapura and Kintamani go to the Kampung Tinggi terminal. The fare from Banyusari to Lovina is Rp500 and from Kampung Tinggi to Gilimanuk and Amlapura is Rp2,000.

ACCOMMODATIONS

As Lovina is only six kilometers away, visitors tend to go there rather than staying in town. But for those who wish to stay in Singaraja, a few places are available. Some have the feel of old

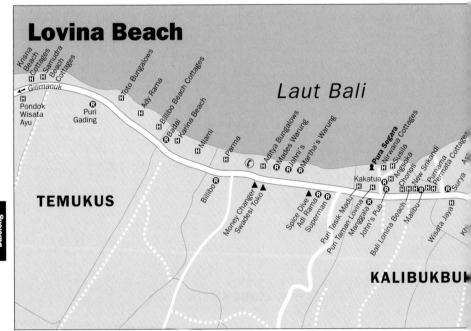

Lovina Beach

Laut Bali

Krisna Beach Cottages · Samudra Beach Cottages · Gilimanuk · Pondok Wisata Ayu · Puri Gading · Toto Bungalows · Ady Rama · Bilibo Beach Cottages · Badai · Karina Beach · Miami · Parma · Billibo · Money Changer · Swadesi Toko · Aditya Bungalows · Mades Warung · Johni's · Martha's Warung · Spice Dive · Adi Rama · Superman's · Puri Tasik Madu · Puri Taman Lovina · Manggala · John's Pub · Bali Lovina Beach · Malibu · Pura Segara · Nirwana Cottages · Susila · Angsoka · Kakatua · Chonos · New Srikandi · Purnama Cottages · Permata Cottages · Wisata Jaya · Surya · As · Kti

TEMUKUS

KALIBUKBU

colonial houses from the Dutch era with spacious rooms and high ceilings. Prices are subject to tax & service charges.Three recommendations: **Gelar Sari** Jl. A. Yani 87. ☎ 21495. 7 rooms with 4 shared bathrooms. $4–$6.

Losmen Darma Setu Jl. A. Yani 46. ☎ 23200. 15 rooms, some with private baths and fan, some without. $4.50, all double, including tea and coffee.

Losmen Duta Karya Jl. A. Yani 59, ☎ 21467. 12 rooms with private baths.$6–$9 fan, $13 AC. Continental breakfast included.

DINING

The Taman Lila complex on Jl. A. Yani has a row of restaurants serving mostly Chinese food. Best known are the **Gandhi** restaurant, No. 25H, ☎ 21163, with an extensive menu and moderate prices. Try the *nasi goreng kepiting* (fried rice crab) or the shrimp satay. Just beside Gandhi is **Kartika**, No. 25I, ☎ 22292. Further west are two intimate restaurants frequented by local lovers: **Cafetaria 99** and next door, **Arina**.

SHOPPING

One place worth visiting in Singaraja is the art shop, **Tresna** on Jl. A. Yani 5, ☎ 25197, which has antiques and fabrics. Another place for fabrics is **Banyusari Market** or go directly to the **Berdikari Hand Woven Cloth Factory** at Jl. Dewi Sartika 42, ☎ 22217, for replicas of antique silk textiles. Open daily, 7am–7pm.

For toiletries and drugstore items go to the

Tirta Dewata mini-market on Jl. A. Yani, in the direction of Lovina. For camera film, go to **Warna Fuji** on Jl. A. Yani 30 and 40, ☎ 22772.

Money

Most places here do not accept credit cards or travellers checks. Banks such as **Bank Dagang Negara** (Jl. A. Yani 60, ☎ 25222), **Bank BNI** (Jl. U. Surapati 52, ☎ 24347) and **Bank Central Asia** (Jl. Dr. Soetomo 3, ☎23760/6) can change money and arrange transfers.

Lovina

The area known as Lovina (actually another name for Kalibukbuk) comprises several villages situated alongside the coastal road west of Singaraja. From east to west they are: Tukad Mungah, Anturan, Kalibukbuk (Lovina) and Temukus. All offer accommodations and other tourist services.

It is quiet and rural here. The black sand beach is beautiful at sunrise. There's no surfing, but plenty of coral areas for snorkeling. The fishermen can also take you to see dolphins offshore; arrange with the boatmen a day in advance. If you have had enough of the sea, the mountainous hinterland is great for hiking.

TRANSPORTATION

Lovina is only 10 minutes from Singaraja by a good road. Public transport runs until 9 pm.

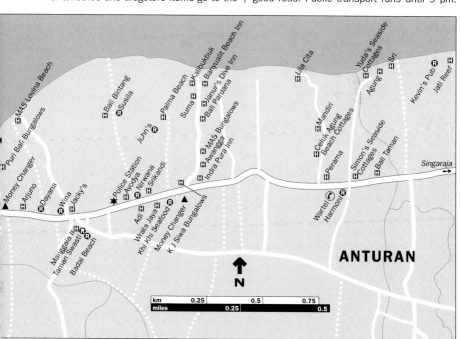

ANTURAN

N

| km | 0.25 | 0.5 | 0.75 |
| miles | | 0.25 | 0.5 |

Bemos to Singaraja (Banyusari terminal) cost Rp300. You can also charter a *bemo* for Rp3,000.

There are direct buses to Java. Buy your ticket from the Perama office in Anturan: Surabaya $10; Yogyakarta $20; Jakarta $25.

Shuttle buses run several times daily to Bali's main resorts: Ubud $7; Candidasa $10; Kuta $7. Buy your ticket from Perama in Anturan or from Ganda Sari, Bina Ria or Arya's Cafe (☎ 21797) in Lovina. Tours of the area, as well as snorkeling and sailing trips can be arranged by your hotel or by these shuttle companies.

For bike, motorbike and car rentals, go to: Bina Ria Transport, Happy Beach Bungalows or Bali Taman Beach in Tukad Mungga; Perama Losmen or Mandhara Beach Cottages in Anturan; or Pringga Guest House and Janur's Dive Inn in Kalibukbuk. The daily rate for a push bike is $2; motorbike $5–$6; car self-drive $15; car with driver $20–$25.

ACCOMMODATIONS

Compared to the beach hotels of south Bali, those here are much less sophisticated. Most fall in the budget and intermediate categories. In general, one gets better value for money in this area than in the main tourist centers.

Almost 50 hotels and *losmen* line the beach at the end of dirt roads flanked by ricefields. Don't expect a traditional village atmosphere such as found in Ubud.

Low Budget (under $10)

Some of the older hotels right on the beach in this category are now well-established and have repeat clients. Newer places are generally not on the beach, but are cleaner and more spacious. Rates include breakfast, unless otherwise noted.

Agung Homestay , Bar & Restaurant PO Box 124, Anturan. 5 rooms. One of the first hotels opened in Lovina, the building uses bamboo throughout. Very friendly atmosphere. No private baths. $3–$4.50. Reservations are needed.

Angsoka Kalibukbuk. 26 rooms. ☎ 41841. Comfortable two-story bungalows, some with hot water. Swimming pool. $4–$7.50 fan, $20–$25 AC.

Astina Kalibukbuk. 8 km west of Singaraja, PO Box 141, Singaraja 81151.☎41803 (c/o Ayodya). 12 rooms, 5 cottages. On the beach. Bamboo-walled rooms around a nice garden. $5.50–$7 with common bath, $8–$9 with private bath. Cottages $11–$12.50 with fan, mosquito net, private bath.

Awangga Tukad Mungga, Banjar Banyualik, Desa Kalibukbuk. ☎ 41561. 8 clean and spacious rooms close to the beach. All with their own private bathrooms. $7, including American breakfast.

Ayodya Kalibukbuk. ☎ 41803. 5 bamboo-walled rooms in a well-kept old house. Despite its location on the main road, it has a pleasantly calm atmosphere. No private bathrooms. $3–$4.

Janur's Dive Inn Kalibukbuk, Tukad Mungga. PO Box 100, Singaraja. ☎ 41056. 5 rooms with fans.

Friendly family place run by Janur, Rose and Gede, who live in the same compound. Very simple accommodation, but special and cozy. Ask Janur to guide you around. $4.50.

Perama Anturan, Jl. Lovina. ☎ 41161. 10 rooms very close to one another right on the main road, so it can be rather noisy. $4.50 for rooms with private shower, $3.60 without.

Puri Tasik Madu/Tama ☎ 41376. 12 rooms. This was one of the first hotels in the area. Rooms are newly-renovated. Pleasant staff, and a very friendly atmosphere. $8.50–$17.

Budget ($10–$25)

Intermediate range hotels in the area are very pleasant, simple and reasonably priced. All consist of bungalows on the beach. Nearly all serve a simple breakfast (coffee or tea with fruit salad, toast and an egg). All rooms in this category have private bathrooms.

Angsoka Seaside Cottages Jl. Lovina. ☎ 41841, fax: 41023. 26 rooms. Special facilities for bungalows include split AC, bathtub and hot water. $7–$18 fan; $12 open Bali-style baths.

Banyualit Beach Inn Jl. Singaraja. PO Box 116, Kalibukbuk. ☎ 41789, fax: 41563. 20 rooms. Simple to newly renovated AC with hot water. Some of the verandahs are literally on the water's edge. Friendly and helpful staff. Ask for a room close to the beach. $12–$15 fan; $16–$23 AC.

Jati Reef Bungalows PO Box 52, Desa Tukad Mungga. ☎ 41052. 16 rooms in four separate bungalows with a short walk through the rice fields to get to your room. $7 fan.

Kalibukbuk Beach Inn Jl. Lafiana, Desa Kalibukbuk. ☎ 41701. 25 rooms. At the end of the Banyualit lane, only a few steps from the beach. $9 budget, $11–$14 fan, $16–$20 AC.

Nirwana Kalibukbuk, Desa Kalibukbuk, Lovina.☎ 41288, fax: 41090. 32 spacious, clean rooms right on the beach. The biggest can sleep four. Two-story bungalows with bamboo trim spread around a lush garden. $14–$18, family suite $23.

Rini Kalibukbuk. ☎ 41386. 20 rooms. Clean and all rooms have a private bath. No breakfast. $15–$30, hot water.

Samudra Beach Cottage Jl. Seririt, Desa Temukus. PO Box 142, Temukus. ☎ 41751. 24 rooms. At the western end of the beach. Very quiet. $7–$11 fan, $9–$16 AC, including Continental breakfast.

Simon's Seaside Cottage Jl. Semit, Desa Anturan. PO Box 151, Tukad Mungga. ☎ 41183.16 rooms in four two-story bungalows. Clean and roomy. Great upper rooms with verandahs front and back overlooking the beach and the ricefields. $11–$14.

Sri Homestay Jl. Singaraja, Seririt, Desa Anturan. 41135. 12 bamboo rooms by the beach. Bathrooms are not the cleanest around, but where else can you look over rice fields while taking your shower? Has a narrow veranda in front. The owner, Sri, is helpful and friendly. $11–$15 family room with fan.

Moderate ($25–$50)

These hotels are all located right on the beach,

facilities include swimming pools, hot water, private bathrooms—some with bathtubs, and AC.
Aditya Jl. Seririt. PO Box 35, Lovina, ☎: 41059, fax: 41342. 75 rooms. Some spacious new suites are available with AC, tub, and a phone. $20–$25 fan, $35–$45 AC, including Continental breakfast.
Aldian Palace Hotel Jl. Raya Seririt, Singaraja, Pemaron Village. ☎ 23549. 34 spacious rooms with AC and lounge. $16 fan, $25–$35 AC, $70 suite.
Bali Taman Beach Hotel Jl. Raya Seririt, Desa Tukad Mungga. PO Box 99. ☎ 41126, fax: 41840. 18 bungalow-style rooms. Tennis court, fridge and TV available. $22.50–$27.50 fan, $45–$55 AC and hot water. Continental breakfast included.
Bali Lovina Beach Cottage Jl. Seririt, Singaraja, Lovina. PO Box 186. ☎/fax: 41285, fax: 41478. 34 bungalow-style rooms. $30–$35 fan, $40–$45 AC, $50–$60 superior, including a generous breakfast of bacon or sausage, eggs and toast.
Baruna Beach Cottages Desa Temaron. PO Box 149, Lovina. ☎ 41746, fax: 41252. 42 rooms. Several cottages overlooking the beach. All rooms with private bath. $17 budget w/fan, $24–$32 cottages w/ fan, $40–$52 AC. Excluding tax, service and breakfast.

First Class ($75–$100)

Palma Hotel Jl. Raya Lovina-Singaraja.PO Box 131. ☎ 41775, 41658, fax: 41659. 45 rooms, standard and cottages, AC, hot showers. Other facilities include meeting room, tennis court and recreation facilities, including boat sailing, push bikes etc. Standard $72–$81, cottages $94–$102, suites $192–$210, including American breakfast.

DINING AND NIGHTLIFE

Nearly all hotels in the area have restaurants. **Janur's Dive Inn** has one that is great value for money. Very pleasant atmosphere, serving standard favorites such as *cap-cay* (mixed vegetables) for $1.

The most famous restaurant is **Khi Khi** in Lovina. If the food is to your liking, go to their open-air kitchen and take notes on the recipes. Grilled fish and fried prawns are the favorites here. Another popular restaurant is the **Kakatua**, near Lovina beach. Try their fried fish for $2. Or you can go to **Srikandi** for fried rice, which you eat sitting on a mat. For those who want live music, go to **Wina** or **Malibu**. The latter turns into a disco on Fridays.

WATERSPORTS

Most hotels can arrange watersports, not only for the Lovina area, but for Pulau Mejangan to the west (around $18). The usual rates are as follows: snorkeling: $3–$4 per person (bargain). Trip to the dolphins: $5 per person. Fishing trip: $5 per person. It may be cheaper to bargain with local fishermen.

SHADOW PUPPETS

Lovina is not known as a center of Balinese culture. However the area is famed for its puppet shows. Hotels with regular performances are: Puri Bedahulu, Happy Beach Bungalows and Mandhara Beach Cottages.

MISCELLANEOUS

Several places **rent books** in the center of Lovina: Dewi Shop, Tiptop and Pub Travel. **Change money** at CV Tali Harta or BPD, in front of Khi-Khi restaurant. There is also a *wartel* telecom office in the same area.

Air Sanih

Driving east from Singaraja along the coast, or north and then east from Kintamani, you will pass through the beach resort of Air Sanih (Yeh Sanih), which is noted for its freshwater springs. It's a nice stop-off before you continue your journey to Karangasem.

You can also enjoy a beautiful sunrise on Air Sanih beach or, by leaving early enough for Karangasem, you may see the first lights hit the peak of Mount Agung near Tulamben—a breathtaking experience. Several bungalows have been built in Air Saneh and the surrounding area, many by the pools which overlook the seashore. There are still no phone lines to the area.

Apilan Beach Front Restaurant Hotel Bukti village, Buleleng. Bookings: PO Box 188, Singaraja 81113; fax: (362) 21108 c/o Telkom Singaraja. A real find: a beach house with open dining room attached. Interesting collection of books and ethnic articles. At dinner a gamelan is played on the patio. Private cottages with verandah and double beds are also available. Set meals lunch and dinner: $2.50.
Bali Dengel Bungalows Jl. Raya Kubutambahan. Mail to Jl. A. Yani 261, Singaraja. ☎ (0362) 22948, 23357. 4 bungalows. Private bathroom, ceiling fan, breakfast included. $12.50.
Puri Sanih Bungalows I & II Jl. Raya Kubutambahan, Singaraja. ☎ (0362) 22990. 12 bungalows, 8 rooms. Private bathroom in all rooms. Breakfast included. $7–$22.50 rooms, $9–$27 bungalows.
Sunset Graha Beach Hilltop Bardens Bungalow Jl. Raya Kubutambahan, Singaraja. fax: (0362) 21108. 6 rooms. Situated on steep hill overlooking beach and spring pools at Puri Sanih Bungalows. Rooms with private bath, shower, fan, mosquito net. Osho Aheeshu Meditation and Creative Center attached. Adjacent Archipelago Restaurant has "back to nature" theme with traditional Balinese style and very helpful, friendly owner, Supartha. $7–$11.
Tara Hotel Jl. Raya Kubutambahan, Air Sanih. 15 rooms with private baths. $5–$11.50 fan; adjoining room $7.

—updated by Debe Cambell/Andy Udayana

Buleleng 10

The main place to stay in Tabanan is the mountain resort of Bedugul, famed for its cool climate and spectacular lakes, mountains and ricefields. Penebel offers hot springs with modern facilities. Krambitan is the place for an unusual stay in a royal palace. Tabanan's west coast is being developed as Bali's newest beach resort—with miles of deserted black sand and a pounding surf. *See area map on page 208.*

Prices in US dollars. AC = Air-conditioning. Telephone code is 0362.

Bedugul

A pleasant climate, splendid views, watersports on scenic Lake Bratan, botanical gardens, fresh tropical fruits and vegetables—these are but a few of the things Bedugul offers. Located 1,500 m above sea level, it gets chilly by late afternoon, so bring your sweater. This is a favorite weekend retreat for Jakartans and the local Balinese bourgeoisie.

ORIENTATION

Bedugul's layout can be somewhat confusing, especially if you arrive in late afternoon after the clouds have descended. Coming from the south,

there are two signposts to watch out for: "Bedugul 0.2 km" and "Bedugul." One might expect to find the village here, but instead the road turns sharply to the left, with a smaller road leading off to the right. The latter leads to the Bedugul Hotel on the southwestern shore of the lake.

The main road continues past a number of hotels on the left until it reaches the village of Bedugul proper. Here you find shops, a few restaurants, a bank, telephone office (*wartel*), a market selling local produce (including flowers, coffee and vanilla) and a lane leading up to the botanical gardens (*Kebun Raya*).

Beyond the village the road descends towards the lake, turning left at the Ashram Hotel. The road then continues north to Candi Kuning. On the right hand side is the entrance to the Pura Ulun Danu and other temples. A line of souvenir shops indicates the way. A fee of Rp1,000 is required to enter the temple.

The walk from Bedugul market to the Ashram Hotel takes about 10 minutes. The temples on the shore are another 10 minutes further on. From the market to the entrance of the botanical gardens takes about 15 minutes on foot.

TRANSPORTATION

Bedugul is situated on the main road connecting north and south Bali. It is the perfect place to stop for a night on an island tour. Rent a car and explore the area at you own pace.

If you are going by public transport, catch a *bemo* from Ubung terminal in Denpasar to Bedugul for Rp3,000. The fare is the same from Singaraja. The nicest way to get around Bedugul is on foot in the invigorating mountain air. Or charter a *bemo*, carrying up to seven persons, for about $10–$20 a day.

The High Road to Bedugul

Most people traveling between the highland resorts of Kintamani and Bedugul travel the cir-

Bedugul & Candi Kuning

cuitous route via Singaraja and the north coast to get from one to another. An alternative route, used by very few people, leads south through the mountains, offering spectacular scenery and a close look at the vanilla and coffee producing area of the island.

The road is good enough for cars or motorbikes, although there are several places where deep potholes make driving fast a big risk. It's best is to allow half a day for the route between Kintamani and Luwus, where you meet the main road between Denpasar and Bedugul. This way you can stop along the way, have a coffee in one of the villages and enjoy a leisurely ride.

From Kintamani, follow the main road north until just beyond Penulisan and the Tegeh Koripan temple. Take the small road that branches off to the left towards Belantih village. Continue west past Belantih to Lampu and the neighbouring village of Catur, where the road bends south. Lawak village marks the beginning of the vanilla-growing region where the harvest can often be seen drying in shelters.

After Belok (keep right) head for Pelaga. Just before the village there's a sharp right turn which leads to a short cut west to Lake Bratan. Not many Balinese are prepared to expose their vehicles to this road though, as chances of ruining it or at least getting stuck are pretty high. Another reason to avoid the shortcut and continue south is that the best has yet to come.

Beyond Pelaga and Kiadan, the elevated area around Nungkung and Sandakan is extremely beautiful. A bit further ahead lies the Islamic village of Angan Tiga with it's small mosque. The next village, Kerta, has a police post and even a bank. Past the bank take the right turn to Bedugul (the road continues straight to Denpasar which is only 32 km away). The stretch of road between Kerta and Luwus via Peria is extremely bad. In Luwus you reach the main road. Turn right for Bedugul or left for Mengwi and Denpasar.

ACCOMMODATIONS

Some hotels are in the lake area of Bedugul proper overlooking Lake Bratan, while others are located on the upper slopes of Baturiti with views over volcanoes, ricefields, and down to the sea. Most rooms cost between $15 and $50, with the best ones having great views. There are budget homestays as well as first-class hotels.

Budget (under $25)

Ashram between Bedugul and Candi Kuning. ☎ 22439, fax: (0368) 21101. 27 rooms. The new cottages on the hill are clean, convenient and overlook Lake Bratan. Restaurant with strict dining times. Huts near the lake are great places to eat or just have a drink. Tennis court and table tennis. Bungalows $13–$31, room with outside bath $7.

Hadi Raharjo Just left off the main road where it forks off to the Bedugul Hotel. 18 rooms. Very simple. Private baths. A small restaurant in front serves Javanese food. $4–$5, breakfast included.
Ibu Hadi A 3-story homestay on Jl. Kebun Raya. 11 rooms with private bath. Proudly presented as "Hotel & Restaurant." $7, including breakfast.
Lila Graha between Candi Kuning and Bedugul. 15 rooms. Across from Ashram. Pleasant individual bungalows. Very private. Go for the rooms overlooking the lake. $12.50–$30.
Mawar Indah Jl. Kebun Raya. ☎ (0368) 21190. 18 rooms. Simple and clean. Restaurant. $7–$8.50.
Mini Bali Homestay On the left side of the main road past the Bukit Mungsu Indah. 7 rooms. Clean and simple, with a restaurant. $2–$5.
Rosela Jl. Kebun Raya. ☎ (0368) 23497. 11 rooms. Simple and clean, situated on small side street. $3.50–$9.
Strawbali Hill south of Bedugul at the Bedugul Hotel turnoff. ☎ 23467. 10 rooms. Managed by famous Poppie's Cottages of Kuta. Clean, simple losmen. Blankets provided for cool nights. Attached restaurant serves Inodnesian favorites, soup, salad, chicken, and burgers. $10.

Intermediate ($25–$50)

If you're into watersports, stay at the **Bedugul** by the lake. Most rooms have private bath with hot water.
Bedugul on the main road south of Bedugul. ☎ 226593. 30 bungalows. One of its restaurants is right on the lake. Rooms by the lake get a bit noisy, especially on weekends. $27–$40.
Bukit Mungsu Indah on the main road southof Bedugul. ☎ 23662/3. 13 rooms. Some of the bungalows face Bedugul's botanical garden. Fireplace in all rooms. $23–$45.
Pancasari Inn Jl. Raya Bedugul, Singaraja, Desa Pancasari. ☎ 21148. 11 bungalows, each with two rooms. North of Lake Bratan. Tennis court. Special rates for groups of five or more. $44–$75.

First Class ($75–$100)

There are several first class hotels in the Bedugul area and more are under construction. The Bali Handara Country Club is geared to the needs of international golfers, while the Pacung, south, on the road to Baturiti, offers a view over ricefields and volcanoes. Both have comfortable bungalows with private baths and hot water. Fridge and TV are standard, as is in-house video. 21% tax and service surcharge.
Bali Handara Kosaido Country Club Pancasari. ☎ 22646, fax: 23048. Located by Mount Bratan. 37 rooms. Has an internationally renown 18-hole golf course, listed among the world's top 50. Rooms in the new wing are hotel style; older bungalows are spread about the garden. Tennis court and gym. $70 (standard)–$350 (executivel suite). Golf green fees for 18 holes: $70 weekdays, $85 weekends.
Lake Buyan Cottages Jl. Raya Baturiti, Desa Pancasari. ☎ 21351, fax: 21388. 16 rooms over-

looking Lake Buyan in Pancasari village. $80–$250. **Pacung Mountain Resort** Jl Raya Baturiti, Desa Pacung. PO Box 3297. ☎ (0361) 262460/2, fax: (0368) 21043. 26 rooms. 9 km south of Bedugul, at the crossroads leading to the Jatiluwih view, Penebel and the Batukaru temple. Rooms with hot water set around a hilly property. Impressive ricefield and mountain vistas. Heated swimming pool, jogging track and two restaurants. Affiliated with Choice Hotel chain. Superior $75–$85, deluxe $85–$95, suite $125–$200. American or buffet breakfast included. Two children under age 16 can share deluxe room or suite with parents with rollaway bed provided free.

DINING

There are only a few restaurants in Bedugul, but they do cover a wide price range. Opposite the road leading up to the botanical gardens, on a right hand bend, there are three small eating places serving cheap meals from 6 am to 7 pm. A good meal costs around $1. Try the ferns (*sayur paku*) at **Ananda I** (40¢). Friendly service.

There are good restaurants in the main hotels: The **Bedugul Hotel's** restaurant by the lake serves meals costing around $5. Try the Chinese food at **Pacung**, especially their crab fried rice (*nasi goreng kepiting*) for $2.50. **Strawbali Hill** serves the same top quality as it's parent, Poppie's in Kuta. The Bali Handara's **Kamandalu Restaurant** is more up market.

Indonesian food is available in front of Ulun Danu temple in small food stalls—not recommended for those with sensitive stomachs. Overlooking the temple and a big banyan tree is the **Perama Tea House**, a small restaurant by the lake. The open-air patio is a pleasant spot for a refreshing cup of tea. Try their *pisang bakar Candikuning*: grilled banana with grated cheese on top.

Ayam Bakar Taliwang Bersaudara is just before the famous Ulun Danu temple and has a view over the temple and the lake. A favorite with locals. The spicy hot dishes from Lombok are just right for the cold weather. Order the satay or *tofu* if you don't like food too spicy. $2. **Jember Indah** is on the higher slopes just outside Bedugul. Cheap east Javanese food and beautiful views down to the sea. Try the *soto* Madura for $2. **Minang Saiyo**, in front of Candi Kuning market, sells spicy Sumatran Padang fare.

SHOPPING

Bedugul is the place to buy fresh tropical fruits, as most of the fruit and vegetables for the island are grown in this area. Go to Pasar Candikuning, a market where you can buy fresh passionfruit, jackfruit, pineapple, carrot and mango. Like everywhere else in Bali, you have to bargain—don't feel reluctant to offer half the asking price. Also available are fresh flowers, in-cluding wild orchids and a number of other ornamental plants.

Some small shops selling souvenir crafts are found around Pura Ulun Danu and the lake. Shops in the Bedugul Hotel compound sell film, but there is no film processing here as yet.

WATERSPORTS

A range of watersports are available next to the Ulun Danu temple and at the lakeside hotels such as Bedugul and Lila Graha. The usual rates, including insurance, are as follows:

Motorboat	$7–$8 for 30 mins.
Covered Boat	$9 for 30 mins.
Watercycle	$4 for 30 mins.
Rowboat	$4 for 30 mins.

Boats are also available on the waterfront beyond the Ashram Hotel for $3 per hour.

Munduk

The village of Munduk, actually in the Buleleng administrative regency, is located on a ridge along the mountain road leading from Wanagiri, just north of Pancasari to Mayong, some 25 kms south of Singaraja as the crow flies. Overlooking coffee and clove plantations, the area comprises the pristine Lake Tamblingan with its traditional fishing community, as well as nearby forests, waterfalls and some of the most beautiful views on the island.

Munduk is a perfect base for treks into the mountainous Balinese hinterland. You can walk to Mt. Lesong (1,860 m), around Lake Tamblingan or visit the area's five waterfalls.

Munduk is the center for an innovative community tourism development project. The village, which has strong links with the Hotel and Tourism Training Institute in Nusa Dua, has set up a number of activites for visitors, centered around Puri Lumbung Cottages (see below).

TRANSPORTATION

Go from Bedugul to the Pancasari *bemo* terminal for Rp200, then take a *bemo* to Munduk for Rp1,000. Alternatively hop on the *bemo* at the Pempatan crossing.

If you hire a car or motorbike, drive cautiously on the road down to Munduk—it's steep and treacherous.

ACCOMMODATIONS

Puri Lumbung Cottages Munduk village, Buleleng. About 13 m from Tablingan Cafe. Traditional Balinese rice granaries converted into comfortable rooms. Reservations and information: Hotel and Tourism Training Institute, Denpasar, PO Box 2, Nusa Dua. ☎ (0361) 772078, fax: (0361) 771985. Or call Munduk direct: (0362) 92514. 10 rooms.

Transport to Munduk will be arranged once your confirmed booking is received. They organize a lot of activities with the guests and local people, including making musical instruments, music lessons, traditional cookery classes, and guided walks. Good restaurant with a milion dollar view. $39–$45, including tax, service and Balinese breakfast.

Pondok Wisata Old Dutch house transformed into a homestay. Simple, clean. $10–$15. Try to bargain.

Jatiluwih and Penebel

The hot springs of Penebel and the rice terraces of Jatiluwih make the slopes of the Mount Batukau (2,276 m) well worth visiting.

These areas are most easily reached by *bemo* from Tabanan or Mengwi in the south via Pacung. The village of Blayu, just north of Mengwi, is worth a stop-off for those interested in handicrafts. It is famous throughout Bali for weaving and woodcarving.

Penebel Hot Spring and Yeh Panes Spa, Desa Penatahan, Penebel. ☎ 262356. Kuta Reservation Office: Jl. Raya Kuta 15 X. ☎ 752411, 754881, fax: 752411. 9 private and semi-private spas, all equipped with air blowers and water jets. Four, six and eight person spas available. 16 rooms. $120–$160.

Soka Restaurant in Jatiluwih serves good Indonesian and Chinese food for $8.

Tanah Lot

Shortly before Tabanan on the main highway from Denpasar a signboard directs you southwest to Tanah Lot. There are a number of shops and restaurants nearby. Tourists congregate at this Balinese landmark, especially at sunset.

Dewi Sinta Cottages Jl. Tanah Lot, Kediri, Tabanan. ☎ /fax: 812933. 11 simple cottages with fan and hot water. $12–$25, including tax, service and American breakfast.

Mutiara Tanah Lot. ☎ 812939, fax: 222672. $30–$35 fan, $40–$45 AC, including tax, service and breakfast.

A number of big hotels are planned in this area.

Krambitan

Located to the southwest of Tabanan, Krambitan is a small town which was once the center of a small principality. Its court culture is retained in the area's particular styles of dance and painting. A branch of the current Tabanan royal family owns the two palaces here.

To get there, continue west from Tabanan until you see an intersection and a road to the left with a sign indicating "Krambitan 5 km."

The main attraction here, besides the quiet, everyday village life, is to order your own dinner and *calonarang* trance play performance in one of the palaces, which also offers rooms for rent. The whole village participates in these "shows," and members of the royal family welcome you as their guests.

ACCOMMODATIONS

The *puri* (palaces) of Krambitan have opened their doors to tourists who wish to experience life in a Balinese palace. The Puri Anyar is recommended, but the Puri Agung Wisata has cheaper rooms. Don't expect hotel-style service, however, as they have no trained staff—which actually adds to their charm.

Puri Anyar Krambitan. ☎ 92668. 7 bungalows. The *saren* bungalows are where the royal family used to live. $40–$55 for the suite. They prepare lunch and dinner for $15. The Puri Anyar stages fantastic torchlit dance dinners on request or for the big Nusa Dua hotels. They also offer village cultural tours and kite-flying parties.

Puri Agung Wisata, Krambitan, south of the Puri Anyar. ☎ /fax: 812667. 8 rooms for rent. Private bath. $20–$35, including tax, service and breakfast, dinner with entertainment is offered.

Beebees Restaurant and Bungalows. 6 bungalows in Tibubiyu, Krambitan. Bungalows set in lush tropical greenery with ocean and village sounds harmonizing in the distance. Very peaceful. $16–$20, including fruit and breakfast.

Western Beaches

A number of small new resorts have recently been opened on the beaches west of Tanah Lot.

Bali Wisata Bungalows, Yeh Gangga Beach, sudimara village, Kecamatan Tabanan. ☎ 261354, fax: 812744. 12 rooms. Swimming pool. $20–$35, including tax, service and breakfast.

Balian Beach Bungalows Lalang Linggah, Selemadeg, Tabanan. ☎ 752669. 9 small bungalows. Look for the sign near the 46 km marker. Set amid palm trees, the rooms face the Balian River near the beach. Bob, the manager, knows a lot about the area. Great surfing.$5–$25, plus a backpackers house at $2.50/person.

Medewi Beach in Pekutatan, Jembrana, 70 km from Denpasar, offers some of the best rolling waves on the island.

Medewi Beach Cottages Medewi Beach, Pekutatan, Jembrana. PO Box 126. ☎ (0365) 40029/30, fax: (0365) 41555. 26 rooms. Modern facilities with hot water, swimming pool and satellite TV situated in a stunning natural setting: coconut-fringed beach with a backdrop of tall mountains. $15 fan, $45–$60 AC. Lunch or dinner for $10.

Tinjaya Bungalows 6 bamboo hut bungalows with private baths located just a hundred meters to the west of the Medewi Beach. $10–$12. You can rent a boat for $20/day.

—*updated by Debe Campbell/Andy Udayana*

Further Reading

Agung, Ide Anak Agung Gde. *Bali in the 19th Century*. Yayasan Obor Indonesia, Jakarta, 1991. A history of the Dutch conquest of Bali focusing on the resistance of the Balinese nobility, by a distinguished Balinese prince and retired diplomat.

Bali. Studies in Life, Thought, and Ritual. Foris, Dordrecht, 1984 (1960). *Bali. Further Studies in Life, Thought, and Ritual*. W. van Hoeve, The Hague, 1969. Two collections of pre-war studies by such eminent Dutch scholars as Goris, Grader, Korn, Liefrinck and Swellengrebel, representative of the "Leiden School" of ethnography.

Bandem, I Made & Fredrik E. deBoer. *Kaja and Kelod. Balinese Dance in Transition*. Oxford University Press, Kuala Lumpur, 1981. An overview of Balinese dance and theater today, bringing together traditional Balinese and contemporary Western approaches to the performing arts.

Bateson, Gregory & Margaret Mead. *Balinese Character. A Photographic Analysis*. New York Academy of Sciences, New York, 1962 (1942). A monograph about the mountain village of Bayung Gede, which attempts to portray the relationships among the different types of culturally standardized behavior by placing a series of photographs next to the relevant text.

Baum, Vicki. *A Tale of Bali*. Oxford University Press, Singapore, 1986 (1937). A fictionalized account of the Dutch conquest of south Bali in 1906. The finest novel that Bali has inspired so far.

Belo, Jane. *Bali: Temple Festival*. University of Washington Press, Seattle, 1966 (1953). A step-by-step description of the rituals composing an *odalan*, the major calendrical feast of a Balinese temple, recorded in 1937 in Sayan village.

Belo, Jane. *Trance in Bali*. Greenwood Press, Westport, 1977 (1960). A detailed description of the various ritual contexts of trance in Bali, recorded in the 1930s by Jane Belo, Margaret Mead, Gregory Bateson and Katharane Mershon.

Belo, Jane (ed). *Traditional Balinese Culture*. Columbia University Press, New York, 1970. Pre-war studies by American scholars such as Jane Belo, Margaret Mead, Gregory Bateson, Colin McPhee and Claire Holt, representative of the "culture and personality" school of anthropology.

Bernet Kempers, A.J. *Monumental Bali*. Periplus Editions, Berkeley, 1990 (1977). A new color edition of the classic handbook on Balinese antiquities.

Boon, James A. *The Anthropological Romance of Bali 1597-1972. Dynamic Perspectives in Marriage & Caste, Politics & Religion*. Cambridge University Press, 1977. On social and cultural dynamics in Bali, showing how the island has been depicted by Western travelers and scholars.

Boon, James A. *Affinities and Extremes. Crisscrossing the Bittersweet Ethnology of East Indies History, Hindu-Balinese Culture, and Indo-European Allure*. University of Chicago Press, Chicago, 1990. By one of America's most versatile anthropologists, an investigation of Balinese culture as a multiple-authored invention.

Brinkgreve, Francine & David Stuart-Fox. *Offerings, the Ritual Art of Bali*. Image Network Indonesia, Sanur, 1992. A delightful album of photographs crammed with an unusual range of Balinese offerings, which is also a thoroughly academic study of that most distinctively Balinese Art.

Covarrubias, Miguel. *Island of Bali*. Oxford University Press, Singapore, 1987 (1937). A beautifully-written account of Bali as seen in the 1930s through the eyes of a Mexican painter who spent 18 months on the island. For the visitor of today, its romantic view of traditional Balinese culture provides a most pleasurable introduction.

Darling, Diana. *The Painted Alphabet: a novel*. Houghton Mifflin, Boston, 1992. An imaginative novel inspired by a Balinese folk tale, Dukuh Siladri.

Djelantik, Dr Anak Agung Made. *Balinese Painting*. Oxford University Press, Singapore, 1986. The religious and social contexts of painting and an overview of regional styles, by a Western-educated Balinese.

Eiseman, Fred B. *Woodcarvings of Bali*. Periplus Editions, Berkeley, 1988. A concise presentation of the history, styles, and contemporary production of woodcarvings in Bali.

Eiseman, Fred B. *Bali: Sekala & Niskala. Vol. I: Essays on Religion, Ritual, and Art. Vol II: Essays on Society, Tradition, and Craft*. Periplus Editions, Berkeley, 1989/1990. Scores of down-to-earth articles on all sorts of Balinesia, from sorcery and trance to cooking.

Emigh, John "Playing with the Past: Visitations and Illusion in the Mask Theatre of Bali" and "Jelantik Goes to Blambangan. A Topeng Pajegan Performance" by I Nyoman Kakul in *The Drama Review*, 23/2: pp. 11-48, 1979. A fascinating account of a *topeng pajegan* performance, providing insights into the complex workings of language and characters which make up traditional theater.

Geertz, Clifford. "Form and Variation in Balinese Village Structure" in *American Anthropologist*, 61: pp. 991-1012, 1959. A seminal essay by a leading American anthropologist, conceptualizing Balinese village structure in terms of the intersection of distinct planes of social organization.

Geertz, Clifford. *The Interpretation of Cultures*. Basic Books, New York, 1973. A collection of essays, three of which bear specifically on Bali: "'Internal Conversion' in Contemporary Bali," "Person, Time, and Conduct in Bali", and "Deep Play: Notes on the Balinese Cockfight."

Geertz, Clifford. *Negara. The Theatre State in Nineteenth-Century Bali*. Princeton University Press, Princeton, 1980. A controversial attempt to characterize the *negara*, the pre-colonial Balinese state, as a "theatre state" embodying the ruling Balinese obsessions of social status and pride.

Geertz, Hildred (ed.). *State and Society in Bali. Historical, Textual and Anthropological Approaches*. KITLV Press, Leiden, 1992. A collection of essays by prominent scholars, examining the changing relationship between state and society in Bali.

Geertz, Hildred & Clifford Geertz. *Kinship in Bali*. University of Chicago Press, Chicago, 1975. An examination of Balinese kinship focused on the *dadia*, defined as a "highly corporate group of people who are convinced, with whatever reason, that they are all descendants of one common ancestor".

Goris, Roelof. *Bali. Atlas Kebudajaan. Cults and Customs*. Djakarta, 1953. An illustrated album, recounting the historical development of Balinese culture from ancient times up to the renewal brought on by Western influence.

Guermonprez, Jean-Francois. *Les Pandes de Bali. La Formation d'une "Caste" et la Valeur d'une Titre*. Ecole Francaise d' Extreme-Orient, Paris, 1987. Based on the study of a particular title group, the *Pande*, a reconsideration of the workings of kinship and hierarchy in Bali.

Guermonprez, Jean-Francois. "On the Elusive Balinese Village: Hierarchy and Values versus Political Models" in *Review of Indonesian and Malaysian Affaires*, 24: pp. 55-89, 1990. A critical assessment of the prevailing Western view of the Balinese *desa* as a primarily political community, which tends to ignore hierarchy as a principle of order and to establish an artificial disjunction between culture and society.

Hanna, Willard A. *Bali Profile. People, Events, Circumstances (1001-1976)*. New edition 1990. A detailed account of the Balinese encounter with Western intruders and its consequences.

Hauser-Schaublin, Brigitta, Marie-Louise Nabholz-Kartaschoff & Urs Ramseyer. *Textiles in Bali*. Periplus Editions, Berkeley, 1991. A sumptuously illustrated book, examining the history and production of textiles in Bali, their ritual and social functions, and the significance of colour, pattern and weave to the Balinese.

Hinzler, H.I.R. *Bima Swarga in Balinese Wayang*. Martinus Nijhoff, The Hague, 1981. A study of the *wayang* focusing on a particular literary theme, the Bima Swarga tale recounting the release of Pandu and Madri from hell by Bima and their subsequent admission to heaven.

Hobart, Angela. *Dancing Shadows of Bali*. KPI, London, 1987. A comprehensive overview of the Balinese *wayang*, describing the repertoire, the puppets, the performance, and the place of the shadow play in Balinese culture and society.

Holt, Claire. *Art in Indonesia. Continuities and Change*. Cornell University Press, Ithaca, 1967. An illustrated overview of the plastic and performing arts of Bali, placed within the context of Indonesia.

Hooykaas, Christiaan *Religion in Bali*. E.J. Brill, Leiden, 1973. A scholarly introduction to the study of Balinese religion by a leading Dutch philologist.

Hooykaas, Christiaan *Introduction à la littérature balinaise*. Association Archipel, Paris, 1979. An introduction to Balinese literature, supplemented by an extensive bibliography.

Howe, Leo E.A. "Hierarchy and Equality: Variations in Balinese Social Organization" in *Bijdragen tot de taal-, land- en volkenkunde*. 145: pp. 47-71, 1989. An attempt at explaining the systematic variations encountered in forms of Balinese social organization, between southern plains villages and the Bali Aga mountain villages.

Jensen, Gordon D. & Luh Ketut Suryani. *The Balinese People. A Reinvestigation of Character*. Oxford University Press, Singapore, 1992. A critical reassessment of Bateson and Mead's study on Balinese personality and culture by two psychiatrists: one Western one Balinese

Krause, Gregor. *Bali 1912*. January Books, Wellington, 1988. A new book containing some of the classic photos from the 1920s which first made the island known to the West, and which prompted so many artists and writers to come and see it for themselves.

Lansing, J. Stephen *The Three Worlds of Bali*. Praeger, New York, 1983. A reappraisal of the role played by literature and theater in shaping and defining Balinese culture.

Lansing, J. Stephen. *Priests and Programers. Technologies of Power in the Engineered Landscape of Bali*. Princeton University Press, Princeton, 1991. A study of water management in Bali, stressing the practical role performed by the traditional system of water temples, which is now threatened by bureaucratic development plans that assume agriculture to be a purely technical undertaking.

McPhee, Colin. *A House in Bali*. Oxford University Press, Singapore, 1986 (1944). The account of how a young American composer came to Bali to study after hearing some gramophone recordings of Balinese *gamelan* music in 1929.

McPhee, Colin. *Music in Bali. A Study in*

Form and Instrumental Organization in Balinese Orchestral Music. Da Capo Press, New York, 1976 (1966). The most comprehensive survey of Balinese music to date, accurately detailed in its descriptions and analysis of musical forms.

Mershon, Katharane E. *Seven Plus Seven. Mysterious Life-Rituals in Bali*. Vantage Press, New York, 1971. A lively description of the 14 Balinese rites of passage, by an American dancer who lived in Sanur during the 1930s.

Nieuwenkamp, W.O.J. *Zwerftochten op Bali*. Elsevier, Amsterdam, 1910. A gorgeous album, illustrated with drawings by the author, who was the first Dutchman to call the attention of his countrymen to the beauty of this island.

Picard, Michel. *Bali. Tourisme Culturel et Culture Touristique*. L'Harmattan, Paris, 1992. An assessment of the role played by tourism in shaping Balinese culture, replacing the touristification of Bali within the context of the colonization of the island and its subsequent Indonesianization.

Powell, Hickman. *The Last Paradise*. Oxford University Press, Singapore, 1986 (1930). The first book in English about the island of Bali and its people, written in the late 1920s by a particularly sensitive American reporter.

Pucci, Idanna. *The Epic of Life. A Balinese Journey of the Soul*. Alfred van der Marck, New York, 1985. A lavish album recounting the Bima Swarga tale as depicted in the paintings of the Kerta Gosa, the Palace of Justice in Klungkung.

Ramseyer, Urs. *The Art and Culture of Bali*. Oxford University Press, Singapore, 1986 (1977). An attempt at studying the arts in Bali by placing Balinese creativity within the all-encompassing unity of *agama* (religion), *budaya* (culture) and *adat* (tradition).

Ricklefs, M.C. *A History of Modern Indonesia. 1300 to the Present*. Macmillan, London, 1981. A comprehensive historical survey of Indonesia, posing the important question of how the diverse but related linguistic and ethnic communities of the archipelago became a unified nation.

Rhodius, Hans & John Darling. *Walter Spies and Balinese Art*. Terra, Zutphen, 1980. The life and work of Walter Spies, the German artist who lived and worked in Bali from 1927 to 1940, and who made an indelible mark on Balinese culture and our understanding of it.

Schaareman, Danker. *Tatulingga: Tradition and Continuity. An Investigation in Ritual and Social Organization in Bali*. Ethnologisches Seminar der Universität und Museum für Völkerkunde, Basel, 1986. A monograph on Asak in Karangasem, looking at forms of ritual and social organization.

Schulte Nordholt, Henk. *Bali: Colonial Conceptions and Political Change 1700-1940. From Shifting Hierarchies to 'Fixed Order'*. Erasmus University, Rotterdam, 1986. An attempt at showing how Western conceptions of Bali shaped Dutch colonial policy, and how these eventually transformed the Balinese political order.

Schulte Nordholt, Henk. *State, Village, and Ritual in Bali. A historical perspective*. VU University Press, Amsterdam, 1991. A study of the changing relationships between state, village and ritual in Bali, arguing that village administration, customary order and public rituals were re-defined and appropriated by the government in order to enhance state authority.

Solyom, Bronwen & Garret. *Museum Bali. Selected Works*. Times Editions, Singapore, 1993. Historical background of the Bali Museum in Denpasar, followed by an illustrated description of its collections.

Stuart-Fox, David J. *Once a Century. Pura Besakih and the Eka Dasa Rudra Festival*. Sinar Harapan, Jakarta, 1982. An illustrated description of the great purification of the universe held at Besakih in 1979.

Stuart-Fox, David J. *Bibliography of Bali. Publications from 1920 to 1990*. KITLV Press, Leiden, 1992. Comprising nearly 80,000 publications on Bali, this long-awaited bibliography continues C. Lekkerkerker's pioneering work which stopped in 1919.

Tenzer, Michael. *Balinese Music*. Periplus Editions, Berkeley, 1991. A highly readable introduction to the musics and orchestras of Bali by a versatile young American composer.

Vickers, Adrian. *Bali: A Paradise Created*. Periplus Editions, Berkeley, 1989. A provocative essay on the invention of Bali as a tourist destination.

Wikan, Unni. *Managing Turbulent Hearts. A Balinese Formula for Living*. University of Chicago Press, Chicago, 1990. A challenging anthropological study, using an empathetic approach to understand how the Balinese confront bereavement, fear and ambition, with the grace they regard as crucial for self respect.

Worsley, Peter J. *Babad Buleleng*. Martinus Nijhoff, The Hague, 1972. A Balinese dynastic genealogy in translation, supplemented by an analysis of its form, theme and function.

Zoete, Beryl de & Walter Spies. *Dance and Drama in Bali*. Oxford University Press, Singapore, 1987 (1938). A fascinating study of the dramatic arts in Bali, as thorough as it is readable, describing the literary background of Balinese dances and the contexts of their performance.

Zoetmulder, P.J. *Kalangwan. A Survey of Old Javanese Literature*, Martinus Nijhoff, The Hague, 1974. The most comprehensive survey of the Javanese literary heritage which is being kept alive in Bali today.

Zurbuchen, Mary S. *The Language of Balinese Shadow Theater*. Princeton University Press, Princeton, 1987. A study of the *wayang parwa*, demonstrating how the linguistic codes used by the puppeteer mediate between social groups, cultural influences, history and conceptual schemes.

— Compiled by Michel Picard

GLOSSARY

adat tradition; customs

Agama Hindu Dharma "Religion of the Hindu Doctrine"; Balinese Hinduism; also called *Agama Tirtha*

Agama Tirtha "Religion of the HolyWaters"

alus refined, smooth; "high level of Balinese language; polar opposite of *kasar*

angklung bamboo shaker rattles

arak clear liquor distilled from palm flowers

arja dance opera; enacts stories of the Panji cycle

arya Javanese nobles

bahasa language

bahasa Bali Balinese language; regional language spoken in Bali

bahasa Indonesia Indonesian language; national language of Indonesia

bale house, pavilion

bale banjar community meeting hall

bale gede "great pavilion"; where family ceremonies and receptions are held; also called *bale dangin* ("east pavilion")

bale kambang "floating pavilion" built on elevated mound n the middle of a pond; meeting hall for kings and their ministers

Bali Aga "original" Balinese; some trace descent to early settlers from east Java prior to Majapahit influx; mountain villages around Kintamani with distinct lifestyle and ritual traditions

balian traditional healer, shaman

banjar neighborhood association

banten daily oferings to gods, ancestors and demons

baris warrior dance; occasionally trance occurs

Barong mythological beast, most commonly a lion-bear, but may also be a tiger, wild boar, pig, or elephant; protector of the village; confronts Rangda, the witch queen

batik process of "lost-wax" dye technique for printing cloth; done primarily in Java

bemo mini-bus; public transport, some can be chartered for private use

beras hulled, uncooked rice

bhatara/bhatari god/goddess

bhuta yadnya rites to appease evil forces and to cleanse humans and their environment

Brahma the Creator; one of the Hindu trinity

brahmana priest caste

brem sweet, mildly fermented rice wine

bulan month; may refer to either Gregorian calendar (January, etc.) or indigenous pawukon calendar which has six 35-day months

calonarang drama which depicts conflict between a powerful widow, Rangda, and an East Javanese king

canang small, shallow palm-leaf trays containing flowers, betel nut, fruit, and coconut-leaf decorations; presented daily as offerings to spirits

candi funerary monument for a deceased king

candi bentar split gate without a roof; often at the entrace to a temple's outer courtyard

dalang puppeteer of *wayang kulit* theater

desa village

desa adat "traditional village"; lowest administrative level of the state

dewa/dewi god/goddess

dewa yadnya rituals to honor the gods, performed during temple ceremonies

Dewi Sri goddess of rice and prosperity

Durga Siva's wife in an evil manifestation

Eka Dasa Rudra greatest of all Hindu-Balinese riturals; purification rite for the entire cosmos; held every 100 years, last held in 1979

endek *ikat*; weft threads are tied, then dyed prior to weaving; most popular Balinese textile form

Galungan Wednesday (*Buda*) of Dunggulan week of *pawukon* calendar; most important festival in Balinese Hinduism; celebrations last for 10 days, ending on Kuningan

gambuh ceremonial dance drama; based on Panji Malat tales; rarely performed; musical accompaniment include meter-long bamboo flutes

gamelan musical ensemble, mainly of percussive instruments; specific instrumentation varies according to dance/theater genre

gamelan gong largest musical ensemble in Bali; 35-40 musicians; ceremonial ritual music

gamelan gong kebyar most common type of *gamelan*; flashy, dynamic music created in early 1900's

gamelan jegog bamboo *gamelan* with large resonant bass instruments; exclusive to Jembrana

gamelan selunding rare iron *gamelan*, considered extremely sacred

Ganesha elephant-headed son of Siva

Garuda mythical eagle-like bird, mount of god Visnu; subject of many woodcarvings

gedong pair of small closed shrines; one with earthenware plate on its roof, other with pointed roof; honor Dewi Sri and her consort Rambut Sedana

Gelgel great dynasty centered in Klungkung; mid-15th through 16th c.; Bali's "Golden Age"

gender wayang ensemble of four metallophones, accompany *wayang kulit* performance

geringsing double *ikat* cloth from Tenganan; reddish brown, eggshell and blue-black natural dyes; magically protective powers

ikat "tie"; tie-dye technique; see *endek*

jaba "outside"; one of the four castes; also referred to as *sudra*, although *jaba* is the preferred term; also refers to the outermost of three temple courtyards, the secular area

jajan multi-colored rice flour cookies for offerings (very colorful, dry, tasteless) and snacks (less colorful, but tastier)

jejaitan leaves cut, plaited, pinned into decorative shapes for ritual offerings

jukung small outrigger boats

kabupaten regency, headed by the bupati; second level administrative unit under the province; Bali is one province consisting of 8 regencies

kaja upstream; toward the mountain

kangin east

kasar uncouth, unrefined; refers to "low" level of Balinese language; polar opposite of alus

kasta birth-determined social group; four Balinese castes are *brahmana, satriya, wesya*, and *jaba* (*sudra*)

kauh west

kebaya women's long-sleeved blouse; often made of brocade or light voile

kebyar dance inspired by gamelan gong kebyar; flashy, electrifying

kecak "monkey dance", features chorus of at least 50 men sitting around an oil lamp; intricate interlocking chanting; dancers enact Ramayana story

kecamatan district, headed by the camat

kelod downstream; seawards

keris daggers, some considered magically powerful; may have eiter straight or wavy blade; part of formal male attire; worn in the back, handle tipped to the right

ketan glutinous ("sticky") rice

klenteng Chinese Buddhist temple

kori agung large temple gate that leads from middle courtyard to inner courtyard

krama desa all-village council open only to men and women born and living in Tenganan who have passed all ritual stages of initiation

Kuningan Saturday of Kuningan week; end of 10-day ritual celebration period that begins with Galungan; *kuning* means yellow; rice offerings on this day are dyed yellow with tumeric

lamak decorated woven coconut leaf mat, usually in the form of a long strip

legong classical dance performed by 3 young girls; grew out of sacred *sanghyang dedari*

leyak witch; one who practices black magic

lingga symbol of Siva; phallic shape set in round or square *yoni*

lontar "book" of palm leaves cut into strips and bound together by a string; engraved with iron stylus then blackened with soot

lumbung rice granary

Mahabharata Hindu epic; centers on story of dynastic struggle between 5 Pandawa brothers and their cousins, the Korawa

Majapahit HIndu Buddhist kingdom of 13th-14th c. east Java; great influence on Balinese culture

manusa yadnya life-cycle rites, ensure personal spiritual and material well-being

mekepung water buffalo races, held in Jembrana

meru Balinese pagoda, has odd number of roofs, increasingly smaller at the top; honors a god or ancestor

nasi cooked rice

nasi campur rice with varied condiments

nasi goreng fried rice

Nyepi first day of the 10th lunar month, usually in March; day of silence and contemplation

odalan temple anniversay based on 210-day *pawukon* calendar; lasts 3 or 10 days

ogoh-ogoh huge bamboo and paper monsters paraded on the eve of Nyepi; to chase away demons

padmasana 8-leafed lotus throne for Sanghyang Widhi; 8 leaves are for gods of 8 directions

Pagerwesi important religious holiday; Wednesday (*Buda*) of Sinta week; celebrates victory of religious duty over religious negligence

palawija cash crops, e.g. soybeans, peanuts, onions, chili peppers

palebon Balinese cremation ceremony; also called *pangabenan*

palinggihan wooden sarcophagus carried in the cremation procession; usually in the shape of mythical animal; also called *patulangan*

pancawara 5-day week, names of days are *umanis, paing, pon, wage*, and *kliwon*

pande clan of smiths and metalworkers

pangabenan see *palebon*

paras volcanic ash sandstone used for carvings

pariwisata tourism

pasar daily market for food, clothing, flowers, utensils, etc.; bargaining is the way of life

pasar malam night market

patulangan see *palinggihan*

pawukon indigenous Balinese 210-day calendar; concurrently running cycles, most important of which are the 3-day market (*triwara*), 5-day (*pancawara*) and 7-day (*saptawara*) weeks; each 7-day week has a name; the cycle governs most auspicious days and religious events

pedanda high priest of *brahmana* caste

pemangku temple's lay priest

penjor tall bamboo poles arching over the streets, hung with offerings

Pita Maha artists' association formed in Ubud in 1936

pitra yadnya ceremonies for the dea

poleng black-and-white checkered cloth; usually worn during rites of passage; associated with demons and death

prada cloth decorated with gold-leaf; traditionally used by royalty; worn during tooth-filing and marriage ceremonies

prahu large boats, may be motorized

prasasti — early historical inscriptions in stone or copper plates

prembon dance created in 1940's; combines elements from older dance drama forms; depicts stories of Balinese kings

puputan mass ritual suicide; most famous was Puputan Badung in 1906 when royalty of Badung committed suicide in the face of advancing Dutch army

pura Balinese temple in the public domain

pura bale agung great meeting hall temple, located in village center; also called *pura desa*; linked to Visnu the Protector

pura dalem — "temple of the nighty one"; death temple, located near the cemetary/cremation grounds; seaward side of village; linked to Siva the Destroyer

pura desa "village temple", see *pura bale agung*

pura kahyangan tiga "three sanctuaries," 3 core village temples: *pura puseh, pura desa/bale agung, pura dalem*

pura puseh "temple of origin," located at mountain-side of village, linked to Brahma the Creator

pura sad kahyangan 6 most important directional temples worhsipped by all Balinese; lists vary, but generally recognized are: Pura Penataran Agung at Besakih (Karangasem), Pura Lempuyang (Karangasem), Pura Goa Lawah (Klungkung), PuraLuhur Uluwatu (Badung), Pura Luhur on Mt. Batukau (Tabanan), and Pura Pusering Jagat (Gianyar)

puri palace; home of the king and his court

purnama full moon

Ramayana Hindu epic, "story of prince Rama"

Rangda lit. "widow," queen of the witches, adversay of Barong

rejang female processional dance; slow steady movement toward altar

resi yadnya rituals to ordain priests

rijstaffel "rice table," full meal of rice with various side dishes

rujak raw fruits mixed with sauce of shrimp paste, chillies and sometimes palm sugar

Saka Hindu-Balinese lunar calendar; one year has 12 months of 29 or 30 days, beginning on the new moon; every 3-4 years a 13th intercalary month is added to maintain sychronization with the solar year

sambal hot chilli sauce

sanghyang "deity"; sacred trance dance

sanghyang dedari sacred dance performed by 2 pre-pubescent girls

sanghyang jaran performed by men who grab hobby horses when in trance

Sanghyang Widhi singular all-powerful God, unification of all manifestations of God

sanggah private or family temple

sangging woodcarvers

saptawara 7-day week of the *pawukon* calendar; name of days are: *Redite* (Sunday), *Coma* (Monday), *Anggara* (Tuesday), *Buda* (Wednesday), *Wraspati* (Thursday), *Sukra* (Friday), and *Saniscara* (Saturday)

sasih lunar month; 12 months in lunar year; names are Sanskrit words for 1-12 (*Kasa, Karo, Ketiga, Kapat, Kelima, Kenem, Kepitu, Kaulu, Kesanga, Kedasa, Jiyestha, Sadha*)

satriya warrior caste

sawah irrigated rice field

sekaha club or group of people involved in communal activity, such as playing gamelan

sendratari abbreviation of *seni* (art) - *drama* - *tari* (dance); created in 1962; dance drama which replaces spoken dialogue with pantomime

Siva the Destroyer; one of the Hindu trinity

SMKI *Sekolah Menengah Karawitan Indonesia*, High School for Traditional Performing Arts

songket brocade; decorative gold and silver threads added to weft threads; traditionally reserved for higher castes

STSI *Sekolah Tinggi Seni Indonesia*; Indonesian Academy of Performing Arts

subak irrigation co-operative

sudra see *jaba*

tegalan non-irrigated dry field

tilem new moon; beginning of Balinese lunar month

tirtha, tirta holy water

topeng mask; popular dance drama in which dancers wear full and half-face masks

triwara 3-day market week; names of days are: *pasah/busaya, beteng/tegeh, kajeng*

tuak mild beer made from palm flowers

tumpek occurs every 35-days when the days *kliwon* (5-day week) and *saniscara* (7-day week) coincide; 6 in the complete cycle; *tumpek landep* (honors weapons, tools), *tumpek uduh/nyuh* (honors useful plants), *tumpek kuningan, tumpek krulut* (honors musical instruments, masks, dance costumes), *tumpek andang/kandang* (honors domestic animals), *tumpek ringgit/wayang* (honors shadow puppets)

usaba temple anniversary festival which is determined by lunar calendar, such as Besakih

warung food stall, small eatery

wayang kulit shadow puppet theater

wayang wong dance drama

wesya merchant caste

Wisnu the Preserver; one of the Hindu trinity

yadnya worship or sacrificial rite; means of maintaining balance of forces in cosmos

yeh water; also *tirta, air*

About the Authors

Rucina Ballinger holds an MA in Asian Studies/ Dance Ethnology and has been studying and performing Balinese dance since 1973. She is a founder member of Gamelan Sekar Jaya, a Californian music and dance group. A resident of Peliatan, she leads study tours for the Experiment in International Living. **Tom Ballinger** has lived and travelled in Asia since the 1950s. He was born in Albuquerque, New Mexico, grew up in Oregon and studied anthropology at the University of Chicago, receiving his BA in 1972. Now living in San Francisco, he travels to Bali whenever he can to study *gamelan gender wayang.* **Kate Beddall** graduated from Yale University with a BA in music in 1988. She spent nine months in 1988 studying *gamelan jegog* in the town of Tegalcangkring, Jembrana. For help with her articles she wishes to thank I Ketut Surung, Ida Bagus Raka Negara, I Wayan Gama Astawa and Michael Tenzer. **Lorne Blair** produced and directed the BBC/PBS TV series, *Ring of Fire,* about ten years' of adventuring in Indonesia. He co-authored a book of the same title with his brother Lawrence in 1988. Born in Britain in 1945, he grew up there and in Mexico. His documentaries, ranging from Africa to New Guinea, include *Lempad of Bali,* which he co-directed. He died in July 1995. **Francine Brinkgreve** is a Dutch anthropologist attached to University of Leiden. She is currently working on a doctoral dissertation on Balinese ritual art. **Debe Campbell** has lived in Indonesia for a decade. First visiting Bali in 1973, she declared it her favorite paradise. She now calls it home. US-born, she is a freelance travel writer, widely published in Asia and the Pacific. **Bruce Carpenter** came to Bali in 1973 after reading an essay by French surrealist Antonin Artaud. From being a performance artist he passed on to academic pursuits, including translations of books by Dutch artist Nieuwenkamp. Presently living in Bali, he is organizing a traveling museum exhibition and writing. **Jean Couteau** was born in Clisson, France in 1945, and came to Bali on honeymoon. Soon divorced, he has been in love with Bali ever since. His PhD dissertation was on Balinese painting. He now lectures on Balinese culture at Club Med, Nusa Dua, and is working on a French translation of the Ramayana. **Diana Darling** was born in the USA (and again in Carrera, Italy and again in Paris and again in Bali). She is a recent subscriber to the Embroiderers' Guild Newsletter (New South Wales Chapter, Overseas Member). **Allard de Rooi** was born in Amsterdam and is the prototype of the Flying Dutchman. He studied Arabic, worked in the Dutch travel business for ten years, wrote a number of books and articles on travel, and in the meantime managed to spend a few years on the roads of all continents except Australia. He now runs his own advertising agency and is manager of Periplus Editions in The Netherlands. **Martijn de Rooi**, sociologist and Allard's brother, is a well-known Dutch travel writer. He has written articles on travel, culture and politics for various Dutch publications, as well as travel guides on Egypt, Cyprus and Indonesia and edited a number of books for Periplus Editions. His first book, *Handelreizigers* (Traveling Salesmen), comes out in 1995. **Fred B. Eiseman, Jr.** first visited Bali in 1961. He has since written for a host of magazines, including *National Geographic,* on the island culture. His two volume work *Bali: Sekala and Niskala* is published by Periplus Editions. He lives in Scottsdale, Arizona and Jimbaran. **Sandra M. Hamid** was born in Jakarta in 1962. She moved to Bali soon after finishing her degree at the Faculty of Social & Political Sciences at the University of Indonesia in Jakarta. She is currently with the Bali Hyatt. **Kunang Helmi Picard** is an Indonesian freelance journalist based in Paris. She studied contemporary history, international law and political science in Bonn, and obtained an MA in political science there, followed by post-graduate studies in London and Hamburg. She contributes photos and articles to German, French, American and Indonesian publications. **Rio Helmi** is an Indonesian photographer and writer who has spent 12 of the last 18 years in Bali. He has published articles and photos in publications throughout the Far East. Recently he served as chief photographer and assignment editor for the book, *Indonesia: A Voyage Through the Archipelago,* which features the work of 45 of the world's top photographers. **Hedi Hinzler** studied archaeology and ancient history, Sanskrit and Old Javanese at Leiden. Her PhD research was on the Balinese shadow play, and she assisted Prof. C. Hooykaas in his researches on Bali from 1972 onwards. After his death she carried on the Balinese Manuscripts Project, and teaches archaeology, epigraphy, modern Indonesian art and Balinese language at Leiden University. **Ida Ayu Agung Mas** studied German as well as Indonesian in Jakarta, Hamburg and Munich. After five years teaching at the Hotel and Tourist Training School in Nusa Dua, she now lectures at Udayana University in Denpasar, and directs her own institute, where courses in Indonesian for foreigners are given. **Garrett Kam** was born in Hawaii and has been involved in Indonesian studies since 1975. He is particularly drawn to the cultures of Bali and Java, where he has lived for many years. He has written and lectured on the arts and dances of both islands and is an accomplished dancer. **Agnès Korb**, born in Neuilly near Paris, graduated from the English department of the Sorbonne University and E.S.I.T. Academy of Interpreters and Translators. She came to Bali in 1980 and began a new career in social anthropology. Attached to the Anthropology Department of Udayana University, she has done research in Bali, Lombok and Sumbawa. **Victor Mason**, born and educated in England, is a specialist in birds of the Oriental Region, his home for over thirty years. Now he watches birds in Bali, where he lives with his Balinese wife and two daughters, and in his spare time plays publican at the Beggars' Bush in Campuan, Ubud.

Kal Muller was born in Hungary, educated in France and the US and lives in Mexico. He has produced several books on Indonesia and his photographs and articles have appeared in *National Geographic*, *Geo* and other magazines. He has a PhD in French literature and is fluent in Indonesian, having spent many years traveling in the archipelago.

Lisa Najoan lives and loves to live in Bali. She was born in Jakarta in 1962 and graduated from the University of Indonesia in 1987 with a degree in marketing management. She has been involved in the garment export business and is now a marketing executive with a major Indonesian bank in Bali.

Sarita Newson first came to Bali when she was 20, lured by its exotic culture and art, and has now spent more than a third of her life here. She has a Balinese family and home, and has worked for the past years in the fields of tourism, art and graphic design.

Eric Oey was born in the United States and has lived for many years in Southeast Asia. He has published numerous books and is the founder and publisher of Periplus Editions.

Nyoman Oka was born in Beratan, Singaraja in 1914 and trained as a teacher in the Europeesche Kweekschool in Surabaya. In 1951 he was elected head of Tabanan. In 1956 he left to manage a travel agency. He has taught at high schools under the Yayasan Saraswati and is now retired.

Michel Picard is a French sociologist attached to the National Centre for Scientific Research (CNRS) in Paris. He is a member of the Laboratoire Asie du Sud-Est et Monde Austronesien (LASEMA) and has recently published a book on "cultural tourism" and "tourist culture" in Bali.

Urs Ramseyer was born in 1938 and studied ethnology, sociology and music at the University of Basel. He was appointed curator of the Indonesian Department at the Basel Museum of Ethnography in 1968. Dr. Ramseyer has organized many exhibitions in Switzerland and directed a Swiss research team on Bali in 1972-3. His publications include *The Art and Culture of Bali* (Oxford in Asia, 1986).

Larry Reed is a film director, writer and performer with a strong interest in intercultural communication. After a trip to Asia in 1972, he began an intensive study of Balinese mask and puppet theater. He then formed the Shadow Play Theater Company, which brings Balinese shadow plays to university campuses in the USA, Canada and Europe.

Raechelle Rubinstein obtained her PhD in Indonesian and Malayan studies at the University of Sydney. She has worked on numerous research projects in Bali; her interests include language and literature both in Kawi and Balinese, and Balinese music. She is currently researching the *Perang Banjar*.

Danker Schaareman was born in Holland and studied cultural anthropology and ethnomusicology at the University of Basle, where he now teaches. Since 1972 he has carried out research in Bali and Lombok. His PhD thesis, *Tatulingga: Tradition and Continuity. An Investigation in Ritual and Social Organization in Bali* appeared in 1986 in Basel.

Amir Sidharta was born in Jakarta in 1964. He received a bachelor's degree in architecture from University of Michigan. He is interested in the art and architecture of Java and Bali, and took the photographs for Bernet Kempers' *Monumental Bali*.

David Stuart-Fox is an Australian scholar who has lived for many years in Bali. He has a PhD in anthropology from the Australian National University. **I Made Suradiya** was born in Apuan, Singapadu in 1963. He is currently completing a thesis for the degree of Bachelor of Arts at the Faculty of Letters of Udayana University in Denpasar. He has contributed several articles to the journal *Kanaka* and to the *Bali Post*.

Miranda Suryadjaya was born in Bali and educated here and in California. She has a BA in foreign languages and an MA in finance. She speaks several languages and has traveled extensively. Since mid-1988 she has rediscovered and fallen in love with Bali, being involved since that time in the travel and hotel industry.

Andy Udayana was born in Negara, West Bali. He is a student at the National Tourism University in Bali and is a research assistant for regional travel publications.

Adrian Vickers has been visiting Bali since the age of 14, and researching and writing about the island since the late 1970s. He received a PhD in Indonesian and Malayan studies from the University of Sydney, with a thesis on the courtly culture of pre-colonial Bali, and has taught at Sydney and New South Wales Universities.

Wayne Vitale has composed and performed both Balinese and Western music. He received a BA in music from Cornell University and an MA in composition from the University of California, Berkeley. His studies abroad have included two years in West Germany, and two years in Bali studying the relationship of music to ritual.

Stephen Walker is a water resources specialist with the Overseas Development Natural Resources Institute of the British Government. After graduating with honours in geography and geology, he took an MSc degree in Engineering Hydrology. He has worked in Indonesia since 1973, including three years in Singaraja.

Tony and Jane Whitten are British ecologists who have lived in Indonesia for nearly ten years, most recently in Bali. Their latest books are *Wild Indonesia, Freshwater Fishes of Sumatra, Borneo, Java and Sulawesi*, and *The Ecology of Java and Bali*.

Made Wijaya was born Michael White in Australia in 1953. He studied architecture at the University of Sydney, and since 1974 has pursued various vocations in Bali: English teacher, columnist for the *Bali Post*, tennis coach, landscape designer and architect. He was an early mover in the revival of *batik* headdresses and the island's first all-male, one-man Scottish *legong*.

Index

Map Index